ROMAN IMPERIAL
CIVILISATION

TO MY WIFE
WHO HAS AFFORDED ME HERE
THE HELP IN WHICH
SHE HAS NEVER FAILED ME

ROMAN IMPERIAL CIVILISATION

BY

HAROLD MATTINGLY

F.B.A., F.S.A., Hon. D.Litt. (New Zealand)

LONDON
EDWARD ARNOLD (PUBLISHERS) LTD.

Printed in Great Britain by
Butler & Tanner Ltd., Frome and London

CONTENTS

MAPS

PLATES OF COINS

INTRODUCTION

Why should we study the past at all ? Why not live in the all engrossing present, letting bygones be bygones ? 'Why indeed ?' say many and act on that conviction. Yet there always have been and always will be many for whom the past has a strange lure. At the worst, this is a mere morbid interest in that which has ceased to have any value—one of the least satisfactory forms of pedantry. But at its best it is something very different. You have only to look at the immense amount of intellectual vigour and curiosity today put into the study of antiquity to realise that. What lies behind this intensely alive study of the past ? Perhaps the wish to gain some warning or instruction from past experience may play a small part. But the dominant motive is a noble curiosity— an intense desire to know how man has lived in other times, meeting other problems and adapting himself to other environments. After all, it is characteristic of man that time for him has three dimensions, past and future as well as present. If that is clearly realised, the look back is as inevitable as the look forward, though naturally, as movement is forward not backward, the forward view is the more important. The remoter past, lying behind all written records, all monuments of stone or brass, is prehistory. History begins when man begins to be articulate, and, as the child who talks is more interesting to most people than the babe who does not—the infant— the interest in history is far more general than that in prehistory. It must be admitted, however, that many fine minds discover a peculiar satisfaction in wresting such information as can be extorted from a difficult material. History is perhaps an adult interest. For boys and girls it is likely to be a matter of colour and pageantry, of battles and kings. The attempt to lift it higher to the range of social studies is nobly conceived, but very hard to achieve. You cannot force adult interests on the adolescent, though you may rightly sow the seeds of them. A deep interest in history may be slowly acquired, but, once acquired, it may become dominant. For almost anything may be looked at from a historical point of view.

In the realm of history the Roman Empire has always had a special attraction for many students. It stands there, impressive by its very mass and duration. Its influence still lives on. Modern Europe cannot really be understood without some knowledge of it. The life of the Empire is, in many ways, so like our own that we can read of it without often feeling shock or surprise ; yet, in other ways, it is so unlike that it stretches our conception of human possibilities. And it is a history of a very special kind. Many times in the past large populations have been brought under one rule. But there are very few examples of peoples of so many races, languages and cultures being held for centuries long in a firm political union. So far as it succeeded, it holds out hopes of a world organisation in the future. Where it failed it stands before us as a grim warning. Periods of strife and revolution may excel in the excitement of the thrilling novel ; but there is more lasting interest in a history that shows clear pattern and logical sequence. There are few episodes in history where pattern can be so clearly seen as in the Roman Empire.

Gibbon had his own vision of the Decline and Fall—a sombre but impressive vision that inspires those long volumes of his. Arnold Toynbee, in our own time, sees the Roman Empire as a late stage in the history of the Hellenic civilisation. It is easy to think of the Empire as something that never was young and very soon grew old. But this is a very partial view that stands badly in need of correction. The cultures that were built into the Empire were many of them old. In the Empire itself signs of weariness and flagging vitality *do* soon appear. But the impression by itself is delusive. There had been gross squandering of vitality before the Empire came into being. Under it there was a relaxation of tension, an economisation of effort. Inside the Empire there were forces slumbering that would in due time wake to new life. Outside it were the unspent energies of the barbarian world. History is like the natural year. It has its changing seasons—its spring of bursting life, its summer of fulfilment, its autumn of ripe harvest, its winter of stagnation. But all belongs to one cycle ; no one phase tells the whole tale.

Should we not balance Toynbee's view just quoted by one entirely different ? Should we not forget for a moment the oldness of the materials with which the Empire worked and think instead of the new aims that it pursued ? Should we not let it rise and flourish before it declines and falls ? This new picture will not show us all the truth, but it will help to correct the faults in other views. It is so easy to employ metaphors and analogies that are never complete and may be misleading. And, in applying this method to the beginning of the Empire, we may also do well to reconsider its end. We have grown accustomed to think far more about the Fall of the Western Empire than of the age-long survival of the Eastern. We have too often forgotten the immense services rendered to Europe by the Byzantine Empire. In the West we have thought too much of the Dark Age—not enough of the impulses transmitted through the Empire that worked on for centuries after it had fallen.

To write the history of the Roman Empire—that is a task almost fantastically difficult, like making ropes out of sand or translating the Odes of Horace into English. Gibbon succeeded marvellously in his own self-chosen task, but only by his peculiar genius and his curious limitation of subject. He writes under a glaring light that makes us see clearly indeed ; but this intense light is also a false light ; it not only shows up, it distorts. The great German scholar, Theodore Mommsen, the one man who might have been held to be *capax imperii*, declined the task, content to give us the ' History of the Provinces under the Empire '. Where he by implication declared his inadequacy, who indeed will dare to venture ? Dessau, that master of research, was not given time to get very far with his history, but, alas, just far enough to show that he lacked the special gifts needed for historical interpretation. Rostovtseff, in his ' Social and Economic History of the Empire ', certainly gained conspicuous success, only marred by some misconceptions of ancient conditions due to the intrusion of modern analogies that do not really apply. Note again that, with him as with Gibbon, success depended on a deliberate restriction of theme.

In what does the special difficulty of writing a history of the Roman Empire consist ? Partly in its sheer mass, the wide range of space and time that has to be covered. The evidence is often broken up into minute fragments, hard to assemble, hard to handle when assembled. For much of the Empire we lack the guidance of any ancient historian of first rank, sometimes even of any of the second. But the main difficulty remains to be told. A target clearly seen may be aimed at, perhaps hit. But what is our target ? The personal history of the emperors, the political history of their empire ? That target we can see and aim at. But, even if we hit it, how much remains undone ? The same objection applies to all special histories—of social and economic conditions, of army and civil service, of literature, art, morals. We gain a series of partial views ; but how combine them into one general view of the whole ? The great ' Cambridge Ancient History ', with its team of experts, interprets period after period with vast knowledge and skill. The editors interpose from time to time an effective synthesis of their own. Yet, even in this magnificent work, we may feel that the rainbow is being broken up into its thousand hues and will not recombine into its perfect bow. The nature of our subject forces us to concentrate on the Many. How are we to find the One of which they are part ? Yet, on the other hand, if we work under the dazzling light of some one dominant idea, our vision will be blurred as often as enlightened.

If complete success in my task is, as I have been suggesting, too much to hope for, to what degree of limited success can I hope to attain ? Regard for the truth, to say nothing of modesty, forbids the pretence that I have had any special revelation of a correct method, hidden from so many wise and learned men before me. All I can hope to do is to draw a number of pictures of different phases of the Empire, as nearly true as I can make them, and to indicate to my readers how they can be fitted together to form the general view. The number of possible aspects is very large and a selection from them must be made. Much will depend on making a wise choice. But I *do* begin with one considerable advantage. Tarn in his ' Hellenistic Civilisation ' and Runciman in his ' Byzantine ' have shown how similar subjects to mine may be treated with success. My debt to both these writers will be obvious to all who have read their books. The mass of material—literary evidence, inscriptions, coins and the rest—is immense, far beyond the capacity of any one writer to handle. So far as I control it, I will try to make it tell its own tale. There is no need, I take it, to exclude some personal prejudices. History, without judgments of value, is poor stuff, desiccated and devitalised, and judgments of value open the door to prejudice. The reader can balance the prejudices of the writer by his own. My debt to modern historians is too general for detailed acknowledgment. It will not often be possible to quote sources. You can quote sources for particular statements, not for general pictures. I shall try to depend on ancient evidence, not on modern fancies or my own imagination. My special interest in coins will be apparent at many points. But, where the importance of the subject is so far from being realised as with coins, a little over-emphasis will do no serious harm. How useful illustration can be in a book of this character has been shown once for all by Rostovtseff. But such illustration adds enormously to the labour and cost of production, and we have had to renounce it here, except for our eight plates of coins. Illustration of other material under its various headings is available in a number of works which will be cited in the bibliography. Good maps of course are essential. A few of the most necessary are given and others may be found in the ' Cambridge Ancient History '. It would be a great advantage to an author to know large parts of the Empire from his own travels. This advantage I cannot claim. But many travellers have recorded their impressions and so, at second hand, this most vital knowledge may be acquired. The final synthesis—the combination of a number of partial views into one—must fall to each reader for himself. From time to time I can put in my own suggestions as to how the synthesis should be made.

Perhaps my readers may be interested at the outset to come with me into my workshop and see some of the tools that have to be used and the use that I shall try to make of them. First of all, let us look at the material on which we have to work. Ancient historians, chance references to historical events in works of more general character, inscriptions, coins, edicts, laws—all are available for study in editions and catalogues. What general principles are we to apply in using these ?

(1) Evidence is to be taken in order of priority—the first-hand before the second, the second before the third. Statements in historians that depend on personal knowledge or documents consulted by them are first-hand evidence. So too, subject to certain necessary precautions, are coins and inscriptions. After that comes second- and third-hand evidence, given not directly, but through one or more intermediaries. The greatest of modern writers can never be a first-hand authority. However wise and authoritative his pronouncements, they must be judged as comment, and comment only.

(2) It is important to treasure one's exceptions—those pieces of evidence that do not fit readily into the general picture. It is from them that future discoveries are to be expected. The temptation to discard them into the wastepaper-basket should be steadily resisted.

(3) *Sint quae ignores.* Admit occasional ignorance. Let there be some things that you do not know. Where the evidence does not justify a positive statement stick to a wise reserve.

(4) On the other hand do not be too afraid of making mistakes. There is no policy of absolute safety. One must take some risks in the quest for truth.

(5) There is very great divergence among scholars in the criticism of evidence. Some divergence, of course, is inevitable, but what we actually find goes far beyond what we reasonably may expect. Here are a few examples where such divergence often occurs.

We may question a statement in an ancient authority, because it seems to us improbable, or even impossible. This is a form of criticism that we cannot avoid, once we give our interest to a subject. We find that the statement, on being admitted to our mind, will not fit in with our general stock of ideas. But this form of criticism has its dangers. Are we really able to judge of the improbability or impossibility of what we criticise ? Probably every scholar has had before now to confess to rejecting what he afterwards discovered to be unobjectionable, when at last seen in its right setting. This criticism applies particularly to the miraculous—that which falls outside the normal order of events. It is not only in the Christian scriptures that such questionings arise. In the pagan writers, too, we find some strange miracles recorded—the cases of healing by Vespasian at Alexandria, for example.

Again, some statement may seem not to fit into the general picture, and we begin to suggest ways in which it may have slipped into our tradition. This is another solvent, of dangerous potency. It has to be employed at times, but it may easily damage valuable evidence. It is a waste of ingenuity to show how the false may have crept into our tradition, until its falseness is really demonstrated. Nor must we be in a hurry to discredit any statement that seems to conflict with others in our authorities. We must first be quite sure that the conflict is real and not apparent.

All forms of literature tend to develop certain set schemes of description that may be applied to varying circumstances. Such schemes may easily deform the truth in any particular case. This leads on to another form of criticism which cannot be avoided, but can easily be abused. Suppose the historian is describing the development of a tyrant. The development follows a general scheme. We at once question the value of this particular description : it is only a particular tyrant, we say, who is being described. But, if the development differs widely from the normal, we may again question it because it is not typical. The evidence gets no chance either way, unless we apply more satisfactory forms of criticism.

Many a passage in an ancient author is susceptible, grammatically, of a wider or narrower meaning. We have to decide just how much meaning to allot to it. There is no natural superiority either in the ' maximum ' or in the ' minimum ' view. We must try to judge each case on its merits. And yet many fine scholars seem to think that there is security in ' minimising '—in refusing to let a passage mean more than the least that it must. I will quote just one special example of this. Strabo reports that the Roman ἡγεμόνες (' generals '—i.e. ' governors ' or ' emperors ') struck ' the gold and silver ' at Lugdunum. The minimum meaning here is that there was a mint in that city, in which the governor struck coins. But the maximum meaning, also quite possible from the Greek, is that Lugdunum was *the* imperial mint for gold and silver. The rest of the evidence to me strongly suggests that the maximum meaning is right here, but it is only fair to add that this conclusion is hotly contested.

A number of arguments, it may be, independent of one another, point towards one general conclusion. By itself none of them is decisive : taken together they make a powerful impression. A favourite method of critics in such a case is to untie the bundle of observations, break the sticks one by one and throw the broken sticks away with the remark that they amount to nothing. It is hard to bring out the point exactly in a metaphor. But the question is, was the bundle a true bundle ? Was it reasonable to bring together the individual sticks to form it ? The method of dividing and breaking may be a very successful debating one, but it may easily stop our advance to the truth.

So far we have been speaking of data as if they were single and isolated. But in a book of this kind our interests will be rather in groups and constellations of facts. Here there is even more room for divergence than in dealing with facts singly. The mind has to undertake a complex process of combination, comparable to the weaving of a cloth. And who can lay down in advance what the rules of such a craft shall be ? Everyone must weave as his taste and judgment direct him. We pass beyond mere narrative to attempts to show its inherent meaning. Facts are presented in patterns, and these patterns are in our own minds. It might seem that here we are completely at the mercy of chance. But, if we have no exact principles to guide us, we have something that may be called ' taste ', something like a correctness in matching colours correctly. Yet it is precisely here, at this point of uncertainty, that fascinating prospects of new discovery present themselves. It is always possible that facts, long known but not satisfactorily interpreted, may suddenly be seen in a new light which, once observed, is quite convincing. The wood is so often lost behind its trees : but one may at last see through the trees to the wood.

All the way we should be directed by a sincere desire to find the truth. There are enemies in our path—bias, intellectual sloth, lack of disciplined judgment. These must be met by sincerity, mental alertness, sound training.

History, when it ceases to be written by specialists for specialists, steps beyond the field of science and becomes an art. It uses all the skills of language to express itself and commend its interest to the reader. Style is therefore no matter of indifference. The first virtue of historical style is clarity. You must say what you mean to say, say just so much and no more, and not inadvertently say something that was quite outside your real meaning. This is far harder to achieve than anyone would at first imagine. Language lends itself to ambiguities. I remember once writing a particular paper in collaboration with a colleague. We had an interesting new thesis to present and were very anxious to present it correctly. It was quite surprising how many doubts and inconsistencies appeared during the revising of the original draft. Imagine something that you have written in the hands of a trained lawyer who is not concerned with what you may have meant, but only with the words that you have used to express your meaning. Meanings that never occurred to you may prove to be derivable from your expression. Firstly, then, let us be clear, and that really implies simplicity too. But, where your subject is rich in emotional content, it is not enough that you should write lucidly ; you must use variety of texture and colour. English with its wealth of synonyms, of native Anglo-Saxon or classical origin, permits an unending variety here. No reader of the classics will quite escape the influence of Tacitus. His fine, terse, ironical style will commend itself as perfect for some themes. The urbanity of our own Gibbon with its balance and deliberation, with its quiet wit and malice, will equally suggest itself in other contexts. But each writer needs to find his own style, the garment that will fit him, even if he may work into it strips borrowed from his predecessors.

History cannot be fully defined either as an art or as a science. It may be most satisfactory to call it a ' humanity ' and leave it at that. That strikes the right keynote. History is concerned with the affairs of human beings like ourselves and that is why it ever claims our interest. That is why we are willing to project ourselves into the past, to imagine ourselves living the lives of the ancients, feeling their emotions, thinking their thoughts. We cannot do this without expanding our own sympathies—and that alone should be reward enough for the effort.

CHAPTER I

HISTORICAL SKETCH

The object of this first chapter is to give a sketch of the Empire which may supply a background to all that follows : to explain what the position of Emperor from time to time was, how it was defined in law, how it was interpreted by the subjects ; then, around the Emperor, to show the different parts of the State in relation to one another and to him. Later chapters will develop particular themes. We shall have to consider at the close how far the constitution of the Empire was satisfactory for its main purposes, how much truth there is in the contention that imperfections in the constitution were a main cause of Decline and Fall.

The dream of a universal Empire had haunted the Near East since the days of the ancient kingdoms of Babylonia, Assyria and Egypt. Persia carried the dream nearer fulfilment, and Alexander the Great claimed it for the Greeks. But with his Successors the dream seemed to fade. The world broke down into a new set of jarring states and uneasy, jealous cities within them. And then came Rome. By slow, hardly perceptible steps she climbed to mastery in Latium, in Italy, then, after the bitter Punic wars, beyond Italy in the Western Mediterranean. Then came involvement in the politics of the Kingdoms of Macedonia, Syria and Egypt, conquest by force of arms, peaceful penetration. Men began to see the ' fortune ' of Rome pushing her forward to the goal of imperial sway by land and sea. For a time Rome handled her problems with admirable skill. The Senate, which had attained a unique moral ascendancy in the State during the wars that culminated in the Hannibalic, succeeded in finding the right policies and controlling its magistrates and generals. But the Empire still grew by diplomacy and arms—and, we should add, by consent. And with its growth its problems did not grow less.

It was just at this point that the Senate, after its brilliant successes, failed. It ceased to be able to impose its authority on the magistrates abroad, above all on the ambitious generals and their devoted, but hungry, armies. The ship seemed to be near port, but the steering was breaking down. Sulla, the first man to rise above the State, found a temporary solution in his dictatorship. But he abdicated—whether quite of his own wish is not easy to decide. After him and his unforgotten example the Senate ruled precariously ;

round it a series of great individuals fought and schemed for supremacy. The Senate itself was partly to blame. It kept its overwhelming pride, but it had lost much of the austere gravity and devotion that had earned it the name of the ' Assembly of Kings '. Its members too often sinned against the traditions of public spirit and incorruptibility. Such weakness was a temptation to the ambitious and powerful to play for their own hand. The first unofficial ' Triumvirate ' of Julius Caesar, Pompey and Crassus dominated Rome for six years ; then, after the death of Crassus at Carrhae, it passed over into a personal rivalry between the two survivors, ending in a great civil war, the death of Pompey and the triumph of Caesar. As Caesar was murdered just before his departure for a Parthian war on the 15th of March 44 B.C. we cannot be sure what his plans for the future government of Rome were. The daggers of the ' Liberators ' prove that many suspected him of aiming at tyranny, whether as dictator or as king. After this there was no true Republic any more. Even Brutus seems to have been moving down the slippery path towards personal rule ; else, what means his portrait on the coins struck just before Philippi ? The picture is at first confused by the quarrels among the Caesarians, particularly between Antony and Octavian. Finally they composed their differences and together struck down their enemies. The second Triumvirate was an exceptional, legalised tyranny ; it never had any prospects of becoming permanent. Men looked to see which of the three would prevail over his colleagues ; for tyranny naturally has one head, not three. Lepidus soon fell out of the race in which the running was too hot for him. The genius of Antony was abashed before that of Octavian at Actium.

Who was this young new master of the world ? He was a grand-nephew of Julius Caesar, chosen by him shortly before his death as his heir ; the judgment of Julius might convince us, if we had any doubts, that there was something remarkable in this young man. For the time his only assets were the adoption and the great name of Caesar ; with them went the debits—the necessity of paying out enormous legacies. Young Octavian faced all his liabilities. He helped the Senate to fight Antony, then, when the Senate proposed to drop him, made his terms with the other Caesarians in time. In the struggles of the next years he showed courage, diplomatic skill, unscrupulous resolution and inhuman cruelty. But he never lost sight of his goal and he won through to it.

Octavian was no mediocrity ; mediocrities do not found empires. Yet he had understanding and sympathy for the ordinary man ; his genius apart, he was in many ways like the ordinary man himself.

He had a peculiarly acute sense of what is possible under given conditions. He had a strong sense of mission—of the need of Rome for reorganisation and of his own ability to meet it. He had the luck to enjoy the help of two devoted friends of the highest capacity ; Maecenas, the diplomatist, and Agrippa, the general and admiral. He is not as exciting a figure as the demonic Julius. But it is something of a mystery that so many historians should exhaust their superlatives in lauding the great destroyer, who could not rebuild where he had destroyed, and sink into lukewarm terms of approval for the man who actually did the rebuilding.

Within four years of Actium Octavian had sketched his new plan for the Empire ; four years more and it assumed something like a final shape. This was very quick work, very sure. The problem was to assure stable government for Rome and her Empire. The Senate had proved its incompetence to undertake full responsibility. Rome was weary of the exceptional powers of the second Triumvirs who had earned just hatred. Octavian, with the general approval, allowed them to lapse. For the moment he stood where he was as leader of the State, Commander of the armies, Consul year by year. But all this was provisional ; what was wanted was something permanent. Rome did not want a dictator or a king. She could not stand either perfect liberty or perfect slavery. Yet ' the interests of peace demanded the concentration of power in one hand '. What is to be done then ? Let Julius be consecrated as the Saint of the new order, but let his political ideas lie buried with him ; restore the Republic, create within it a position for a leader who can sustain the government, but define that position in old Republican terms. The resulting system will not, of course, be quite what it seems. There will be an element of acting, of hypocrisy in it. But that very hypocrisy is a sign of willingness to conciliate public opinion and as such may be condoned.

In 27 B.C. the Republic was ' restored ' ; so Rome was assured and she accepted the assurance. Octavian, now named Augustus, the ' Revered ', for his merit, continued to be Consul year by year. He also continued to command the armies as their *Imperator*—the old word used in a new sense. To him as Proconsul were assigned almost all the provinces that still required the presence of armies ; the other, ' peaceful ', provinces were left to the Senate. Four years later, in 23 B.C., Augustus found it desirable to modify his position. He gave up the consulship, but received the proconsular power in an extended form. To express his peculiar position within the State he chose to develop the tribunician power in a new and enlarged form. He had already held it in some way not quite clear to us ;

but now he made it the expression of his *fastigium*, his supremacy. He was not actually tribune, but received the power year by year and could use it to date his reign. He inherited the tribune's personal sacrosanctity, his almost unlimited power of veto, his right to protect the Roman citizen. To all this were added a number of special rights, as for example the right to convene the Senate and present the first bill at each meeting. Augustus was not censor ; he refused the offers of a perpetual censorship. But he *did* receive and exercise a general responsibility for public morals. He was not yet *pontifex maximus*, head of the State religion. But that office was only waiting for him till Lepidus, who had received it after Caesar's death, should die, as he did in 12 B.C. Above all Augustus enjoyed a unique *auctoritas*; men looked to him to take the initiative in all that wanted doing. This *auctoritas* was in its essence undefined. We shall not be far wrong if we regard the tribunician power as its vehicle. In course of time Augustus assumed a number of *curae*—charge of the corn supply, of the *vigiles*, the night watch of Rome, of the public roads. Augustus did not go out of his way to seek them ; rather were they imposed on him by the stress of need.

The Senate was to retain its traditional honours. It was to be the partner of the Emperor in government, but on two conditions—that the Emperor asked for its co-operation and that it did not shirk its responsibilities, but found the courage and independence to face them. It sent out the governors to a number of the provinces ; it was the supreme authority in Rome and Italy. Its members filled most of the main posts in the Emperor's service. It began to function as a great court of criminal justice. A great deal of public business was transacted in the Senate. But we must not be too ready to talk of a ' dyarchy ', a government shared between Emperor and Senate. When the Senate dealt with the business of the Emperor, it was the will of the Emperor that was decisive. One might say impatiently that it made no difference whether the Emperor governed directly or through the Senate, but that will not be quite true. In politics it is not only the ultimate authority that counts ; it makes a lot of difference how that authority is exercised. When the Emperor consulted the Senate he was showing his respect for ancient tradition and its representative ; he was showing that his intention to maintain the old Roman *respublica* was sincere. We must not forget that the word did not mean ' Republic ' in our modern sense. It signified the commonwealth of Rome, the Senate and people ; and it did not cease to exist because it had become necessary to devise the new office of Emperor at its head.

The second order of the Roman nobility, the Knights, had also their place in the plans of Augustus. They supplied him with a few high officials, such as the prefects of the Guard and of Egypt, with many of his young officers and with men of business experience to assist him as procurators in his financial administration. The class of freedmen supplied him with many minor officials. The lowest tasks naturally fell to imperial slaves. While the nobles enjoyed their *otium cum dignitate* the Roman people were contented with their *panem et circenses,* lavish provision for their material and intellectual (?) needs. Rome and Italy ' attended at the tribunal of the consuls and the Senate '. The charges undertaken by Augustus infringed this rule at particular points, but did not break its general validity. The provinces, divided, as we have seen, between Emperor and Senate, were inclined to welcome the New Order. They had suffered long and bitterly under the tyranny of magistrates, imperfectly controlled from Rome. They found new hopes under the Empire. The governors were mainly senators ; only a few small provinces were given to knights. The governor of a senatorial province was a propraetor or proconsul, the governor of an imperial province a *legatus,* a deputy of the Emperor. Over both classes a strict control was now exercised, especially in the imperial. It was not the interest of the government that its provinces should be robbed by individuals. The army was reduced to reasonable proportions and set on a basis of professional service. Pay and length of service were fixed and arrangements were made for the payment of pensions on discharge. Augustus set his face against military anarchy and kept his armies well in hand. They swore allegiance to him and to him only.

Such was the system Augustus founded. That he had builded well is proved by the durability of his building. We know how Augustus wished his new system to be regarded—as a continuation of the old *respublica* with only such modifications as pressing need required. We can see at once that it was never quite what he represented it to be. The Senate had now at hand just such a chief, a citizen of predominant power and authority, as Cicero had imagined. But the real importance of this chief had far outgrown anything that was ever in Cicero's mind. Whatever you called him, he was the one great man of the State, not a king, because Rome disliked the name, but more than any king, an Emperor or king of kings in fact. The realities of the position were more readily grasped from the first in the provinces than in Rome. About the provinces in their relation to Rome there was less pretence. Rome and Italy were the queens of the world. The provinces, in return for obedience and punctual discharge of liabilities, might expect a good government and the benefits of the Augustan peace. There was no suggestion yet that they were effective partners in a joint concern. The motto of the Empire was ' defence not defiance '. The frontiers were to be defined and protected. There was to be no greedy expansion ; the great thing was to conserve the vast values already contained within the Empire.

Augustus had not been unmindful of the future, of what might happen after his death. He had picked out various candidates for the succession—first his nephew, Marcellus, then his loyal assistant, Agrippa, married to his daughter Julia, then the two young sons of that marriage, Gaius and Lucius Caesar, adopted by Augustus as his own sons. One by one, unkind fortune swept them away and the choice of Augustus had finally to fall on his stepson Tiberius, whom for all his services and abilities he never loved. When Augustus died in A.D. 14 Tiberius was his colleague, holding the title of *Imperator* and the tribunician power ; there was no possible rival, unless Germanicus, his nephew and son by adoption, chose to become one. Tiberius, then, at once took over power and received the formal grant from the Senate. But he showed a reluctance to shoulder the whole burden that was not entirely hypocritical, and the Senate a hesitation that was not entirely innocent. Tiberius ruled on the principles of Augustus, using the same formula for his power. Judged from the point of the Empire at large it was emphatically a good reign. There were no great disasters abroad and some notable successes. Government was orderly and firm traditions began to be established. But Tiberius was very unpopular. He lacked sympathy for the masses ; the traditional arrogance of the Claudian family clung to him like a curse. He tried to induce the Senate to co-operate with him, but could not win its confidence and detested it for its servility. His family life was unhappy, from faults on many sides. Germanicus, his son by adoption, was a thorn in his side. He had resisted the attempt of his legions to make him emperor in the mutinies of the first year of Tiberius's reign. He had commanded with some show of success in Germany. Sent on a great mission to the East he had discharged his duty of settling Armenia, but became involved in a feud with Piso, Governor of Syria, and died under circumstances that to some suggested poisoning. The trial of Piso, which ended in his suicide, was a grave embarrassment to the Emperor. Germanicus had given more trouble by tactlessness and courting popularity than he could have done by open disaffection. Drusus, Tiberius's own son, died suddenly in A.D. 23, soon after receiving the tribunician power.

He had shown initiative and resolution on some occasions, but there is a question mark about his real character.

After his death Tiberius had to look for heirs in the family of Germanicus—in his two eldest sons, Nero Drusus and Drusus. Agrippina, the widow of Germanicus, lacked any kind of wisdom or tact. She allowed herself and her family to become the centre of something like a party against the Emperor. Sejanus, the praetorian prefect and all too powerful friend of Tiberius, rose to supreme influence, especially after he had persuaded Tiberius to retire from Rome to Capri. According to Tacitus Sejanus was mainly responsible for the quarrel between the Emperor and his relatives. Perhaps the quarrel was ready enough to develop without any special assistance. When Livia, widow of Augustus and mother of Tiberius, died in A.D. 29 the latent enmity broke out ; Agrippina and Nero were disgraced and banished. Sejanus used the absence of Tiberius to draw all power to himself. He aspired to marry Livilla, widow of Drusus, and gain a share in the imperial power. At last, in A.D. 31, when he thought himself near his goal, he was suddenly struck down. Tiberius found a new agent, Macro, to supplant him, denounced him to the Senate and so caught him before he could launch a counterstroke.

The political world was now turned upside down. The friendship of Sejanus changed from an asset into a deadly liability. The sins of Sejanus, real or imagined, came home to roost. It was now discovered that Sejanus had actually murdered Drusus and seduced his wife while he yet lived, but it is permissible to hold the story in some doubt. The friends of Sejanus were struck down without mercy, but there was no mercy for his enemies either. Agrippina died by suicide, her sons, Nero and Drusus, were involved in the same destruction. The fall of the house of Germanicus, then, cannot be solely attributed to the one villain, Sejanus. The closing years of the reign were stormy and unhappy. The weapon of *maiestas*, high treason, was remorselessly used against all whom the Emperor disliked or suspected. Tiberius lived on, lonely, hated and hating all, despising and despised, till 37.

For his heirs he chose Caligula, younger brother of Nero and Drusus, and with him his own grandson, Tiberius Gemellus ; but he is said to have foreseen that Caligula would not long tolerate his young rival. Even so, the verdict of the Senate on the dead Emperor should have been favourable. But Caligula lacked the resolution to enforce consecration and Tiberius was left in a kind of limbo, not numbered among the gods of the State but still ensured by his record of the respect of succeeding Emperors.

Caligula succeeded his great-uncle unchallenged. As Tiberius had foreseen he soon disposed of his colleague, the young Gemellus. He was welcomed by an outburst of popular enthusiasm. But he was unbalanced, morose, trained by his servility to Tiberius to play the tyrant himself. A serious illness in his first year seems to have wrecked his health. He began to show signs of megalomania, aspired to divinity on earth, acted with a mixture of cruelty and wild caprice. History has chosen to concentrate on his vagaries. But there may have been some method in his madness. For example, his expedition to Germany may have been necessary to forestall rebellion. But he quarrelled with all his friends including his own family, to which he had at first paid extravagant honours. One sister, Drusilla, died, to his bitter grief ; the other two, Julia and Agrippina, were banished. In the end he insulted an old officer of the guard and was murdered in the conspiracy set on foot by him. The coinage of the reign maintains its original course throughout, discreet, insisting on the greatness of the Augustan House, avoiding all extravagance. One might suppose that it was an open secret that the Emperor was not quite in his right mind and that his deputies contrived to limit the mischief resulting.

The murder of Caligula in 41 left Rome without an Emperor, and the Senate could dream of an Emperor of its own choice or even of a restored Republic. But the praetorians had got ahead of it. They found Claudius, uncle of Caligula, hiding in the palace, hauled him off to the camp and proclaimed him Emperor. The Senate had to bow to the will of the soldiers, which had been confirmed by a donative, an evil precedent for the future. Claudius was a surprise. He drooled and mumbled—probably the effect of some illness of childhood. He was very learned in a somewhat pedantic way and a trifle ridiculous in all that he did. But he had a good deal of the ability of his house. He carried through the conquest of Britain speedily and economically. The armies were kept active and disciplined. The efficiency of the Civil Service was increased ; the great Bureaux of correspondence, finance and petitions were developed under freedmen ; the imperial chest, the *fiscus*, assumed permanent form ; the imperial procurators received power to decide fiscal cases in court. But there were less satisfactory features of the reign. Claudius was incalculable in mood and could be cruel. He was too much under the influence of his wives and freedmen. How much he was to blame for the wantonness of Messalina and the hard ambition of Agrippina the Younger is hard to say. He certainly tried to do too much and often ended by leaving the necessary undone. But the record is on the whole a good one, and Claudius, hastened on his way by the mushrooms that his wife served him in 54, was yet enrolled among the State gods.

Nero, son of Agrippina and Cn. Domitius Ahenobarbus, was adopted as son by Claudius, married to his daughter Octavia and preferred above his own son, Britannicus. From his father the unruly blood of a turbulent family flowed into the Julio-Claudian line. Abroad, the reign was signalised by great wars—a long struggle with Parthia, ending in a good peace, revolts in Britain and Judaea, both serious, but both soon brought under control. At home there were two distinct periods—constitutional government under the tutelage of Seneca and Burrhus, followed by wild capricious tyranny under Tigellinus and his like. Rome now learned what absolute power, when married to the artistic temperament, could be. Nero murdered his half-brother, his mother and his wife. He was even suspected of causing the great fire of 64. He violated all rules of morality and decency ; but good Romans loathed almost as much as his crimes his appearances on the stage or in the circus. But the bad loved him as much as the good loathed. He was endured for fifteen years, and even at the last it was he who threw in his own hand. Many refused to believe that he was dead, and no fewer than three times false Neros appeared in the East to trouble the peace of the Empire.

In 68 Vindex, a governor in South Gaul, called the world to revolt against the tyrant. Galba, in Spain, announced his adhesion to the cause. The legions of the Germanies, however, led by Verginius Rufus, treated the movement as a Gallic revolt, and cut to pieces Vindex and his army at Vesontio. But the victorious legions threw down the statues of Nero and tried to force the Empire on Verginius. For a moment there was an impasse. Nero was obviously falling, but no one could foresee who would take his place, since Verginius declined. The matter was settled when Nero lost his head and prepared for flight from Rome. Then at last the Guard was bribed to declare for Galba, and Nero only escaped execution by suicide. Galba was an old senator of wealth and reputation ; but he was past his prime and in the hands of greedy and unwise advisers. He offended the Guard by refusing them the promised gift, he offended the legions of the Germanies by favouring what was left of the cause of Vindex, he offended his own lieutenant Otho by not choosing him for adoption. On the 1st of January 69 the legions of Upper Germany refused to swear allegiance to Galba ; two days later they and their comrades of the lower province proclaimed Vitellius Emperor. Galba tried to save his tottering throne by an adoption. But his choice, Piso, lacked all qualifications

c

except a stern respectability. Otho, disappointed of his hopes, seduced the praetorian guard and Galba and Piso were brutally murdered in the streets of Rome. Neither Otho nor Vitellius commanded much respect ; but they had behind them armies determined to fight the issue out. Otho was defeated in a sharp campaign in North Italy and committed suicide. He might still have won had he waited for reinforcements to come up from the East. But he probably judged—and rightly—that his record as murderer of his old friend damned him and that, even if he won, he would soon be discarded for some other rival. Vitellius owed almost everything to others—his initial reputation to his father, Lucius, the great general and diplomatist, his elevation to the ambitions of his legates and armies. He was a gross sensualist and glutton. But he was not usually cruel and he had a certain kindliness and simplicity that deserved more friends than he won. His troops gave him an extravagant devotion. But his reign did not last long. In July the troops of the East set up their own general, Vespasian, as rival, and, after a little fighting in Italy, all was over by the end of the year. Vitellius wished to abdicate, but his followers insisted on fighting it out and in the last struggle the Capitol was burned to the ground.

The Civil Wars of 68–69 taught men several lessons. An Emperor could be made outside Rome—by an army as well as by the Guard. An Emperor need not be of the Julio-Claudian House ; hitherto it had been, as Tacitus puts it, an inheritance of one family. The coins of the Civil War usually lack any mention of an emperor, but dwell on the Senate and the people of Rome. It is very unlikely that any large number of people thought seriously of a restoration of the Republic ; what they had in mind was a constitutional principate on the model of the Augustan. The Civil Wars shook the prestige of the whole Empire. The revolt of Vindex had not been primarily nationalist. But Civilis, the Batavian, and his allies in North Gaul and Germany were definitely against Rome, dreaming of new power for the Germans or of an ' Empire of the Gauls '. The warning was clear to read. Fortunately for Rome the warning was taken in time.

Vespasian had been selected by Nero for the command in Judaea precisely—the irony of it—because he combined the necessary military requirements with the lack of social distinction that seemed to guarantee his harmlessness. Solid rather than brilliant, he was just the man for the occasion. He restored unity in the Empire, checked licence in the army, recovered the desperate finances. He soon showed that he meant to govern along the lines laid down by

Augustus. He introduced a new morality into Rome, his own country parsimony and honesty in place of the luxury and display of the Neronian court. He became censor in 73 and recruited many new senators from Italy and Narbonese Gaul. The disputes over the succession had set men wondering whether it was reasonable to leave it to chance at the end of each reign. Was not some general principle needed ? And was there not much to be said for Galba's idea of a son by adoption rather than by birth ? Such thoughts were certainly in the minds of men like Helvidius Priscus, the leader of a kind of opposition party in the Senate. But Vespasian had no understanding for this very reasonable view. He had two sons—Titus, a proved soldier, and the younger and untried Domitian—and he let it be known from the first that his sons were to be his heirs. Titus was advanced to be his colleague ; Domitian, while kept in the background, received the title of Caesar, suggesting future inheritance. It was on this point that Vespasian quarrelled so bitterly with Priscus and his friends. Vespasian again was no doctrinaire moralist. He looked at what needed doing and used the most suitable instruments, including notorious agents of Nero. Yet Tacitus summed him up correctly : Vespasian was the one man whom Empire improved.

Titus succeeded his father in 79 without question. Domitian claimed that he should have been partner in the Empire, and it looked as if a party supporting him made trouble for Titus. The quarrel was patched up, but Titus never made his brother his colleague and Domitian continued to feel aggrieved. Titus's short reign was marked by two natural disasters—the eruption of Vesuvius and a great fire at Rome. Abroad all was quiet, except that the advance in Britain, already begun under Vespasian, was pressed forward. Could Titus have retained his good intentions and his popularity through a long reign ? He was very much inclined to waste money—and that is the shortest way to ruin. As it was he died within two years and Domitian succeeded him.

Domitian was a man of much ambition and some ability. Kept back by his father he had developed an inferiority complex, but sought compensation in arrogance and display. Abroad, the advance in Britain was carried as far as it was wise to go. The bitter fighting on the middle Rhine led to an improved frontier. Even the hard wars with Sarmatians, Suevians and Dacians on the Danube were not of Domitian's seeking, but by a vigorous resistance and judicious concessions he strove to become master of them. The real trouble was at home in Rome. Domitian was ungenerous and suspicious. He failed to reach a full agreement with the Senate.

Governing like an autocrat, yet observing the forms of constitutional Empire, he required the Senate to be his partner in his actions, even the most unpopular—such as the condemnation of offending senators. A few bold spirits defied him and met death or exile ; the majority ground their teeth and submitted, waiting for somebody else to do something about it. By assuming a perpetual censorship Domitian made himself master of the composition of the Senate. The army loved him because he had raised its pay by a third. The people, pampered with food and shows, were at least not unfriendly. The one military rebellion, that of Saturninus on the Rhine, was speedily suppressed. Domitian fell a victim to a conspiracy of his wife, chamberlain and Praetorian prefect, all of whom feared for their own lives. So ended the second imperial dynasty, the Flavian. Domitian had founded the temple of the Flavian family, had consecrated most of his relatives and nominated two young nephews as his heirs. But their father fell into disfavour in 95 and that was the end of imperial chances for the sons. It is hard to believe that the lads would have been allowed tranquil succession, even if Domitian had died a year earlier in his bed. The dynasty had not had time to impress itself on the public imagination either by military prowess or by munificence in Rome. At the last it had alienated the Senate.

The conspirators selected an elderly lawyer, Nerva, to succeed Domitian in 96. Nerva had secured honours rather than honour under Nero and had since then walked delicately. As Emperor he exceeded the best that could have been hoped of him. He let the violent outcry against the fallen tyrant run its course, then judiciously applied the brakes. He showed respect for the Senate and Roman liberty. He sought popular favour by generous and enlightened reforms—improvement of the corn supply, relief for Italy of the burdens of the state post, abolition of abuses in the special chest that raised the tax on the Jews. One institution of Nerva—the *alimenta*, arrangements for the nurture of orphans, based on loans to Italian farmers—was one of the noblest charities of ancient times. One thing Nerva lacked, strong military support. The praetorians at Domitian's death, lacking a leader, had only growled in secret. A year later they called upon Nerva to surrender the murderers to justice. The demand might be considered just. Nerva pleaded with the troops, but finally had to give way. His imperial dignity was fatally damaged. But Nerva again showed that he had a head to plan and a heart to dare. He adopted as his son Trajan, the darling of the army, and rebellion died away or was quietly suppressed. It is probable enough that the plan of adoption had already been formed ; the mutiny of the Guard gave the signal for its announcement.

Trajan succeeded Nerva in 98 within four months of his adoption. He paid the dues of piety to his adopted father—that and no more. His policy was to be his own. He would command the love and respect of the Senate by a loyal observance of its rights. He would dazzle the public by his munificence. He would control the army and astonish the world by a new display of Roman valour and a resumption of the offensive. The conquest of Dacia, the invasion of Parthia and conquest of new provinces in the East, showed this policy in action. Trajan was remembered by the name the Senate conferred on him, ' Best of Emperors '. He certainly achieved stability in Rome and restored Roman prestige abroad. But he overspent and overstrained the resources of the Empire. That probably accounted for the great revolts of Jews over all the East that blotted the page in his final years.

Galba had set the example of adoption with Piso in 69. It was a dismal failure. Nerva repeated the experiment in 97 with Trajan. It was a brilliant success. Experience had shown the difficulties involved in succession within one family. Free election to the Empire was barely conceivable. But election under the form of adoption of the man approved by Emperor and Senate seemed to meet all requirements. As things fell out, the experiment of Nerva became the norm ; a great dynasty of adoption ran from Nerva to Commodus. Trajan apparently had no son of his own and so lacked the temptation to promote his own flesh and blood. But it is quite uncertain what he meant to do. He was on his way back to Rome from the East in 117 when he died, and up to the last he had not named his successor. Hadrian, his kinsman, whom he had left as Governor of Syria, succeeded him. But men whispered that the deathbed adoption, which was reported, had not really been Trajan's act, but the result of the plotting of his wife Plotina and her favourite Hadrian.

The new Emperor, like Trajan a Spaniard—the provincials thus entered on their inheritance—was a man of extraordinary genius, interested in everything, restlessly active, ever ready to try new ways. He spent a large part of his long reign in visiting province by province and studying their requirements at first hand. But the peace of Hadrian was no weak pacifism ; it was based on a strong and well disciplined army and an elaborate frontier defence. The one serious revolt of the reign, that of the Jews (132–135), was crushed without mercy. Hadrian had no son and, as his reign drew towards its close, he decided on adoption. His first choice, L.

Aelius, disappointed him by dying prematurely.   His second choice
was more fortunate.   It was the respected senator, Antoninus, who, at
Hadrian's wish, himself adopted L. Verus, son of Aelius, and the young
Marcus Aurelius ; Hadrian had marked him out as the real promise
of the future.   Antoninus ruled with wisdom, firmness and justice for
twenty-three happy years—perhaps as happy an age as any great
Empire has ever enjoyed.   His loyalty to Hadrian earned him his
title ' Pious '.   Marcus married Faustina, daughter of Antoninus,
in 148 and received the tribunician power.   When Antoninus died
in 161, Marcus was bound to succeed him, but he chose to admit
Lucius Verus as joint Emperor with him.   It was the first example
of two Augusti reigning together.   Verus went out to a Parthian
war as nominal Commander-in-Chief, but he was of little real help
and might have become a serious hindrance.   The skies were now
clouded.   Plague came back with the armies from the East.   The
Eastern Germans broke into Italy and Verus died on the first
expedition against them.   Troubles on the Danube occupied
Marcus for the rest of his reign.   The philosopher Emperor was
called by duty to spend weary months and years in a frontier camp.
In spite of the revolt of Avidius Cassius in the East, the war was
nearly over when Marcus died in camp in 180.   Yet for all the
virtue and devotion of the Emperor the gods seemed to be wroth
with Rome.   At Lugdunum the angry mob demanded the punishment of the ' atheist ' Christians, and a grim persecution followed.
The one surviving son of Marcus, Commodus, had become a
colleague during his lifetime and succeeded him unquestioned.   The
test of the dynasty of adoption had come.   Four Emperors, from
Nerva to Antoninus, had died leaving no sons and adoption had
supplied the vacant places.   Now came an Emperor who left a son
behind him.   An Emperor of the calibre of Marcus must surely be
concerned with the public good.   If, then, he promoted his son and
marked him out as successor, he must have supposed him worthy,
apart from the accident of birth, of holding the imperial post.   If
Marcus so reasoned, he was wrong.   Perhaps it was impossible to
foresee what the temptations of imperial rule in Rome would do for
a disposition like that of the young Commodus, not at first hopelessly
perverse, but impressionable and not confirmed in virtue.

Commodus patched up a peace on the frontier and made haste to
return to Rome.   There were no serious wars, but there was serious
trouble in some of the armies, with desertions on the grand scale.
In Rome, Commodus played the part of an Eastern despot, devoted
to the pleasures of his harem and the delights of circus and amphitheatre.   He had exceptional skill with the javelin and slew vast

numbers of wild beasts for the public amusement. Lacking any serious capacity for government he was controlled by diverse favourites in turn—the able but ambitious Perennis, the adroit, low-born, unscrupulous Cleander. The Emperor lost the respect of all good citizens and when, like Domitian, he fell a victim to his inner circle of friends at the end of 192, the Senate exulted over his corpse.

Again an imperial house was extinct ; again the succession was undetermined. Pertinax, prefect of the city, one of the best generals of Marcus, was the man chosen by the conspirators. He governed with excellent intentions and some little success for three months. Then the discontent of the praetorians broke out and a band of desperadoes murdered Pertinax in his palace. The praetorians of 69 had been ready with their candidate, Otho. Not so the praetorians of 193. They found no better expedient than to put the Empire in their gift up to auction. An elderly senator, Didius Julianus, chose to regard himself as a suitable candidate and won over the Guard by an enormous present. But the people of Rome loved Pertinax and called for an avenger of his murder. The provincial armies were quick to answer the call. No fewer than three avengers arose—Clodius Albinus in Britain, Septimius Severus in Pannonia, Pescennius Niger in Syria. Didius, lacking any firm support, was lost. Septimius, being nearest Rome, struck first ; Didius collapsed without a struggle. Septimius secured Albinus by offering him the rank of Caesar. Taking the field against Niger, he concluded what might have been a serious war in a brilliant campaign of three victories. Within a few months of the last of these he had broken with Albinus and promoted his own little son, the future Caracalla, to be Caesar. It is hard to believe that there had been any sincerity in his previous dealings with Albinus. Septimius quite deliberately broke with the principle of adoption. He put aside a tried colleague and substituted for him an untried lad. Septimius however gained a quick victory. Albinus was killed, his supporters were mercilessly persecuted, the Senate which had secretly favoured his cause fell into disgrace.

To establish his new dynasty Septimius betrayed Rome. He enriched and pampered the army to ensure its unquestioned support and so opened the way to the military anarchy of the 3rd century. Septimius was a man of great energy and ability. He was one of the greatest of Roman generals, victorious in the Civil Wars, victorious over Parthians, victorious in his last years over the Caledonians in North Britain. A provincial himself, from Leptis Magna in Africa, he showed consideration for provincial interests

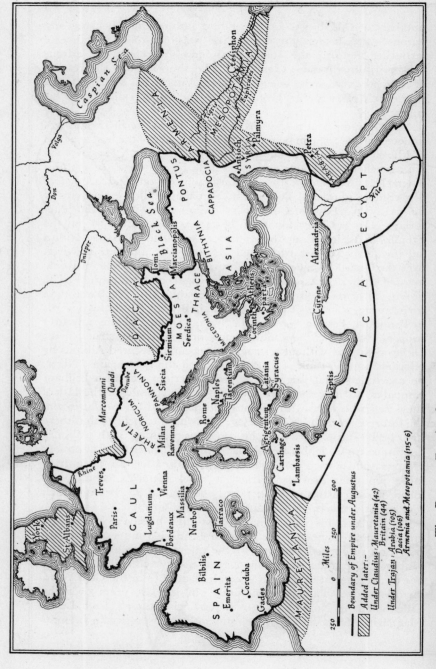

Added later:—
Under Claudius : Mauretania (42)
  Britain (44)
Under Trajan : Arabia (105)
  Dacia (106)
  Armenia and Mesopotamia (115–6)

——— Boundary of Empire under Augustus

Miles
250 0 250 500

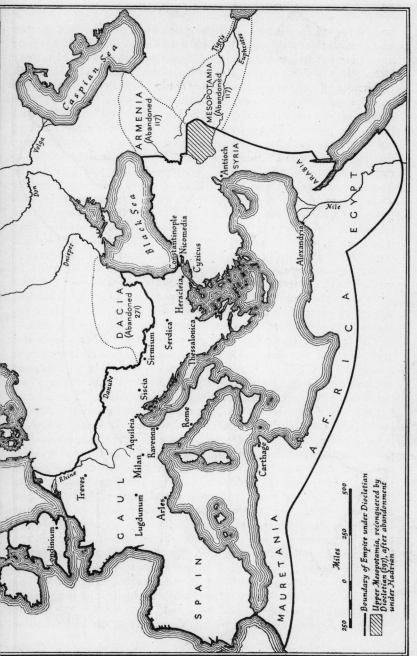

The Roman Empire under Diocletian

and disregard for Rome.   But the prize for which he had plotted
and sinned, the establishment of his dynasty, seemed likely to elude
him.   He left two sons to succeed him, Caracalla and the younger
Geta.   But it was vain for him to leave them the advice to enrich
the army and despise the rest, if they could not take the third part of
his advice and keep the peace between themselves.   Within a year
of Septimius's death in 211, Caracalla had murdered his brother and
seized sole power.   Hated and feared by all classes of society he had
only the army left him.   He spent his remaining years in the camp,
first fighting on the Danube, then conceiving a grandiose scheme to
unite the Roman and Parthian Empires by his marriage to the
daughter of the Parthian king.   Coming to Parthia as a friend he
gained a scandalous victory by treachery and returned home with
many captives and vast spoils.   He had made himself hated by his
extortions and by a peculiarly callous massacre at Alexandria.   But
it was something like an accident that led to his fall.   Macrinus,
one of his praetorian prefects, fell under his displeasure, but learned
of his impending disgrace in time.   Caracalla was murdered by
soldiers with a private grievance and Macrinus was accepted *faute
de mieux* by the army.   His responsibility for the death of Caracalla,
though suspected, could not be proved, and his choice by the army
was accepted at Rome though he was only a Roman knight.

The tradition fostered under the succeeding Emperor is hostile
and unjust to Macrinus.   He did not abandon himself to luxury at
Antioch.   He could not return to Rome and disband his army
because he was tied by a Parthian war, for the Parthian king came
breathing vengeance and, after some protracted but unsuccessful
fighting and long negotiations, Macrinus bought a peace.   Now at
last in 218 he might have returned to Rome.   But new complica-
tions at once arose.   Julia Domna, widow of Septimius, had shared
in the administration of her son.   In spite of some show of friendli-
ness from Macrinus she despaired of her fortunes and committed
suicide.   Her sister, Julia Maesa, with her immense fortune, withdrew to her native Emesa.   She had two daughters, Julia Soaemias
and Julia Mammaea, and each of them had a son, one the future
Elagabalus, and Alexander.   Elagabalus was paraded before the
troops at Emesa as the son of Caracalla by one of the daughters.
The conspiracy took root and grew, for Macrinus refused at first to
grasp the extent of his danger.   A final decisive battle near Antioch
turned against him and he fled ; he was caught and captured just
before he could carry his flight into Europe.   Against all expectation
the dynasty of Septimius had returned.

Young Elagabalus—he took his name from the chief god of

Emesa whose priest he was—was an immoral and irresponsible debauchee. His only serious interest was in the worship of his god whom he tried to foist on Rome as the one supreme power. He lasted just four years. He was then replaced by his cousin, the gentle Alexander, whom he had been persuaded to nominate as Caesar. We cannot help admiring the skill with which Julia Maesa had played her cards. She had made adroit use of her great wealth and of the dynastic feeling of the troops. She had waited for Macrinus to end the Parthian war and had then struck before he could return to Rome. When Elagabalus proved himself impossible she contrived to replace him by Alexander. But the imperial dignity had suffered irreparably. The Empire was apparently the prize of anyone who cared to grasp for it, and a series of short-lived usurpations showed that the lesson was not neglected. Alexander, who now took the name of Severus, reigned for thirteen years (222–235). The Senate was treated with consideration, the public conciliated by wise and moderate government, the troops were held in check. But the dynasty really needed a soldier to represent it. The new Persian Empire, which replaced the Parthian, was a deadly threat. Alexander had to lead an expedition which only won very partial success. When Alexander was called to a new war on the Rhine, he was soon supplanted by the giant Maximin, a barbarian by birth, commended only by his vast strength and military efficiency. The greed of his mother, Julia Mammaea, is blamed as responsible for his fall ; that probably only means that she failed to glut the insatiable avarice of the troops.

The dynasty of Severus was at an end, but the evil harvest of his faults was still to be reaped. Maximin fought with success against the Germans on Rhine and Danube, and there he served the Empire well. But he was quite out of touch with the Senate. He had no regard for the interests of the civil population. They were simply there to pay for his campaigns. He persecuted the Christians. A revolt in Africa threw up two new Emperors, the Gordians, father and son. Accepted by the Senate they were soon overthrown by Maximin's general in Numidia. The Senate, already committed beyond hope of pardon, found the energy to resist. It nominated two new Emperors, Balbinus and Pupienus ; the clamours of the people soon compelled them to admit a child of the younger Gordian as Caesar. Maximin, mad with rage, moved against Italy. But defence was well organised and resolute. Held up by the siege of Aquileia, the first town of Italy he encountered, Maximin lost the confidence of his men and, with his son, was murdered in camp. The Senate to the general surprise had won the trial by combat ; the next pretender might hesitate to challenge its authority. But peace was not yet won. Balbinus and Pupienus did not trust one another, and, when the Praetorian Guard rose and set up the little Gordian against them, they were speedily overthrown.

The young prince was at first under the influence of unworthy favourites ; but, when he married the daughter of his praetorian prefect, Timisitheus, he gained a friend and adviser who could teach him how to rule. New trouble with Persia took him to the East. The campaign had some successes to show, but Timisitheus most untimely died and his successor, the new prefect Philip, was ambitious and disloyal. The army clamoured for the removal of Gordian, and Philip, after some hesitation, let him fall (244). For the moment it seemed as if the prefect of the Guard might become a kind of Mayor of the Palace of the Emperor and finally supplant him. Philip was an Arabian by birth, a local sheik. His short reign, after his ugly beginning, ran an even course. But troubles arose on the Danube and Philip was compelled to send out his best general, Decius, to quell the revolt. The result was what Decius had foretold to Philip. The rebellious troops forced the Empire on him and, when he invaded Italy, Philip and his young son fell. Philip showed some intention to govern well. He was supposed to favour the Christians. At any rate, pagans complained of a lack of devotion in his celebration of the Secular Games of 248–249, the thousandth year of Rome. He fought with success against the Carpi on the Danube. His weakness lay in the sins of his relatives whom he sent out to govern provinces. Decius took to himself the proud name of Trajan and strove to re-enact the part of the restorer of Roman valour. He fought courageously against the Goths on the Danube, but finally lost his life on the stricken field of Abrittus (251). Hating what he considered to be mere weakness he instituted the first general persecution of the Christians ; in fact he forced all subjects of the Empire to sacrifice to the national gods. The coins show us that to Decius the gods meant mainly the imperial deities, the *Divi*.

On the death of Decius his younger surviving son, Hostilian, was associated in Empire with Trebonianus Gallus, the commander of the Danube army. Hostilian soon died and Volusian, son of Gallus, took his place. The new reign was gentle ; the persecution died down and the Emperors won a deserved popularity by ministering to the sufferers from the plague that smote Rome. But troubles soon arose. The Persians again threatened the East and Antioch, it seems, fell into their hands. On the Danube a bold general,

Aemilian, refused to pay the barbarians their subsidies and distributed the monies to his troops. The grateful soldiers hailed him as Emperor and he invaded Italy, to try out the issue with Gallus. Gallus was deserted by his own men and Aemilian entered on his short reign. The historical record at this point is most imperfect ; it is probable that the reign of Aemilian lasted for a good part of a year, not the mere three months that the epitomists give him. Gallus had sent a trusted general, Valerian, to the North to bring in reinforcements from the Rhine frontier. Too late to save Gallus he was quick to avenge him. When he marched south to Milan, Aemilian in his turn was abandoned by his men and killed. Closely scrutinised, the conduct of Valerian has a sinister look. Still, Valerian bore a high reputation and men looked to him and his son, Gallienus, whom he raised to partnership, to restore the State. Valerian seemed ready to meet the crisis in the spirit of Decius. He gave Gallienus charge of the West and himself marched eastward to meet Sapor, the Persian, who was threatening the whole of Syria and Asia Minor ; to make matters worse, the Goths were again on the move, this time by sea as well as by land. To impress the public the persecution of the Christians was resumed. For a time things went not too badly. Gallienus gained some successes in the West and Valerian could claim to be restoring the East. But in the winter of 258–259, facing Sapor on the Syrian frontier, he became involved in difficulties of supply, perhaps caused by a disloyal prefect, Macrianus. He lost the confidence of his men and found himself driven to negotiate with Sapor. He was treacherously seized and carried off to captivity. In that humiliating bondage he died some years later.

The crisis of the Empire had now reached its height. A Roman Emperor a captive ! What a shocking disgrace. The Christians saw in the disaster of their persecutor the direct punishment of God. The pagans, accustomed to blame everything on the Christians, must have faltered in their confidence ; the gods had not troubled to save their champion. On almost every frontier danger threatened and, to make matters worse, pretenders sprang up like mushrooms—the so-called ' thirty tyrants ', though they were neither thirty in number nor tyrants in quality. It did not help much towards overcoming these troubles that at just this moment Gallienus excluded senators from all military command. The coinage, which had long been tottering, crashed. The silver was hopelessly debased and the value of money became quite uncertain. Through this confusion of troubles, which can only be sketched here, Gallienus contrived to steer some sort of course. The East for a time

was lost. Sapor returned home laden with booty, but harassed
by Odenathus, Prince of Palmyra. The two sons of the prefect
Macrianus were set up as Emperors and challenged the rule of
Gallienus. A single battle in Thrace decided against them. For
the moment Gallienus was glad to recognise Odenathus as Roman
general and virtual regent of the East. Pretenders rose and fell ;
but in Gaul and the West an able general Postumus slew Saloninus,
the younger son of Gallienus, and established a separate Empire.
In the East the Goths returned to renew their raids. A considerable
success had been won over them before Gallienus died.

Gallienus has been seriously misjudged by historians. For the
calamities of the Empire in general he was certainly not responsible.
When he could meet them in person, he fought with resolution and
not without success. If he did not attempt to recover his father,
it was probably because the attempt was hopeless from the first.
Sapor would have demanded whole provinces for ransom. In the
part of the Empire that was left him Gallienus wished to reign as
a prince of peace. He checked the persecution and granted the
Church what amounted to toleration. In 268 one pretender the
more threatened North Italy, the rebellious general, Aureolus.
Gallienus shut him up in Milan and his fall seemed imminent. But
at this point the staff of Gallienus intervened ; they arranged the
murder of Gallienus and conferred Empire on the gallant Claudius.
The rising of Aureolus was more dangerous than it looks in the
history books, for Postumus was behind it. This fact, lost in our
wretched scraps of history, is securely recorded by coins of Postumus
at Milan, struck at the moment when Aureolus held the city.
Perhaps the staff had wasted their crime, for the worst was already
over. But, to the Roman, good fortune ranked as next to valour,
and no one could say that Gallienus had been lucky.

In the years of agony, 258–259, the Empire had come near to
foundering. Rome could cope with the recurrent dangers from
abroad on one condition, that she retained some degree of peace and
stability at home. But the constantly disputed succession, the
decline of the Senate, the blind interferences of the army in politics—
all damaged Roman prestige and encouraged her enemies to strike
harder. But the will to live was still sufficiently strong. The new
Emperors, the great line of restorers, were, in the main, of Illyrian
stock, tough, only recently civilised, not too subtle, but virile and
determined. Claudius ended the menace of the Goths by a decisive
victory on Mount Haemus. He died, honoured and lamented, of
plague in 270—one of the few Emperors of the age to die in his bed.
Aurelian, commander of the Horse, pushed aside Quintillus,

brother of Claudius, and was joyfully accepted by the Empire. After meeting serious invasions of Germans and Vandals, not without serious danger and loss, Aurelian applied himself to his task of restoring the frontiers. Palmyra was aspiring to an empire of her own. Zenobia, widow of Odenathus, seized Egypt and ruled for her little son, Vaballathus, as virtual Queen of the East. She held Syria and aspired to Asia Minor too. In two sharp campaigns Aurelian struck down his rival and carried Zenobia captive to Rome.

Meanwhile in the West the Gallic Empire of Postumus had aged and lost vigour under his successors. In 274 Tetricus, the last of the line, weary of precarious rule at the mercy of a disobedient soldiery, deliberately gave away the battle to Aurelian and surrendered on honourable terms. Aurelian could celebrate a well earned triumph as ' Restorer of the World '. The walls of Aurelian, set up round Rome, attested the sad fact that the Queen of the World was no longer safe against sudden assault. In 273 or 274 Aurelian put down a serious revolt in Rome, which sprang out of disorders among the moneyers, called in the base money and issued new. It was a serious attempt to restore confidence ; perhaps it was not Aurelian's fault that it only partially succeeded. In 275 Aurelian, on his way to a Persian war, was murdered by a conspiracy of his officers. It seems to have been a peculiarly stupid crime and the army resented the loss of their general. In remorse they begged the Senate to appoint the next Emperor. Months were spent in negotiations before the Senate would consent to risk making a choice. At last they chose an elderly senator, Tacitus. Despite his age he manfully took the field and repulsed his first enemies, invaders from Pontus. . But the management of his disorderly army was too much for him and he died in camp, worn out and discouraged. Florian, his brother, grasped at power, but Probus, the best general in the Eastern army, contested his claim and soon gained the decision (276). The Senate accepted the verdict of the army.

Probus continued the great work of Aurelian. He successfully dealt with several pretenders and recovered the province of Gaul from the Germans. We see how fast danger from abroad follows on civil war. He claimed to be the restorer of true peace and spoke of days to come when an army would no more be needed. Meanwhile, he kept his men busy on endless works of land reclamation, tired out their patience and was finally murdered by them. Carus, the praetorian prefect, seized the throne and simply announced his accession to the Senate, not asking, as form required, for its approval. We have not the materials for judging Carus ; we only know that he appointed his sons, Carinus and Numerian, Caesars, left Carinus to

rule the West and with Numerian marched against the Persians.
A brilliant campaign and victory was ended by the Emperor's
sudden death.   Whether Carus had a hand in the killing of Probus,
whether he wantonly flouted the Senate, whether his attack on
Persia was justified on political and military grounds—these are questions that await an answer.   A peace was patched up with Persia
and the army turned back home.   When it arrived back in Asia,
it was found that Numerian, Emperor after his father, was a corpse,
though still being carried in his litter.   The army assembled to find
a successor and chose Diocles, commander of the bodyguard.   His
first act was to strike down the praetorian prefect, Aper, as murderer
of Numerian.   Diocletian, as he now called himself, as avenger of
Numerian, might have looked to an understanding with Carinus.
It was probably the jealousy of rival army groups that made war
inevitable.   The decisive battle, fought on the river Margus, was
desperately contested ;   Carinus seemed likely to come out the
victor, but in his hour of triumph he was struck down by a jealous
husband.   Diocletian was now generally accepted and crowned his
victory by mercy to his defeated enemies (284).

Most of the great Illyrians were men of action and no more.
Diocletian added to courage and resolution an acute perception and
a scheming brain.   He had pondered over the events of the preceding years and had drawn the conclusion that, if Rome was to
survive, she must be rebuilt from her foundations.   It would be a
rewarding task to examine in detail how far the reforms of Diocletian were already foreshadowed during the troubles of the 3rd
century.   It is probably true that in nearly every case what he did
was to make permanent what had already been tried by way of
experiment.   Let us take the constitution first.   Rome had had
experience enough of soldiers making emperors and murdering their
' comrades ' when they were tired of them.   One possible remedy—
to set up the Senate as arbiter—seems never to have entered the
mind of Diocletian.   What he did was to remove the emperor from
all vulgar contacts and surround him with the awe of Eastern
royalty.   There was no longer a ' Prince ', an ' Imperator ' even,
but a ' Lord and God '.   The Empire was too large for a single
governor.   Diocletian solved this difficulty, while retaining imperial
unity, by taking to himself a colleague, Maximian, who should rule
in the West as he himself did in the East.   After a few years, in 293,
he attached to himself and his colleague a junior colleague apiece,
a Caesar, to rule a sub-division of the Empire.   Under the undis-
puted leadership of Diocletian this team worked with brilliant
success.   The Persians under Narses, again invading Syria, were

humbled. The revolt of Britain under Carausius and Allectus was at last quelled. Troubles in Gaul and Africa were suppressed. On the difficult Danube frontier the Caesar Galerius laboured fruitfully. Diocletian reduced the size and increased the number of the provinces—probably to lessen the danger of rebellions ; the process had begun before him. He did the same with the legions ; again, the example had been set when detachments of legions were frequently sent off on errands far from their permanent camp. He created a field army, ready to strike when required. This had always been needed ; in the 3rd century concentration of troops, particularly of cavalry, at Milan and Ticinum had shown the way. He set the provinces on the same level as Rome and Italy and developed the great provincial capitals, like Nicomedia, Treveri, Antioch and the rest. This was only to carry the previous development to its logical conclusion. The special prerogative of Rome had ceased to have any meaning. The whole Empire now claimed to be Roman. Diocletian made a new survey of the Empire ; he established the number of units of labour and land (*capita* and *iuga*) that it contained and based on this survey a new taxation, revised every fifteen years. He reformed the coinage, re-issuing gold and pure silver in quantity. He attempted to check a vast inflation that overtook the Empire by an ' edict of maximum prices ' in 301. The work of Diocletian was carried further by Constantine the Great and, in some cases, we cannot be sure to which of the two the credit for a particular reform belongs. It is safe to give credit to Diocletian for the whole general plan, while admitting that he may not have had time to carry it out in all its details. In the field of religion Diocletian seems to have hoped to carry on the toleration of Gallienus and perhaps to improve on him by finding a religious formula of agreement. If so, he failed. Late in his reign he was induced by his Caesar, Galerius, to outlaw the Church and attack its leaders, its churches and its sacred books. The battle was still on when Diocletian and Maximian abdicated in 305.

Here we must reduce a complicated history to its simplest terms. In 305 the Caesars, Constantius Chlorus and Galerius, succeeded in West and East according to Diocletian's plan. Two natural candidates for power, Constantine, son of Constantius, and Maxentius, son of Maximian, were passed over for two hitherto unknown friends of Galerius, Severus and Maximin Daza. The system of Diocletian was at best a delicate mechanism ; intrigues like those of Galerius made its smooth working impossible. Constantius died in 306 at York. Constantine, who had been held as a hostage by Galerius, with difficulty reached his father's side. He was proclaimed

D

Emperor by the troops, but Galerius grudgingly conceded the lesser title of Caesar and with this, for the time being, Constantine was content. Discontent in Rome led to the elevation of Maxentius, and old Maximian came back from retirement to help his son. Severus, the Augustus of the West, was repulsed in an attack on Rome and shortly afterwards compelled to surrender and put to death. Galerius, following him, only escaped a similar fate by a hurried retreat. To save his system, Galerius held a conference at Carnuntum, to which the old Diocletian was invited. A new Emperor, Licinius, was created by the side of Galerius; Constantine and Maximin Daza were to be left as Caesars, or at best 'sons of Augustus', while Maxentius and Maximian were ignored. Within a few years all the surviving rulers were claiming the title of Augustus. Old Maximian quarrelled with his son, took refuge in Gaul with Constantine, who had married his daughter, Fausta, plotted against him and was driven to suicide. Galerius died in 311, 'eaten by worms' said the Christians. The pattern of rule now began to clear. Constantine, aiming to dethrone Maxentius in Rome, drew close to Licinius, who was at variance with Maximin in the East. Constantine attacked Rome and destroyed Maxentius at the battle of the Mulvian Bridge. Soon afterwards Licinius declared war on Maximin and gained an unexpected victory. The Empire was back to a simplified form, with two Augusti, one ruling in the West, one in the East. For over ten years Constantine and Licinius maintained their uneasy partnership, interrupted by one short war. In 323 new quarrels broke out and the resulting war ended in the complete defeat of Licinius and his execution a little later. The Empire had once again a single head.

Constantine was a general of great force and drive. He was direct in attack and in sheer ruthlessness he could outdo his barbarian enemies. His foreign wars were in the main successful and there was no serious breach with Persia. His enemies accused him of showing too much favour to the Goths on the Danube. At home he ruled equally forcefully, successful for the moment, if not necessarily for the future. We have already seen that he was the completer of the programme of Diocletian. He left three sons to succeed him; but his home life had been clouded by the terrible tragedy of 326 when first his eldest son, Crispus, then Fausta, stepmother of Crispus, were in succession put to death. Crispus may have been suspected of conspiracy—but surely unjustly. Fausta may have trumped up a charge of assault on her virtue to pull down a stepson who blocked the way of her own sons; but the black imperial secret was well kept. Constantine is, of course, best remembered as the

man who made the Empire Christian. Constantius, father of Constantine, had himself been a refined monotheist ; he had done his
best to check the persecution in his own part of the Empire.
Constantine, succeeding to this inheritance, was impressed by the
heroism of the best Christians under persecution. The Church,
though sorely pressed, had not collapsed, and even Galerius on his
deathbed acknowledged failure and granted them grudging toleration. Constantine fought against Maxentius under the banner of
the Cross, and, after his victory, joined Licinius in making the terms
of toleration more precise. Henceforward he showed marked
favour to the Church and concerned himself with promoting its
welfare and its unity.

Judgments on Constantine have varied and will continue to vary.
He was a man of vast ambition, a scheming statesman, a lover of his
own will. His conversion to Christianity, though it cannot be
doubted, did not imply any deep reform in morality or any profound philosophical understanding. What *did* draw Constantine
was power, and he had concluded that power resided not in the
pagan gods, but in the God of the Christians. The Church could
not be crushed ; it must then be taken into partnership with the
Empire. For this purpose its prestige must be fostered and, above
all, its unity must be maintained ; otherwise its usefulness in the
unified Empire would be maimed. The Roman world bowed, as it
must bow, to the will of the Emperor. Many were suddenly converted. Many more conformed up to the point of referring in vague
general terms to the ' divine power '. The devout pagans fell back
on the toleration promised by the Edict of Milan. Despite his
gradual advance towards the full Christian position, Constantine
never, it seems, declared war to the death against the old religion.
But his new capital, Constantinople, on the site of the old Byzantium, was from the first a Christian city, the capital of the new
Christian Empire.

Revolution in religion thus came to crown the general reform.
Logically, Diocletian should have carried it through, but he was
deflected by the insistence of Galerius. In the new world to which
Diocletian was trying to give form the old paganism had lost its
place. The Christian Church had learnt the Roman art of government and had perfected its social organisation. It made terms with
Greek philosophical thought. This sharply different attitude to the
religious problem separates the two men, who otherwise stand so
close to one another as the shapers of the new world. The elaborate
system of Diocletian had proved too complicated to stand. With
Constantine we are back to a united Empire and to hereditary

succession. The Emperor by Grace of God can no longer be 'master and god'. But the old conceptions of the Emperor as Head of the Republic, or Commander-in-Chief were gone for ever. The new Emperor was the complete autocrat. But his nominal autocracy now left little room for personal initiative ; he was a prisoner in his own serf state.

Constantine had devised an elaborate scheme of succession. The Empire was to be divided between his three sons and two nephews. This careful balance was upset by the troops at Constantinople, who swore that only sons of the great emperor should rule them and, in a blood-bath at Constantinople, murdered almost all the side members of the House. Constantine II, Constantius II and Constans now redivided the Empire between them (337). But Constantine tried to exercise over Constans a tutorship—which his father may have designed for him—and was killed in the attempt. Constantius II was now left to reign in the East, while Constans held the West. Constantius had the harder task, as the Persians were again assailing the frontiers in a series of unrelenting attacks. Constans had better luck in defeating barbarian invaders on Rhine and Danube. The Arian heresy had been banned at Nicaea, but it lived on and was espoused by Constantius. In 350 Constans was murdered by one of his captains, Magnentius, and in the civil war that followed Constantius had much difficulty in gaining the upper hand. The decisive battle at Mursa drained the Empire of blood that it could ill afford, as the defeated Gauls of Magnentius continued to sell their lives dear for one whole hopeless day. Constantius, having no son of his own, was forced to look for cousins to help him in ruling. He found them in two survivors of the massacre of 337, Constantius Gallus (351–353), who proved unreliable and was executed, and his half-brother, Julian (355–360), who revealed unexpected abilities and recovered Gaul from the barbarians. In 360 the order to withdraw troops from Gaul for the East led to grave discontent in the army, and Julian was proclaimed Augustus by his men at Lutetia (Paris). Constantius treated this as plain rebellion ; Julian moved East against him, but natural death removed Constantius in 361 and Julian could succeed without serious bloodshed.

Constantius had favoured the Arians after their sufferings under Constans. Julian, though brought up as a Christian, was at heart a pagan and now threw off the mask. All Christians—Arians or Athanasians—were alike to him. He knew the Faith from the inside and could with cool malice point to its shortcomings. He did not actually persecute, but he *did* show marked favour to pagans and tried to bar Christians from the ordinary pagan education. Julian

was an honourable man and aspired to cleanse the corrupt administration, but his intentions were not backed up as they should have
been. He was also a man of valour. He decided to resume the
offensive against Persia and thus free the Empire of an incubus. He
planned the attack with great determination and launched it with
fiery energy. But he got into trouble by burning his fleet on the
Tigris—an unexplained piece of folly—was hard pressed by the
Persians and finally died from a chance spear cast. He is a strange
figure in history—hero, reformer, pedant—noble, isolated, a trifle
ridiculous—but a true man in contrast to the many mediocrities and
sinners of his time. His revolt against Christianity was too personal, too philosophic to command any wide following. The
strength of the pagan resistance lay in the City of Rome and its
ancient traditions, and these to Julian had no great appeal.

To succeed Julian Jovian, a Christian of moderate type, was
chosen. He patched up a peace with Persia and led the armies
home ; but he died before he could define any policy. A notable
soldier, Valentinian I, was chosen by the army in his place. He soon
set up his brother, Valens, in the East as his colleague. The great
task of Valentinian was the defence against the barbarians who were
beginning a new series of deadly attacks. Here he showed himself
vigorous and skilful. He had the will to cleanse the administration,
but lacked the power. How could you relieve the overburdened
taxpayer when the wars kept on increasing their demands ? In
religion Valentinian maintained a noble tolerance. His only clash
with paganism was over the trials of senators for magic practices, in
which the political aspect was always prominent.

Valentinian died in 375, leaving a young son, Gratian, to rule
beside his brother, Valens. Three years later came one of the
acutest crises of the Empire. The Goths, hard pressed by the Huns
from the Steppes of Asia, appeared on the Danube, clamouring for
admission to the Empire as federates. Valens granted their re-
quest ; but supplies were not forthcoming according to schedule,
and the mass of emigrants soon turned to plunder and then to
formal war. Valens led the forces of the East to meet them and
would not wait for reinforcements from Gratian. On the lost field
of Adrianople the flower of the Roman army and the Emperor himself were lost, ridden down by the Gothic cavalry. It was disaster,
complete and unredeemed. Gratian's only resource was to appoint
the best soldier he could find, Theodosius the Great, and leave him
to settle the Gothic problem by admitting Goths in masses to the
Eastern army. In 383 a pretender, Magnus Maximus, rose in
Britain, won over Gaul and put Gratian to death. Italy continued

to be ruled by the younger brother of Gratian, Valentinian II, who had been set up by an army group after the death of Valentinian I. For the time Theodosius accepted Maximus as colleague ; but, when in 388 Maximus attacked Valentinian II in Italy, he moved to repel him.   Maximus was defeated and executed and Valentinian was restored.   In fact, if not in theory, Theodosius was effective ruler over the whole Empire.   Valentinian II, rebelling against his impotence before his Master of the troops, Arbogastes, committed suicide, and the general, unable to find an accord with Theodosius, set up as Emperor a Greek man of letters, Eugenius.   The rebels adopted the pagan gods as champions of their cause and the world watched to see how the ordeal would be decided.   Theodosius, triumphing at the battle of the Frigidus, proved to all the virtue of the Christian Faith.   When he died in 395 he left two young sons to succeed him, Arcadius in the East, and Honorius in the West. Theodosius owes his name of the ' Great ' to his championship of the Catholic Faith, which he established as the religion of Rome. Paganism was persecuted and driven out of its last hiding places.

We are now drawing near the end of our period.   The division of the Empire into East and West was from henceforth permanent.   Succession was no longer really hereditary ; the influence of the Masters of the soldiers usually decided.   Constantinople triumphed over her immediate dangers.   First, she got rid of the immediate danger from the Goths by a general massacre.   Then she contrived to shift the drive of the Visigoths and, after them, that of the Ostrogoths from East to West.   For more than a generation she paid tribute to the Huns, and then shook off the yoke.   The Huns, too, turned to the West, were repulsed by Aetius at Chalons and broke up after the death of Attila.   A great joint expedition of the two Empires against the Vandals in Africa failed, it is true, but it was Rome that had to pay most of the price of failure.

The history of the West was stormier.   Rome was sacked by Alaric in 410 and the world had to envisage a future in which the Eternal City no longer ruled.   A series of weak Emperors was dominated by Masters of the troops.   Even a strong Emperor could hardly assert his personal authority.   The Empire became dependent on half-barbarian soldiers, and at last in 476 one of them, Odoacer, deposed the little Romulus Augustulus, and reigned himself under the vague suzerainty of the Eastern Emperor, Zeno. Why Constantinople survived when Rome fell is one of the fascinating problems of history.   The exceptional geographical position of the capital is probably at the root of the solution.   There will have been other factors that are hard to evaluate—a better relation between the Emperor and his generals, a better basis for authority in the Eastern peoples, who felt their unity more than the tribes of the West. The issue we know. Rome moved on to her early doom, though destined to rise in a new form under the Papacy ; Constantinople entered on her millennial watch at the Eastern gate of Europe.

It remains to sum up the results of the developments that we have been considering. What was a Roman Emperor ? He began by being a Roman magistrate, exceptional in the range of his competence, but holding no power that was strange to old Republican ideas. He came more and more to be the representative of the army or of some dominant army group. Diocletian escaped from his turbulent comrades by surrounding himself with the pomp and ceremony of a Great King of the East. After Constantine he was Emperor by the grace of God. So much for the form. What of the fact ? From the first the Emperor was only not a king, because he was more than that, a King of Kings. The Greek East recognised this from the outset. Throughout the whole process the real autocracy of the Emperor was never long in doubt. The development of royal ceremonies around his person in court is eloquent of the true state of things.

Autocracy can take any one of several forms. An autocrat may exercise his authority capriciously and wilfully ; it is not given him for that purpose, but, if he chooses so, who can check him ? Several of the earlier Emperors were autocrats of this type. They interpreted their imperial power as licence to indulge their whims and lusts. Or autocracy can take a military form ; it can express the fact that the army represents the force that in the last resort decides. Or autocracy can mean a totalitarian state, in which the Emperor is the figurehead, but the Government really depends upon the machine that has been created over generations. After all, it was a weary and complicated task to govern the Empire. Many weak Emperors were quite incapable of governing in any real sense ; they were bound to leave the running of the machine to their experts. In general, it is safe to say that the personal idiosyncrasies of the Emperor came to matter less and less.

At no time was the Emperor an absolute lord over slaves. He was not above the laws. He ruled because he had the support of the army ; but who was to control the army for him, if it began to claim too much for itself ? There was no final answer to this recurring question. Quite vital was his relation to the Senate, still the only possible repository of constitutional tradition. If the

Senate were flouted, military anarchy was at the door. That was why the best Emperors tried to establish cordial relations with the Senate, why even bad Emperors made some attempt to work with it and hesitated to renounce its support. In our historical authorities the test of a good Emperor is often sought in his treatment of the Senate. Even in the 4th century, when the political power of the Senate was almost extinct, the Senatorial class continued to hold great prestige and to supply high officers of state. The other orders who contributed to imperial government, the knights in particular, had their own importance ; the Emperor could not do without their expert services. In the late Empire, when the Civil Service became more professional, numerous and meddlesome, it acted as an effective brake on the personal government of the Emperor.

The Emperor from the first was worshipped in the provinces, venerated with something very near divine worship in Rome and ' consecrated ', if good, after death. He was also the head of Roman religion, the *pontifex maximus*. The Romans were always deeply concerned for the ' peace of the gods ', the right relation between man and God. Their political leaders must enjoy the divine sanction. In the 2nd century the thought of the ' piety ', the religious duty of the Emperor, comes more and more into prominence ; in the 3rd century the thought that the divine powers are companions and protectors of the Emperor is especially emphasised. In the 4th the Emperor comes under the protecting hand of the Christian God. The sense of the sanctity pertaining to the office is never quite absent. You might think of the Emperor as appointed by divine providence or, alternatively, by the great capricious deity of fortune. In any case you sought in the Unseen for something to correspond to the visible greatness.

Apart from any defined powers the Roman Emperor could rely on his prestige, his ' authority ', a good Republican word for the kind of influence that a man of ability and position draws to himself. It meant that the Emperor was expected to take the initiative whenever new action was required. The actual powers of the Emperor served as vehicles for his ' authority ', but ' authority ' was not itself such a power, was not even contained in any of them. The great imperial lawyers, especially from the age of Septimius on, translated this ' authority ' into an absolute and universal thing. What the Emperor enacts is by virtue of his position valid. The developed sense of ' authority ' is never given up, though the emphasis shifted a little from law to religion. The Emperor of the 4th century ruled by the grace of God. He and everything connected with him was ' sacred ' and obedience was owed to him as the representative of

God on earth. He had now come very close to the Persian Great King, who, according to the old Persian ideas, though not actually divine himself, stood in a specially close relation to the gods.

There were other general conceptions that helped to interpret the meaning of an Emperor to his subjects. He could appeal to the natural relationship of father to children and claim to be the ' Father of the country '. The title *pater patriae* was conferred as a mark of special honour, and the Emperors affected not to treat it as a matter of course, but to defer it till they had deserved it. The best Emperors *did* care for their subjects with a fatherly devotion and the answering feeling could be deep and spontaneous. More constant was the conception of the Emperor as the great patron. It was at the bottom of Roman ideas that the natural relation of the great man to the small was that of patron to client. The patron was expected to protect his client and advise him in his affairs ; the client repaid such services by political support and civil attentions. The relationship was sanctioned by religion ; to defraud a client was a grave breach of ' piety ', unnatural conduct only one degree less heinous than sin against one's own son. Under the Empire the old ideas lived on ; but we get a false idea of clients from poets like Martial and Juvenal who concentrate on the degrading features of a client's life. The fact was that the Emperor was now the great patron and that all lesser patrons faded into insignificance before him. He supplied the Roman people with their food and their pleasures. They liked to have him with them in Rome, where he could be immediately conscious of their desires. If he failed them, they could demonstrate in their masses at the public shows. It was vital for the Emperor to keep his clients contented.

There was no one form of appointment to the office of Emperor. Recognition by the Senate was necessary, if a reign was to rank as truly constitutional. The senate would pass a ' law of Empire ', conferring the necessary powers on the new potentate. This, after a form of approval by the people, gave the required authority. In times of trouble, such as recurred again and again, the act of the army was decisive ; all that the Senate could do was to stamp with its authority the accomplished act. The swearing of the oath of allegiance would be the normal form of election by the army. The raising on a shield, which sometimes took place in the late Empire, was borrowed from the German barbarians. In the East we find the Byzantine Emperor solemnly anointed by the Patriarch of Constantinople after choice by the chief officials of State and Church.

The Empire was an authoritarian, a totalitarian State. There

was no regular opposition—that is to say no party that, while con-
tinuing its loyalty, could expressly disapprove of the measures of
the Government.   In the early Empire there was often a silent
opposition in the Senate, particularly among the Stoic zealots.
Under Nero the provincials read the ' acts of the Senate ' with a new
avidity to learn what Thrasea Paetus had abstained from doing.
When the Senate congratulated Nero on the murder of his mother,
Thrasea walked out of the House.   This not very efficient opposition
gradually faded away.   The later Senate would occasionally blaze
out into fury against a dead Emperor ; it seldom found the courage
to say a word against the living.   The one great exception—the
rising against the brutal Maximin I—was prompted by sheer
desperation.   Outside the Senate the Cynics sometimes carried
their contempt of authority and orthodox morality as far as attacks
on the Emperor's person.   They were not numerous enough to be
dangerous and an Emperor could dismiss them, as did Vespasian,
as ' barking curs '.

And yet there were certain checks on the Emperor's power to act
as he pleased.   Of the checks of the Senate and the army we have
already spoken.   We have suggested also that the Civil Service, in
its fullest development, must have kept the Emperor imprisoned
within its frame.   It was his medium of expression and, as often,
the medium might be in control.   The personal entourage of the
Emperor, his court, should always be at his will and disposal.   But
from early days the imperial freedmen held great, if irregular, power.
The imperial chamberlains, with their close access to the Emperor,
held far more real influence than they should have done.   In the
4th century the eunuchs, the barbers, the cooks about the court
represented a set of interests, selfish and detrimental to the public
welfare, but very hard to control, impossible to eradicate.   Another
check lay in public opinion.   Unpopular measures might evoke
outcries in circus or amphitheatre, and such outcries were dangerous,
whether you neglected or suppressed them.   If the Emperor too
obviously lost support in Rome, discontent might spread from the
people, who could do nothing immediately, to those who could—
the soldiers with swords in their hands.   We shall come back to this
subject when we discuss the moulding of public opinion.   A final
check lies in the nature of all earthly rule—it is subject to mortality.
However much you may insist on the eternity of Rome, the individual Emperor is obviously not eternal ; even the dynasty has its
term of life ; the Emperor must rule, then, with an eye to the judgment of the Senate on his career, when he comes to die, and the
subsequent fate of those near and dear to him.   A bad Emperor now

and then would follow the whim of the moment with no regard to the future. Any man capable of calculation would take it into account.

This brings us to the vital question of the succession. What happened when an Emperor died? There was no one rule ever formulated or accepted. Very often the choice fell on a son or near relative of the dead Emperor. He might be set up by the army or approved by the Senate. The hereditary principle is so simple, so natural, that it recurs, however often you cast it out. But it was never laid down in so many words that sons must necessarily succeed father. To the Roman, adoption made a son as fully as birth. It was natural, then, that adoption should be called in to make good the lack of a natural heir, that the Emperor, by adoption, should mark out the man whom he deemed worthiest to succeed him. If the Senate approved him and the armies concurred, succession was more or less guaranteed in advance. The great dynasty that ran from Nerva to Marcus Aurelius was a dynasty of adoption and it gave the Roman Empire its greatest peace and prosperity. Where neither birth nor adoption decided, the place fell to the pretender, usually representing an important army interest. Such chance promotions were beyond control and led to a contempt for a position that was so much at the mercy of chance. There was a strong general desire for some regular rule—by birth, if must be, if not by adoption. In the strange *Historia Augusta* of the mid-4th century (?) the question of birth as against adoption is again and again argued out. The cases discussed are of the 3rd century, but the author's real interest is in the 4th. The writer (or writers) are concerned with the events of their own day. It is the age of the sons of Constantine ; his dynasty has broken down and Constantius II is driven to adopt cousins in default of direct heirs. With Valentinian I and Theodosius I heredity returns and continues to be the guiding principle in the East. In the West succession was mainly determined by the tyrannical marshals.

It was probably too much to expect that a regular rule of succession should be established. Varying circumstances are bound to throw any possible system into discredit from time to time. But there are such great advantages in the absence of uncertainty that even the occasional succession of an unworthy Emperor may be better than succession disputed. England has an hereditary monarchy. That principle, long established, has not saved us from all disturbances ; but it has served to minimise them. In Rome it was disputes about the succession that cost the Empire dearest and most sorely vexed the imperial peace. Witness the civil wars that followed the deaths of Nero and Commodus, the Emperors who rose

and fell in the 3rd century, and the bloody fields of Margus and
Mursa. The lesson was often written clear. Civil war in the
Empire added virulence to dangers from abroad. We shall see
later that the Empire had never much to spare either in man-power
or in money. Against the casual trouble within the provinces,
against the normal pressure from without it could cope, but only on
condition that it did not squander its resources on unproductive
strife. A regularised succession might conceivably have spared
Rome much loss of blood and prolonged her powers of resistance
against barbarian pressure. We can discern a sort of basic commonsense at work which limited the destructive effect of civil wars. The
decisive campaigns were generally fought out very swiftly—as if both
contestants realised that the long grinding down of the forces of the
Empire must be disastrous for both sides, that victory, to be worth
anything, must come quickly. It is a sad reflection that care for the
ultimate interests of the State, even when these are manifest enough,
is not enough to check the natural movements of ambition. Septimius should have known that his selfish desire for his own family
aggrandisement must spell disaster for Rome ; yet he snatched at
quick success and left his successors to pay the price. There was
always too much room under the Empire for the careerist.

We have tried to show how the Empire appears to the student
today ; let us ask for a minute how it looked to the ' man in the
street ' who lived under it. By ' the man in the street ' we mean
primarily the ordinary member of the Roman people, resident in
Rome and closely related to the Emperor as his client. We may,
at will, work out varying points of view for the privileged orders of
society, senators and knights, the freedmen and slaves and the mass
of taxpayers in the provinces. But much that is true of our ' man
in the street ' will be true also of them. The Empire was universal ;
it included almost all the civilised world. The far empires of China
and India seemed almost to belong to another planet. The barbarians were different—not full human beings as yet, destined perhaps some day to be, but not yet arrived at the goal. The Parthian
Empire was a weak rival to the Roman ; the Persian Empire that
succeeded it was more formidable. As a member of the Empire you
had your share in its peace and prosperity; there was the incidental
disadvantage that, if you did not like it, there was nowhere to escape
to. A Roman senator under Tiberius got into great trouble for
trying to leave Italy for Parthia. The advantages of this universal
Empire were realised in varying degrees. It was not everyone who
had time, money and energy to travel. Trade was not forbidden
within the Empire, but it was not exactly encouraged—what with

custom duties and taxes on sales. While things went well, you could take your pride in being a partner in such a great concern. But, when things went ill, as they did in the 3rd and 4th centuries, you might find the Empire a very uncomfortable boat to be in, over-crowded and likely to capsize.

The Empire was not only universal, but eternal—as far as any-thing on earth can claim to be. Having once arrived at supremacy, Rome seemed destined to stay as immovable as sun and moon in the natural order. It is hard to define just when this conception became fixed. In the early Empire the Jews, perhaps also the Gauls, may have doubted its continuance, may have seen in the burning of the Capitol the omen of its fall. But yet the idea of eternity *did* become set and the theme of ' Roma Aeterna ' haunts all pagan thought. The Christians, when once they had forgotten the apocalyptic dreams of the first age, conceived the Roman Empire to be the order instituted by divine providence to govern the world until the terrors of the last times. As a defence against that grim horror the Empire could be approved, even loved. The sack of Rome in 410 shocked the world ; the unimaginable had occurred. It was not everyone who could rally as quickly as did St. Augustine and reconceive the whole position, see Rome, the City of the World, not eternal in her own right, but only as a symbol of the City of God that endures. Nothing gives one a surer impression of what Rome has meant to the imagination of the world than this concep-tion of her eternity. It is to be seen behind the temporal power of the Pope. Even today, Rome holds her place as one of the few cities that belong not to one time or people but to the whole world order—to eternity as far as we here can conceive it.

Such an Empire, universal, eternal, is clearly very near the Divine. It stands under the Divine protection, its rulers themselves are not far removed from the divine sphere. To fight against its ordinances is not only foolish and hopeless ; it is also impious—a protest against what God has ordained. The Christian Church early learned to preach obedience to the powers that be. When Constantine became a Christian the Church gained a new interest in the Empire ; it was now home, defence, protector of the Church. Constantine saw in a united Church a strong support of his united Empire. Perhaps we have here one reason the more why Con-stantinople stood, while Rome fell. The Eastern city was Christian from its birth, the new capital of the Christian Empire. Rome stood out in obstinate defence of her ancient past, her religion included. In Rome, too, the Faith finally triumphed, but the delay may have made impossible that close growing together of

Church and State that Constantine had had in mind. Gibbon has accused Christianity of being, with the barbarians, the destroyer of Rome. The charge is obviously overstated. The Church survived in Rome ; if the Empire could not survive with it, the fault will have lain in the State. But Gibbon has, as usual, seen something vital. Christianity did not win quickly enough to pour its new life into the body of the Western Empire.

For direct opposition to the Empire there was no vehicle. The Senate or the army might terminate an unsatisfactory rule ; it could not control it while in action. Something, of course, could be done by judicious criticism, though that always involved danger for the critic. The only safe method was by way of eulogy. You might so praise the ruling Emperor as to suggest, in the most indirect and discreet of ways, how his admirable administration might be even better. Pliny's panegyric of Trajan is a good example. He praises without stint and yet conveys an occasional hint or warning. The Emperor, for example, is almost too generous ; such generosity is lovely to watch—but can State finances really bear it ? Dio Chrysostom, Aristides and other writers follow similar paths. They hardly affect to criticise at all. But their pictures of the perfect state, realised under the best of rulers, contain more than is yet perfectly worked out. Naturally, you would be careful not to preach to the Emperor what he would be too reluctant to hear. But you might occasionally make a new suggestion or encourage him to proceed with a policy for which he was awaiting support.

Public opinion counted for a good deal. The expression of the popular will in circus and amphitheatre could not safely be neglected. You could not easily silence or coerce a mob of tens of thousands. Often the demand would be only for ' bread and games ', a demand easy to satisfy. But the demand might be political. The fall of an unpopular minister might be called for ; an unpopular war might be denounced. When Septimius entered on the civil war with Albinus, the crowd shouted to him : ' How long is this nonsense going on ? How long are we to be kept at war ? ' To govern a great people is always a laborious task. To govern a discontented people is in the long run almost impossibly difficult and painful. You cannot do everything by force ; there must be a large measure of consent. You cannot coerce all the people all the time. And this brings us to a matter of great import-ance, the regard of the Emperors for public opinion and their endeavours to control it by propaganda.

The imperial coinage carries a wealth of type and legend, which, on closer investigation, is found to be very purposeful. The coins steadily carry out to the world their little messages about what is happening and about what the Emperors have in mind. Sometimes the messages are definite enough ; sometimes they carry only vague suggestions. But we have only to study their careful idiom, their skilfully varied changes, to be sure that they were deliberately chosen and that the choice of what to say or not to say was usually taken at a high level. Apart from the language of the legends the types are found to have a language of their own. The attributes of the various gods and virtues are carefully distinguished ; where they are mixed, it is with full intention. We must not forget that the ancient world had not our modern means of publicity. There was no popular press, no wireless, no broadcasting. The Emperors had to do their best with what they had at their disposal. Of course, imperial letters and edicts carried exact messages into the provinces. But for the messages to be really carried into every corner the coins could be brought in to help. They passed from pocket to pocket ; and, as men knew that they were always changing, they would study them with a care that we have forgotten, to see what new thing they might have to say. For a study of this neglected aspect of the Empire the coins are vital. They do not tell us all the truth or only the truth. But they persist in putting the official point of view—a point that is often not too prominent in our historians.

Augustus presents himself as the victorious prince of peace. He writes large the tale of his Parthian and Armenian successes, has less to say of the German wars and, not surprisingly, nothing at all of the revolt of Pannonia and the disaster of Varus. The coinage, as far as it is central, flows in two main channels, (1) the gold and silver issued by the Emperor, primarily for the pay of army and Civil Service, (2) the coinage in the base metals, issued at the will of the Emperor by decrees of the Senate and therefore marked S.C. (*senatus consulto*). Apart from these central coinages there are sundry provincial issues and, above all, a mass of city issues, especially in the East. From the local issues one may learn much about local myths, local government and festivals. Tiberius on his gold and silver confined himself to a very few themes—his great predecessor, the victory of the Augustus and the ' Peace of the gods ', secured by the Emperor as Chief Priest. The S.C. coinage is much more eloquent and celebrates such triumphs of the reign as the restoration of the cities of Asia after earthquake. Caligula boasts of the grandeur of the House of Augustus and Germanicus. Claudius advertises to the world the debt that he owes to the praetorians who made him Emperor, celebrates the conquest of Britain and, towards his close, honours his third wife, Agrippina, and her little son, Nero, with a

1. *Obv.* Augustus. *Rev.* Civic Oak (OB CIVIS SERVATOS). Aureus. *c.* 18 B.C. Spain. (p. 13.)

2. *Obv.* Augustus. *Rev.* Agrippa (M AGRIPPA PLATORINUS IIIVIR). Aureus. *c.* 13 B.C. Rome. (p. 14.)

3. *Obv.* Claudius (TI[berius] CLAUD[ius] CAESAR AUG[ustus] P[ontifex] M[aximus] TR[ibunicia] P[otestate] VI IMP[erator] XI). *Rev.* Arch (DE BRITANNIS). Aureus. A.D. 46. Rome. (p. 47.)

4. *Obv.* Nero and Agrippina (AGRIPP[ina] AUG[usta] DIVI CLAUD[ii] NERONIS CAES[aris] MATER). *Rev.* Civic Oak (NERONI CLAUD[io] DIVI F[ilio] CAES[ari] AUG[usto] GERM[anico] IMP[eratori] TR[ibunicia] P[otestate]. In centre : EX S[enatus] C[onsulto]. Aureus. 54. Rome.

5. *Obv.* Domitian. *Rev.* Minerva (GERMANICUS COS XVII). Aureus. 94. Rome. (p. 50.)

6. *Obv.* Trajan (IMP[eratori] TRAIANO AUG[usto] GER[manico] DAC[ico] P[ontifici] M[aximo] TR[ibunicia] P[otestate] COS V P[atri] P[atriae]). *Rev.* Trajan presents a Dacian to the Senate (S.P.Q.R. OPTIMO PRINCIPI). Aureus. *c.* 107. Rome. (pp. 21, 50.)

7. *Obv.* Hadrian (HADRIANUS AUG[ustus] COS III P[ater] P[atriae]). *Rev.* Hispania. Aureus. *c.* 135. Rome. (pp. 21, 60.)

8. *Obv.* Septimius Severus (SEVERUS PIUS AUG[ustus]). *Rev.* Dea Caelestis of Carthage riding on a lion (INDULGENTIA AUGG IN CARTH[aginem]). Aureus. *c.* 205. Rome. (pp. 23, 216.)

9. *Obv.* Trajan Decius (IMP TRAIANUS DECIUS AUG). *Rev.* Genius of the Army of Illyricum (GENIUS EXERCITUS ILLYRICIANI). Aureus. 249. Rome. (p. 28.)

10. *Obv.* Postumus (IMP POSTUMUS AUG). *Rev.* 'The Loyalty of the Cavalry' (FIDES EQUIT[um]). Antoninianus. 268. Milan. (pp. 30, 283.)

11. *Obv.* Probus (IMP PROBUS AUG). *Rev.* Trophy and captives from German victory (VICTORIA GERM[anica]). Aureus. 277. Siscia. (p. 31.)

12. *Obv.* Maximian (MAXIMIANUS P AUG). *Rev.* Hercules killing hydra (HERCULI DEBELLAT). At foot : P[rima, s.c. officina] T[icinum]. Aureus. *c.* 300. Ticinum. (pp. 33, 51, 233.) (*Note.* Letters at the foot of the reverse of coins are often mint-marks, as here. Letters—P, S, T—or numbers— A, B, Γ (Greek) or I, II, III (Roman)—denote officinae (shops) of the mint. On gold the letter P may mean ' percussus ' (struck at).

13. Constantine I (CONSTANTINUS MAX[imus] AUG). *Rev.* Victory (VICTORIA CONSTANTINI AUG). At foot : CONS (for Constantinople, place of issue). Solidus. *c.* 330. Constantinople. (pp. 34, 53, 234.)

14. *Obv.* Constantine I (CONSTANTINUS P[ius] F[elix] AUG). *Rev.* Emperor riding down enemy (VIRTUS AUGUSTI). At foot : TR[eviris]. Solidus. *c.* 320. Treviri. (p. 52.)

15. *Obv.* Constantius II (D[ominus] N[oster] CONSTANTIUS P[ius] F[elix] AUG). *Rev.* Emperor and captives (FEL[ix]TEMP[orum] REPARATIO). At foot : CONSA*. Aes. *c.* 348. Constantinople. (p. 36.)

16. *Obv.* Valentinian I (D[ominus] N[oster] VALENTINIANUS P[ius] F[elix] AUG). *Rev.* Rome and Constantinople (GLORIA REI PUBLICAE). At foot : TR[eviris] OB[ryzum]. Solidus. *c.* 368. Treviri. (p. 37.) Obryzum means ' pure gold ', and the abbreviation OB probably means, at the same time, 72 (in Greek numerals), the number of solidi to the pound. For the inscription on the shield (VOT X MULT XV) see Pl. VII, No. 9.

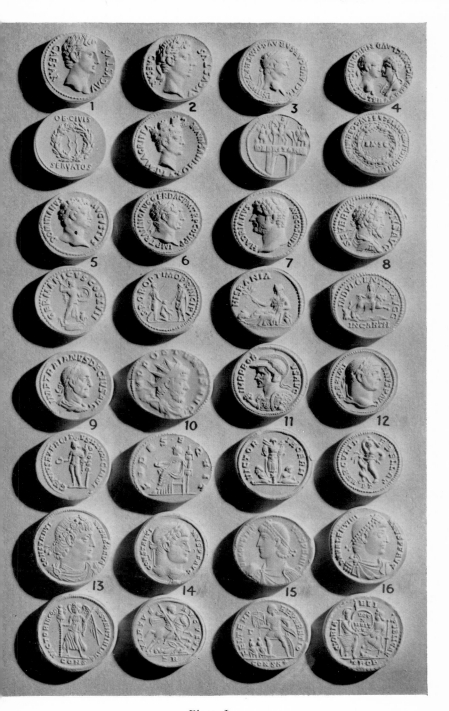

Plate I

Plate II

1. *Obv*. Vespasian (IMP CAESAR VESPASIANUS AUG). *Rev*. Judaea captive. Aureus. 70. Rome. (p. 50.)

2. *Obv*. Hadrian (HADRIANUS AUG COS III PP). *Rev*. Hispania. Aureus. *c.* 135. Rome. (pp. 21, 61.)

3. *Obv*. Antoninus Pius (ANTONINUS AUG PIUS PP TRP COS III). *Rev*. Italia as Queen. Sestertius. *c.* 144. Rome. (p. 60.)

4. *Obv*. Antoninus Pius (ANTONINUS AUG PIUS PP). *Rev*. Mauretania offering crown. Sestertius. 138. Rome. (p. 61.)

5. *Obv*. Trajan Decius (IMP[erator] CAE[sar] TRA[ianus] DEC[ius] AUG[ustus]). *Rev*. Dacia. Antoninianus. 249. Milan.

6. *Obv*. Constantius II (FL[avius] IUL[ius] CONSTANTIUS PF AUG). *Rev*. Rome and Constantinople (GLORIA REI PUBLICAE). At foot: R[omae]s[acra] M[oneta]Q[uarta]. Aureus. *c.* 354. Rome.
   For the inscription on the central shield (VOT XXX MULT XXXX) see Pl. VII, No. 9.

7. *Obv*. Probus (IMP C M[arcus] AUR[elius] PROBUS P AUG). *Rev*. Personification of Siscia between two rivers, the Save and the Kulpa (SISCIA PROBI AUG). At foot: XXIQ. (See p. 191.) Antoninianus. *c.* 277. Siscia. (p. 91.)

8. *Obv*. Constantine I (IMP. CONSTANTINUS PF AUG). *Rev*. Great gate of Treviri (AUGG GLORIA). At foot: P[rima sc. officina] TRE[viris]. Double solidus. *c.* 320. Treviri. (p. 90.)

9. *Obv*. Constantius I (FL[avius] VAL[erius] CONSTANTIUS NOBIL[issimus] CAES[ar]). *Rev*. Emperor entering London (REDDITOR LUCIS AETERNAE). Below: LON[dinium] and P[rima] TR[eviris]. Gold Medallion. *c.* 296. Treviri.

coinage. Nero's coinage falls into two periods, corresponding roughly to his more or less worthy youth and his debauched manhood. In the first, he is the gentle young prince, reigning in harmony with the Senate ; in the second he is a kind of Sun-King, bent on self-glorification.

The Civil Wars produced coinages illustrating their varying fortunes. There was much talk of Senate and people, but what was meant was simply a constitutional rule like that of Augustus. The Empire of the Gauls produced its own defiant little coinage, but Vespasian was at pains to obliterate all traces of it afterwards. Vespasian recalled to mind the glories of Augustus, celebrated his own Jewish triumph and outlined the policy of a new dynasty. Domitian revealed to Rome his intense devotion to Minerva, boasted of his German victory and celebrated the Secular Games, but was decently reticent about the difficult and dangerous wars on the Danube. Nerva sketched a programme, generous and liberal. Trajan revealed Roman valour in its revival. His coinage is full of his wars, Dacian and Parthian, of his buildings, of the richness and hope of Roman life under his vigorous rule. Hadrian gives the fullest expression to his passionate interest in all his Empire. Antoninus Pius reveals an Empire, strong but quiet in its assured strength. Under Marcus and Verus the war trumpet sounds again for wars in the East and on the Danube. Under Commodus serious interests fall into the background—all except the religious ; Commodus shows a new interest in the Eastern cults of Cybele and Isis and takes on himself the role of the Roman Hercules. Septimius Severus strikes notes of his own ; he has many a military success to boast of, he has the hopes of a new dynasty to unfold. Elagabalus was mainly concerned in presenting his Sun God to an admiring Rome. A quiet reaction under Severus Alexander was followed by a simple coinage with warlike emphasis for Maximin I.

The coinage of the next troublous years has much to teach us when closely studied. We find what may happen at any time, what now happens very frequently—that the coinage speaks of what is hoped for rather than of what is enjoyed. The theme, ' loyalty of the troops ', might be said to be the main one of the military anarchy. Gallienus casts a glint of gold on the dark clouds of his reign ; he dreams of a blessed peace in that part of the Empire that was wise enough to stay loyal to him. Many of the ' tyrants ' of the reign have left their record on coins ; it was one of the first acts of a pretender to open a mint. The great restorers of the Empire expressed their new confidence in a coinage full of pride and promise. The tetrarchy of Diocletian has an impressive coinage, honouring the four rulers, glorifying the dynasties of Jove and Hercules, speaking of the exploits of the four and of the divine protection. The coinage shows clear as life the blunt, thickheaded, efficient Illyrians. With Constantine comes a new refinement. But the old rules are now falling into neglect. It is not so much the changing pageant of the days that is presented as the eternal course of imperial rule—the vows—the victories—the triumphal entries. The pagan gods fall into the background. At the same time, the Christian references are few and mainly indirect. Something like an armistice is observed ; most of what is said and shown can be interpreted as you please. It is what one finds in literature too— a vague form of reference to the ' divine power ' without precise definition. This armistice goes on until Theodosius and even later. Vetranio and Magnentius each have one definitely Christian type ; but the general rule of neutrality still holds. It is more remarkable that Julian, in his reaction, uses only one purely pagan type—the bull, Apis, to suggest the ' security of the State '. Under Theodosius Christian emblems take a permanent place on some issues of bronze ; but most of his types still speak of ' restoration of the State ', ' harmony of the Augusti ', the imperial vows and so on. In the 5th century the cross or monogram of Christ appears frequently on small denominations of gold ; we find an occasional devout legend such as the ' Salus Mundi ' of Olybrius. It was left to Byzantium from the 7th century onwards to show how a true Christian coinage might develop, with its types of the Saviour, Virgin Mary and a number of saints.

These are but a few examples drawn from a very large store. They are worth pondering. Coins are still not nearly as familiar to students as they deserve to be and the historical gain from the imperial coinage has only recently begun to be realised. What is true of imperial coins is also true in a different sense of the local city issues. They throw occasional gleams of light on the history which, apart from them, hardly exists. In the case of the central issues much is still to be learned from a comparison of the gold and silver with the bronze issues. By the 3rd century the distinction between the two had been much reduced. But in the early Empire the difference between them is extraordinary, and, since we are now sure that the Emperor had virtual control of both, the difference must be one of deliberately varied approach to the same theme. Most of the work on these lines has still to be done ; but Dr. C. H. V. Sutherland has given us a fine lead on the Empire down to Nero.

It must not, of course, be imagined that imperial propaganda was conducted only through coins or even most effectively through them.

Edicts, letters, responses must have continually gone abroad to the
provinces.   But of all the mass of material that was once there, only
the coins survive in bulk.   For the rest we have an occasional inscription, an occasional quotation in literature.   The coins have the
same function here that they have in art.   There they often preserve
some faint memory of a great building, group of statuary or painting
that is lost to us today.   Here they remind us of a phase of imperial rule, which was a deep and steady concern of the holders of
power, but which can easily be forgotten, if the active touch between
ruler and ruled is no longer realised.   The world of pagan thought
lent itself admirably to the expression of political ideas.   The gods
themselves were realised in human form, with their distinguishing
attributes.   They were associated in men's minds with the various
departments or activities of life and could be used to symbolise them.
Mercury will stand for trade, Neptune for the sea, Ceres for the
harvest and so on.   To the gods we must add those less definitely
conceived powers, the ' virtues ' or the ' blessings ', such as peace,
felicity and hope.   These too are gods or goddesses and can receive
cult ; but they are not so clearly realised as persons, are rather
powers (*numina*) of the old Roman type, divine powers realised in
special actions.   These ' virtues ', like the gods, have their distinguishing attributes.   Like them they express different sides of
life—*Pax* peace, *Virtus* war, *Felicitas* luck in trade, *Salus* health,
salvation and so on.   The imperial mint-master learnt to make use
of these gods and powers to express and define the quality of the
imperial government.   Add the adjective *Augustus* (*Augusta*) to the
name and you have an imperial blessing ; add a genitive (*Augusti*)
and you have an imperial virtue, a power that works through the
Emperor to produce its benign effects.   *Pax Augusta* is the imperial
peace, seen more or less objectively as we see it.   *Pax Augusti* is the
peace in the spirit of the Emperor, creating peace in State, in home,
in religion.   Ancient thought diverges a little from ours here ; but
its idiom is quite easy to learn and, once we have learned it, much
that strikes us at first as odd becomes matter-of-fact.

Again, we have only room for a few examples from an abundant
store.   We will take in turn a few of the virtues that were used as
slogans in the imperial campaign for support.   Liberty was naturally quick to appeal to a Roman, and many an Emperor boasts of it
under his rule.   It clearly retained a considerable sentimental value.
But wherein could liberty under the Empire consist ?   Quite a lot
of different answers can be given.   Liberty may mean that the
Emperor claims to be constitutional, not a mere tyrant.   It may
refer to the generosity of the Emperor that enlarges the personal

freedom of his subjects by putting money into their purses. Later
on, it may even mean liberty in religion. But it never means
political liberty. Ruskin used to speak of liberty as a will o' the
wisp, sure to lead men into the quagmire. Perhaps this was too
extreme, but Ruskin was right up to a point ; liberty can be very
vaguely conceived and can then lead men into darkness. It seems
to us that one of the most obvious facts about the Empire was that
a large measure of liberty was sacrificed without reserve and for ever
for what seemed the sufficient price of peace and security. The
coins seem to show that even the ghost of liberty was loved and
honoured.

Pax is perhaps the symbol *par excellence* of the Empire. She can
carry a number of meanings—the absence of foreign or civil war,
the general rule of order inside the Empire, the good relations existing inside Rome between Emperor and Senate or the State at large.
Hope will often run ahead of realisation. When Otho speaks of the
' peace of the whole world ' he is stressing the fact that the East and
the Balkans were supporting him ; but the West and the mighty
German armies were against him. At the very crisis of the 3rd
century Gallienus struck an amazing reverse, ' victory on every
hand ' (*Ubique Pax*) ; ' Everywhere ' here must have meant ' everywhere that matters '—in the remains of the civilised Empire. The
Augusta in Pace of Salonina, wife of the same Gallienus, perhaps bears
a Christian reference. Salonina herself was a Christian and Gallienus granted toleration to the Church. It is this peace of the
Church that the type might represent. Peace was one of the last
pagans to live on into the Christian era. She could enter the new
scheme of things as the ' Peace of God ', a Christian angel.

Victory should perhaps be treated rather as goddess than virtue.
She is a Valkyrie of Jupiter, sent on her wings by him to carry
triumph to the side that he favours. Victory belongs to the
Emperor ; she, with valour, is part of that *imperatoria virtus* which, as
Tacitus reminds us, should not be allowed to a subject. Every
Emperor should feel in himself the divine urge of these two powers.
' Augustus, may you conquer ' is still the acclamation of the Byzantine Emperor. The proper field of Victory is the field of battle ;
but she may also be used to mean other successes—the prowess of
a Nero or a Commodus in circus or arena, for example. Valour
goes very closely with Victory. She is a goddess, almost identical
with Roma. Like Victory she is close to the throne of Jupiter and
hies at his bidding to put heart into the good and brave. Valour
is the goddess of war, as also of the mimic warfare of the chase. The
last struggles of paganism centred round these sister goddesses—

round the altar of Victory and the statue of Valour. Valour only survived so far as she could under the title of Eternal Rome. Victory was baptised a Christian angel ; it is no accident that the typical angel of our imagination wears the wings and bears the wreath and palm of victory.

Pietas is more than our piety. She expresses goodness—duty in many a relationship. She may be directed towards the gods, near kin, clients, subjects or foreign peoples. She implies strict regard for obligation, strict honouring of your bond. When the style *Pius Felix* came to be applied to every Emperor, the religious meaning was certainly to the fore. The Emperor enjoys peace with Heaven and, as a result, he cannot fail to prosper. Antoninus Pius won his title by his loyalty to Hadrian who had adopted him. In the imperial family Pietas will express the love of husband and wife, the care of mother for children.

Providentia may move in the divine sphere ; she may be the providence of the gods, the general expression of divine government. Thus she is often claimed to sanction the imperial rule. But providence can carry several more earthly meanings. The providence of the Emperor may be looking far ahead to ensure the corn supply, to frustrate the designs of the usurper, to provide for his succession.

Fortune, like Victory and Valour, is goddess rather than virtue ; but she often falls rather into the virtue class. She expresses, in a less religious form, the sense of the ordering of human life from without ; only here, the outside agency is thought of not as super-human wisdom, but as some strange power of unknown caprice. The supreme ' luck ' is that of Empire, that which raised a man to the dizzy eminence. To the Emperor Fortune is above all the homebringer after campaign. Many saw under her Roman form an Eastern goddess, Isis or Atargatis, the ' Syrian goddess '.

A whole group of virtues moves about the imperial mint and corn supply. Moneta is the spirit of the mint itself. Aequitas, a closely related figure, is the spirit of justice in observing true weight and measure. Abundantia and Ubertas represent the overflowing wealth of the imperial store ; Ceres is the major goddess who presides over them. It is a curious form of reference. You want to assure the public that the coinage is being issued in accordance with good tradition, that the corn supply is in sure hands. You give the public a picture of the goddesses who inspire the Emperor in these parts of his duties. By choosing among these powers, by varying their appearances and their combinations you can sketch your picture of imperial administration to suit all requirements. You can sometimes produce unusual effects by borrowing an attribute from one power and allotting it to another—by giving Peace the palm of Victory, or Victory the branch of Peace. The imperial virtues on the coins are so many claims, not so many proofs of achievement ; they often promise precisely what was not fulfilled. But they preserve for us a view of history that often falls into the background.

It is impossible to write a book on Rome without saying something about Roman Law, the greatest gift of Rome to the world. Rome began with an exactly conceived, narrow system of law, tied up in set actions and unalterable formulae. Then, through her praetors, the City and the ' peregrine ', she advanced to a new, developing law that was being continually geared to meet fresh requirements. The praetors, practically speaking, created new law, by stating in advance in their edicts how they proposed to treat cases where there might be doubt. The cases were usually arbitrated ; what the praetor did was to issue a formula within which the controversy must be fought out. Already under the Republic eminent jurists had begun to teach and give advice. Augustus took over and developed this system. He gave to certain approved specialists the formal right to give legal advice. Imperial recognition naturally added to the prestige that they had won by their own efforts. The great development of Roman Law under the Empire was mainly due to the imperial jurists, who worked out the theory of political power under the new order and at the same time developed private law according to new ideas. The old Roman rigidity was gone for ever. Cases were more and more judged in the light of equity, of what is reasonable according to the ideal common law of nations, or even of the still more transcendental ' natural law '.

Hadrian brought the praetor's edicts to an end ; after him the edict was frozen, a part of the system unchangeable for ever. Practically all new legislation was by act of the Emperor, by his will expressed in any one of a number of forms—edict, letter, response. The final fruits of this vast work were the great imperial ' Codices ', those of Theodosius II and Justinian I. The collection of the latter was accompanied by a vast apparatus of commentary. Perhaps the surest way to a deep knowledge of the later Empire is through these Codices. The general history shows how the Emperors actually behaved, how they fought their wars, managed their subjects, filled their treasuries. The coins show how they wished themselves to be regarded ; they reflect the imperial achievement, with a good deal of interpretation. The laws and the Codices show how the Emperors considered themselves required to act. The statement should be calm and dispassionate ; the individual will of the Emperor should hardly enter into the question. The question really is what is demanded of the Emperor in his imperial quality. The Codices, in fact, let us into the secrets of the imperial conscience, show us how the Emperors felt themselves bound to act. When we study the career of a particular Emperor, we may hesitate whether to attribute some particular act to any kind of policy or to mere caprice. In the laws we are sure ; policy is deliberate ; if wrong is done, it is with the eyes open. The Emperors regularly profess a strict sense of duty, an active care for the good of their subjects. They not infrequently hold out the thread of a rigid punishment that seems to us vindictive rather than deterrent. They thunder against economic abuses which they cannot fathom. They try to check the natural movements of coinage. They screw up the taxes to impossible heights. But, even if theirs was in many respects a painful government, it was still a conscientious one.

It is in Roman Law that the Roman genius for social organisation culminates. In some countries it is dominant even today. No study of Law can neglect its influence. It is a tragic sign of our times when some legal faculties give up the compulsory Latin of earlier days. It is like writing off all one's past.

There is just one more aspect of the Empire that deserves a moment's attention—its attitude towards time, its devotion to the past, its lack of interest in the future. The myth of the Golden Age is the stock expression of this attitude. Once, far back in human history, men were perfectly good and perfectly happy ; it was in the days when old Saturn fled to Latium to find a safe retreat or when the baby Jupiter was nurtured in Crete by the goat Amalthaea. That Golden Age is always returning in the imagination of the panegyrist ; every reign may be the Golden Age restored. The ' Age ' by itself as spoken of by Trajan, when he protests that anonymous denunciations are out of keeping with his age, is this and nothing else. In general, men's eyes were on the past. The great models have been set ; you could copy, hardly improve on them. Men were always linking the present to the past, not infrequently celebrating anniversaries with a zeal now shown only by occasional individuals.

The best feature of this interest in the past was a careful conservatism, a refusal of disastrous change. The curse of it was that it so often spelt stagnation, a refusal to do any more thinking, to consider the future as something to plan for. The world felt tired and behaved as if it were. Roman thinkers turned over in their minds the idea that the world had really reached an old age, in which all production, natural and human, was long past its prime. To us, with our hopes of progress not quite forgotten, there is something dispiriting in this attitude. With this is mind, we may turn back to ask what the Empire in the movement of history really means. We are compelled by our natural make up to seek patterns in the historical scenes that come under our view. Where no such patterns can readily be found we are inclined to say that such life does not really belong to history, even if lived within the historical epoch. Let us still form our patterns ; they are a sign of our concern for our subject and our will to understand it. But let us also understand that here we pass over from what is objective to what is highly subjective, that must vary with the observer.

For the Roman Empire we have a choice of a number of patterns. The best known, which has largely ruled thought since his day, is Gibbon's vision of ' Decline and Fall '. It comes like a flash of lightning in the night, illuminating, dazzling, blinding. There is something to be dug out of Spengler's flamboyant, ' Untergang des Abendlandes '. Korneman has recently presented the History of Europe, including the Roman Empire, in one synthesis. And then we have Arnold Toynbee's classification and schematisation of cultures and their growth and decay and his identification of the Roman Empire as a late phase of Hellenistic culture, a stage of universal Empire. There is some vision in all these views, perhaps some truth in them. But I want to suggest—and here I shall have Byzantinists with me—that all these views suffer from being too negative. They make enough of what the Empire was not—of where it failed—not nearly enough of what it was and did. The stuff out of which it was made was, it is true, the stuff of the Hellenistic world, but that stuff was already composite enough. And are cultures determined entirely by the human stuff of which they are made ? Is not the indwelling spirit—if such a spirit there be— much more important ? I would suggest that, for a change, we think of the Empire as a new culture, working in an old environment —as an attempt, only partially successful, to express national and social relations in a new way—as a civilisation which should, had fate been kinder, have found its proper literature, religion and art. If the Empire is to be regarded as a child, it must be admitted that it was born with an old head on young shoulders. The world was tired ; men of the time felt it and we can trace its tiredness in many of its doings. May not the reason for that be that the Empire came too late, that too much energy had been consumed in the strife of nations, so that the supernational society began with a dangerously low stock of vitality ? This pattern is not complete in itself, but it has more claim to be true than the more negative ones. What nonsense it is to think only of Decline and Fall in connection with an Empire which lasted nearly five centuries in the West and, in dying, left its mark on the whole life of the Western world—which in the East, where it found a more congenial home, only reached its peak after the West had gone and, for a millennium, kept the door of civilisation closed against Eastern invaders and kept the torch of understanding alight? According to Toynbee, the Empire must die in part, in part prolong a strange, almost unnatural existence. Is it not much fairer to regard the Roman Empire all along its course as something that was to grow into the Byzantine without any radical change of character?

It matters not a little to our hopes of the future what view we take. If we regard the Empire as only a phase in a culture, and a phase of decline at that, we shall be confirmed in a pessimistic outlook. If the Empire not only fell, but was always doomed to fall, what hopes can we have of repetitions of the experiment in the future? Unified government is no guarantee of the good life ; at some points it even threatens it. But we see in past history and in the grim prospects of the present the threats to supreme human values that are involved in the continuous and unfruitful struggles of nations. Survival may depend on a solution of the problem which the Empire posed. There must always be the fight for freedom, the power of man to realise the possibilities of his being. The antithesis of authority and freedom will always be with us, demanding harmonisation. But if what we want is undiluted freedom, it is easier realised in a state of barbarism than of civilisation at all. And, as we have already said, survival may depend on securing a safe framework of international life, even at some sacrifice. It must be the task of men who love freedom to see that such sacrifices are made in the right directions, that the essentials are safeguarded. The ancient world was craving for peace and security ; in Rome she found the power with the peculiar qualifications that enabled her to answer the need. And are we to see in it all no more than a phase of decay—one of the ways in which a civilisation can run down? There is every reason for the more hopeful view—that an experiment was made which achieved a large measure of success, that such an experiment might be repeated with better prospects later ; and this is just as well, for we shall probably be compelled to make it. If we can bring ourselves to take the plunge, we shall follow the fortunes of the Empire in its diverse manifestations with something more than vague curiosity, blended with pity ; we shall find in it lessons for the future —both as to what to seek and what to avoid.

CHAPTER II

THE EMPIRE AND ITS PARTS

In the Roman Empire the opposite principles of unity and diversity are nicely balanced. Unity is the principle that arrests our interest first. For our main interest in the Empire is just this—that it for the first time gave the Mediterranean world a single political form. Up to a point the unity was complete ; there was one Emperor over all, one army, one Civil Service—in the end, one religion. But you could never speak of one nationality or one culture. Centuries of living together brought races and cultures nearer to one another. The inhabitants of the Roman Empire, the inhabitants of the Byzantine Empire after her, could with some reason call themselves ' Romans '. But beside the unity diversity in many forms persisted. Our first chapter aimed at sketching the unity of the Empire ; our second shall aim at painting its diversity—in geography, in race, in culture, in politics, in economic and social life, in religion. Many of these points will find fuller treatment in later chapters ; for the sake of completeness they will be briefly included here.

To do justice to the geographical variety of the Empire would require a range of reading and of travel to which I can lay no claim. Yet, with the help of many admirable books on the subject, the attempt shall be made. Perhaps we may get the outlines of our picture correct. Let us move from West to East. Our own island came late within the Roman sphere. Ireland remained unknown except for a little trade or raiding. Scotland was half in, half out ; the Lowlands were held for some time, the Highlands were never really conquered. In Britain the Romans found a lowland area with too much woodland for intensive cultivation, but easily controlled ; outside it, an upland area was loosely held and little exploited. The conquerors came, expecting to find considerable mineral wealth ; they were disappointed. The best tribute that Britain could bring was her man-power for the armies. In the 4th century Britain enjoyed a short-lived prosperity before the final storms broke. If we compare the after-history of Britain and Gaul, we shall be led to believe that the Roman occupation of Britain was never very extended or very intense ; if it had been, the Anglo-Saxon conquest could not have had such devastating results.

Gaul was a rich and varied country, with plenty of land for

agriculture and herds, with a wonderful system of rivers and canals, for the considerable growth of native towns, ready to develop into Roman cities.   Rome first took hold in Provence (the ' province ') in 118 B.C., conquered all Gaul under Julius Caesar, 58–49 B.C., and sealed the conquest under the Empire.   Gaul abandoned most of her old culture for the Roman : that is why French of today is a developed dialect of popular Latin.   Gaul had from of old great wealth of metal, though her own mines were not of the first rank. Under the Empire, manufactures of various kinds developed ; several Gallic cities rose to fame as universities.   The Roman Germanies were frontier strips of military occupation.   In course of time, great cities and trades grew up there.   Beyond the Rhine lay free Germany, unlovely to Roman eyes, ' either bristling with woods or festering with marshes ', with little cultivation, few towns—not to say cities—a population sown far and wide.   Tacitus cannot conceive that anyone could wish to wander there ' unless it were his home '.

The mountainous districts to the North of Italy—Rhaetia, Noricum, the little Alpine provinces—could show a few notable cities.   The country was not very suitable for human uses.   The romantic beauty that draws the modern visitor had little appeal for Romans.   Sublimity combined with cold did not attract them.   It comes as a pleasant surprise when we find one Roman procurator in an inscription showing some sense of the natural beauty of his province ' where he directs justice and manages the fortunes of Caesar '.

Spain from early times was a land of cities.   Many parts were rough and mountainous, the natural lair of wild peoples.   The plains were fertile and grew the olive in plenty in imperial times. Above all, Spain was distinguished by her mineral wealth in gold, silver and lead.   Slow to be conquered, in time she became almost as Roman as Gaul.   Spanish is as much a dialect of late Latin as is French.   The variety of the country is illustrated by the fact that a second language, Portuguese, rose in the North-West.   Spain was almost the first of the provinces to give the Empire great men of letters, and, after them, Emperors.

Italy stood beside Rome as an equal partner in Empire, a queen of nations.   We may read the praises of Italy in the Second Georgic of Virgil—her wonderful ancient cities, her fair country, her harbours, her climate, her human wealth in men.   Only the Po valley could rank with the great agricultural countries.   The South was given up to herding.   But the cultivation of the very profitable minor crops—choice vegetables and flowers—throve round the cities, and manufacture for export grew in many centres. Italy was not unworthy to be the centre of Empire and the Roman showed supreme wisdom in admitting her to full partnership; otherwise the basis would have been too narrow. The words of Virgil

Sit Romana potens Itala virtute propago

exactly express the truth. Of the islands, Corsica was a wild country, given over to brigandage, which was not a profitable article of export. Sardinia was in her minor way one of the granaries of the Empire. Sicily, an ancient centre of civilised life, had still her crown of fair cities and something of her old agricultural fame left. But, for her, the Empire was an age of slow decline.

In Africa there was a sharp contrast between the desolate interior and the strips of coast where cities could grow, where corn could be produced for imperial use, where vine and olive could be cultivated with profit. The desert peoples—Moors, Numidians, Musulamii, Gaetulians, Garamantes—were nomad wanderers and the enemies of civilisation. But the prosperity of the coast—at times spreading inland—was remarkable. Africa is one of the few parts of the world in which a marked decline from Roman standards can be noted today.

The Balkan lands came to Rome still undeveloped. Under the Empire they put off much of their barbarity. But despite the growth of city life, especially in Thrace, they were ever lands of war rather than peace. They were storehouses of man-power. The Pannonians of the 3rd century supplied much of the fighting strength of the armies. Greece still had her ancient fame and such little prosperity as that might bring. Athens was still the first university of the Empire; its schools of philosophy continued to draw students from all quarters. But the country, never rich, was sadly impoverished. Servius Sulpicius, the correspondent of Cicero, draws a moving picture of the dead or dying cities of Greece. In Pausanias we see Greece as the land of the curious visitor and the archaeologist, no longer anywhere near the centre of actual interests.

In the vast extent of Asia Minor there was room for strong contrasts. The inner districts were largely wild and uncultivated. But the coasts, especially in the ancient provinces of Asia and Bithynia, were swarming with famous cities. They drew wealth from trade by sea, from natural sources, from highly developed manufactures, from land trade with the far interior of Asia. To the contending war lords of the late Republic Asia was a never-ending source of supply. Already vital for Rome, Asia was to be the main basis of Byzantine power for centuries.

Syria might rank beside Asia as one of the most valuable parts of the Empire. Here, too, city life flourished ; here, too, trade throve by land and sea ; here, too, famous factories continued to create and diffuse wealth. Syria inherited the old Phoenician genius for trade ; the Syrian was the most successful trader of the Empire. As you went inland, you came to the desert, with its unsettled life, its tribal feuds, its caravans. You came to the great caravan cities of Palmyra, Bostra and Petra, and to the Arabs ' who dwell in tents '. Armenia was always an Iranian country, never closely attached to Rome, though often under her suzerainty. Mesopotamia came for a time under Roman rule. Here a number of famous cities diversified the monotony of the desert and won wealth and consideration by the through trade between the Far and Nearer East. Across the frontier lay the Iranian kingdom of Parthia, with one or two great Greek cities, such as Seleucia on the Tigris. Here was a life alien to the Roman norms—an hereditary autocracy and feudal lords, a land where the old simple virtues of shooting, riding and telling the truth replaced the more sophisticated Greek or Roman moralities.

Egypt remained essentially unchanged. The Nile still brought down from its mysterious fount its fertilising streams, the fellahin still tilled the land for foreign consumers. Egypt was one of the great granaries of the Empire. There were few cities. Alexandria, the capital, was one of the greatest centres of manufacture and handled the trade from far India. Cyrenaica had lost her ancient wealth, the silphium plant, which died out under the Empire, and only plays a minor role. Of the islands, Cyprus and Crete lay just outside the main currents of life. The smaller islands served mainly as convenient places to which exiles might be consigned.

Within this vast geographical setting there was room for great diversity of race. In the West we find the Celts, in several streams— the oldest stream, the Goidelic, from whom come Gaelic and Erse— the Brythonic, from whom come Welsh, Cornish and Breton—the Belgae of Gaul, the latest comers to Britain. Gaul was mainly Celtic, with strong admixtures of German blood in the North and Iberian in the South. In Spain, the old Iberian stock was largely intermingled with Celtic, making the peoples which we call the Celtiberians. In Italy, we find the Latin and Oscan peoples, traces of Sicel blood and also Illyrian. The tough Ligurians of the North-West seem to have been pre-Indo-European, perhaps kin to the Iberians. In Africa, the chief racial ingredients were the Phoenicians of Carthage and the other cities and the Berbers of the Coast. The Balkans contained an intermixture of Germans,

Thracians and Sarmatians. Behind the frontiers were the East Germans, later the Goths, and behind them the Slavs, hardly known as yet to history—also Iranian peoples from Asia. In Asia, the welter of peoples defies analysis. There were ancient peoples, descendants of the Hittites or even earlier stocks—Indo-Germans, Phrygians and the rest ; strange little races like the Lycian and the Carian, obstinately holding on to their own languages ; then the latest comers, the Galatians of the interior of the North. Syria had its old stock, the Phoenicians, the Canaanites, the Arabs, the Philistines. Egypt had its mixed population of Egyptians, Macedonians, Greeks and other foreigners. Cyrenaica was Greek, intermixed with native Berbers. It is only the politician, anxious to make capital out of history, who rushes in with positive interpretations of racial problems. To the serious student they are amazingly hard to interpret, even to understand. Races as they appear in history are not to be classified under any one heading—physical type, language, habitat or any other. Race in fact is always something composite. The dominant racial types of the Empire continued to exist distinguishable from one another. There was certainly intermarriage, for there was much to induce it, no bar to prevent it. I do not think that any statistics are available which would enable us to conclude how far interbreeding went.

Nationality is definitely not the same as race. A nation will usually be based on some one prevailing race; but political conditions may bring several races under one rule, and a strong national feeling, which is not purely racial, may develop. Under the Empire the complete domination of Rome meant the complete supremacy of the Romans. Other nationalities might survive, but it was as cultures rather than as nations proper. Isocrates had already laid down the principle that a ' Greek ' meant the man who shared Greek culture rather than the man of Greek blood. As a political factor nationality ceased to count for much. The Jews alone refused to acquiesce in imperial rule, and, as a result, lost their national home. But they retained their strong national consciousness. In the early Empire there were stirrings of national feeling in Gaul. An independent ' Empire of the Gauls ' rose for a moment out of the Civil Wars of A.D. 69. But, when we come to the Gallic Empire of Postumus and his successors in the 3rd century, we find it by its own declaration only a separate version of the Roman. Britain rose in revolt against Nero's procurator, but it was definite wrongs to individuals, even more than offended national pride, that nerved the rebels. The British Empire of Carausius and Allectus in 289–296 was as avowedly Roman as the Gallic.

1. *Obv.* Augustus. *Rev.* Victory sacrificing bull (ARMENIA CAPTA). Aureus. *c.* 20 B.C. Asia Minor. (p. 47.)

2. *Obv.* Claudius. *Rev.* ' De Britannis ', Arch. (See Pl. I, No. 3.)

3. *Obv.* Trajan (IMP[eratori] CAES[ari] NER[vae] TRAIAN[o] OPTIM[o] AUG[usto] GER[manico] DAC[ico] PARTHICO). *Rev.* Emperor crowning kings (REGNA ADSIGNATA). Aureus. 115. Rome. (pp. 21, 104.)

4. *Obv.* Trajan (IMP CAES NER TRAIANO OPTIMO AUG GER DAC PARTHICO PM TRP COS VI PP). *Rev.* Emperor triumphant over Armenia and Mesopotamia (ARMENIA ET MESOPOTAMIA IN POTESTATEM P[opuli] R[omani] REDACTAE SC). Sestertius. 116–17. Rome. (pp. 21, 104.)

5. *Obv.* Antoninus Pius (ANTONINUS AUG PIUS PP TRP COS III). *Rev.* Emperor giving diadem to the king of the Quadi (REX QUADIS DATUS SC.). Sestertius. *c.* 143. Rome. (p. 109.)

6. *Obv.* Antoninus Aurelius (M. ANTONINUS GERM[anicus] SARM[aticus] AUG). *Rev.* Arms taken from the Sarmatians (TRP XXXI IMP VIII COS III PP). At foot : DE SARM[atis]. Aureus. 178. Rome. (pp. 50, 109.)

7. *Obv.* Constans (FL[avius] IUL[ius] CONSTANS PIUS FELIX AUG). *Rev.* Emperor triumphing over barbarian peoples (TRIUMFATOR GENTIUM BARBARARUM). At foot : TES[i.e. Thessalonica]. Silver Medallion. 346. Thessalonica. (pp. 36, 108.)

8. *Obv.* Augustus (AUGUSTUS DIVI F[ilius]. *Rev.* Nero Drusus and Tiberius presenting laurels to Augustus (IMP X). Aureus. *c.* 14 B.C. ? Lugdunum.

9. *Obv.* Claudius (TI CLAUD. CAESAR. AUG. P.M. TR.P.). *Rev.* Emperor in Praetorian camp (IMPER[ator] RECEPT[us]). Aureus. 41. Rome. (p. 47.)

10. *Obv.* Claudius (inscription as above). *Rev.* Emperor receiving allegiance of praetorians (PRAETOR[ianus] RECEPT[us, sc. in fidem]). Aureus. 41. Rome. (p. 47.)

11. *Obv.* Nerva (IMP. NERVA CAES AUG PM TRP COS II PP). *Rev.* ' The concord of the armies ' (CONCORDIA EXERCITUUM). Aureus. 96. Rome. (pp. 20, 147.)

Plate III

Plate IV

1. *Obv.* Domitian (IMP CAES DOMIT[ianus] AUG GERM COS XI CENS[oria] POT[estate] PP). *Rev.* The Oath of Allegiance ('sacramentum'). Sestertius. 84. Rome. (p. 138.)

2. *Obv.* Hadrian. HADRIANUS AUG COS III PP). *Rev.* The Army of Britain (EXERC[itus] BRITANN[icus]). Sestertius. *c.* 135. Rome. (p. 148.)

3. *Obv.* Commodus (M. COMM[odus] ANT[oninus] AUG P[ius] BRIT[annicus] FEL[ix]). *Rev.* Emperor reconciling army groups (PM TRP XI IMP VII COS II PP). At foot : CONC[ordia] MIL[itum]. Aureus. 186. Rome. (p. 148.)

4. *Obv.* Septimius Severus (IMP CAE. L. SEP[timius] SEV[erus] PERT[inax] AUG) *Rev.* Standards of Legion XIV Gemina (LEG[io] XIIII GEM[ina] M[artia] V[ictrix]). Aureus. 193. Rome. (pp. 149, 284.) Septimius took over the name Pertinax from his predecessor.

5. *Obv.* Gordian III (IMP. CAES M[arcus] ANT[onius] GORDIANUS AUG). *Rev.* The loyalty of the Army (FIDES MILITUM). Aureus. 244. Rome. (p. 150.)

6. *Obv.* Gallienus. *Rev.* Badge of the Legion I Adjutrix, 'six times loyal and faithful' (LEG[io] I ADI[utrix] VI P[ia] VI F[idelis]). Antoninianus. 260 (?). Milan. (p. 151.)

7. *Obv.* Gallienus. *Rev.* The loyalty of the Army (FIDES MILITUM). Aureus. *c.* 264. Rome. (p. 151.)

8. *Obv.* Victorinus (IMP C[aesar] VICTORINUS P[ius] F[elix] AUG). *Rev.* Badge of the Legion IV Flavia, 'loyal and faithful' (LEG[io] IIII FLAVIA P[ia] F[idelis]). Aureus. 270. Gaul.

9. *Obv.* Carausius (IMP CARAUSIUS PF AUG). *Rev.* Badge of Legion II (LEG[io] II). At foot : M[oneta] L[ondiniensis]. Antoninianus. *c.* 288. London. (p. 33.)

10. *Obv.* Julian II (FL[avius] CL[audius] IULIANUS PF AUG). *Rev.* The Valour of the Roman Army (VIRTUS EXERCITUS ROMANORUM). At foot : ANT[i.e. Antioch] A[i.e. 1st officina]. Solidus. 362. Antioch.

11. *Obv.* Titus (IMP T[itus] CAES VESP[asianus] AUG PM TRP. PP COS VIII). *Rev.* Imperial corn-supply (ANNONA AUG[usti]). Sestertius. 80. Rome. Titus took over the name Vespasian from his predecessor. (p. 19.)

There is something almost comic in the claim of the Menapian Carausius to ' restore Rome '. Spain had ended her protests against enslavement when Agrippa subdued the Cantabri. The Pannonians said their last word in the great revolt late in the reign of Augustus. One episode of the 3rd century constitutes an exception. When Palmyra first repulsed Sapor and then ruled as Vicegerent for Rome in the East, when she went on to bid for an independent Empire against Aurelian, Rome met a definite challenge—not so much national as racial and cultural. A Palmyrene Empire would not have been a mere variety of the Roman. But here fortune decided for Rome against the brave adventure.

Close to the problem of races and nations stands that of languages. In the Empire Latin was, of course, dominant. It was spoken universally in the West ; it must have been known in all the centres of government and trade in the East. The survival of so many Romance languages in Europe tells its own tale—French, Spanish, Portuguese, Italian, Romans in Switzerland, Rumanian. That Dacia, the latest of Roman provinces in these regions and the first to be abandoned, should yet speak a Latin language, while all the rest do not, is an amazing fact. Trajan's resettlement with Latin-speaking people must have been very thorough. Even so, it is hard to understand how the original Dacians can have disappeared so completely and how the new settlers can have had time to plant their own language so firmly. There is something in the transmission of language that is not immediately to be understood. Consider the political history of Britain and Gaul—both conquered by Rome, both held by her for centuries, both then given over to barbarian peoples. Can we readily find anything to account for the completely different fate of their languages—Latin in its French form surviving triumphant, the Celtic which the Roman province of Britain used almost completely lost?

Greek was predominant in the East as Latin was in the West. Among the educated classes everywhere a knowledge of Greek might be presumed. The Emperor had his Greek as well as his Latin secretary. The barbarian languages of the West yielded the field to Latin as far as administration and literature went; they only survived in private life. Punic lasted down into the 4th century, at least in Africa. The old languages of the Balkans and Asia Minor seem to have sunk below the surface. In Syria, Syriac and Aramaic must have had a vigorous life, for both of them found expression in literature. Hebrew lived on in the sacred scriptures of the Jews. In Egypt the old language continued, to be revived in a late form in the religious literature of Coptic. Over the whole of the Roman East there was one language readily accessible to all—the ' common ' Greek, the κοινή, still unmistakably Greek in vocabulary and construction, but shot through with borrowed words and very far adrift from the pure Attic of Plato or Xenophon.

We have left to the last the most interesting feature—the cultures associated with the races, nations and languages that we have been discussing. Culture can be observed but not easily defined. It tends to be associated with nations and races, but it is not identical with them. A strong culture draws aliens into itself ; after a time it will include not only birth members, but others also who, so to say, join it voluntarily or are co-opted. Culture includes the many details that go to make up a way of life—social, literary, artistic, religious as well as political and economic. The main culture of the Empire can only be described as Greco-Roman. Some parts of it may be traced to Greece, others to Rome. But it was by now a composite that could be seen and accepted as a whole without analysis. The lover of Greece is tempted to complain that the heritage of Greece has come down to us in what he will feel to be a debased form. But ought he not to be thankful that it has managed to survive at all ? Greece herself could not mould any vessel strong enough to contain the wealth of her genius. Rome, for her own ends and half blindly, discharged this great service. This culture imposed itself on the Empire at large and seldom met with any direct opposition. The Jews, we have seen, *did* fight, and their fight was cultural as well as national. The Jewish way of life had its appeal for many who were not born Jews. Other cultures contrived to survive within narrow limits. The Phoenician stock still retained its vast aptitude for trade. The Egyptian was still recognised as a distinct type, with a strong religious bias and with something mysterious and, it might be, sinister in his religion. The Corybantic element in the Phrygians found expression in Montanism, an enthusiastic movement within the Christian Church. The influence of the ancient cultures of the East—Syria, Babylonia and Persia—was still felt along the Eastern frontiers. In the form of astrology, the science of the stars as governors of human destinies, the Babylonian mage exercised a potent and evil influence on men and affairs. To pry into the secrets of the future is for Horace ' to tamper with Babylonian numbers '.

The business of government, the ' ruling the peoples under its sway ', was at first entirely in Roman, or we should rather say Italian hands. But it could not remain exclusively so. Province after province offered its best men to Rome, to take their share in the administration and, step by step, they found admission to the inner circle—first, Gauls from Narbonese and Spaniards, then other Gauls and Africans and with them Asiatics and Syrians ; but some peoples, the Egyptians for example, hardly penetrated into the central shrine.　The 2nd century saw Emperors from Spain, its close an African ; the 3rd century saw Emperors from the East and even from the barbarian frontiers.　It was next the turn of the great Pannonians.　Roman citizenship spread beyond Rome and Italy by grants to whole communities or to individuals.　The process was at first deliberately retarded by wise Emperors, but in 212 Caracalla extended citizenship to all but the lowest class, the *dediticii.*

Next to citizenship came the Latin right, a relic of old Italian public law ; it was used under the Empire as a preparation for the full citizenship.　The Latin community had a constitution modelled on the Roman and its magistrates proceeded to citizenship.　The privileged communities in the provinces were (1) the Roman colonies, enjoying full civic rights and counting as little models of Rome, and (2) the *municipia*, which, without citizenship, enjoyed the forms of Italian civic life.　The cities of the Empire were bound to Rome by alliances of various grades.　The *civitates liberae et immunes*, cities free and exempt from taxation, enjoyed the equal alliance, under which only actual predominance of power gave Rome, the advantage.　It was a special favour if a city received the ' Italian right ', the privilege of a share in Italy's exemption from direct taxation.　Famous ancient cities like Athens and Sparta were nominally free cities.　Other cities possessed alliances of lower grade.　The treaty would normally regulate relations with Rome— would determine, for example, to what extent a community was exempt from the jurisdiction of the provincial governor.　Beyond them lay the remaining mass of subjects of the Empire, not protected by any special favour other than that of the general law and liable to pay taxes.　The status was indeed a low one—the status of the *dediticius*, who surrendered himself at discretion to Rome and took from her hand what she was pleased to give.　If the *dediticii* of the edict of Caracalla were just this class of subject, the exceptions to his bestowal of citizenship were wider than has sometimes been supposed.　But the question is much debated and not yet settled.　The direct tax demanded might be considered as a natural levy on the conquered by the conqueror.　The Roman lawyers worked out a theory that provincial land became the property of the Roman people and, as such, paid its tax as a kind of rent.　It mattered very little to the taxpayer what the tax was called.

Italy stands beside Rome as the most favoured land, queen not servant. The provinces stand on a lower level ; they are subject and tributary. Between the provinces differences can be noted along a number of lines. The older and more peaceful provinces were governed, not by the legates of the Emperor, but by the pro-magistrates of the Senate. In status this meant little difference ; in both cases the Roman state was the master. Imperial Syria and Gaul could be balanced against senatorial Asia and Africa. In practice, imperial rule was found on the whole more tolerable than senatorial. Provinces were sometimes transferred from Senate to Emperor, to give them rest from their burdens. The presence or absence of an army too must make a difference. There was also a strong contrast between East and West. The West became Romanised earlier and was earlier admitted to partnership. In the East the process took longer and was in some cases never carried through. Hadrian showed a readiness to rethink the Empire in terms of its provinces, as individuals with wishes of their own, not merely as satellites of the central sun. But he found no worthy successor ; perhaps the whole idea was too far in advance of or too wide of the views of the average man. Septimius Severus showed some interest in the provinces, but though he gave lavishly it was with little settled policy. Yet the supremacy of Rome and Italy was contradicted by the logic of facts and came to count for less and less. When Diocletian divided the Empire into its four sections under two Augusti and two Caesars, there was no reason left why any one section should be more highly privileged than another. When the Empire ultimately found one capital that ranked above all others, that capital was not Rome but Constantinople. It is one of the fascinating, unanswerable problems of history : could the Empire have developed along more hopeful lines ? Could it have become politically alive in its parts ? Could it even have developed into a friendly society of allied states ? All that we can say for certain is that it did not. But, when we see how inevitably the special privilege of Rome and Italy gave way before the necessities of the 4th century, we cannot but wonder whether it might not equally well have given way earlier to considerations of wisdom and conciliation.

One of the vital considerations in judging the efficiency of the State is that of communications. A great state with little con-nection between its parts may actually be far behind a much smaller one with its parts effectively linked together. In this respect the Empire advanced far beyond any predecessor. The Persians had been the first to organise a great state post along a network of roads.

Rome brought with her her instinct for road-making as part of her military efficiency. An army must march before it can fight ; if it is to march, it must have roads to march on. So, with the victories of Rome, spread the Roman roads. The Empire also used its road system to establish an effective state post for official business. The costs were heavy and normally fell on the local communities. Nerva could boast of his generosity in relieving Italy of the expenses of the *vehiculatio*, as the post was called. The Empire, then, was linked up by an admirable system of roads, military in purpose in the first place, but continually improved for general public uses. One of the most attractive interests for an archaeologist in any country that was Roman is the tracing of what is left of the roads. The general pattern was simple and plain —a raised track with a ditch on either side, driving as straight as possible across country in the desired direction. What was meant in the first place for public uses could not altogether be denied to private. After the soldiers traders made their way to and fro along the roads. The minor roads, which received less attention, served private rather than public ends.

Not so easy were communications by sea. The Romans in dire need might take to the sea and dispose of their enemies there. There is the first Punic War to attest Rome's capacity for learning warfare on a new element, the war of Pompey with the pirates to show how Rome could deal with a dangerous nuisance that had gone on far too long. Pompey, by the bye, was responsible for the grand slogan

Navigare necesse est, vivere non est necesse
(' keep the seas we must, live if we may '.)

But how poorly the Romans lived up to it ! The Empire brought some improvement. Italy received a fleet on either coast— at Misenum and Ravenna ; auxiliary fleets kept watch on the Channel, on Rhine, Danube and other rivers. But the service was not held in the same honour as the army and, in emergency, the fleets proved inefficient. When the Goths seized ships in the Black Sea and descended on Greece and Asia Minor, there was no immediate staying of them ; the imperial fleet, which should have been in reserve for such an emergency, was just not there. When Carausius drew off the Channel fleet and seized Britain, the Empire was again without resource. A new fleet had to be constructed and its first efforts against the island pretender were disastrous. Carausius himself died, murdered but undefeated ; had he lived, Constantius Chlorus might have had a much harder task to deal with him than with his murderer, Allectus. Navigation, of course, did develop. The regular voyage to India began with the discovery of the monsoons in the Early Empire. The adventurers sailed up and down the Mediterranean and passed the Pillars of Hercules to Britain and Ireland. But the sea was dangerous in the winter season; even the boldest captain preferred to hug the shore—and that meant more risks from rocks. We do not hear of any effective charting such as the British Admiralty undertook in the 19th century. Development at sea reached a certain point and there stopped short. The belief lingered on that the seas had been set by Heaven to divide the land and that there was something presumptuous in man's attempts to reverse the benign decree. We might have much the same feeling about the air—those of us, that is to say, who have never become fully air-minded. Communications by water—rivers and canals—were very highly developed in a country like Gaul and the results must have been excellent for trade. The special conditions of movement in the East—travelling in caravans—concerned the Romans only indirectly; they might draw their profit from the trade, but they left it in the main to its old holders.

We have so far been speaking of those communications by which human bodies and goods in bulk are transferred from place to place. What of those other purposes that are served today by our letter and small parcel post? The difference here is that bulk matters far less, speed far more. Along the great roads the postman, *tabularius*, as well as the soldier or trader, travelled. The rich might still send their private postman to their friends. What we really want to know is how imperial edicts, how public news was transmitted quickly from place to place. Our modern methods, which almost annihilate distance, were of course entirely unknown. It took days, if not weeks, for the most important news to travel within the Empire. There was no telegraph, no telephone, no wireless. What the Emperor wished to communicate to his subjects will have travelled far and fast along the network of roads. His edicts would have been posted up at an early date in the chief provincial cities. The *Res Gestae Divi Augusti*, known to us in three copies only, were almost beyond a doubt published in every province. The setting up of the monument in bronze would take some time after the text had been received. The *acta diurna*, the short official chronicle of Rome, was read in the provinces; the *acta senatus* were presumably available, like a modern Hansard, to the few who would take the trouble of ordering them. Books and treatises would go out from the centres to outlying parts; they would have to use the ordinary means of transference, but their small bulk may have helped speedy transit. To carry news quickly into every street and market place, into every small city or village off the main track, the coins, especially the small change, were invaluable. They passed, inevitably if not very quickly, from hand to hand. It was well known that types were not fixed once for all, that they were constantly changing to reflect the changes of events. Men therefore looked and looked again at what came into their hands, learned the news, were impressed, if impressed they could be, with the latest propaganda. The Epistles of St. Paul give us some idea of how thought can travel under the Empire. Neither the Apostle nor his friends were in most cases wealthy people ; yet correspondence was carried on about vital matters with little waste of time. But there was nothing like a penny post.

The Empire, so large and so varied, included in itself the most diverse kinds of lives. The first great cleavage is between country and city—the latter far the more important. Let us take the country first. The cultivation of grain took first place in those favoured provinces where it flourished. Egypt, Africa, Sicily and Sardinia were the granaries of the Empire ; a few other provinces produced enough for their home use, but not for normal export. There was money in land, but not much for the labourer. When it came to the vital corn-supply, Government kept a tight rein on the whole business of production and transport, controlling not only the producer but also the guilds of shippers and carters. Great country estates, with some farmland, were very common in some provinces—Africa, for example; they might even have a closed economy of their own. The vine and olive flourished in places new and old. Olive culture increased to a vast extent, especially in Spain and Africa. Protective measures against provincial vine culture, in the interest of the Italian, might be taken, as once by Domitian. Both vine and olive were essential to ancient life and there was money in them. Market gardening, in many profitable forms, was prosecuted in the neighbourhood of large cities, which could take up the produce quickly. Many a fortune was made near Rome by ingenious producers, who guessed right about a new possible market. Wide spaces of open country, which had proved too hilly or wild for grain, naturally lent themselves to the keeping of herds or flocks. South Italy was largely taken up with immense tracts of grazing land, where few ventured except the wild shepherd slaves. The Empire over, such pasture lands must have been common. We hear of famous breeds of horses from Gaul and Sicily. The Arabian breed of horse was as yet unknown. The

roughest parts of the Empire were useless even for sheep and cattle ;
they lent themselves best to hunting. But, though you might hunt
for pleasure, there was not much money in it. But under the
Empire there was an almost unlimited demand for animals, tame
or wild—let them only be of some special interest—for exhibition
in the amphitheatre. This gave rise to a kind of luxury trade in
beasts—the lion, tiger, panther, wild bull, hippopotamus, rhinoceros. The elephant was domesticated in Rome as a peculiarly
imperial beast, used to draw chariots in solemn processions. In
those wildest districts of the Empire you came close to the great
barbarian world that lay outside, to its lawlessness and lack of
control. The deserts on the fringes were denied to civilised life,
except in the East, where men knew their deserts from of old and
priceless treasures came in, pillaged and overtaxed, to glut Roman
luxury.

So much for the country, usually dependent on the nearest cities,
except in the case of the very large estates (*saltus*) which might be
administered as little communities by themselves. The cities
offered a very wide range of employment. The rich and noble
might aspire to a share in the Government, might enjoy a selfish
leisure or busy themselves with a range of social engagements, they
seldom worked in the sense in which most of us use the word. The
clients, dependents of noble families, still as of old paid their respects
to their patrons—attending their levies, running their errands. The
dole that they received was not a living, but a modest contribution
to one. The client-patron relation was for Rome a vital one. It
still survived under the Empire—only now the private patron was
overshadowed by the Emperor, the great *patronus publicus*, whose
clients all Romans came to be. Freedmen were tied by some
obligations to their former masters. They often displayed wonderful energy and enterprise ; they had one great advantage—they
need not ask about every possible source of money Vespasian's
question ' Does it smell ? ' Freedmen often waxed presumptuous
and used their money and influence to defy the strict letter of the
law that bound them to their patrons. The slaves were everywhere
—in the great city houses, where they rendered an infinite variety
of personal services ; on the country estates, often used for punishment, where there would be sure to be hard work and might be
bitter sufferings ; in small trades where their masters let them earn
money with which ultimately to buy their freedom. One proposal
—to introduce a distinctive dress for slaves—was turned down on
the ground that it would be too dangerous to let the slaves realise
their numbers. The free population of the cities must have had

at its disposal a variety of ways of making a living. There were small businesses ; there were the various arts and crafts ; there were the transport workers from near and far. Especially when the slave supply began to fail, the prospects for free labour should have been good. Yet it seems as if a large part of the Roman people lived precariously from hand to mouth, depending on the free or cheap corn and on the occasional imperial largesses. Rome herself was not a great industrial city. But cities like Antioch and Alexandria were famous for their manufactures, which employed thousands of hands.

In modern times the professions tend to pride themselves on a superior social status, even if they may have to accept financial inferiority as part of the bargain. In antiquity the case was somewhat different. The Law held a high place in Roman esteem ; it was an occupation fit for a gentleman. Legal experts, officially recognised by the Emperor, gave their advice to all comers. Barristers pleaded in the courts. Services were in theory given free ; in practice, means were found to evade the strict letter of the law. Many adroit advocates made fortunes by skilful practice. Higher up, the great barristers, often men of quick but not noble ambitions, rose to wealth and power by serving the Emperor against his more prominent enemies. Roman Law reached its zenith with the great lawyers of the age of Septimius—Papinian, Ulpian, Paulus. The praetorian prefect was by now expected to act as deputy for the Emperor in his legal capacity, and the great jurists held that office. A good acquaintance with the Law must have been the qualification for many posts in the Civil Service of the late Empire. The teaching profession set out from humble beginnings ; neither the grammarian who taught children their rudiments nor the rhetorician who carried on the training in public speaking ranked very high. To a Roman the capacity to speak reasonably well in public was a necessity for an educated man ; but the rhetorical training of the Empire was too often artificial, insincere and unreal. But the status of teaching rose when the Emperors gave it official recognition. Highly salaried professors began to be appointed for cities. In the 4th century the rhetorician was very highly regarded. He could master the curiously contorted style that was considered proper for official pronouncements, or he could discourse to the public on themes grave or gay, of high political import or bordering on the farcical. Themistius and Libanius received high honours from Emperors. Ausonius, the tutor of Gratian, became praetorian prefect and for some years sprinkled honours in the West over his friends and relations. Medicine was at first in the hands of slaves or freedmen. Doctors were often of Greek or, at least, Eastern extraction and were regarded with some suspicion by the Roman nobles, who did not like being at the mercy of those whom they despised socially. But the profession in its very nature is both dignified and essential, and it rose in status as the Emperors recognised it and appointed public doctors for the cities.

In pagan Rome religion was not a profession. Priesthoods were held by men of affairs, often of singularly irreligious character. Regular priesthoods became known to the Romans in the worship of the Great Mother, of Isis or of Mithras. Christianity developed its fine organisation in the true Roman spirit of discipline and efficiency. When Constantine brought the Church out of darkness and oppression into the light of his imperial favour, a new profession stood open. There was room within the Church for ability of many grades—the organising ability of the Bishops, now called on to be men of affairs as well as of the spirit, the teaching work of the clergy, the administrative ability of the deacons and the rest. Rome must now recognise a clergy that was set apart, into which men might try to escape from their civil obligations as senators of the local cities, as members of state-controlled guilds, as possible soldiers.

Literature could hardly be considered as a profession, though a certain number of men lived by it. Virgil and Horace, for all their popularity, depended on their patrons for their comfort if not for the bare means of livelihood. It is not probable that the reading public was large enough to guarantee large incomes for those who lived entirely by their art, though a poet like Martial seems to have done fairly well. But then, it has always been the privilege of the literary genius to starve in an attic. The stage was a profession and a vastly popular one, but not held in any honour. Yet the great pantomimes often won immense fame and might intrude into the domesticities of the imperial house. Domitian put to death the Paris who was accused of being the lover of the Empress Domitia. The malicious whispered that Commodus was no true son of Marcus Aurelius, but of an actor, Tertullus. It was always considered a disgrace for a Roman noble to sully himself with appearances on the public stage, though even the austere might make an exception for private performances. Nero disgusted Rome by his shameless defiance of this prejudice. For women the profession never rose in dignity ; to be an actress was almost tantamount to being a woman of easy virtue.

On something like the same level of wild popularity, wealth and influence, combined with social degradation, stood the professions

bound up with the great popular amusements.   The gladiator was
the lowest of the low.   Tacitus can hardly bring himself to admit
the awful truth that the Curtius Montanus who rose to be governor
of Africa was the son of a gladiator.   But the public made heroes
of these desperadoes who risked wounds or death to delight them.
Noble Roman ladies were known to leave home and luxury for the
company of these fleshly lovers.   Under bad Emperors the profession might profit by imperial favour.   Commodus had all the
makings of a skilled gladiator himself.   At the time of his murder
he was preparing to ' proceed ' to the consulship from the quarters
of the gladiators.   This last disgrace was narrowly averted by his
murder.   Wilder if possible was the passion for the circus.   The
rivalry of the colours took up much of the party spirit that was
denied vent in public life.   Successful drivers made huge fortunes
and were extolled to the skies by the excited mob.   Nero gave a
boost to the profession by his passion to excel as charioteer, here
as in music and poetry emulating his chosen god, Apollo.

Next come the social distinctions, largely bound up with distinctions of profession.   At the top we find the imperial circle, the
court and its hangers-on.   Next to it comes the Senate of Rome,
still acknowledged as the first order of the State, still mighty in its
landed wealth, its public activities and its social pull.   Next come
the knights, the second order of the nobility, comprising many
men of wealth who preferred money to political distinction.   They
served the Emperor well both in army and in Civil Service.   Then
come the freedmen of Rome, of various social grades, the better of
them often bound to noble families by ties of clientage.   The lower
orders, the *plebs*, enjoyed the imperial liberalities and supplies of
corn, cheap or free, and all the lavish entertainments.   In their
assemblages in circus and amphitheatre their voices carried a not
to be despised political influence.   The conditions of Rome were
repeated, on a smaller scale, in the provincial cities.   The local
senate led the state ; Roman senators or knights would enjoy a very
special prestige.   Retired centurions could rise to rank and honour.
The country as a whole took a lower rank.   Living away from the
main currents of life, you counted but little politically or socially—
except so far as wealth anywhere will make itself heard.   Freedmen
were despised by the old-fashioned.   Tacitus is never tired of insisting on the degradation of allowing these base newcomers to take
so much upon themselves.   Slaves did not count in the social scale ;
their only hope lay in winning or buying their freedom.   The rigid
division of society into classes that were almost castes is a vital feature
of the life of the Empire.   Some movement, upwards or downwards,

was possible ; but you could not escape from the system. You were placed from birth and only the man of exceptional energy could escape from the wheel. Tacitus has a supreme contempt for the socially underprivileged. He despises even the members of Italian municipalities ; he despises the aspiring freedmen. Against this rigidity of opinion the philosophers and the Christians fought, but for long with little success. It was one thing to assert in noble tones the equality of man before the Universe ; it was quite another thing to give value to the assertion in practice. Things became even worse under the new Empire of Diocletian. Society was frozen in its hereditary classes and occupations. Free movement of the individual was, as far as possible, forbidden. The Church triumphant could assert a certain degree of freedom, but only for itself.

Of religion itself we shall speak in a special chapter. Here we will confine ourselves to looking at it as one of the principles that diversified the Empire. The great mass of the inhabitants of the Empire were at one in recognising the existence of many gods, worshipped under a vast number of names and in a great variety of forms. Their worship was mainly a matter of state ; private devotion played no large part. The great Eastern cults brought to Rome the ideas of priesthood set apart and religious secrets shared by the faithful. The worship of Cybele, with its eunuch priests, with its picturesque ritual, with its solemn processions, made a great impression on men's minds. Its *taurobolium*, the bath in bull's blood, by which a man could be ' reborn into Eternity ', seemed to the Christians an indecent parody of their own sacred mysteries. The cult of Isis was imposing in its dignity, its purity—defiled by an occasional abuse—its high moral claims. Mithras spoke above all to the soldier. The Mithraic grades, the ordeals through which they were attained, the solemn services in the underground caves— all had their strong appeal. All these cults linked together many believers in many walks of life and in far distant lands. To the relations that bound men together in social life was added the sharing in a common cult, often transcending race and rank. The Jew continued to hold to his old religion and national consciousness ; he refused to be merged in the mass of imperial subjects. The Christians, under the strain of persecution, perfected their own organisation. Julian the Apostate acknowledged with sadness that they had found something which appealed to the masses and which the pagan cults had missed. It was not as easy as he conceived it to be to borrow the form without the Christian spirit. As a persecuted body, the Christians had come to be considered as a race apart, the ' third race ', beside the pagans and the Jews. Admitted to imperial favour, they retained their organisation, but had to make terms with the society in which they now held a prominent and permanent place. One of the reasons of the Decline and Fall of the Western Empire may be seen in the slowness with which the Church assimilated the dying remains of paganism.

Such then is the Empire as seen under the aspect of diversity— one in its government, its social structure, its systems of thought— diverse in its races, cultures, economic interests, religions. If we can neglect for a moment the political and military history, the significance of the Empire may be seen largely to consist of varying interests struggling to survive and express themselves within forms that could not be abolished, only slowly modified. If it is true, as we have suggested, that a civilisation is to be realised in its form of life, its art, its literature, its religion, as well as in its politics and social conditions, the partial successes and failures of the Empire politically may be set beside its similar successes and failures in harmonising the discords that existed within it. The Empire, to succeed fully, needed a common culture, an accepted scheme of thought. When Christianity is charged with having helped the barbarians to pull the Empire down, what is really meant is that the Empire, at least in the West, failed to assimilate the new religion fully, so that in the end the Church triumphed while the Empire fell. The conflict of Empire and Church in the Middle Age echoes this unresolved discord. Both were conceived to be essential under the divine providence, but the right relations between them were never satis-factorily defined. In the East, an easier solution was found in the definite subordination of Church to State.

Divided and diversified within itself, the Empire offered some-thing like a united front to the world outside. It stood for civilisa-tion against barbarism or the oriental kingdoms of the East. The breakdown of the sense of unity under the stresses of the 4th century was the main cause of the Decline and Fall. The provincial ceased to feel himself at one with the government that continually over-taxed, but could not effectually protect him. The barbarian came so constantly as a visitor that his presence was hardly resented. The price of being a member of the great civilised community came to be too high. It was left to the Christian Church to maintain some at least of the values of civilised life in a world that sank wearily back into the barbarism out of which it had through centuries so laboriously climbed.

Martin Charlesworth, that much beloved, too early lost, Cam-bridge scholar, had the happy idea, in his book entitled ' Four Men ', of illustrating the immense variety of Roman life under the

Empire from four careers—three real characters of history, one a composite portrait. We will borrow the idea from him and imagine what life had to offer to various people in various places and times of the Empire.

Our first example shall be a Jew, born of good family in Judaea under procuratorial rule. He might confine himself to the traditions of his own people and become a Pharisee, devoted to a study of the Law. He might take the desperate part of defiance of Rome and become a zealot. But, if personal ambition was strong, he might decide to make the best of the world as he found it and seek honour and wealth in Roman employment. Migrating to Rome, he might attach himself to some noble family. Though Jews were generally unpopular, there was something of a craze for Jewish ways in high places of society. He might hope to become a Roman knight, enter the imperial service and devote the financial talent that distinguished his race to his official career. If he were fortunate he might rise above the lower procuratorial posts and even end in high employment as a prefect. We know of one such case—the Tiberius Alexander who was prefect of Egypt in A.D. 69 and took a large part in making Vespasian Emperor.

Let our second example be a young man of good family and decent fortune from a municipal city of North Italy under the Flavians. Vespasian had opened the doors of the Senate to Italy and Provence and our young man, with sufficient recommendations, might hope to be promoted to that body. All the splendours of the senatorial career were opened to him. He must be industrious, must not show undesirable independence ; it would help if he were a good speaker at the Bar. If all went well, he might end, as did Tacitus or Pliny the Younger, as governor of one of the major provinces.

For our third example we will look to a later date, the reign of Septimius Severus, and to another district, the province of Syria. Take a young Syrian whose father has been able to afford to send him to the University of Berytus, where he may study law. The Empress, Julia Domna, is a daughter of the noble priestly house of Emesa. So the Syrian may hope to find friends at court. He enters the imperial service as *advocatus fisci*, ' Counsel for the Treasury', advances in this career and at last finds the higher places of the profession open before him. It is not everyone who can be a Papinian, stand as praetorian prefect next to the Emperor, be related by marriage to the imperial house. But our man may satisfy a reasonable ambition as an assessor of the prefect.

We will take next a lad from one of the few cities in Pannonia at a date about A.D. 260. The life to which he is brought up is still simple and rough.   His family has only moderate wealth, he has no special taste for the civil professions.   But war has ever been the main interest of his people and he is drawn towards the army service. He is a Roman knight, but he decides not to pursue the prospects of his rank, but rather to do as many others have done and enter the military career by a privileged way.   He will ask by petition for the centurion's staff of vine-wood.   He receives what he has asked for. He likes his profession, works hard, attracts the attention of his superior officers.   He is promoted grade by grade, until he reaches the prized rank of chief centurion, *primipilus*.   The Pannonians are high in favour ; they are supplying the Empire with most of its best generals and not a few Emperors.   Our centurion may end in a high military command and may finally retire to enjoy much honour and consideration in his native Siscia.

Our last example shall be from Britain in the late 4th century. Our lad shall come of a good old British family, long reconciled to Roman ways.   He might, like Kipling's Parnesius, take a post as centurion in the legion.   But we will suppose that his trend is rather towards learning.   His father sends him to the University of Bordeaux, for Gallic universities rank very high in this age.   He shows a marked aptitude for study and learns the rhetoric of the time, the art of the panegyrist and the official style of the imperial chancellery.   Luck comes to his aid, for he has become acquainted with the most famous Gallic professor of the time, Ausonius, the tutor of the Emperor Gratian.   Ausonius uses his high official position of praetorian prefect in Gaul to advance his relatives and friends.   Our young man ends up as governor of one of the Gallic provinces and lives long enough to see the great barbarian invasions of the early 5th century.   His life has been a happy one and he dies without realising that the world in which he made his career is fast vanishing away.

CHAPTER III

CITIES AND CITIZENSHIP

Any student who would understand the Roman Empire needs to meditate on the whole ancient conception of the city state and to re-read such a famous book as that of Fustel de Coulanges on ' La cité ancienne '. Much of what he will find there is simple, obvious even ; but it is vital to understanding what ancient life really was.

When man emerges from the stage of hunting and grain gathering and begins to cultivate the soil and expect its yearly harvests, he soon tends to leave his forest home and to assemble himself in communities within common walls for mutual convenience and protection. The city usually follows close on the change from nomadic to settled life. But this is not all. The city is not only a place of assemblage for security or trade ; it is not simply the centre of a country district. The fully developed city is also the beginning of something quite new—a new unit of consciousness, the unit of man as a social and political being. The city is the place in which man as such a being exists. The city gives him the necessary environment—the protection of the fortified citadel, the altars of the common gods, the places where senate and council meet. Human life takes on a new dimension and it is in and through the city that the new idea is expressed. The city is something more than the place where you live and make your money ; it is the place where you draw political breath. When the writer of Hebrews says ' Here we have no abiding city ' he means more than that our home is elsewhere. He means that we are sojourners on earth, not earth's citizens. We are like Roman citizens resident in foreign parts ; our citizenship is away, in Rome. The place where we reside has nothing permanent in it for us. All our fundamental terms in politics—city, citizenship, civilisation—are all derived from the Latin *civitas*, state or city. The Greek πόλις gives us ' political ' and its correlatives. Men have lived in communities other than cities, but no other form of life has so impressed the imagination as to establish itself as a normal political thought.

The Roman Empire had at its head a city state ; many of its members were likewise cities. In the larger units, the provinces, there were many cities, more or less removed from the general administration. But the city was much older than the Empire. Rome inherited what many ages, many races had built up.

G   81

When the curtain rises on civilisation in ancient Sumeria and Accad, the city state is already vigorous. It is of a special and peculiar type, ruled by kings who stand in very close relationship to the gods. The interests of life are narrow but intense—cultivation of the soil, building with brick, worship of the gods, rivalry with neighbours. The Phoenician cities rose to fame as traders. Tyre, built on its high, narrow island, gathered wealth from the whole Mediterranean. Here trade was the main interest, with religion as its second. Here again the government was kingly ; the city republic was a creation of Greece.

Egypt was never a country of great cities ; the few that existed were residences of the god-kings and priests. Persia had its few great capitals and treasure cities ; but its life centred more on the country districts. As we can trace this development with peculiar clarity in Greece, Greece must stand for us as representative of many another country. The Greek city states were mostly small, confined to narrow tracts of territory. They were usually in want, usually at strife with their neighbours. They went through every phase of government—kings, tyrants, aristocracies, oligarchies, democracies. The forms that interest us most are those that were more or less special to Greece—the republican forms, in which there was no one ruler, but power was shared among the few or the many. It was a confederacy of Greek cities that by a miracle of courage, good counsel and good fortune threw back the advance of Persia. But that glorious morning prime was soon passed. The Greeks wasted their vital energies in civil wars and, in the 4th century, are found carrying purely Greek disputes to the court of Susa. The end was the domination of the half-Greek Macedon, which patriots like Demosthenes somewhat strangely thought worse than submission to the Persian.

With the Empire of Alexander and the kingdoms of his successors the city state met a new rival—the autocrat armed with powers against which no single city could fight. The cities held on to their independence as best they could ; they never ceased to count as pieces in the great game of politics, but very seldom could they meet the kings on terms of equality. The frequent payment of divine honours to the kings marked a noted decline in religious feeling ; it has certainly also a political aspect. The peculiar position of the king, as something above the level of the city state, was expressed by the concession to him of divine status. In this new age the city state still maintained itself, albeit with diminishing power. The republican forms which tended to assert themselves often gave way to renewals of one-man rule under tyrants. The

city had to survive in an environment not entirely kind which compelled certain adaptations. But it *did* survive and could still play
an important part under the Roman Empire. In the Seleucid
kingdom of Syria the city was deliberately used by the Greek kings
as an instrument of government and Hellenisation. New cities,
often stocked with soldiers and named after members of the royal
family, grew up far and wide—Antiochs, Seleucias, Laodiceas.

In Italy, city life flourished from an early date. The Etruscan
power was expressed in a league of cities, governed by rulers called
Lucumones. From the 8th century or earlier, Greek cities arose in
the South—Cumae, Naples, Tarentum, Metapontum and the rest
—and among the Latin and Oscan peoples too the city became the
prevalent form of government. The early history of Italy is largely
that of the struggles between rival cities, though in some parts, such
as Samnium, the country confederacy held its place against them.
There is no need to suppose that city life did not develop independ-
ently in many places ; but the idea of the city was so specially Greek
that Rome very early could be described as a ' Greek ' city.

In the West, cities flourished in Spain, but not in Gaul, where the
towns were originally only the centres of country districts. In
Africa, there was a string of Phoenician cities, with Carthage at their
head. Here, a form of republican government, comparable to the
Greek, had been evolved and interested Aristotle sufficiently to make
him include it in his studies of constitutions. Already when Rome
took the reins of power, the city was the dominating form wherever
civilisation flourished. But the world did not belong to it alone ;
there were competing forms of political life—the country confederacies and the great organised monarchies.

There were some things that every city supplied to its inhabitants.
It gave them the protection of city walls and fortresses ; it gave them
a focus for their religion ; it gave them too the centre of their social
life. Further than that a city need not go ; it might be ruled by a
king, as autocratic as an Eastern monarch. But, where circumstances were favourable as in Greece, the idea of the Commonwealth,
the *respublica*, developed—the state that is not simply the possession
of the reigning house, but a concern and interest of all. In the
development of the republican form of government the ancient city
found its fullest realisation. The State, belonging to all, should be
run in the interests of all and, to realise this purpose, all possible
forms were tried. You can hardly expect that a single ruler will be
the best at expressing the common interest. Government becomes
the concern of the whole community. The question has next to
be answered : ' How can a community govern itself ? ' Some

principle of choice must be adopted, be it noble birth, wealth in lands or commerce, or just to be free-born. In every case, self-government was aimed at and it had come to stay—government of the people, by the people, for the people. The single ruler was never quite at home in the city state of the Greek type. He is generally called not king but tyrant, an expression of aversion, suggesting irregular and lawless rule. There might be good tyrants, but the genus tyrant was bad. Tyrannicide is a term of high praise.

When Rome triumphed, it was a signal victory for the city state. The Greek cities had waged a long and unequal war with the Successor kings, to keep what was left of their freedom. Now Rome, a city state, proved herself stronger than all the kings and their solid military powers. The city state came back into full honour. There could not be much real freedom under the new Empire, but the city state was privileged and offered itself to Rome as a most useful instrument in the government of her vast estate.

The cities of the Empire may be classed as (1) Roman and Italian, (2) Greek, or (3) divergent types. The Roman and Italian city had its senate, its popular assembly, often with little power, its magistrates, usually few in number and distributed over two or three Boards. The Roman colony, not now confined to Italy, was a small model of Rome, copying as closely as possible all the chief features of the capital. The *municipium*, the community organised on the lines of an Italian city, was run very much like a colony but lacked its special rank. The Greek city conformed in general plan to the same scheme ; the details varied, the magistrates were different, but the shape was the same. There was often a preference for larger boards, for the ' ten chiefs ', δεκάπρωτοι, for example. The Greek form predominated in Greece itself, in Asia Minor and in other Eastern provinces, as they developed city life.

In Gaul, the old towns often developed into cities. Spain early adopted Italian forms ; Vespasian gave the whole province the Latin right, the step before full citizenship. In Africa, the Punic forms persisted, but new foundations followed the Italian model. Cities in the East, in Syria for example, grew up as a rule on the Greek plan. But some features of old local ways persisted. In Syria, there were a number of priestly kingdoms—little dominions based on cities, where the cult of the chief god was the main interest, and political power was in the hands of his priest. Such cities were Emesa and Chalcis. Egypt had its one great city, Alexandria ; in the rest of the country city life was sparse and slow to develop.

The development of cities under the Empire is a fascinating

theme. It may be studied conveniently in A. H. M. Jones's great book. It is a study in which correctness of detail is everything. We have not to guess how things might have developed ; no, we have to collect the bits of evidence which show how they actually did develop. Inscriptions, coins, occasional references in literature, all must be pieced together to yield at last something of a consistent picture. Here we can only draw together a few conclusions. In one sense, the Empire was a golden age for the city. The city was the privileged form of government, placed at the very centre of the Empire. Rome honoured the great cities of the provinces, used them as instruments of government, subordinated outlying country districts to them. But there has been a vital change. The city was essentially individual, the expression of diversity against unification. Its glory had been its freedom, its readiness to think and act afresh. Its shame had been its factiousness, its quarrelsomeness with its neighbours, its inability to find harmony even within its own walls. There was small room for this type of city under the Empire. Even sovereign Rome was hardly free in the old sense ; her reign over others meant heavy burdens for herself, not only honour and wealth. The city, as used by Rome for her Empire, plays a new part : it is the cell out of which the whole organisation is built. The cities have still a full life but it is not as independent entities—rather, as useful parts of a whole. We will come back later to this most important phase of imperial life.

An empire on the scale of the Roman cannot be conveniently administered until it is subdivided into manageable parts. The city supplied the most satisfactory means of division. A province could be divided into a number of cities. This system was so convenient that it was even applied where the city was not naturally prominent. Some parts of the Empire could at once be run on the city basis. Italy first—only the wild districts of the South and East lay apart from city life. Gaul readily accepted the city form. But it is to be noted that *there* the city was still felt as the centre of a tribe. That is why modern French names of cities often preserve the tribal name—Paris of the Parisii, not Lutetia ; Amiens of the Ambiani, not Samarobriva ; Rheims of the Remi, not Durocorturum. Spain had always had her many towns, which soon took Italian forms. The Germanies and the Alpine districts developed a few great cities, generally in close connection with the armies. The Balkans were slower in growth, but barbarian Thrace had become a great home of cities by the 2nd century. Along the coasts of Asia Minor there was no need to foster cities : they had been there from the first. But in the interior the city was deliberately used as a means for simplifying the government of wide country districts. In Mesopotamia there was a great development of cities —some of them, such as Edessa and Nisibis, of great strategic and economic importance. Egypt, as we have seen, was almost restricted to her great Alexandria, and even she had for long no city council. Cyrenaica had few cities. Further west, the old Punic cities lived on ; Carthage grew to be one of the great capitals of the West. In the general prosperity which blessed Africa under the Empire, city life grew and throve. The desert sands are still yielding the record of flourishing communities of the Italian pattern.

In the centre stood Rome, ' the loveliest sight on earth ', as Horace calls her. Augustus found Rome brick and left her marble ; the queen of the world was to be royally arrayed. Emperor after Emperor took pride in beautifying his capital. Augustus restored the temples, built the Augustan forum and the Julian basilica, and encouraged his lieutenants to add theatres, temples, libraries. Vespasian built the temple of peace and the Colosseum, Domitian a multitude of temples. Trajan was one of the greatest of all builders ; he was never tired of creating or restoring. The column of Trajan, the forum, the Ulpian basilica come at once to mind. Hadrian built the temple of Roma and Venus, Septimius Severus the famous Septizonium. The history may be read in the great works on the topography of Rome. A glory was achieved which all the centuries have not been able entirely to destroy. Rome was the normal residence of the Emperor, the seat of the nobility, the Senate and knights. She paid no direct taxes, but rather drew to herself the tribute of the world. Africa, Egypt and Sicily combined to supply her with the bread, free or cheap, for her teeming thousands. Luxuries of all kinds flowed in to satisfy the lusts of the wealthy. The far distant provinces sent their strange beasts, wild or tame, to delight the Roman multitudes. Such was the attractive power of Rome that not only material wealth but also intellectual and artistic ability was magnetically drawn to the centre. To Rome too flowed less welcome acquisitions ; as Juvenal writes, ' the Orontes flowed into the Tiber' ; or, as Tacitus tells us, ' all that anywhere is shameful or horrible flows to Rome and there finds a ready welcome '. The population was large, something in the neighbourhood of a million, free and slave. The old and insanitary Rome perished in the great fire of Nero. The new city that rose on the ashes of the old was salubrious and delightful. There was more open space and far fewer blocks of unhealthy flats, the *insulae*, ' islands ' as they were called. The urban cohorts under the prefect of the city discharged police duties, the *vigiles* kept night watch and fought fires. Juvenal enlarges vigorously on the various miseries of city life in Rome, but his picture is certainly a one-sided one. Rome was not to any large extent a manufacturing centre. But she was a vast emporium for receipt and exchange. There were special markets for various classes of goods, and special streets were appropriated to special businesses. But there was an essential weakness in the position, only to be dealt with by continual vigilance. Rome had a vast concentration of population, without means of support near at hand. She did not live mainly on the near parts of Italy, but on distant parts of the Empire. Hence, beside all the opulence of the capital, we find a latent insecurity. Even the vital corn-supply may occasionally be imperilled by exceptional storms. Against such insecurity the Emperor wages eternal war ; he cannot risk the discontent of a starving capital.

Rome, we have suggested, was the great centre of intellectual and artistic life ; but it was not in these two forms that the world then found its chief expression. What impressed the visitor most about Rome, after her general magnificence and wealth, was her immense resources for amusement. Juvenal talks of bread and circus races as the main delights of the Roman people—amusements are close seconds to necessities. Entertainment of a superior character was not lacking. There were great libraries to satisfy intellectual curiosity. Contests like the Capitoline contest of Domitian were festivals of culture, even if the talents which they fostered were likely to be forced and artificial. The theatre enjoyed great popularity, but the most popular forms, the mime and pantomime, gave more scope to virtuosity than to literary skill or dramatic talent. The pantomime must have had much in common with our modern cinema—an immense and immediate appeal, a vast temptation to fall into sensationalism and unreality. But the main amusements of Rome were even more debasing. In the circus, the mad passion for excitement, bitter partisanship, gambling—all found their expression. The ' colours '—blue, green, yellow, red—attracted the same mad following as our modern professional clubs. The passions that had once poured themselves into politics, now denied that outlet, vented themselves in the sham contests of the circus. Emperors would announce themselves as patrons of one or another colour; but it is curious that no trace of political influence of the colours is to be found till very late—in the Nica rising under Justinian, when the Emperor almost lost his throne through riots in the circus. Victorious jockeys and horses received honours almost divine. Nero, we know, aspired to fame as charioteer ; he was crowned victor in all the great games of Greece, although, it is said, he actually took a fall at Olympia. It was a madness which radiated out from Rome to the Empire at large. Salvian tells us that the people of Treviri, often taken by the barbarians and still threatened by them, asked from the Emperors restoration not of walls, but of the circus. When Sapor suddenly came down on Antioch in 252, the people were so absorbed in games that they only began to take notice when Persian arrows fell on the concourse. It was one of the characteristics of bad Emperors to overdo their patronage of the circus. But even as good an Emperor as Trajan prided himself on his patronage of the races and his improvement of the building. The Contorniates—those odd, coinlike pieces of the late Empire, which look as if they were men in some sort of game— preserved the memories of many Emperors, especially those who, like Nero, Trajan and Caracalla, had been munificent patrons of racing.

At the best, the circus was an outlet for unruly passions ; at the worst, it encouraged desperate gambling and diverted men from national interests. It did not encourage any virtue or in- tellectual ability. But the thirst for excitement at all costs found an even uglier expression. In the circus there was continual danger to life and limb ; you could watch with desperate intentness to see whether your favourite or his rival smashed the wheel in turning the goal, but, after all, victory, not bloodshed, was the main thing here. In the amphitheatre, the great Colosseum of Vespasian, the thirst for blood was the very first thing to be slaked. Men took a terrible pleasure in seeing others in peril of their lives, enjoying vicariously what they would never taste for themselves. These awful shows came in from Etruria, that home of strange cruelty. They soon acclimatised themselves in Rome and ruled there, in defiance of morality and humanity, till a Christian monk by his martyrdom brought them to a close. Some serious thinkers tried to condone the games because war was the Roman profession and, for that, a contempt for wounds and death is to be desired. But the excuse was half-hearted and not sincere. The lust for blood was its own justification. But one need not ask for any particular sym- pathy for the gladiators. Most of them followed the profession of their own free will. They enjoyed immense popularity during their prime and considerable wealth. If the satirists may be trusted, it was not unusual for a gladiator to win the love of a lady of fashion. We must remember too that good gladiators were too expensive to be sacrificed too readily to the demands of the public. But bloodletting there always was, even if it was usually cheap blood.

The vilest feature of the games was the demoralisation that they produced in the vast crowds that haunted them. We see it in one of its ugliest forms when the Christians were sent to the lions and hordes of ignorant folk gloated over the sufferings of innocent people of whose supposed crimes they had no real evidence.

The wild beast shows were little better. Sometimes they were organised on more civilised lines. Creatures of interest from distant lands would be promenaded as in an ancient Whipsnade. But, even here, the innate brutality broke out. At the end would come an insensate slaughter of beasts, harmless as well as wild. It was the chief boast of the preposterous Emperor Commodus that he was a better shot than any professional of his time and could sever the neck of an ostrich with a special curved javelin. Apart from all the other evils attendant on circus and amphitheatre, there was an incredible waste of time. At the height of the Empire nearly half the year was devoted to games or shows of one kind or another. It meant that the vast population was continually being fed on evil food and distracted from any worthier interests that it might ever have had. When we seek the causes for the lack of tone and energy that crept over the life of the Empire, we must not forget the influence of these favourite amusements. Passions so constantly indulged became norms of life. Apart from the games there were many interesting public occasions in Rome—religious ceremonies, imperial advents and departures, marriages and deaths and births in the imperial family. These all drew their crowds and prevented city life from being dull ; but they were rather quiet after the major excitements.

Much that has been said of Rome applies in varying degrees to other great cities of the Empire. The circus was an almost universal mania. But gladiators were never popular in the Greek East—a certain sign of superior refinement and taste. In their place, athletic contests were immensely popular ; but the Romans always tended to despise them as too tame.

It would be an endless task to cover the whole Empire, city by city, or even to record all the great cities without exception. It will be enough to select a number of the most famous. Britain was never a great land for cities. York, a Roman colony, the camp of a legion, was perhaps the most notable. London was already a port of some importance, but never gained city rank. Verulamium (St. Albans) was a *municipium* and enjoyed a certain consideration. It is one of the last places in Roman Britain to be recorded before darkness came down on the island. Gaul was a home of famous cities. Massilia ranked high as a university city and centre of Greek culture ; with her political importance all was over since her resistance to Julius Caesar. Narbo, the capital of the ' Province ', held her rank over the centuries and developed an important trade. Lugdunum (Lyons), a Roman colony, was the focus of the road system, in the early Empire the seat of an important mint, a great centre of trade, sometimes even a seat of Empire in times of crisis. The neighbouring Vienna, also a colony, maintained its steady rivalry with Lugdunum. The rise of Treviri (Treves) to the rank of imperial capital and great manufacturing city belongs to a later date. Many another city won fame for trade or culture. Gaul came to be a home of universities ; Burdigala (Bordeaux) held high rank in the late Empire. Lutetia (Paris), no very considerable place, won the favour of Julian II and, as his residence, makes its début in history.

Spain, of old a land of cities, flourished under the early Empire. She gave Rome men of letters like Seneca, Lucan and Martial and Emperors like Trajan and Hadrian. She had many cities noted for one thing or the other—literary fame, wealth or trade—but hardly one of the first rank. Tarraco, the capital of the nearest province, was an important port and seat of an imperial worship. Emerita was an important garrison town. Corduba (Colonia Patricia), and Bilbilis—all were famous in their different ways. Gades, with its ancient trade and wealth and its famous cult of Hercules, continued to hold high rank. But Spain as a whole, after its early prime, declined in the scale of imperial importance.

The Alpine districts to the North of Italy had few towns of any size or importance. Italy prided herself on her crown of lovely cities ; you need only re-read the second Georgic of Virgil. Many of them could look back on days when they had been not unequal rivals of Rome. Such were Praeneste and Tibur and the great cities of Etruria. There were the famous settlements of the Greeks—Naples, Cumae, Tarentum and the rest. There were many other cities in the centre and north, some of them Latin colonies of the olden days, some of them modern creations of industry or trade. The Romans of the city continued to despise the municipals ; such contempt is a comic part of the snobbery of Tacitus. But the solid worth of these communities counted. Vespasian in his censorship refreshed the Senate with new blood drawn mainly from the Italian municipalities. Many of these cities retained their ancient pride. Under the Empire we find bitter feuds between neighbouring cities. On one occasion the city of Sena drew severe punishment on itself by insulting a Roman senator. But as a rule the municipalities moved quietly in the wake of Rome. In the late Empire, Milan and, after her, Ravenna in the north reached the rank of imperial capitals and residences. Rome by now was a little remote from the critical points and yet not quite safe from their dangers. There were no important cities in Corsica or Sardinia. Sicily had her cities of ancient fame—Syracuse, Agrigentum, Catana—but the island was on the decline and none of them added materially to its reputation. In Africa the Punic cities retained something of their old importance, still with a Punic flavour. The new cities that embellished the desert, such as Timgad and Lambaesis, were creations of the military occupation and in a striking way attested its success. The great city of Roman Africa was Carthage. Rome's ancient rival, refounded by Julius Caesar, was destined to come near to being a true rival of Rome in the West. She was wealthy, luxurious, a great centre of trade, a famous bishopric, university, capital and residence city of one of the two chief senatorial provinces. Her favourite goddess, the ' Dea Caelestis ', was worshipped far beyond the confines of Carthage herself. Hardly a city in the West apart from Rome did as much as Carthage to set the tone of the whole.

The Balkan districts were originally country tracts with very slight trace of city life. With the full Roman occupation city life increased. Thrace, in the early Empire a backward country under client princes, was crowned with a coronal of cities, many of them named after members of the imperial family—the famous Adrianople, Marcianopolis and the rest. There were Roman cities of some importance along the line of the Danube and even beyond it in Dacia. In some cases the city grew originally out of the civilian settlements (*canabae*) round military camps. The 3rd century saw the rise of the Illyrian armies that gave so many Emperors to the world. The 4th century again witnessed the rise of many a Balkan city to imperial rank, as capital or residence. Siscia, Sirmium, Serdica—all were seats of important mints ; the mint is always a sign of importance, sometimes of imperial residence. Constantine the Great once thought of developing Sirmium as his new Rome.

The ancient cities of Greece—Athens, Sparta, Corinth—were still known to all the world. Fame, for what it is worth, they did not entirely lose. But they lacked wealth and the power that it brings. Corinth on her two seas could not fail to rank fairly high in the commercial scale, and she was still the Paris—the gay city—of the ancient world. Athens was the Mecca of many a pilgrim. She was the first university of the Empire ; in her, the schools of philosophy carried on the great traditions of Plato, Aristotle, the Porch and the Garden. Sparta had its wealthy and powerful families, but no assured basis of prosperity. Pausanias, who wrote his 'guide round Greece' in the 2nd century, gives us a good idea of what Greece meant to the Empire—a country a little removed from the main currents, but of perennial interest to those who had a relish for antiquities.

Asia, with which we may throw in the coasts of Thrace, the Propontis and the Black Sea, was above all other places the home of cities. Asia herself had so many cities of old fame that it could be a very difficult question to choose any one of them for such a special honour as the site of the temple of Rome and Augustus. Ephesus, Smyrna, Sardis, Pergamum—all these and many others had their several claims to distinction. In some, possession of a famous cult added fame ; we think of the great Diana of the Ephesians. Sardis had been a royal residence of the kings of Lydia and after that the seat of the Persian satraps. Pergamum had been the capital of that kingdom out of which Roman Asia developed. Smyrna had very old relations with Rome and very notable services to plead. Along the coasts of Thrace there were a number of cities—Thessalonica, Aenus, Abdera, Maronea ; of these, Thessalonica came to be an important residence and mint city. In the Propontis, Cyzicus retained her ancient reputation, though once, in the early Empire, she incurred chastisement for insolence to Rome. In the 3rd century she became an important mint city.

The cities of the Black Sea, Greek foundations originally, learned to look to Rome as their natural protector against the wild peoples of the interior and as the natural recipient of their raw materials. Their importance was mainly for trade. Tomi has gained a special fame as the place of exile of the poet Ovid. Bithynia had its famous cities, especially Nicomedia and Nicaea, eternal rivals. Nicomedia was selected by Diocletian as his Eastern capital and enriched with buildings on the imperial scale ; down to Byzantine times it was one of the main mints of the East. In the interior—Galatia, Cappadocia and the rest—cities were few and mostly of late growth. One or two of the most important were the centres of important worships, as, for example, Pessinus of the worship of Cybele. In the South Lycia had still her cities, with their old strong sense of nationality and their fine civic pride ; but none of them held high rank under the Empire. In Pisidia Antioch, in Cilicia Tarsus stood high above the average. Antioch was a colony and a settlement of veterans, Tarsus, the seat of an old Persian satrapy, a centre of commerce, a university city. It has a special claim to remembrance as the home of St. Paul, who was proud of his citizenship there. The little cities of Lycaonia and the neighbourhood, where St. Paul preached the Gospel—Iconium, Lystra, Derbe—were late creations and of no great importance. The south coast was mostly wild and bare of cities except in one or two sheltered spots.

One city must be selected for special mention—the great city that Constantine founded on the site of the old Byzantium and named after himself Constantinople—the new Christian Rome, an artificial creation, but destined to rank beside the great historic cities of the world, beside Jerusalem, Athens and Rome. The site had unique advantages. It commanded one of the great sea routes, it had free access to the land on three sides. In time of danger it was almost impregnable, except against overwhelming superiority of force. From A.D. 330 onwards Constantinople rises beside Rome and finally overshadows her. She was closely modelled on Rome, with senate, knights, even a Roman people ; she too received exemption from taxes and a corn dole. In contrast to Rome Constantinople was from the first a Christian, not a pagan city. Constantine chose to be buried there rather than in the old capital. Rome refused to buy imperial favour at the price of the surrender of her past.

Syria and the adjacent districts were homes of city life in almost as high a degree as Asia. But there was some difference in the prevailing type. The great cities of Asia were in general Greek foundations, sometimes set on foundations older still. In Syria the cities were of three main kinds : (1) foundations of the Greek kings, the Seleucids—Antioch, Seleucia, Laodicea and many more ; (2) old cities of native type, Phoenician or other, such as Tyre, Sidon and Ascalon ; (3) cities centred on the worship of some widely honoured god ; such were Emesa with its sun god Elagabalus, Heliopolis with its special Jupiter, Doliche with its Jupiter Dolichenus. Jerusalem of the Jews will fall under this heading, until its re-founding as a pagan city, Aelia Capitolina, by Hadrian. As a fourth class on the edge we may add the desert cities—Damascus, Palmyra, Bostra, Petra. Some of these were closely in touch with the settled world ; but, one and all, they opened out to the East and drew most of their wealth from its caravans. Palmyra was destined to have its short hour of fame, when it represented Rome in the East and finally challenged her supremacy. The outposts of civilisation that grew up in Mesopotamia—Nisibis, Edessa and the rest—throve on the trade between Rome and the East and proudly held up the imperial banner in the face of a hostile Persia.

Among the Syrian cities Antioch on the Orontes deserves a special notice. It came to Rome as the capital of the once great kingdom, the Seleucid. It was the inevitable capital of the Roman province of Syria. It was the centre of Syrian trade, and the Syrians were the most adventurous and successful traders of the Empire. Political consideration and material wealth were there from the first. To these were added other advantages. There was the famous cult of Apollo at Daphne, with its fervent devotions and its wild abandonment to indulgence. And there was a lingering tradition of freedom in political life. The mob of Antioch kept much of its cockney impudence and often ventured to criticise imperial decrees with unusual and possibly dangerous impudence. Julian the Apostate found himself at loggerheads with the Antiochenes. His 'Beardhater' leaves us with a feeling that Julian, though he had more of the right on his side, hardly gets the better of the exchanges. Antioch had a genius for catch-phrases and nicknames ; 'in Antioch the disciples were first called Christians'. On more than one occasion Antioch was the seat of a pretender to Empire ; in the late Empire it was commonly the imperial residence when campaigns were on foot in Persia. It was probably not so very far behind Rome in population as in rank and wealth ; it may have had its half million inhabitants or more.

Alexandria, the chief city to bear the name of the great conqueror, was really the only city of Egypt that mattered. It was only one— but that one was enough and more than enough. To Alexandria most that we have already said of Antioch applies. Alexandria had long been the capital of a great Eastern monarchy, that of the Ptolemies. She grew strong and wealthy with the trade of the Red Sea and the East as well as the Mediterranean and Syria opening at her doors. She had a huge mixed population, perhaps somewhere between Rome and Antioch in size. There together dwelt Greeks, Egyptians, Romans, Jews—the latter in a special civic body (πολίτευμα) of their own. Religion was a vital everyday concern of the population. This passion, often rising to mania, had begun in Egyptian times, continued under the Ptolemies and Romans and led on to the street battles of monks and pagans in the 4th and 5th centuries. The city was factious, unsettled, ready to flame up at anything that might touch its religious instincts. It had little respect for government and often called down chastisement on itself. The horrible massacre that Caracalla ordered could never be justified, but there may have been considerable provocation.

This short geographical survey of the Empire may well be balanced by a study of these cities in order of time. The order will of course not be absolutely the same for all parts of the Empire, but the lines of a general development may be successfully sketched. Augustus was favourable to cities ; he saw them as integral parts

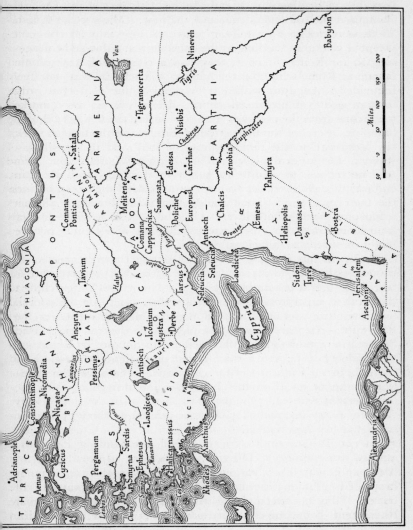

Cities of the East

of his kingdom, intelligible and congenial to the Roman mind, capable of helping him greatly in his task of government. He honoured the old and encouraged the new. Many of his foundations were designed for military purposes, especially for the settlement of veterans. As long as the cities showed a due and courteous regard for Roman honour, they had a comfortable task allotted them as Rome's humble coadjutors. Citizenship was not freely extended ; Augustus wished it to stand as the goal—but rather distant goal—of provincial effort. There was no very marked departure from the norms of Augustus during the first period of the Empire. Perhaps the most striking features are the favours shown by Vespasian to the municipalities of Italy and to the whole of Spain. Of political power nothing serious was left. But Rome did not choose to meddle in purely local affairs, and the cities, subject to their good behaviour, could manage their own business in their own way. They could even make honorary alliances (ὁμονοίαι) with other cities. They held their religious festivals and their games, and there was much going and coming between cities on such glad occasions.

Rome, in fact if not in theory, encouraged governments of the same type as hers—with senates based on landed property, care for the poor—but a minimum of liberty. The wealthy often chose to lavish their superfluity on the needs of their cities—on the imperial cult, on games, on buildings. For such munificence they received the appropriate honours of complimentary decrees and statues. There is no reason to think that the burdens imposed by Rome were excessively heavy ; they certainly were much lighter than those laid on Asia in the confusion of the civil wars. There was the chance for prosperity on a considerable scale, and this chance was to a large extent realised. But there was a worm in the bud. There was a very serious qualification of the general prosperity ; and this brings us to a new section.

In 111 Trajan sent his trusted friend, the Younger Pliny, as a special commissioner to Bithynia. The cities had been falling into debt and, with that, various irregularities in their government appeared. Trajan interfered—of course in the interests of the cities. Pliny's correspondence with Trajan enables us to estimate the extent of the imperial interference. It goes right down into the minutiae of city life—the suppression of unlawful societies, checks on building operations, fire brigades and so on. Pliny in Bithynia was just one case of note among many. Similar disorders in many provinces gave the Emperors cause for alarm and led them to appoint curators for cities to supervise their affairs, especially their finances. For finance was the vital difficulty. Private munificence and rivalry between cities had led to an absurd race to embellish oneself above one's needs or means. As long as the phenomenon was isolated, it might be neglected ; but, as soon as it became general, the Emperor must interfere, for on the finances of the cities the financial stability of the Empire depended. Imperial control no doubt removed the worst abuses ; but a blow had been dealt to the independent feelings of the cities from which they never recovered. They must realise how precarious was any show of freedom left to them, how entirely dependent they were on the indulgence of the Emperor, who could interfere at will, if he thought fit.

The increase of control from the centre might have been no bad thing, if it had been accompanied by any increased provincial responsibility—if the provinces, while controlled from the centre, could have been encouraged to assist the central government in its tasks. Hadrian may have cherished hopes of such renewed vitality of the Empire in its parts ; but he had no time to carry through his plans and he had no immediate successors in his policy. The provinces had their councils that met for religious celebrations, especially for the cult of Rome and Augustus, and were allowed to present petitions to the Emperor touching their interests. But these councils were firmly controlled by tradition ; the men who rose to their head were men of wealth, position and approved loyalty. There was little chance of serious reform starting from such a source. But there was as yet no general decline. Cities went on their way of festival and service ; the world seemed to some observers to be keeping eternal holiday. Cities were still springing up in new provinces ; Roman citizenship was still being extended.

In 212 Caracalla gave the citizenship to all subjects of the Empire except the *dediticii* ; this class may have been a considerable one, including many subjects of the Empire living outside the charmed circle of the cities. But city dwellers with few exceptions must from now on have been Roman citizens. A process, long since begun, now reached completion—a little prematurely through the whim of an Emperor, but still not against the run of history. Perhaps it helped the solidarity of the Empire that the citizenship should now belong to nearly all. But the sad thing was that the equalisation was downwards rather than upwards, that it was rather a case of Rome and Italy losing privilege than of the provinces gaining it.

The miseries of the 3rd century, due to such natural causes as plague and famine, the civil wars and barbarian invasions on a

H

scale as yet unheard of, all struck hard at the cities. Many a famous city was sacked by Goths coming from the Balkans and the Black Sea. Land that had long been free from foreign invasion had to suffer new terrors. These sufferings were aggravated by the financial collapse that followed on the political. The coinage was debased to such an extent that its value became quite uncertain. The finances of the city, already compromised, could not stand the strain. The weakening of the provinces and their cities compelled the imperial government to undertake far more of local administration than ever before. We are already well on the way to the fully centralised empire of Diocletian.

The Empire of the 4th century, set beside that of Augustus, looks like something entirely new. It is now governed from the centre, or rather from a number of centres. Rome is no longer the only capital. Each Augustus and each Caesar of Diocletian's tetrarchy has his own residence. There is an increasing efficiency, but with it also an increasing clumsiness and expense. The cities are now in a parlous plight. They have only a shadow of independence left even in local affairs. The local senates were made responsible for the collection of the taxes ; what had once been a coveted honour became a crushing burden from which men tried to escape by every means, fair or foul. The defender of the city, appointed late in the 4th century for the protection of local interests, only imperfectly fulfilled the purpose of his institution. The old city mints were no more ; the last had finally disappeared under Diocletian.

The hope of the Empire had been that its more backward sections might gradually be raised to the level of the higher. The sad fact was that they dragged them down. Seeck, the great historian of the 4th century, was haunted by his conception of the ' Ausrottung der Besten ', the systematic elimination of all excellence. Seeck is undoubtedly extreme. The war on outstanding merit was far less systematic than he conceived it to be. But the fact on which he based his conclusions cannot be denied. The centralised state was not much interested in individual excellence ; it tended to reduce all to one level of hopeless subservience. The vigour of local life was fatally impaired. The Empire looked in vain for the loyal support that it so sorely needed in face of the increased virulence of barbarian invasion.

The subject of any ordered community becomes liable to certain duties and susceptible of certain privileges. He has to pay his taxes ; he may be called upon for military service. The city does not alter this, but it intensifies the sense both of duty and of privilege. The citizen is called on to take a part in political life, to use his franchise, perhaps to share in public office. The subject of an empire enjoys such protection as his ruler can give him against foreign invasion and disorder at home ; against the ruler himself he is hardly protected at all. The citizen of a city, on the other hand, is much more conscious of the laws both as protecting and constraining him. Civic consciousness is expanded and enhanced. But when, as the world changed, the place of the individual was no longer secure, new problems arose that demanded solution. Cities must combine, if they were to face the new monarchies. Thus arose the demand for something wider than the citizenship of the single city. In Greece, the Leagues, the Achaean and the Aetolian, brought a number of cities into a larger political block. The city of such a League had its local citizenship, but it had also its share in the life of the League. The Achaean cities, when they struck their coins, all described themselves as ' Achaeans ', only adding the name of the city in a subordinate place. There had also been examples of two cities sharing citizenship, Corinth and Argos, for example, in the early 4th century B.C. Rome had her own new contribution to add. From an early time she had established firm relations with the Latin cities. The Latin colonies were planted out from Rome as little offshoots of the Capital, destined for mutual assistance and defence. The principle was established that, subject to certain limitations that varied from time to time, the Latin could claim Roman citizenship if he moved his residence to Rome. For a long time the principle held that no man could be a citizen of two cities at once ; if he took on a new citizenship, he must surrender the old. It is hard to say at just what stage this general principle broke down before the logic of facts. But under the Empire, when more and more provincials became Roman citizens, it was obvious that the old ideas no longer applied. A citizen of Antioch who became a citizen of Rome did not thereby cease to hold his initial right. Citizenship now takes on two distinct meanings. There is the old meaning—the belonging to the community where one was born and bred—and a new meaning—the sharing in the higher privilege of citizenship in the Empire. Once discovered, this duality of meanings has never been lost. It is a permanent enrichment of our store of political conceptions. A possibility is suggested of reconciling local with wider loyalties. If the course of events had been entirely favourable, the advance to Roman citizenship might have meant the advance of the backward sections of the Empire to the best in culture that had yet been achieved. But what actually happened was that citizenship lost value just when it was being made free to almost all. Here we see

the measure of the success and failure of Rome. She produced
the new and fruitful conception ; she failed to realise it to the best
effect.

Rome has impressed her stamp on the world in a way that
cannot be mistaken. She gave something of a civic complexion to
a vast and variegated world—

Urbem fecisti quod prius orbis erat.

Men could hardly conceive of a world in which Rome was not.
When Alaric sacked the Imperial City, men drew their breath in
apprehension of what new darkness might be coming on the world.
It was then that St. Augustine applied his magnificent powers to the
elucidation of the riddle. He found his own solution. Rome had
never been more than a city of the world, a very imperfect adumbra-
tion of the true city, the City of God, that has foundations, that
must endure. The idea of the city, the true home and heart of
civic life, once found could not be lost. It was almost overshadowed during the Dark Age. The revival of the cities in their
vigour was one of the chief signs of the coming of the new times,
when the old arts and civilisation could revive.

CHAPTER IV

THE OUTSIDE WORLD

If we look at a modern map, we can set the Roman Empire neatly in its place. We can see at a glance what proportions of the world it included, what vast tracts lay quite beyond its ken. But to see things as the Romans saw them, we must forget our modern geography and go back to ancient views of the world. Europe was sufficiently well known, likewise the nearer parts of Asia ; but no one knew the full extent of that great land mass or where India or China fitted on to it. Africa was known along its Northern coasts, and the Carthaginians had done some exploration of the West. One bold mariner seems to have rounded the Cape of Good Hope. But virtually the whole of the interior, centre and south was quite unknown.

What lay beyond the known world ? A very old idea which for long continued to satisfy many minds was that of a stream of ocean running round the world on the outside and neatly delimiting the whole. Where you could check it—in the extreme West—it seemed to work out all right ; you really found the ocean there. There was complete ignorance about the North of Europe beyond those Germans with whom the Romans came in contact.

It is important to remind ourselves of differences in fundamental conceptions between us and the Ancients. Of course, we are far nearer the truth than they were. But for the moment that does not so much matter. What does matter is that difference in such conceptions involved differences in thought about many problems of human life and destiny. We think sometimes of the shock to old ideas which the discovery of the New World brought. The shock to an ancient thinker could not have been less, could he have been confronted with our modern geographical knowledge.

However we choose to define it, by whatever metaphor we choose to describe the Roman Empire—house, domain, fortress—there is always very prominent the idea of an inside and outside. Inside, civilisation ; outside, barbarism or civilisation alien to Rome. In the early days the distinction was not quite as acute as it became later. The frontiers were not yet fully marked out, the interior had its pockets of disorder and discontent. But the chief troubles within were soon overcome. Rebellion was crushed in Spain, Gaul, Britain, Pannonia, even in stiff-necked Judaea. The client kingdoms came one by one into the provincial system. Only in a few corners—in Isauria, for example—did barbarism or something near it persist within the sacred confines. At the same time the frontiers were clearly marked. Rivers, seas and mountains showed where the Roman Empire ended and the outside confusion began. The Empire was not entirely sealed against this outside. Some going and coming in the way of trade was allowed. But there was no complete freedom of movement ; there was control for all who wished to remain inside the law. As time went on, as the invasions from without became almost a matter of course, as barbarians came more and more to settle within the Empire as federates or take service in the Roman army, the distinction of inside and outside grew fainter. In the later times some of the frontiers had become almost fluid ; they are no longer a solid obstacle, obstructing barbarian movements. They are hardly more than marks on the beach which define, without controlling, the extent of the encroachments of the tide. The history of the Empire must as a rule be written from the inside—the history of a garrison, not of its assailants. But it will be good for a change to take the other view—from the outside. Things will look quite different, and the unusual point of view will be found to be not without interest.

Of the world that lay outside their ordinary direct observation, the Romans knew something about India and China. Trade with India developed greatly under the early Empire as traders learned to use the monsoons. Roman gold and silver in considerable mass is still found in South Indian hoards. Later, it is in Ceylon that imitations of late Roman bronzes are found. Since the days of Alexander the Great India had ceased to be an entirely unknown country. Indian elephants had come to play an important part in war. But the land route was a very long one. Apart from its costly treasures that came in the way of trade, India was chiefly known as the home of wonders—of strange beasts and birds, the basilisk and the phoenix, or wise men of strange powers and saintliness, the Gymnosophists. It was remarked as quite exceptional that an Indian embassy visited Augustus at Samos in 20 B.C. The way to China was even longer and more difficult. Caravans might make the golden journey to Samarcand and beyond ; but to Rome and Italy the great central land routes were barred. The Chinese were known only as a distant mysterious people ; their chief product was the silk, worth its weight in gold. For centuries the silk-worm was unknown outside China, and its precious product could not be matched at home.

With the interior of the Empire the Romans were well acquainted.

After the surveys made for Augustus by Agrippa, knowledge of distances and direction was, for all practical purposes, almost as good as ours today. Ignorance of the vast tracts of land and ocean quite outside the ancient view could not matter. They might as well have belonged to another world. The ignorance that *did* hurt and hamper was ignorance of what lay just beyond immediate observation and yet was closely connected with the known. It was a serious handicap to the men who tried to direct the Roman fortunes to have no exact knowledge of what lay behind the Germans and Sarmatians who pressed immediately on the frontiers. Ignorance of the interior of Asia was less harmful, though it might lead to an occasional ill-judged project, such as Nero's proposed expedition against the Caspian gates. Ignorance of Africa was not serious. The deserts supplied the natural frontier and the natives of the deep interior were not yet ready to emerge from the dark of their primeval forests.

On one frontier only did Rome confront a rival power of anything like equal stature. This was the Parthian Empire beyond the Euphrates. The Romans of the Republic had clashed with the Parthians as with other Eastern powers. Pompey had had a brush with them ; Crassus in a vain attempt at conquest had lost life and standards at Carrhae ; Mark Antony had failed in his attempt at conquest. Julius Caesar himself had spent his last months in preparations for a Parthian expedition which never came off. There was, then, a Parthian problem awaiting Augustus. Rome had lost prestige and men looked for a war of revenge. Augustus contented himself with a diplomatic victory ; the standards were restored and friendship was established between the two powers. Augustus seems to have judged—and judged correctly—that the Empire was already sufficiently extended, that in Parthia began the real East, impervious to Western ideas, not easily to be subdued by force, by no means to be won by cultural assimilation. Parthia was a monarchy, not a republic ; a state of country districts, not cities ; of landed nobles and dependents ; of heavy-armed knights and mounted archers. In their own country the Parthians were deadly enemies, as Roman armies learned more than once to their cost. The principle of Augustus—to confine the Empire within its natural limits—found complete justification here.

On this one frontier, then, there was room for diplomacy, for permanent foreign relations. Parthia could not dream of conquering even the Eastern part of the Empire, and, as Rome soon abandoned the dream of conquering Parthia, there was no real bar to peaceful living side by side. The Empires could trade together for mutual benefit. Rome might be jealous of Parthia for controlling so much of the lucrative Eastern trade, but she could do nothing about it. Thus there were in fact long intervals of peace and they might have been longer and more frequent, except for one permanent factor in the problem. This was the kingdom of Armenia, touching Parthia to the North, touching provinces of the Empire on the West, definitely Iranian in national culture and sympathies, but drawn this way and that as rivalries between princes and nobles led one party to appeal to Rome, the other to Parthia. It was over Armenia that most of the wars between Rome and Parthia were fought. Several solutions of the problem were tried. Armenia could be virtually abandoned to Parthia ; but Rome did not like this solution, as it damaged her prestige, perhaps even her material interests. Armenia might be dominated by a king nominated by Rome. But the natives did not like this solution, as their sympathies were with the other side ; the Parthian king also resented it, because he liked to think of Armenia as an appanage of the Parthian crown. There was a third solution—a compromise— a Parthian prince, nominated by the king, but acknowledging a vague Roman suzerainty and accepted by Rome. This was the most successful of the three policies, but none of the three was in force for very long.

Wars with Parthia were intermittent, often troublesome, seldom very dangerous or costly in life. Under Nero Rome suffered one considerable disaster, but retrieved it by careful generalship and diplomacy. Trajan came near to conquering Parthia and forced her for a time to accept Roman suzerainty. Marcus Aurelius subdued the reviving pride of the Arsacids in a series of hard campaigns. Septimius Severus gained a notable victory ; the Parthians had offended him by interference in the civil wars. His son, Caracalla, conceived the wild scheme of uniting the two empires by marrying the daughter of the king of Parthia. The end of this wild wooing was a disgraceful conquest and plundering of the Parthian capital. Macrinus, the successor of Caracalla, had to meet and with difficulty fend off—or rather buy off—a Parthian expedition of revenge. The Parthians were a civilised people, with something of the old Persian culture plus a small admixture of Greek. There was room for diplomacy in your dealings with them and even wars did not reach the heights of barbarian fury. There was a certain *status quo*, recognised by both sides, which both might seek to modify, neither would wish entirely to subvert. Rome did occasionally aim at conquest, but she always recoiled before national resistance and the natural difficulties of the task. The Parthians seldom pressed their counter-attacks far home. Pacorus and the renegade Labienus in 41 B.C. had indeed penetrated far into Asia Minor ; later attacks usually stopped at the Syrian frontier. Invasion of Parthia was another matter. The Parthians bitterly resented it and would often punish it heavily under the conditions which they understood so much better than their enemies.

Under the reign of Severus Alexander, the kingdom of the Arsacids fell before the dynasty of the little land of Persis, which suddenly revived its ancestral glories and raised the banner of the old religion of the Magi, the worship of the sacred fire. The Parthians were overthrown without serious resistance and the new dynasty of the Sassanids ruled. In some ways the situation was little changed. The stranger power, potentially hostile, still con-fronted Rome on the Euphrates. But there was now this difference. The new dynasty brought with it fresh life and vigour, and among its first kings were several men of exceptional energy and power, notably the great conqueror, Sapor I. National and religious feel-ing were raised to a new intensity. All this meant that the Persians were aggressive where the Parthians had been defensive. The kings claimed the whole of the ancient empire of their Persian ancestors as theirs by right, to be resumed as soon as might be by conquest. Rome was thus faced with a new situation, always threatening, often positively dangerous. Wars with Persia were fought with varying issue under Gordian III, under Valerian I and Gallienus, under Carus, Diocletian and Constantine. Rome was usually on the defensive. Valerian was actually captured by Sapor and was long kept by him in unhonoured captivity. Sapor came within an ace of a permanent conquest of Syria, if not of Asia Minor itself. Carus went over to the attack, but died in the moment of victory. Under Diocletian, Narses renewed the ambitious attacks of Sapor. After one great victory over Diocletian's lieutenant, Galerius, he lost his baggage and harem in a heavy defeat and was glad to purchase peace by the surrender of several small provinces. Constantius II, son of Constantine, spent much of his reign in a laborious, only partially successful, defensive against Persian attack. Julian tried to wrest the initiative from the Persians and penetrated deeply into enemy country. But he suffered the usual fate of the invader ; he was hard pressed on his return journey and died by a chance spear cast. His army under Jovian had to buy itself a safe retreat. The troubles on this frontier never came to rest. Rome had to live beside a power ready to snatch any opportunity of stripping her of her Eastern possessions. Not till the 7th century did a vital change come. Persia and Rome fought one another to a standstill.

Heraclius was defeated and driven in on his capital, Constantinople. By a magnificent rally he first threw back, then completely routed the Persians. But on the ruins of the two Empires the new Arab power asserted itself. Persia went down under the shock and Byzantium forfeited two of her fairest provinces, Syria and Egypt.

So much for the Eastern frontier, with its civilised enemies and its diplomatic exchanges. Beyond all the other frontiers lay something quite different—the barbarians. To begin with, we must get it clear in our minds what the word ' barbarian ' meant to a Greek or Roman. The word probably suggested unintelligible speech, a natural token to a civilised man of lack of acquaintance with his ways. The barbarian was not necessarily a savage. He might be capable of assimilating culture when it was presented to him. He might even have some rudimentary culture of his own, but he would know little if anything of city life ; his economic system would be elementary. He would be not purely nomad, but only half settled, still half inclined to lead a nomad life. Government would often be by kings, otherwise by princes, distinguished by birth, ability and wealth. Men would live dotted about the land in scattered settlements, where hill, lake or wood took their fancy. They *did* cultivate the soil, but extensively, not intensively. Territories of tribes were wide and might vary as tribe fought tribe for local advantages. Precious metals would be little known ; barter would be the general rule. Foreign trade would mean chiefly the exchange of raw products for Roman luxuries. The peoples nearest the frontiers would get by assimilation something of the Roman stamp. They would become what we should call ' tame ' barbarians. Behind them would press the ' wild ' barbarians, not yet tempered by any contact with a near civilisation.

It will make the position clearer if we look in turn at the barbarians as they presented themselves to the Romans along the various frontiers. When you reached the Britannic islands in the extreme West, you could have no doubt about being at Land's End indeed ; for was not the very ocean flowing around ? ' The Britons completely divided from the whole world '—that was how it would seem to a Roman. Those twenty miles of channel meant a separation far more complete than that of any river. The conquest of Britain, envisaged by Julius Caesar, was delayed until Claudius, who carried it through with skill and vigour. Once begun it went steadily ahead ; the revolt of Boudicca was only a momentary check. The barbarian tribes of the island were reduced to obedience. The tribes of the South and East, subject to Belgic princes from Gaul, already knew something of Roman ways and accepted civilisation readily. There was more trouble with the Welsh tribes, the Silures and Ordovices, and the Brigantes of the North. The Roman conquest of Scotland was never completed. The Highlands remained almost untouched, even the Lowlands were not fully Romanised. The Picts in the South West were to prove a thorn in the flesh to the lost province of the 5th century. Ireland, inhabited by peoples from Spain and Scotland, was unviolated by Roman arms ; there was a little trade, a little raiding. But the wonderful development of culture on a religious basis in the later period should stand as a warning to us not to class the ' barbarian ' in the Roman sense as necessarily completely barbarous.

Gaul, after the conquest of Julius Caesar, might rank as a civilised country. Nationalism lost its sting. Gaul settled down to be one of the most prosperous, most favoured of the provinces. In the Roman Germanies and in the parts of Gaul near them, you found peoples of German blood, with sympathies for their kin across the river. Beyond the Rhine came the Germany that Tacitus has described for us—a vast extent of land, some plain, much forest and marsh, a reservoir of peoples—Germany long fought, never conquered by Rome—an indefinitely troublesome peril for the future. Augustus aimed at extending the frontier to the Elbe. His scheme was more or less accidentally defeated, by the exceptional cunning of the Cheruscan, Arminius, and the exceptional fecklessness of the Roman general, Varus. Perhaps the scheme was always beyond Roman capacities ; the Germans were too numerous and too fond of freedom to be easily held down. For the time, the Germans were not a positive menace. The kingdom of the great Maroboduus in Bohemia was viewed with mistrust by Augustus and he would have broken it up but for the Pannonian revolt. Under Tiberius, the kingdom collapsed of itself and Maroboduus found refuge at Ravenna under Roman protection. Trouble arose from time to time with special tribes—with the Batavians in the great Civil War of A.D. 69, with the Chatti on the middle Rhine under Domitian. But fortune gave Rome one precious gift—disunion among her enemies. Still, the danger was always there. Under Marcus Aurelius the East Germans, the Marcomanni and Quadi, broke into the North East of Italy, and the rest of the Emperor's life was spent in repulsing them and repairing the damage to the Danube frontiers. The menace had for the time shifted from West to East, from Rhine to Danube.

Troubles began again during the crisis of the reign of Valerian and Gallienus. New people appear on the scene, some of them known before, but not so close to the Roman frontiers—such as

Vandals and Langobardi—others new to history and probably representing new confederacies of tribes hitherto known under their several names—the Alamanni, the Franks, perhaps the Juthungi. Postumus, Emperor in Gaul, defended the Rhine frontier with success ; under his successors the Germans flooded Gaul ; it was left to Probus to sweep them out. From this time on German invasion never ceases for long. The tides as they flowed constantly crossed the line. There was successful defence and occasional counter-attack under the Tetrarchy and Constantine I. In the revolt of Magnentius, the waste of Roman blood in the terrible battle of Mursa and the fall of the pretender exposed Gaul to barbarian assault. The task of Julian in the years 357–360 amounted to reconquering most of Northern Gaul. Finally, the tide ceased to be stayed by the frontier at all. Barbarians flowed not only into Gaul, but through it into Spain and even Africa. Vandals in Africa, Visigoths, Suevi and Alans in Spain, Franks, Visigoths and Burgundians in Gaul—that was now the picture. Roman government only lived on in odd corners. The West was being lost to Rome and partitioned among a number of successor states. These barbarians had lived long in contact with Roman civilisation ; they could appreciate and assimilate some of its ways. When the wildly barbarous Huns under Attila threatened to engulf the West, Visigoths fought side by side under Aetius with his Romans to repulse them. Despite the long centuries of barbarian occupation France today speaks a Latin tongue.

Spain was early clear of her own barbarians, when the Cantabri and other wild tribes of the North West were broken by Agrippa. Apart from an occasional threat from the Moors in Africa, the province enjoyed long intervals of peace and prosperity. Spain began to suffer in the disorders of the 3rd century, when the Rhine frontier temporarily collapsed. But full disaster only came in the 5th century when Visigoths, Suevi and Alans descended from the Rhine overland to Spain and settled there. The Vandals passed on to Africa ; the Visigoths established a kingdom that lasted into the 8th century. In Spain as in Gaul, Romanisation had been so thorough that a Romance language held its own there—or rather two languages, Spanish and Portuguese.

North of Italy the Alpine districts had continued to harbour wild marauding peoples down to the reign of Augustus. His settlement was final, and permanent order was established. Italy for the future was only to be threatened by the occasional surge of peoples in mass from the frontiers. Even so, barbarians penetrated into Italy several times in the 3rd century and Aurelian thought it necessary to gird

Rome with a rampart of new walls. In the 5th century Italy at last was as much exposed as the provinces had been. Rome was to be sacked by Alaric the Visigoth and Gaiseric the Vandal, to be threatened by Attila the Hun. She was finally to fall victim to latecomers among the barbarians, the Ostrogoths and after them the Langobardi. The whole of the West became a barbarian sea, with only a few small islands of civilisation standing out above the foam.

Augustus had found the Balkans very slightly civilised. He had to break the revolt of the Pannonians and Dalmatians. His successors had much trouble with freedom-loving Thracians. But the work of civilisation though slow was sure ; Roman arms were advanced to the Danube. For a long time the Danube was only a second front, far behind the German in importance. It was under Domitian in the years from 86 on that the balance shifted. Domitian had to cope with dangerous invasions of Sarmatians and Suevi and with the more deadly designs of Decebalus, the able and ambitious king of Dacia. Domitian patched up the trouble without finding a final solution. Trajan ended the Dacian question by destroying the kingdom of Decebalus in two wars and creating a new, Latin-speaking Dacia across the Danube. It was along the Danube front that the main army of the Empire was now deployed. It was East Germans on the Danube that Marcus Aurelius had to meet. When serious trouble broke out in the middle of the 3rd century, we find Rome at grips with a new enemy. The Goths, coming from homes near Denmark, had crossed Europe and were now near the Black Sea. It was against the Goths under Kniva that Trajan Decius fought the lost battle of Abrittus ; they had raided deep into the Roman provinces of Moesia and Thrace and were carrying off vast quantities of booty and prisoners. Henceforth the Goths were one of the main factors to be reckoned with. But they seem to have been a people of very superior gifts, capable of arriving at a *modus vivendi* with their Roman neighbours. It was a new factor, the coming of the Huns, that threw the Goths on to the Roman provinces in 378. Admitted as federates within the Empire they found themselves cheated by the imperial officials. They took first to plundering, then to open war, and, when Valens led the army of the East against them, they rode it down in the battle of Adrianople. Theodosius patched up a peace, admitting Goths in great numbers into the Roman army. And Gothic the Eastern army largely remained down to the great massacre just after 400. Constantinople narrowly escaped falling into the hands of Gainas and his Goths. But the future belonged largely to them. In their two great divisions of Visigoths and

Ostrogoths, they were both in turn deflected from East to West, the Visigoths to found a kingdom in South Gaul and Spain, the Ostrogoths to rule for a short time in Italy.

The peoples further behind the frontiers seldom impinged on the Roman sphere. Far back in the Steppes of Russia the Slav peoples were already huddled ; they were not yet ready to enter history. The Huns were creatures of another world, wild nomads of Mongol type, who seemed to the terrified provincials hardly human. After throwing the Goths on to the Empire, they founded a vast but short-lived empire behind it, forcing a multitude of diverse tribes to follow them. Attila, ' the scourge of God ', plagued both Empires, Eastern and Western, for a generation. Constantinople long paid him tribute. Then, turning westwards, he came near defeating the combined forces of the Empire, Goths and Burgundians, at the great battle of the Catavellaunian fields. When he died, his Empire melted away and his Huns were swallowed up among the neighbouring peoples.

Asia Minor was in the main a land of peace. Not till the 3rd century was it heavily punished by raids of the Goths, by land and sea. It had its own little pockets of barbarism, but they could be sealed off. The wild people who lived towards the east end of the Black Sea were not as a rule aggressive. Between Rome and the more easterly barbarians lay the Parthians, later the Persian Empire. In the desert Rome had a new class of neighbour—the Arabs ' living in tents ', the ' Skenites ' as the Romans called them. These folk were not exactly barbarian in the usual sense. They had their own form of life and they often played a large part in land commerce. But they lay outside the ordinary scope of Greek and Roman life.

With South Arabia and Ethiopia Rome had only rare dealings. She made occasional attempts to get in closer touch with what were conceived to be important springs of wealth ; but she overestimated the wealth, underestimated the difficulty of reaching it. At the back of Egypt a poverty-stricken people, the Blemmyes, caused frequent trouble. In the deserts behind the African coast lay sundry barbarous tribes—the Marmaritae, the Gaetuli, the Garamantes, the Numidians, the Moors—all more or less removed from civilisation, often plundering the settled life near them, rarely breaking out into serious war. These border people knew nothing of city life and were even more barbarous than the barbarians of the Northern frontiers. But here there was not the same seething tide of peoples, and the danger to the Empire was far less.

Barbarians inside the Empire, as we have seen, came to be well controlled. Barbarians outside were kept out by the frontiers—natural ones such as great rivers, Rhine or Danube, or artificial ones such as the ' Limites ', fortified lines between the two great rivers, or the walls of Hadrian and Antoninus Pius in Britain. The first use of a frontier was military or defensive. It was there to ensure that those outside stayed out. At suitable points just on or behind the frontier stood the great permanent legionary camps ; they could not stop every violation of the frontier, but they were near to punish it. In serious troubles defence had often to be organised well in rear of the line. The Romans learnt much wisdom in the making and holding of frontiers and were amazingly successful, in all but desperate times, in keeping their lines intact. Aggressive war beyond the frontiers was usually reserved for great and definite provocation. The permanent camps supplied suitable bases, but all advances into barbarian territory were fraught with danger and were not lightly undertaken. Germanicus in the early years of Tiberius crossed the line on several occasions to demonstrate the might of Roman arms and magnify Roman prestige—perhaps even to suggest that Germany might still be conquered. But there was serious risk and little profit in such bravado. On one occasion the disaster of Varus came near to being repeated.

Relations with the barbarians were, of course, not always hostile. On frontiers where the two worlds lived long in close contact with one another there had to be some regulation of civil relations too. The conditions under which the frontier might be crossed had to be fixed ; arrangements for markets must be made. The Romans commonly insisted that the barbarians should not cross the frontier except at certain appointed times and places. Tacitus notes it as a special privilege of one tribe, the Hermunduri, that they come and go as they please ; he adds that they do not abuse their privilege. In some cases Rome kept a strip of unoccupied, untilled territory on the far side of the frontier, a sort of ' no man's land ' between the two spheres. The barbarians, not without reason, resented such withdrawal of good land from cultivation.

In quiet times such warfare as went on along the frontier was rather a fight of police against smugglers than one between armed enemies. Trade with the outside world had to be regulated. The custom dues had to be levied, raw materials would come in, certain manufactured articles of use or luxury would go out. The balance would usually be in favour of the Romans, who found a market for their goods and got raw materials cheaply. One luxury import, the amber from the Baltic, is an exception. Tacitus tells us that the Germans who find it are astounded at the prices they are paid

for it.   In the East, of course, the luxury goods brought by the ships
and caravans cost the Empire dear and drained it of its bullion.

Barbarians could not usually be expected to have anything like a
foreign office.   Discussion would take place directly with their kings
or princes.   And yet there was some room for diplomacy in Rome's
dealings with them.   It suited neither side to fight it out every time
with arms.   And so some settlement by compromise was indicated.
We can point to such diplomacy in the case of Maroboduus the
Marcomannian or Decebalus the Dacian.   In some cases both sides
would make concessions, in others the barbarians would give up
something for peace, in others again it would be Rome that paid.
Examples of peace by subsidy may be seen with Domitian and
Decebalus in 93.   Historians are very fond of stigmatising such
bargains as disgraceful.   But as a matter of fact such bargains are
to be found in every record of border relations between civilised
and less civilised powers.   There is nothing essentially disgraceful
in using the method of spoiling with the troublesome child that the
barbarian often is.   Naturally Trajan, when he decided to destroy
the Dacian power, rejected the old policy as contemptible, unworthy of Rome ; but we must not swallow his propaganda blind-
fold.   It is obviously more flattering to a nation's pride to get its
way by victorious arms, not by any form of concession or purchase—

Non cauponantes bellum sed belligerantes.

But, because you prefer one way of doing things, it does not follow
that you will always be able to take it.

We have been looking at the barbarian outside the Empire.
What is to be said of him so far as he entered it ?   Barbarians could
come in as slaves ; they might be captives taken in battle and thrown
on to the slave market.   They might in some rare cases sell themselves into slavery.   There was probably some scope for the kid-
napper.   The barbarian slave could not readily compete with a
trained and educated Syrian or Greek ; but he had a sound physique
and a rough natural beauty which might please some masters.
There was employment for strong men in such jobs as litter-bearing.
The barbarian was by nature a soldier ; war was still the main
occupation of his adult life.   Tacitus has an amusing description of
the weariness of the intervals of peace, when the great warriors idle
away their time, leaving the work to the old men and women.   The
early Emperors enrolled Germans for service in the little private
bodyguard of the palace ; the men were loyal and brave.   But
barbarians were more widely used than this in the Roman army.

The Batavians—actually just inside the Empire, though close in blood and sympathies to the free Germans—supplied levies in place of taxes. They were a corps d'élite and played a prominent, if turbulent, part in the Civil Wars of 69–70. In 83 we find a cohort of Usipetes serving in Britain, apparently just recruited from along the German frontier. It was in the auxiliary forces that barbarians first began to be employed. Later, there was much barbarian blood in the legions. The intention of the Government was good, to let the Empire bear the burden of its own defence. But the run of life was the other way. The world was full of a false pacifism, a pacifism that had nothing to do with a strong moral or rational objection to war, but just a personal reluctance to be troubled with a painful and laborious business. What good was it to have conscription in theory if it would not in practice find the men needed ? Where you have two lots of people—the qualified who won't and the unqualified who will if they are given a chance—it is fairly clear what must be the outcome. The people who will get their chance. The barbarisation of the army had already gone a long way by the 3rd century. If Maximin, a mixed barbarian, could rise to Emperor, there must have been many like him who could at least rise high in the army. The ranks were recruited more or less from the few frontier provinces ; there, the barbarians could easily get in with the rest. The disaster of Adrianople in 378 made things even worse than they had ever been. The Goths had almost destroyed the Eastern army of the Empire. Theodosius had to let them in to refill it. Eastern Rome lived through the period of barbarian domination in the army ; it found its own internal barbarians, the Isaurians, who helped to supply their place. But the Western Empire went down under the barbarian masters of the troops and their equally barbarous bands, the *buccellarii*. It might have been thought that civilisation would retain its advantage in superior ingenuity, in technical perfection of armament. This was not the case. The new developments in war came from the barbarians or, if not from them, from the alien East. Such were the archers or the heavy knights, the ' catafracts ', men and horses heavily cased in armour. Byzantium later was to produce the dreaded ' Greek fire ', which could set hostile navies on fire. Rome produced no such useful invention. The anonymous author of the little book of inventions, addressed to two Emperors of the 4th century (Valentinian I and Valens), actually proposes various devices for facilitating transport or damaging the enemy. He is ingenious, but not very practical. But his work is the exception that proves the rule ; inventiveness was sadly lacking. The whole art of war became

I

something like a preserve of the barbarians. When the West lapsed into barbarism it only followed where its army had long gone before.

There was one other way—a most important one—in which barbarians could enter the Empire. They might come in as ' federates ' in mass and receive settlements in frontier provinces. They would normally undertake a share in the defence of their new homes. Such a quickening of provincial life with fresh blood might obviously be very advantageous to Rome, and the practice was often employed from early in the Empire. The Empire gained new subjects, so many new friends where enemies had been. Marcus Aurelius settled great numbers of barbarians on the Roman side of the Danube. Under Diocletian we find the settled barbarians recognised under special names, as *laeti* or *limigantes*. The process of turning foe into friend would normally be proceeding along the frontiers. These barbarians could become tamer and tamer till they ceased to be barbarian at all. These settlements on the large scale simply hastened on a natural process that never ceased.

So far we have been looking at the problem of the barbarians from the Roman point of view. We have been members of the garrison, looking forth from the frontiers on to the troublesome human problems that keep presenting themselves. It is the natural view with which to begin, for it is the view given by most of our evidence. But it is also possible to do something quite different— to forget Rome for the moment and try to see the world as it would look if viewed from above or outside. We shall see movements of which we had no suspicion at first. We shall find ourselves asking for answers to questions that we had never asked. We shall give up the point of view of the garrison within and see instead a whole world of which the precious garrison is only a part. Franz Altheim, that scholar of wide outlook and quick imagination, has essayed a picture of the Roman Empire in the time of the troubles as seen from without, from the circumference and not from the centre. Altheim's attempt is only partially successful ; how could it be otherwise when evidence except from the Roman side is so hard to come by ? But Altheim *does* contrive to give us glimpses and suggestions that will enrich our outlook for all time to come. Kipling had success of a rather different kind in the Roman stories in ' Puck of Pook's Hill '. On the Roman wall, we are enabled to see not only the points of view of Parnesius and Pertinax, the Roman officers, but also of the Winged Hats from the far North and the little Picts under their foxy old chief Allo. There is fine imagination there, and *that* may sometimes help us more than erudition. If we engage in such an attempt we must shift our view. We must no longer concentrate on Rome and the lands between Rome and the frontiers. We must try to focus our gaze on the darkness, total or partial, that lies beyond. On the frontiers themselves, the movement must always be towards stabilisation, the setting of relations on a footing more and more peaceful. We shall seldom find there the causes for the storms that so often break in suddenly from far outside.

Human life is at the mercy of change and chance ; no system of government will alter that. But a society which has gone over completely to ordered life in cities has limited the sphere within which change and chance can work. Stability has been reached in society and state. Even if that stability is challenged from time to time through uncertainties as to the succession or the ambition of great individuals, disturbance will not be total ; much will stand unchanged and there will be the tendency to return to a new stabilisation on similar lines. The Roman Empire in the course of its history had to undergo most of the vicissitudes possible. It groaned under famine and plague ; it endured wasteful civil wars, misgovernment and cruel taxation. But throughout all it kept its main form and returned again and again to the old foundations. There were many factors making for change, but they were not quite incalculable ; they were not past human power to manipulate. Along the frontiers, as we have suggested, the example of the settled Empire exercised its steady influence. The barbarians were brought into some semblance of imitation of Roman ways. Life is no longer purely nomadic ; the ways of settled peoples are at least partly understood. But, as you move further away from contact with civilisation, you come to the pure nomad life, with no cities, no regular agriculture, no fixed settlements. The Roman poets were much impressed with this formless life ; when they allowed their eyes to wander abroad to it, they might even see in it a strange purity, free from the artificial evils of civilisation. Here everything flowed, nothing remained the same. If there was movement here, what determined its direction ? The great movements of the barbarians which from time to time menaced the Empire can seldom be explained by anything to be observed close on the frontiers. The wave which ultimately sweeps them has gathered somewhere far in the dark background. It is these mysterious tides from far away that we have to investigate.

Buckle in his great book on civilisation has seen in climate the chief formative influence on nations. By ' climate ' he means something more than weather—he means the sum of all conditions under which men live. This ' climate ' of his will effect even the most civilised peoples ; but its influence will be more immediate and decisive on peoples which have not reached settled life and respond to every drive. There is endless room here for speculation if not for exact knowledge. But we can be sure that climate had much to do with the movements of the further barbarian peoples ; we can even guess some of the ways in which it may have worked. Periods of unusual drought or rain would alter the desirability of grazing grounds. If such periods were of any length, they might induce peoples to change their habitat. They might be thrown on to other peoples ; those peoples might in their turn be thrown on to others, and thus a movement might begin which only ended when it met the solid obstacle of the Roman frontier. Apart from such climatic causes, there might be causes more intelligible in human terms—the ambitions of a nomad chief to extend his bounds or the restlessness of a nomad people. In both cases, a movement would start far back and advance till it encountered Rome. The true story of these movements is for the most part hidden from us. But, whenever peoples near the frontiers suddenly begin to assault them, we must suppose some such hidden drive from behind. In several instances our darkness is partially lightened. The great migration of the Cimbri and Teutoni in the years 113–101 B.C. began with floods that drove the peoples from their homes on the Baltic. The movement swept Gaul and Spain and was with difficulty halted at the gates of Italy. There was probably pressure from behind to explain the drive of peoples against the Danube front under Domitian and again under Marcus Aurelius. Later, the Goths were visible as the chief disturbing agency. Their trek from the Baltic to the Balkans was probably responsible for many of the troubles of the 3rd century. It may have been the threat of these formidable new enemies that led the German tribes to combine into the larger alliances which we find later—the Franks, the Alamanni and the rest. In the 4th and 5th centuries, it was something new that caused the trouble—the incursion from the Steppes of Asia of wild nomadic peoples, Huns and Alans, who pushed their way among the Goths and other tribes, shook them out of their quiescence and hurled them on the Empire. The pressure of the Huns gave the Empire no rest till, with the death of Attila, the unwieldly empire broke up into its parts.

Civilisation and barbarism—here are two of the great contrasts in history. To those who have once embraced it, civilisation seems to have all the advantages. It enriches and embellishes life ; it substitutes some degree of law and order for confusion and caprice ; it allows religion and morality to grow. Its danger is that it may grow stale, lose vitality, cease to be able to defend the values that it has created. Barbarism, on the other hand, makes up in vitality what it lacks in quality. It is free, uninhibited, ready to follow its natural drives. It comes into the civilised world, prepared to conquer and enjoy the wealth that it could never create for itself. The problem of the civilised state is to tame and control its barbarians, whether they be within or without, to teach them respect for its law and order, to harness their energies to its own purposes. On its success or failure here its destiny depends. The Roman Empire, as we have seen, succeeded well in one part of its task. It created a peace within which men might live and enjoy their life. The fact that all civil wars failed to destroy the Empire shows how well this task had been performed. With the barbarians outside, success was much less complete. For a long time the frontiers were maintained. The barbarians grew accustomed to a life not their own ; they came to take their part in the defence. They were settled in large numbers within the Empire. But, at the end, as the pressure from without grew ever stronger, the assimilation of barbarians became less thorough. There was a permanent barbarian element in the army, not only in the rank and file but up to the highest posts. At last the balance had fatally shifted. Civilisation ceased to impress itself upon the barbarians ; it yielded to them and in turn took their stamp. The different fates of East and West never cease to arouse our interest. The West went down under the barbarian tide ; the East emerged safe and sound. The element of chance cannot be overlooked. The Goths threatened the East no less than the West ; yet it was only on the West that the full fury of their onslaught fell. Something may be allowed to the unique geographical position of the capital, Constantinople ; it could so easily be assailed, so hardly taken. Something too may be due to superior diplomacy ; this was certainly manifested in the handling of the Goths. But there were probably other causes latent. The East seems to have accepted the later Roman civilisation—its strongly centralised state, its rigidly organised society, its new Christian religion—much more completely than the West. It was more unified in itself, more loyal to the imperial idea, more resistant to threats from outside ; and, after it had thrown off its Goths and been rid of its Huns, it found itself for a time without a serious barbarian danger.

The problem of civilisation and barbarism is not out of date. We have it with us in our modern world. The problem is more complicated than it used to be. There are several civilisations that may compete with one another—the civilisations of China and Japan, and India, apart from the European and its derivatives in the United States and the New World generally. These civilisations might conceivably ruin themselves by wasteful conflict ; but the waste would need to be very heavy before it could endanger the cause of civilisation generally. One might look to Africa as a possible source of barbarian menace for the future. But there still seems to be some chance that the Africans may accept civilisation in time to share its blessings instead of destroying them. But we have now learnt to sense a new danger—the breaking out of barbarism in new forms inside our civilised systems. Science, the chief glory of our modern world, has shown a perilous tendency to advance technical mastery without regard for the permanent values of our civilisation. Atom bomb warfare is just about as barbarous as anything could be ; but atom warfare is the prerogative of just those peoples that claim to be most civilised. We have to do some fresh thinking and to do it quickly. Our civilisation has developed lopsidedly. Vast improvement in technical methods has gone far ahead of the development of the arts of government and social organisation. A society that gives everything for material wealth, that shrinks from nothing in the pursuit of power, is barbarous, however great its mastery of nature. Still, there is hope. The abilities that determine the growth of Science are abilities of the trained, the civilised mind. Many of our greatest scientists are fully aware of the false direction Science has taken. If these abilities could be awakened again, to control as well as to advance technical progress, we might still have cause to bless the Science which at the moment we are tempted to curse. It may be a salutary warning for us to look again at the Roman Empire of the 4th century, with its barbarians in the army, with the encroachment of barbarous arms and methods of war on the old Roman traditions. If we can only realise that it is our own home-grown barbarism that threatens us, we may yet recoil from it before it is too late.

CHAPTER V

THE IMPERIAL CIVIL SERVICE

There are two reasons why we should dwell rather carefully on the Civil Service of the Roman Empire. One is that we happen to be well informed about it. A great number of inscriptions give us details of the careers of Civil Servants and several poets have sung the praises of patrons who rose high in the service. The other is that the question is of vital importance for our judgment of the Empire. There may be a great difference between the look and the reality. The man you see first is not always the one who is really doing things. Behind the Cabinet may lurk the permanent Civil Servant. The man in the background will not as a rule get any of the kudos ; but, if a man is content with real as against nominal power, the backroom job may be the right one for him. What the Roman Government looked like we have seen in an earlier chapter. What it meant to its subjects will become more apparent when we have studied the Civil Service, which translated the intentions of the government into practice for the subjects of the Empire. A good executive may redeem the failures of a bad government— and *vice versa*.

We British have in our national experience quite a lot that may help us to take an interest in and understand the Roman Empire. In India we long maintained a Civil Service with very high standards of efficiency, devotion and hard work. And yet that service was bitterly resented by the Indians. It might prevent or mitigate famine or plague, but it was felt as a foreign body and could not please the people it served. At home we began with a Civil Service, mainly appointed by influence, not very energetic, lacking in energy and ambition. Then came an enormous improvement. Conditions of appointment were regularised and improved, higher standards were demanded and the work began to be handled with a much higher efficiency. The public showed little appreciation of its good luck. The comic papers were never tired of being funny at the expense of the Civil Service. *Punch* was a notorious offender. That the service was well organised and, almost beyond suspicion, honest was not allowed to count for much. It was drab, unexciting, inert. We should have learnt by now how lucky we were. The requirements of the modern state have saddled us with a Civil Service, swollen in numbers, vastly grown in extent, prying into every detail of business and private life. We shall find in the Roman Empire something to compare with all these different states of the public service. Our experience in India will help us to understand how the provinces regarded the Roman Civil Servant. The Civil Service of the late 19th century may not unjustly be compared with the service organised by Augustus. The Civil Service of today will suggest comparisons with the Civil Service of Diocletian and Constantine.

Augustus found a vast task awaiting him, with very few instruments ready to his hand. The Roman Republic had been very economical in its arrangements. It had run itself and its provinces with magistrates, elected by the people, assisted by modest staffs recruited for each occasion. This system was not good either for the governors or for the governed. The State was not well served ; the provinces suffered under these exactions of large numbers of more or less irresponsible hangers-on of the governors. There was no large, well-organised service for Augustus to take over. What had he to direct his actions ? The experience of the Republic, such as it was, was, as we have seen, not very helpful. Next came the lessons to be drawn from the kingdoms of the Greek East. From them something might be learned. The kings of Syria had had long experience in administering the affairs of an extensive kingdom. The Ptolemies of Egypt had shown how a country might be run on the lines of a profitable private estate. From both these sources Augustus may have learnt much. Again, he could draw on the experience of Roman private life, the way in which Roman nobles handled their often complicated affairs. But what taught him most was the task itself with its urgent necessities. The tasks to be done could be seen clearly and it soon became obvious to Augustus what kind of instruments he required for them. It will be worth our while to consider with some care just what Augustus did. The foundations that he laid stood unshaken ; the development of the service ran for long on the lines that he had indicated.

For nearly all the higher posts Augustus employed senators, for the chief provincial governorships and for the chief prefectures. For the posts of the second order—and a few of the first, the prefectures of Egypt, the guard, the corn-supply—he employed knights ; below them came the various financial posts, the procuratorships ; there were also governorships of a few minor provinces. For some minor procuratorships and for the personal officers about the court he employed freedmen. For the subordinate positions he employed slaves. The free population below the rank of knights seems to have played but a small part in his arrangements. The details of the service have been worked out with great care by that fine German scholar, Otto Hirschfeld, and can be consulted in his great work. What we must not omit is to bring into prominence the guiding principles of the arrangements of Augustus.

In the first place the service was still very personal, not fully professional. Augustus selected the men who were to serve him much as the Roman noble had selected under the Republic. It was in fact a State service, but selection was made by an individual and loyalty was owed to him alone. There was room for personal considerations, for caprice even, to enter in. It was only gradually that appointments came to follow a fixed course, that norms for the service were established. For some reigns the immensely important imperial secretariats were in the hands of freedmen, answering only to their patron, the Emperor. In such a system the Emperor should have his hands free. But by the reign of Claudius the imperial freedmen were exercising an excessive influence. The tales of the subservience of Claudius to his freedmen may be exaggerated ; they cannot have been completely invented.

One passes easily on to a second point, the question of responsibility. In the early Empire responsibility could rest only on the Emperor. His servants had to do exactly that which was delegated to them—so much and no more. When Cornelius Gallus in Egypt exceeded the bounds of his commission he was met at once with the loss of favour that led to his suicide. When a procurator of Asia under Tiberius was accused of various oppressions, the Emperor declared plainly that he had only given him authority over imperial monies and slaves and that, if he had trespassed beyond his sphere, the law must take its course with him. But Pallas, the financial secretary of Claudius, when forced by Nero to retire, bargained that his accounts with the State should be taken as cleared. He had in fact won almost complete independence of the Emperor whose agent he was.

In theory, then, the servants of the Emperor acted only in his commission ; in fact, they often took a great deal on themselves. Augustus showed his sense of public obligation by leaving behind him long detailed accounts of the budget of the State. No one could call him to account, but he chose to justify his stewardship. This was perhaps going further than the later Emperors liked ; at any rate we cannot find that the publication of such budgets ever became normal. The real responsibility belongs to the Emperor—and to the Emperor in his public capacity ; that is to say, the responsibility belongs to the State in the person of its chosen representative. The Emperor delegates part of his responsibility to various assistants ;

they often take on themselves more than is their due. It is only gradually that a new influence arises—the influence of the Civil Service itself, as it assumes a set form and develops its own traditions. This service comes to play an important part in the game, exercising its influence not only on its servants, but also on the Emperor, its master.

We have already seen that Augustus drew his helpers from various grades of society. The tasks he had to delegate were of varying grades of difficulty and it was only natural to find for them suitable men in various walks of life. It also suited Augustus to have society as a whole looking to him for employment and reward. This was entirely natural, but it had a curious and half unexpected consequence. Men who served the Emperor belonged from the outset to their several classes ; they continued to rank as senators, knights, freedmen ; they would not be grouped together as ' Civil Servants '. This at first helped to prevent the growth of a professional Civil Service. The advantages and disadvantages of this might be argued and no decision would be easy. Probably, for a time, the advantages prevailed. It is perhaps connected with this that the free population took so little part in Augustus's plans. For his higher posts he must look to the two first orders of Roman society. When he fell below them, his own freedmen suggested themselves. It might have been well if the Emperor could have found more room for the free-born of lower rank to share in his service. But his attitude towards them seems to have been that of the patron towards his clients. He gave them protection and spoilt them with games and food ; it does not seem to have occurred to him to employ them freely in his service.

As far as the senators and the knights were concerned, the Civil Service was closely tied to the military. The young senator or knight had to perform his term of military service in an officer's post before he passed on to civil employment. This was deliberate policy here. Augustus did not intend that the growing reluctance to undertake military service should be encouraged among the higher orders. They must set a good example to their humbler fellow-citizens. The results on the whole were good. Neither the army nor the Civil Service stood apart from the general life of the State. Everyone might expect in his time to see something of both. It suited the general policy of the early Emperors to discourage any states within the State—and it is into such that professional services tend to grow.

The early Civil Service was not very numerous and not very complicated. It was planned for its jobs ; jobs were not yet made for it. It seems to have been fairly efficient and fairly honest. Abuses crept in ; under a bad Emperor, the men who brought him what he wanted might count on some short-sightedness as to their own sins of omission and commission. The Romans had a genius for illicit exactions and that genius was not unemployed under the Empire. The revolt of Boudicca in Britain under Nero was provoked by the cruelties and extortions of the procurator and his tools. But, as a whole, the imperial administration ranks as superior to the senatorial, and examples are known of provinces, ' pleading the weight of their burdens ', being transferred from Senate to Emperor. When we compare the simplicity and economy of the service with the vast extent of the Empire and the immense volume of business to be done, it will be obvious that a very great deal was left to be dealt with locally. The cities might be feeble enough compared to Rome, but they still transacted a great mass of minor business. Only in the 2nd century does the Emperor begin to take over much of city administration—and that at first only by appointing his curators of senatorial rank. The detailed work must still have been done by local talent. The service was not yet tyrannical and it was not unduly resented.

An ugly feature of an intrusive Civil Service is its passion for knowing everything about financial—yes, and even about social and private life. This may to some extent be necessary ; it is always unpleasant. Government employees, not recognisable as such until their service done, they declare themselves, are unpleasantly like spies. This feature was not very prominent in the early Empire. Spying was not unknown. Procurators were often used to report secretly on the governors in whose provinces they served. We could pick out here and there an example of information being brought in to a suspicious Emperor. It was under Hadrian that something like a regular system of spying was introduced. Soldiers selected for confidential employment were sent abroad into the provinces—nominally to make enquiries into details of the vital supply of corn, actually to report to the Emperor on anything they thought likely to interest him. These *frumentarii* soon began to extend the range of their activities and became justly unpopular.

In a Civil Service as personal as that of Augustus, there is no clear distinction between the Civil Servants proper and the various appendages of the court. Court chamberlains, barbers, cooks— they are not public servants but they are close to the Emperor and are often employed by him in tasks a little outside their nominal competencies. Under bad Emperors these excrescences of the court multiplied and became vexatious. Public money was squandered on such unworthy favourites. But the abuse was an occasional one, not a permanent cancer. Access to the person of the Emperor might be valuable in the market. It might enable its possessor to recommend a certain person or to deal out private information that could be turned to account. If our history is correct, the selling of such private information became very prevalent in the 3rd century. There was a special word for such reports of what the Emperor said or did ; they were called *fumi*, ' smokes ', presumably because so often there was some fire behind them. Much worse was to come in the 4th century.

The system of Augustus continued without violent change until the days of Diocletian. No ancient writer has left us any record of the service as a whole, though we are fortunate enough to have an informed account of the water supply of Rome by an able official, Frontinus, who himself had held that charge. But changes there were and we can follow them with sufficient clearness. Tiberius was peculiarly faithful to the arrangements of Augustus. He was loyal to the person of his great predecessor and he admired his wisdom and foresight. His own great contribution was to encourage long terms of service. He was slow to approve, but, when he found a man to his liking, he would continue him for years in the same place, till he grew old or died in it. He contributed thereby to the growth of firm traditions and forms. Caligula seems to have left no mark on the service. The Emperor himself was unbalanced and irresponsible. This seems to have been so notorious that the imperial example was as far as possible ignored. The coinage of the reign continues throughout on the same decent, normal course of eulogy of the great imperial house, of respect for the Senate and religion—there is not a trace of divine honours for the megalomaniac Emperor. In the East, too, we know that Petronius, the wise governor of Syria, contrived so to temporise that Caligula's mad design to be worshipped in Jerusalem was frustrated by his death.

Claudius introduced changes of some importance. The imperial secretariats now assumed a new significance ; they now appear as virtual offices of state, departments of correspondence, finance, petitions, law cases, literary research and so on. Claudius to the Romans was always a figure of fun. He could often enough be laughed at, and the opportunity was never to be missed. The freedmen of Claudius certainly made colossal fortunes and abused their power on occasion. But the development was healthy and normal. The Emperor's business was outgrowing the scope of any private individual and the great bureaux had to be organised. In this reign the *fiscus*, the imperial treasury, first comes into prominence. This may mean that only now were the imperial finances balanced in one account ; before, there may have been a number of chests ; the balancing of the whole may have been left to the Emperor. Claudius also armed his procurators with the power to try cases in which the *fiscus* was concerned. Tacitus, who reports the action, confuses us completely by identifying the new powers of the procurators with the right to sit on juries in Rome—a piece of confusion so ridiculous that we may even believe it innocent. Fiscal cases often depended on disputed questions of property or privilege and might drag on indefinitely. Claudius no doubt aimed at dealing summarily with such dragging claims. But that the Emperor through his procurator should appear as judge in his own case was bound to be resented, and Nerva appointed a special praetor to decide such cases in Rome.

Nero in his early days proposed to abolish all indirect taxes—a noble, but vain ambition. He *did* succeed however in abolishing many illegal exactions that had hardened into practice. His lust for gold in his later days—gold to be squandered on his grandiose architectural schemes, on his pleasures, on his low friends—led him to seek wealth from any source, even such an unlikely one as the supposed treasure that an African dreamed he had found on his estate near Carthage. Nero's agents were busy for him in all the provinces, stealing statues to adorn new-built Rome or plundering the wealthy provincials. There was no change of principle here— only a sad example of how a good service might be corrupted to please an irresponsible head.

Vitellius in his short reign made one change that attests his insight and good sense. He gave to Roman knights those court appoint-ments that had hitherto been given to freedmen—correspondence, finance and the rest. These posts were so important and so public that they could not reasonably be left to freedmen. Hadrian fixed a practice, first introduced by Vitellius, as the norm for the future. Domitian will certainly have exercised some influence on the service, but we cannot measure it closely. When he took on himself the perpetual censorship he must have had need for new assistants. Nerva appointed the praetor to try fiscal cases—in this, as in other things, trying to win public opinion to his side by judicious reforms. Trajan was too much concerned with war and building to spare much thought for the details of the Civil Service.

The influence of Hadrian was considerable. As we have just observed, he gave the imperial bureaux to knights. It was a great advancement of the equestrian order, which in these posts con-trolled business of the highest importance and stood very close to the

Emperor himself. Hadrian also developed the Civil Service in its earlier stages by opening a new civil approach to the career as an alternative to the military ; the prospective Civil Servant served, not as prefect of cohort or squadron or tribune of cohort, but as an *advocatus fisci*, a counsel for the *fiscus* in cases with the general public. Septimius Severus is chiefly notorious for his spoiling of the army. He needed the unquestioning loyalty of his troops and he was prepared to buy it, no matter what the cost. But the Civil Service also felt his influence. It is in his reign that we first find the prefect of the praetorian guard blossoming out into a high legal authority. The prefect was appointed to decide cases on appeal, *sacra vice*, representing the sacred emperor. This demanded legal qualifications ; but the sudden emergence of men like Papinian, Ulpian and Paulus can only be explained if the Emperor now insisted with a new urgency on them. It was probably the multitude of appeals, due to the trials and confiscations arising out of the civil wars against Pescennius Niger and Clodius Albinus, that developed this new activity of the prefect to such an extent.

These same confiscations led to another development of the highest importance. The vast sums of confiscated money were not lodged either in the Emperor's official chest, the *fiscus*, or in his personal fortune, the *patrimonium*, but in a new private fund, the *res privata*, under a procurator of the highest rank. This sinister fund, fed by extortion and devoted to the pleasant task of bribing the army, deserves more attention than it always receives from historians. It marks a terrible advance of sheer autocracy, when funds due to the State were placed at the private disposal of the Emperor. It also tended to confuse ideas of the Emperor's financial responsibility everywhere. If the Emperor had undoubted right to dispose of part of the State monies, how call him to account for the rest ? The accounts that our authorities give us of the *fiscus* and the Emperor's relation to it seem to be complicated and confused by the new conception of the *res privata*.

After the fall of the dynasty of Severus, the Empire entered those dangerous rapids in which it came nigh to foundering. The terrible years of the troubles cannot have failed to leave their mark on the Civil Service. It would not be so much a case of reforms as of partial collapses under the stress of events and improvisations to make them good. It is reasonably certain, though it can only occasionally be proved in detail, that most of Diocletian's reforms already existed in plan before him. One development we can trace. The senators in military employment came to be supplanted by knights. The process was completed by Gallienus, when he closed the military career to the senator.   It would be natural to place the responsibility in the first place on the barbarian Maximin I, who ruled without regard or respect for the Senate and would naturally distrust that hated body.   The way in which the ousting of senators took place was probably that of replacement ; a senatorial governor, commanding an army, might be replaced by a knight, acting in the first place *vice legati*.   The triumph of the Senate over Maximin I must for a moment have checked the development.   But the causes continued to operate and Gallienus took the decisive step of excluding senators from military commands.   One cause was undoubtedly the breach between Emperor and Senate, which became acute under Septimius and was never for long healed.   On the side of the Senate we may postulate a growing reluctance to launch out on the dangerous waters of a military career.   For the army we may imagine a growing sense of separation as a profession.   If the army was beginning to demand a man's whole allegiance, it may have seemed far easier to win that from a knight, with his lower range of hopes, than from a senator with his ancient pride.   Whether the service was growing in numbers we cannot say.   The troubles of the State would work both ways.   The loss of provinces reduced the sphere to be covered.   The need for collecting the taxes and the *annona* would tend to multiply collectors and spies.   It is fairly safe to assume that the service steadily grew in unpopularity.

A few words must be added about the conditions of the Service as far as we know them.   Appointment was made in every case by the Emperor ; he might consider the opinion of the Senate when he selected noted senators for high positions, but he was in no way bound by it.   Appointment would be for merit as far as it came to the notice of the Emperor ; recommendations of friends would of course count.   The aspirant unknown to the Emperor might present his case in a petition which would be duly considered by the bureau, *a libellis*.   There was no general limitation of term of office.   All posts were held at the Emperor's pleasure.   Rules for different offices of course appeared as time went on.   All posts in the Civil Service were paid—a vast improvement on the Republic, when so many men were supposed to be giving their services free, but were really recouping themselves fourfold by irregular exactions.   There was a far better chance for the provincial when his possible oppressor started well fed.   The salaries of procurators were on four grades : at 60,000, 100,000, 200,000 and 300,000 sestertii—*sexagenarii, centenarii, ducenarii* and *trecenarii*.   The procurators of the smaller provinces were on the lowest level, those of more important provinces and important services on the next, a few superior procuratorships

on the third ; the highest grade of *trecenarii* was reserved for a
very few high posts at the top, such as the *a rationibus* and the head
of the *res privata* (high financial officers). These salary grades were
at the same time grades of rank, a clear sign of the increasingly firm
organisation of the service. Attempts have been made to work out
the equestrian course of office and have been successful up to a point.
After military service came the various procuratorships of smaller
provinces or of special branches of finance, such as the 5% on
inheritances, then the procuratorships of large provinces, then, at
the head, the few major prefectures. The senatorial career was
rather more exactly ordered—a post on the board of twenty, then
quaestor, aedile or tribune, praetor, consul ; then employment as
governor of senatorial province or legate of imperial ; finally, a
number of important prefectures, of which the prefecture of the city
may be considered the most important.

The system which we find after Diocletian and Constantine is so
unlike that of the early Empire that we might almost be tempted to
regard it as a completely new invention. It will be best to describe
it in some detail, to show how it was developed out of the earlier
system, finally, to point out its chief merits and defects.

The Emperor, the centre of the government, had always had
around him a number of high officers who together made up what
we might call the government. In the new age this central organisation stands out much more clearly than before. One officer, the
quaestor sacri palatii, was at the head of all legal business, the drafting
of edicts, etc. ; he represents the *ab epistulis* (imperial secretary)
and also the *a cognitionibus* (legal adviser) of the earlier system and
was perhaps the most important officer of all. The master of
offices, *magister officiorum*, was a kind of official chief of the Civil
Service, with all the minor officials under him. He was also the
head of the Secret Service, the hordes of *curiosi* or *agentes in rebus*.
We know what degree of power such a chief of police can wield.
The *comes sacrarum largitionum* was the chief officer of finance, corresponding to the old *a rationibus*. *Largitiones* were a euphemism for
the exactions which the Emperor had to make from his subjects.
The epithet *sacra* could bear two meanings—a bad as well as a good.
The *sacrae largitiones* will have been freely translated as ' damned
exactions '. A number of other *comites*, or Counts, were in charge
of other departments. There was, for example, a special ' Count of
the gold ' in charge of supplies of the precious metal in the West
of the Empire. *Comes* becomes one of the main civil titles, just as
dux, duke, marks the military commander. These were the central
offices of the Empire. But the Empire was no longer one. The

division into East and West was always there. Only for short
periods, under Constantine and Theodosius, was the unity of the
Empire restored. That meant, not one central government, but
two or more according to the number of Emperors. Marcus
Aurelius had let his cousin L. Verus share Empire with him, but
there was no clear division of function between them. Valerian,
when he marched East in 255, left the West in the charge of his son,
Gallienus. On this occasion there was certainly division of power ;
Gallienus will have had his own armies, his own Civil Service.
These conditions were repeated when Carus, setting out on his
Persian expedition, left his son, Carinus, in charge of the West.
Diocletian adopted the plan and made it permanent, but he carried
subdivision one stage further, when he added to the two Augusti
two Caesars. The Empire now had its four divisions and, though
these did not outlast the Tetrarchy, the fourfold division persisted in
the permanent division of the Empire into its great praetorian
prefectures.

The governorships of provinces were multiplied with the increase
of the provinces. The distinction between imperial and senatorial
had ceased to exist. All governors were appointed by the Emperor.
They were now purely civil officers and had no contacts with the
army. In Asia and Africa the old title of honour, proconsul, persisted. The usual title was *praeses*, a vague term, or *iudex*, more
closely defining the judicial functions which now made up the main
part of a governor's duties. Over the governors stood the praetorian
prefects—of Gaul, of Africa, of Illyricum and the East. (The
question of these prefectures is a complicated one ; they were not
always of the same number.) Each prefect has deputies (*vicarii*)
under him. This was a considerable step towards rationalisation
and efficiency. The provinces were no longer administered as
separate entities ; the interests of whole blocks of the Empire were
brought under the unifying rule of one prefect. In the praetorian
prefect the transition from military to civil career is seen at its most
perfect. The praetorian prefect originally was the military man
who stood next to the Emperor, on whose efficiency and loyalty the
Emperor depended. The new prefect has nothing to do with the
army directly. He is the supreme judicial instance, hearing appeals
as the deputy of the Emperor. He considers as a whole the district
in his charge. He controls the *annona*, the supply of commodities
of the most various kinds for imperial requirements. We will consider a little later how this astounding change of function took place.

Financial officers were numerous ; they were now called *rationales*
and corresponded more or less exactly to the earlier procurators.

K

The staffs, the *officia*, were vastly swollen in numbers. There were more governors for the increased number of provinces and the tendency was always to multiply such posts. The spy service was now placed on a new and more permanent basis by the creation of a corps of ' spies ' or ' busies ' (*curiosi, agentes in rebus*). This was an ugly business. The government avowed its intention of continually prying into all secrets. Security may have been one reason. Diocletian had the intention of ending for ever the incessant revolts of the 3rd century. But even more to the point was the need to find out exactly what a man's financial position was. The demands of the State were excessive, bad enough in time of peace, almost insufferable in war. Excessive demands cannot be enforced without some compulsion.

How this system grew out of the old we shall never know in all details. The tradition of the critical years of the 3rd century, when the changes were being silently prepared, is incurably corrupt. But some points do emerge. We have just seen how the division of the Empire into sections had been carried out by Valerian and Gallienus and by Carus and Carinus. The rival Empires—the Gallic of Postumus, the British of Carausius, the Palmyrene of Zenobia and Vaballathus—carried the idea forward. We can see here the germ of the later manifold prefectures. The change in the character of the praetorian prefect may be partly explained from the logic of the position. As the man who stood closest to the Emperor he was bound to find himself interested in functions other than the military one of commanding the Guard. I think we may trace the decisive change under Septimius Severus. He undertook four major expeditions from Rome—to the East against Pescennius Niger, to Gaul against Clodius Albinus, to the East against Parthia, to the West against Britain. The organisation of all these expeditions will have fallen largely to the praetorian prefects ; in particular, the vital question of supply will have been in their hands. Septimius chose to put large trust in his prefects ; we think first of Plautianus, later of Papinian. The other main development, on the legal side, may have come a little later. Of Plautianus as a lawyer we know nothing ; but Papinian ranked as the greatest of all. Is it too much to guess that it was the trials of the supporters of Clodius Albinus, the confiscations and the creation of the *res privata*, that accelerated the process that had already begun ?

The complete separation of civil and military careers which we find in the new order had long been preparing. It represented a very general tendency of the Empire. The civil population showed an increasing distaste for military service. The natural result was that the army drew apart as something special and that the barbarian element in it grew unchecked. The withdrawal of the Senate from military life, partly of free choice, partly enforced, is of the same tendency. The senators feel themselves less and less inclined to venture into the hard conditions of the camps ; they are suspect both to the military class and to the Emperor.

It is time now to assess the effects of the late Civil Service on the Empire as a whole ; it will be convenient to divide the subject under a number of headings. First of all, the new service was vastly increased in numbers and complexity. The Emperor now proposed to divide his Empire into many more small parts, to look more closely into their affairs, to co-ordinate all his arrangements for each section. He was concerned to know all that could be known of the conditions of his subjects. All this demanded large staffs, and staffs devoted to special tasks.

Secondly, the new service was professional in a far higher degree than the old. It was completely separated from the military service ; yet it too was entitled a *militia* as a kind of analogue of the service in the army. This meant, of course, that the new service felt itself more distinct from the general public, more conscious of its own class interests than before. With this went the fact that the service, like everything else in the State, tended to become hereditary. The son of a Civil Servant would normally follow in his father's footsteps. The Emperor was always needing men for his service and, distrusting the adequacy of the man-power of his Empire, he found it simplest to hold fast to what he had.

Thirdly, the new service was tyrannical, the chosen instrument of a tyrannical State. The State creates a vast service to enforce its demands on its subjects ; the service is hungry, grows ever hungrier, opens its mouth wider and wider. There is a natural hostility now between government and governed—the one greedily demanding, the other resisting demands. But in happier times the hostility is mitigated by some restraint on the part of government, some answering compliance on the part of the subjects, who must acknowledge that for their sacrifices they do get something back in the form of security and protection. In the late Empire the hostility was bitter and unmasked. The government and its servants stood apart from the general population, hated and distrusted, but able to have their way. As the tone of imperial edicts shows, the Emperor claims to provide in perfect love and wisdom for the needs of his subjects. The claim may be honestly made, but it is not readily admitted. Whatever authority said, the public was convinced that government would take as much as it could and give as little.

Taxation was no longer borne as a voluntary burden ; it had to be enforced by brutality and trickery. The loss of confidence in government was a main cause of the collapse of the West. Before the outer frame gave way, the inner firmness was undermined. The ugliest feature of this tyranny was, as we have said, the developed system of spying. The *frumentarii* of the 2nd and 3rd centuries had been a plague, but they had been an occasional visitation. But the new spies and ' busies ' were a different matter. They were organised as a permanent corps under a high chief of State. They were ever running to and fro, leaving no stone unturned, no secret uncovered. We have seen too much in modern Europe of the hateful effects of such systems of secret police. They exasperate the general public, they corrupt government—which ought to be able to carry out its policies without such repulsive assistance—they pollute the sanctities of home and social life by making sons spy on fathers and friends on friends. Such a system can only be defended on grounds of necessity. The State, it may be said, must have the necessary information ; if the public will not volunteer it the State must take its own steps to secure it ; private suffering must give place to the public good. A State which is really in such a parlous position has only one need—the need for thorough reform. A system that can only be maintained by consistent spying and bullying has no right to survive. A State that can devise no better system has no right either.

The next question is that of the relation of the new Civil Service to what was left of local and city government. The general tendency was to centralise everything and to oust the local authorities from the functions they had held. We have already seen how the cities had abused their limited freedom and had forced the Emperors through their curators to assume control of their finances. It is not likely that, as the Empire staggered out of the troubles of the 3rd century, much of the old semblance of local liberty survived At one point we can see clearly—in the matter of the local senates, the *curiae*. Traditionally, they were the centre of the cities, the foci of local ambition, local nobility, wealth and talent. In what condition do we find them in the 4th century ? They still exist ; the government still recognises them—in fact, finds new uses for them They are required to guarantee the payment of the local taxes Unable to be sure of payment in full, the government passes the burden on to the local magnates. The result was lamentable. The financial position was obviously desperate ; more was demanded than could easily be paid. The State protected itself by ruining the local senates and draining them of what wealth they had left

There were desperate attempts at flight from the *curiae*. Men sought refuge in the army, in the Church, on the estates of local country magnates. Government thundered out its threats at all who tried to escape ; but attempts at escape were still made. Conditions were so desperate that no degree of intimidation could keep men still. They would say to themselves ' things at least cannot be worse '.

The personal service of the Emperor had never been quite distinct from his Civil Service. Such officials as the chiefs of finance and correspondence had sprung out of the private entourage of the Emperor. The imperial chamberlain had always had considerable influence ; under a bad Emperor he might play an important part in politics. An already existing tendency grew far worse in the 4th century. The imperial chamberlains, and, in general, the eunuchs round the Emperor's person, became a force to be reckoned with. Under Constantius II, who was peculiarly liable to such influence, the eunuchs dominated the government ; fine officers were at the mercy of their intrigues. Julian the Apostate was always fighting against their malign influence. The Augustan history has much to say of such court intrigues in the 3rd century ; this is perhaps one of the points at which what was specially true of a later date has been thrown back on an earlier. The worst evil of such a eunuch régime was that it lurked in the background and could not be fully detected or controlled. The mischief went further down than the higher or more influential offenders. There were hordes of court cooks, court tailors, court barbers—all eating up the public revenues if not engaged in anything worse. Julian, with his fine instincts for order and decency, tried valiantly to prune away this evil growth, with some immediate success. But it is hard to exterminate vermin from their chosen haunts, and Julian worked no lasting good.

The picture that we have drawn of the Civil Service of the late Empire is no pleasing one. We have depicted it as overgrown, imperfectly efficient, devoted to special selfish class interests, tyrannical to its clients, the general public. We have just seen how Julian at one of its worst points tried to reform it. It may be said without fear of contradiction that men both feared and loathed it. Government had become something to be dreaded, to be avoided as far as possible. It was no longer felt as anything that belonged to the people ; it was something alien that threatened and oppressed— something not so very unlike the invading barbarians ; they too took all that they could get—and what better off were you when all was given ? We should like to know how much protest these

undoubted evils provoked. Unfortunately, there are few independent observers who speak to us from the time. Our best
witness is Ammianus Marcellinus, that admirable soldier who
towards the end of his career took up the pen in place of the sword.
Reading him carefully we can form our own judgments.

But if things were as bad as this, was there no one in high circles
who could see the possible danger likely to arise and attempt reform
before it was too late ? If we read in the pages of the ' Codex
Theodosianus ', we cannot escape the impression that there was
some sincerity behind all the protestations of the wisdom, clemency
and justice of the Emperor. After all, he was trying to perform a
tremendous task—and that alone makes for sincerity. I think that
we must conclude that the main fault on the imperial side was a lack
of understanding of the real causes of evils. When violent punishments are threatened against evil-doers, the intention is not purely
vindictive ; it seems essential to banish at all costs what is so detrimental to the public interest. But it is of no use to thunder out
judgments, if you cannot identify the guilty. Diocletian was certain
that the rise of prices against which he issued his edict *de maximis
pretiis* was the direct result of extreme wickedness and greed. We
can understand him ; it is only the natural effect of such vexations
on the temper. But, in that case, there were certainly economic
causes which were really to be blamed and should have been
sought out for cure. It was perhaps a well-meant, but ill-judged
measure of Diocletian himself that had precipitated the last rise
of prices.

Abuses in the official mints were very common ; the baseness of
the coinage began very near home. Remedy was sought in savage
punishments ; but the frequent repetition of such inflictions proves
that they were not very effective. There is difficulty in enforcing
the government's regulations about the calling in of old coinage and
the prohibition against selling coins as merchandise. Again,
violent abuse and prohibition. There were clearly economic
factors involved which should have been dealt with first. The
trouble was that government would never admit that it might be
wrong about its first assumptions. Men are continually fleeing
from the *curiae*. Everything is done to block the ways of escape ;
punishments are multiplied ; it is ensured that not many shall
escape, that very, very few shall have any benefit from it if they do.
What government will not do is to admit that its policy of tax
collection may be wrong ; it will not do anything to make the
burden that rests on the senators less intolerable. Government is
eternally denouncing abuses in the mints and in connection with the

coinage. Threats and fury, savage punishments, but never an attempt to find out what was really wrong. The state of the mints, by the by, must really have been very bad; the anonymous author who suggested reforms to Valentinian and Valens can find no better remedy for mint abuses than to place all moneyers on one island where at least the contagion of their defilements cannot spread. The taxpayer is persecuted all along the line. It never occurs to the authorities that what he really needs is not more bullying—but a little rest.

Professor Alföldi, in his recent study of the reign of Valentinian I, has painted in vivid colours the corruptions of the life of the times and the savage repression that they called forth. He has also shown how the Emperor cherished noble plans of reform. There is the remarkable story of the praetorian prefect, Probus. The Emperor trusted him fully and put him in charge of the great district of Illyricum. Under the administration of Probus the taxes came in and so did the customary addresses of compliments and congratulation from cities within his jurisdiction. But on one occasion the spokesman of one of these addresses, who was personally known to the Emperor, contrived by his tone to convey some doubts about the sincerity of the address. Valentinian asked him point-blank whether the compliments were really intended. ' My people paid them ', replied the spokesman, ' with weeping and gnashing of teeth.' Deeply shocked, Valentinian pressed his enquiries and found to his horror that many of his former acquaintance were either dead or in prison. Probus fell into disgrace, but the Emperor's death intervened to save him. Here we have one case of the Emperor being brought face to face with flagrant, undeniable wrong. It is to the credit of Valentinian that he recoiled with horror ; he did not like the things that had been done in his name. But what was the right answer ? As long as the Emperor demanded that his praetorian prefects should bring him in more than the provinces could properly pay, there was no way out but by extortion. Probably here, as in most other similar cases, radical and intelligent reform might have produced a cure. Economies of inessentials would have made it possible to provide without disaster for essentials. But such reforms demanded a fine conscience on the part of the Emperor and a steady support from public opinion. Sometimes one was present, sometimes the other—seldom the two together. What made the situation hopeless was the pressure of the barbarians on the frontiers. An empire, already seriously embarrassed within, was continually being subjected to these strains and stresses from without. But perhaps this is only an excuse, not

the real reason ; perhaps the Empire, even if not harassed by barbarians, might still have failed to find the energy to reform itself.
It all depends on how seriously we estimate the decline of morality
and worth in the late Empire.   If we take the extreme view of
Otto Seeck, we shall see a world declining in culture and intelligence and falling victim more and more to its own worst elements.
If that diagnosis is correct, the disease was really deadly.   Christianity, it must be admitted, did little to minister to the diseases of
the State.   It was too busy settling its own doctrinal disputes.   It
must occur to every careful observer, whether he be Christian or not,
that the energy of the Church might have been better spent on
reforming the worst abuses.   Perhaps it was easier to hold Councils.

The Emperor of the early days had been in an extraordinary
position—a new magistrate with abnormal powers, the centre of all
authority, commander-in-chief, head of the State religion, guardian
of the people's rights.   Everything depended on his personality ;
he had to choose and make his own systems.   What chanced if he
happened to be unequal to his own task ?   Serious duties fell by
default to unsuitable people.   The Emperor played the rogue or
fool and let his responsibilities go to rack and ruin.   As the system
solidified, as more and more was carried on from reign to reign, and
became, if not law, regular form, the evils of bad Emperors were
much mitigated.   Much of the government now ran itself on the
lines once laid down.   There was no need of continued decisions
from the Emperor.   To sum up, the system counts for more and
more, the individual character of the Emperor for less and less.   In
the 4th century this process reaches its natural end.   The Emperor
is as much autocratic or even more ;   he is the glorious head of the
colossal system—but he is on the way to becoming a figurehead.
As a symbol of the omnipotent State he is unchallenged.   But how
much individual choice was left to him ?   We shall see in the next
chapter how he became the prisoner of his military chiefs, how they
practically deprived him of all freedom of movement.   In a lesser
degree, he must have been the prisoner of the heads of his Civil
Service, tied by all the red tape of the time, hampered by weight of
precedent, forced to rely on advice of officials by the enormous mass
and complexity of the business he must transact.   It was an age of
serfdom, and the Emperor, like the humblest serf, was *glebae
adscriptus*, bound to his own sod.

This chapter has been much taken up with detail ;   but, in such
a case, on detail depends our judgment on matters of vital moment to
the whole character of the Empire.

CHAPTER VI

THE ROMAN ARMY

Rome rose to greatness, not by the path of philosophy and science, but by that of political wisdom and war—of war in the first place. The Roman army, therefore, was always one of the vital factors. In the early days it was an army of citizens, of farmers who left the plough to wield the sword for their country. But, as the Empire spread abroad outside Italy, these emergency levies became unsuitable for their purpose. The State was not well served, when she had to keep on raising fresh armies for campaigns that followed one another almost without interruption, and the farmer found it more and more intolerable to have his life divided between the harvest field and the camp. The natural solution was only reached near 100 B.C., when the great captain, Marius, recruited his army from volunteers without regard for their census qualifications. He was certainly only making a rule of what had already been done in special cases before. From this time we meet armies of a new kind, armies drawn largely from the dregs of civil society, tolerably loyal to the commander from whom they expect everything—pay and rewards after campaigns—but very dubiously loyal to the State. It was these armies, together with their ambitious commanders, that overthrew the Republic. The last of the civil wars, beginning with Mutina and going on to Actium, had swelled the already swollen numbers. Octavian after Actium found himself with something over sixty legions, his own or Antony's, on his hands. Their claims were not of the kind that could safely be kept waiting. What was Octavian to do with them? On the answer to this question the most fateful issues depended.

Let us first sketch the problem as it confronted Octavian and then briefly describe his solutions. There were more troops under arms than could well be retained. The army must be reduced to reasonable proportions. At the same time, it must be kept up to its responsibilities ; it must be able to defend the frontiers, to maintain peace in the provinces within the Empire, in rare cases to take the offensive. It must as far as possible be eliminated from politics—not allowed to bully its general into unwise concessions or to intrude its influence on political decisions. The answers that Octavian found were perhaps as wise as any human brain could have devised. He reduced the army to something like a half its strength, pensioning off the discharged men. Having to decide between voluntary enlistment and conscription he deliberately chose the former. Not that conscription was or ever could be abolished ; according to Roman ideas, the duty to serve the State with one's life was one of the primary ones that could not be evaded. But conscription was only used in times of special emergency, such as invasion of Italy. For the ordinary supply of troops the State took recruits as they offered themselves, and the supply seems at first to have been adequate. Even an army of conscripts has to be paid and fed. How much more important to pay and feed when the men have to be invited to the service ! Octavian (or Augustus, as we may now begin to call him) decided at once on fixed rates of pay and length of service, with a pension at the end. The terms offered might not be over-generous, but at least they could be known in advance. The legions, as reduced in number by Augustus, were obviously inadequate for all the needs of the Empire. But Augustus had his remedy near at hand. He developed the forces of allies, already often employed by the Roman Republic, into a second branch of the service, nearly equal to the legions in number and not far behind them in efficiency. All these troops, legionaries and auxiliaries, took the oath of allegiance directly to the Emperor, their Commander-in-Chief—only indirectly to the State through him. The Emperor also held in his own hands all army appoint-

---

LEGIONS AND THEIR HEADQUARTERS (see map opposite)

Britain
II Augusta (Isca Silurum = Caerleon)
VI Victrix (Eboracum = York)
XX Valeria Victrix (Deva = Chester)

Lower Germany
I Minervia (Bonna = Bonn)
XXX Ulpia Victrix (Vetera = Xanten)

Upper Germany
XXII Primigenia (Moguntiacum = Mainz)
VIII Augusta (Argentoratum = Strassburg)

Pannonia
X Gemina (Vindobona = Vienna)
XIV Gemina (Carnuntum = Petronell)
I Adiutrix (Brigetio, nr. Komorn)
II Adiutrix (Aquincum, nr. Budapest)

Upper Moesia
IV Flavia (Singidunum = Belgrade)
VII Claudia (Viminacium = Kostolac)

Dacia
XIII Gemina (Apulum = Karlsburg)

Lower Moesia
I Italica (Novae = Sistof)

XI Claudia (Durostorum = Silistria)
V Macedonica (Troesmis = Iglitza)

Cappadocia
XV Apollinaris (Satala)
XII Fulminata (Melitene)

Syria
XVI Flavia (Samosata)
IV Scythica ⎫
III Gallica ⎬ (nr. Antioch)

Judaea
X Fretensis (Jerusalem)
VI Ferrata (from Syria to Caparcotna, nr. Jerusalem, after 132)

Arabia
III Cyrenaica (Bostra)

Egypt
II Trajana (nr. Alexandria)

Africa
III Augusta (Lambaesis)

Spain
VII Gemina (Legio = Leon)

Not shown on the map are :—
IX Hispana (destroyed in the British revolt between 119 and 122)
XXII Deiotariana (probably destroyed in the Jewish revolt in 132)

Distribution of Legions under Hadrian and his Successors

ments from the least to the greatest. There was to be no question about it ; the Commander-in-Chief must have unchallenged authority.

The legions varied in number from 23 in 27 B.C. to 25 at the end of the reign of Augustus ; after him, there was a slow but steady rise in numbers. The legion was a brigade, complete with all arms of the service—infantry, cavalry, artillery. At full strength it totalled about 5,000 men. The legions were generally stationed in permanent camps on the frontiers, sometimes singly, sometimes two in one camp. There were no legions in Italy, none in the main peaceful provinces. Legionary service was a duty or privilege, call it which you will, of the Roman citizen ; in exceptional cases Roman citizenship was conferred simply to make enrolment possible. Even when the number of the legions rose to 30, the 150,000 men represented were far too few for the needs of a far flung Empire. The auxiliary forces, the *auxilia*, were approximately equal in numbers to the legions ; this balance seems to have been deliberately maintained. Drawn from semi-barbarous peoples on the frontiers, the auxiliaries were often raw troops, but of fine military quality. They were not Roman citizens, but received citizenship after honourable discharge. At first they often served in or near their homes and were commanded by native officers ; but when these arrangements had led to serious dangers in A.D. 69–70, they were changed. It often suited Roman convenience to expend auxiliary blood rather than Roman in action, as auxiliaries were easier to replace and less expensive to train. It is hard to understand why Tacitus should find anything ' glorious ' in this canny economy of Roman soldiers.

The peaceful provinces and Italy saw few regular soldiers. The local militia was at the disposal of the governor, if he needed it ; but it had no serious military value and would only serve such minor purposes as combating brigandage. In Rome and Italy, the Empire could not be without some military support. Augustus developed a praetorian guard—the personal guard of the Republican governor—into a special privileged branch of the service. At first spread out over Italy, the praetorian cohorts were concentrated under Tiberius in one camp, just outside the Colline Gate. They were the unfailing support of the Julio-Claudian dynasty down to Nero and soon began to realise and use—or abuse—their influence. Beside the praetorian guard stood the urban cohorts, under the command of the prefect of the city, a police force of Rome, and the *vigiles*, the night watch, an inferior branch of the service, which, nevertheless, exercised occasional power in the political field. Immediately around his person the Emperor had a bodyguard of Germans. There was no regular central reserve. That must be found, in case of need, in the praetorian guard, which, however, was not really trained or adapted for that purpose. The neglect of the fleet, a gross error, repeated again and again after the most urgent warnings, was to some extent repaired by Augustus. He placed two main fleets on the East and West coasts of Italy, at Ravenna and Misenum, and auxiliary fleets at strategic points in the Empire—on the great rivers, Rhine, Danube, Euphrates, and in the Channel. But the service was still considered inferior to that in the army and was supplied from lower orders of society. And, now as ever, the fleets in peacetime were allowed to fall far below their highest standards of efficiency.

The commander of the legion was the *legatus*, the brigadier, the nominee of the Emperor. Under him were colonels, *tribuni*, of senatorial or equestrian rank, sometimes efficient, sometimes only mechanically following the necessary steps in their official career. Under the tribunes were the centurions, sixty to the legion, one to each century. It was the centurions who made the Roman army what it was. They were often cruel, often mercenary and greedy, but they were almost without exception brave—the custodians of the best traditions of the service. It was on the centurions that the wrath of the privates first fell in cases of mutiny, but it was also the centurions who restored a wavering line or died in defence of the regimental colours. Apart from the centurions there were subordinate officers and special branches of the service, such as the *beneficiarii* (orderlies) and the *evocati* (veterans recalled to the colours under special conditions of service). The army had its own engineers under the *praefecti fabrum* and its own medical army service. The auxiliaries were commanded by prefects of cohorts of infantry and prefects of squadrons of cavalry. The praetorians were under the supreme command of the prefect or prefects of the guard with tribunes and centurions under them. The urban cohorts, under the prefect of the city, had their tribunes and centurions, as also had the *vigiles*, though these were regularly drawn from the freedmen class. The praetorians in the early Empire were a special service, recruited only from Rome and Italy ; but this strictness had gradually to be relaxed. When an army comprising a number of legions or auxiliaries had to be concentrated, the command would be given by the Emperor to a legate, carefully chosen and chosen perhaps for political harmlessness as much as for military efficiency.

Augustus certainly wished to fix conditions of pay and service

that would content his men.   From the first he contributed gener-
ously to the needs of the army from his private resources.   In A.D.
6 he established the special military chest, the *aerarium militare*, with
its own revenues allotted to it and the special task of arranging for the
pay and pensions of the troops.   At the death of Augustus the pay
of the legions was ten Asses a day ;   after his death, the legions
mutinied to obtain a denarius, 16 Asses.   What Pliny the Elder
means when he tells us that in the soldier's pay a denarius was
always given for ten Asses is a mystery.   As a matter of fact, the
whole question of Roman army pay is obscure.   In the times of
Polybius, *c.* 150 B.C., it was two obols, which probably means four
Asses a day.   We might expect the figure to be raised to about six
and a half Asses when the As sank to being a sixteenth of a denarius.
Julius Caesar is reported to have doubled the pay.   As the soldier
had to pay out of his allowance for food and clothing, he cannot
have been very well off.   To judge more exactly we should have to
know just what was provided and what had to be paid for and how
liberally the soldiers were treated when it came to charging them
for food and equipment.   It is unfortunately quite certain that the
gallant centurions levied a regular tax on the privates at their
mercy.   Service was fixed at a normal twenty years, but the
exigencies of the service kept many worn-out veterans with the
colours much longer than that.   Upon discharge, the veteran
received a pension on a fairly generous scale ;   but the value of the
gift might be much reduced, if the lands allotted were in some dreary
swamp or on some waste mountainside.   The praetorians enjoyed
higher pay, two denarii a day, and only twelve years' service.   The
prestige of the corps stood supreme—even if the frontier armies
might growl that the prestige was undeserved.   Of the military
gods, Honos and Virtus, prestige and valour, Virtus was common
to all branches, Honos was peculiarly the guardian spirit of the
guard at Rome.   Urban legions and *vigiles* ranked below the
praetorians, but above the legionaries.   The fleets, as we have
already noted, tended to be neglected.   The men need not be
Roman citizens ;   they were largely recruited from such districts
as Dalmatia with its population inured to the sea.   The chief
command, the prefecture, might even be given to a freedman.   No
Mahan had yet arisen to call attention to the possibilities of sea
power.   The fleet of Misenum might find its chief activity in
carrying a Nero to and fro between pleasure resorts on the south-
west coasts of Italy.   The stupid contempt of the Romans for the
sea has to be carefully observed to be believed.   Under the Empire
it continued tu cost them dear.   When the Goths in force invaded

the lands round the Aegean in the 250's and 260's, their raids might have been nipped in the bud by an efficient navy—but it was not there and the Goths knew that it was not. Our British Emperor, Carausius, when he revolted with the Channel Fleet, was able to survive for some seven years and inflict at least one decisive defeat on the central Empire.

Let us now try to form an idea of what life in the army was like. We can draw a fairly clear line of division between the quiet times of peace and the stirring times of war.

In time of peace the legions were stationed in permanent camps, round which grew up civilian settlements (*canabae*), in which the soldiers could live with their concubines ; marriage was not permitted before Septimius Severus. Children born in the camp could not become Roman citizens, until, as usually happened, they themselves enlisted. In the East the soldiers often lived in the cities, formed marriage connections with the local people and grew soft and unfit for war. The life was a round of fatigues, guard duty, drill, physical training and route marches. But the soldiers might be employed on more ambitious projects, such as the building of roads, forts or canals. Some generals tried to win glory for themselves by such adventures, which were resented by the troops as unnecessary encroachments on their ease. One Emperor, Probus, was murdered by his troops for thus over-exerting them. Army food was simple—a porridge made from pulse, soup, bread, lard, vinegar, vegetables, etc., and a little wine. Meat was not relished, and, when no other food was available, the soldiers bitterly resented it. For this food, as well as for arms, clothes and tents, the soldier himself had to pay. It tells us much about the high purchasing power of money that something was left over for social clubs and burial societies and even for saving. The centurions and officers of course were paid on a higher scale.

In time of war, it was quite different—a matter of marching, camping, fighting and looting. The line of march (*agmen*) was commonly formed thus—cavalry in front, on flanks and in rear, legions and baggage in the centre. In circumstances of great difficulty and danger the army marched in a hollow square, enclosing its baggage and ready to fight on any side. A fortified camp was laid out each night, with ditch and mound about it, roads crossing it at right angles and the headquarters in the centre. In battle the usual form of arrangement was one in three lines (*triplex acies*) ; in the 2nd century, the solid block of the phalanx was again introduced. The auxiliaries fought in their native style, often in wedges or blocks.

The chief items in the soldiers' dress were tunic, military cloak and military boots (*caligae*). For defensive armour he had his breastplate of leather, probably backed by metal. He would also wear helmet and greaves. For offensive armour he had his casting javelin (*pilum*), his thrusting sword (*gladius*), his dagger in his belt—occasionally a long lance. The auxiliaries mostly had their spear and long sword (*spatha*).

Military rewards were numerous—bracelets, torques or metal discs (*phalerae*) for common soldiers, and the *corona civica*, the ancient V.C., for saving the life of a comrade ; for higher officers, there were crowns, spears and flags ; for the general, in case of notable success, the ornaments of triumph. Punishments were severe, going from flogging to dishonourable discharge and even the death penalty. A regiment that had disgraced itself might be ' decimated '—each tenth man beaten to death. In less extreme cases it might be ordered to camp outside the camp wall—a position of dishonour and, possibly, of danger.

The fighting quality of the troops was high, much higher in the West than in the East. In the early Empire their superiority in training and tactics normally sufficed to make good great numerical inferiority. But later, when all the chief innovations in fighting came from outside the Empire—heavy cavalry from the East, archers from Osrhoene, Moorish javelin throwers—this advantage was largely lost and, as the barbarian element in the army grew, there was little difference between those who fought for and against Rome.

What of the Roman generals ? They were usually competent, seldom remarkably brilliant ; but, with the material at their disposal, competence usually sufficed. The victory of Suetonius Paulinus over Boudicca's rebels in enormous numerical superiority shows what general and legions could do together.

How much good there was in the arrangements of Augustus is sufficiently proved by the fact that they lasted so long substantially unchanged. But several serious criticisms of them could be made. In the first place, Augustus budgeted for too small an army. He no doubt knew, as we cannot know, the difficulties of finding the men and money for more legions. But there was something seriously wrong when the whole Empire could be seriously embarrassed by a single local disaster, such as the destruction of the three legions of Varus. The legions were fully taken up with the defence of the most exposed frontiers ; they had not many men to spare for occasional service in the peaceful provinces. In the case of really serious trouble on any one frontier, reinforcements could only be drawn piecemeal from other frontiers. There was no army ready to take the offensive, in case an extension of the frontier were decided on. It may or may not have been wise for Augustus to suspend, for Tiberius to abandon, the scheme for the conquest of Germany up to the Elbe. But the real reason for the abandonment—shortage of men—is a bad reason ; the Empire should have had men enough for all necessary services. But this is not an argument for a jingoistic policy.

But more than most armies the Roman army performed the function of guardian of the peace, which was best served by its maintenance at a high level. The aversion to military service among the subject people had nothing to do with high ideals ; it was simply a natural preference of a people beginning to grow soft. Augustus undoubtedly chose restriction of numbers as the lesser of two evils. Soldiers in masses about the Empire might be not a protection only, but an explosive—a threat to the legitimate Emperor, a temptation to the ambitious subject. Augustus tried, by keeping the army on the lowest scale consistent with security, to minimise a danger that could not be eliminated.

This leads us on to a second criticism closely connected with our first. The defence of the Empire was almost purely static—legions and auxiliaries on the frontiers, praetorians and urban troops in Rome—no real link between the two, no central strategic reserve. On military grounds, the arguments in favour of such a reserve are overwhelming. It was, strictly speaking, a sheer necessity, and a heavy price had often to be paid for neglect of it. We may be assured that the political arguments against it were even more convincing than the military ones for it. A strong reserve in or near Italy would have been an irresistible temptation to the greedy adventurer. Augustus chose to reduce the political danger at the sacrifice of military efficiency. The fact that the Empire was held by the one Julio-Claudian House down to Nero may blind us to the real hazards involved. But the early Emperors never felt themselves secure.

Despite the general principle laid down by Augustus—that the Empire should be kept within its boundaries—additions were made from time to time—Britain, Dacia, Arabia—and the number of legions rose to answer the growing need. By the time of Trajan the number had risen to thirty. The centre of gravity too had shifted. The Rhine at first and for some long time was undoubtedly the most vital frontier. Then attention had to be shifted to the Danube. By the reign of Trajan the shift of emphasis is clear ; legions have to be transferred from one river to the other. There

L

was a new front created in Britain, a new front in Cappadocia. Spain lost all but one of its legions and became almost as much a peaceful province as the neighbouring Gaul.

Turning now to the developments after Augustus, we learn by the way how his system worked out in practice. Tiberius made it a principle to be loyal to all that Augustus had laid down. The mutinies at the beginning of his reign, in Pannonia and Germany, forced him to grant extra pay and reduced terms of service ; but the concessions were extorted under duress and were withdrawn as soon as it appeared safe to do so. The cautious conservatism of Tiberius allowed the improvisations of his predecessor to harden into established rules. The crazy Caligula might have demoralised the army had he lasted longer, but he was gone before he could do much harm. Claudius is more important. He went back to the offensive and conquered Britain. In the Empire at large he encouraged his legates to be active, building roads and bridges, if there were no fighting campaigns, and he earned more acclamations as ' Imperator ' than any other Emperor except Augustus. The reign of Nero was in a military sense not inglorious. He ended a serious war with Parthia by a very satisfactory compromise and broke the dangerous revolts of the Britons and the Jews. But he did what no member of his House had done before him : he forfeited the loyalty of the praetorian guard, first by his crimes, then by his fatal indecision, and he created widespread discontent in the legions by striking down their most distinguished generals. After him, the relation of the Emperor to his armies had to be restated and redefined. The civil wars that followed the death of Nero revealed new dangers and new problems. As Tacitus has expressed it in a memorable phrase, ' an Emperor can be made outside Rome ', by a provincial army as well as by the praetorian guard. Otho, of course, owed even more to the guard than the Julio-Claudians had done ; he and they had shared in a ghastly crime and must stand or fall together. Galba had lost the support of the guard by a parsimony that might sound honourable, but was certainly undiplomatic. Vitellius at the head of his German legions, the premier corps of the army, rewarded their victory over Otho with admission to the hitherto closed guard. Vespasian, raised up against Vitellius by his Eastern legions, won complete victory by land and sea, over foes foreign and intestine. He founded the Empire afresh, on the basis already designed by Augustus but now re-established. The guard was again reserved for Roman citizens from Italy or the near provinces. Its loyalty had still to be secured by a donative, but that was limited in extent and lay within the Emperor's discretion. Vespasian, a distinguished soldier himself, with a son, Titus, also of approved merit, restored the imperial prestige and won the loyalty of the troops for his new imperial house.

One or two minor details may be noted. Otho, finding the privates of the guard distressed by the extortions of their centurions, and being unwilling to vex the centurions by curtailing their gains, paid the sums that they demanded out of his own *fiscus*, and this expedient worked so well that it became a part of army discipline for the future. The legions came to be recruited more widely from the provinces. The auxiliaries were no longer employed near their homes, nor so readily entrusted to native officers. The dangers of these practices had been exposed when the Batavians revolted under Civilis and drew a large part of Gaul after them, to create a separate *imperium Galliarum*. Domitian was a great fighter, partly by choice, as when he regulated affairs on the Middle Rhine and curbed the powerful tribe of the Chatti in a series of hard but not unproductive campaigns, partly by hard necessity, as when he had to endure long and dubious fights with Sarmatians, Suebians and the Dacians on the Danube. The complete conquest of Britain, apparently a design dear to Vespasian and Titus, was abandoned just when it seemed about to be realised. Domitian was popular with the army and not without cause, for he raised the soldier's pay by a third. The guard at Rome, helpless for the moment when he fell, avenged his death a year later. Nerva had to submit to the indignity of surrendering the murderers of Domitian to them. But he soon restored the damaged imperial dignity by adopting the darling of the army, the great Trajan, as his son. The mutineers were overcome by a mixture of subtlety and force.

The Empire had too long been standing on the defensive. Trajan reverted to the idea of the offensive. It was time to show the world that Rome had not lost the capacity for vigorous action. Decebalus of Dacia, who had defied Domitian in a series of bloody campaigns and had extorted a not unfavourable peace from him, was broken and destroyed in two terrible wars. A new Roman Dacia was erected on the wreck of the old native state. Arabia was incorporated in the Empire without serious resistance. Finally Trajan turned to grandiose schemes of Eastern conquest. He would settle the Parthian question once and for all by making Parthia a client state and advancing the Roman frontiers far to the East. Like a second Alexander the Great he penetrated as far as the Red Sea and reported to a wondering Senate victories over peoples whose names had never been heard. But the strain of these campaigns, aggravated by the widespread revolts of the Jews following them, forced him to abandon his more ambitious programmes. The new Eastern provinces that he had added to the Empire, Mesopotamia and Assyria, were at once abandoned by his successor, Hadrian. Tacitus thoroughly approved of the new manifestation of Roman valour by Trajan. But there can be no doubt that he overstrained Rome's resources. His acquisition of Dacia proved to be of doubtful value. It was the first of the provinces to be abandoned when the great crisis of the 3rd century struck Rome. In the East the case is even clearer. Trajan tried to go too far. If we ask why the Jews chose that moment to revolt, when the Emperor was present in person with a large army, the answer can only be that Roman resources were so overstrained that enemies of the Empire could not fail to see it. Hadrian was a man of peace, in the sense that he gave up the Eastern acquisitions of Trajan and went back to the defensive. But he was no pacifist. His peace depended on the highest standards of courage and efficiency in his troops. He took the greatest interest in them on all his travels, reviewed them at their exercises and found occasion to criticise or praise. It is curious to find him encouraging local pride in the provincial armies. His coins celebrate the great armies of the Empire by name, ' Germanicus ', ' Britannicus ', ' Dacicus ', ' Syriacus '. What pleased Hadrian probably shocked most Romans. We hear no more of such sectional interests for many a long year after his death

The immense majesty of the Roman peace stood almost unquestioned through the long reign of the gentle Antoninus Pius. But troubles soon followed after his death, whether or not they were caused by his too great gentleness. A serious conflict with Parthia had to be settled in a series of hard campaigns that required the presence of one Emperor, Lucius Verus, colleague of Marcus Aurelius. More dangerous was the new threat to Italy from the Marcomanni and Quadi on the Danube. The philosopher Emperor had to spend his declining years in camp, warding off the immediate danger and building sure defences for the future. Had Marcus only lived one or two years more, he would probably have secured a frontier that would have held for generations. But his young son, Commodus, who succeeded him, chose to patch up an easy peace and return to the enjoyments of Rome, thus sacrificing much of what his father had by hard effort won. Commodus reverted to the example of a Caligula or a Nero. The imperial power was a dear prize, to be used for the expression of the Emperor's personality in every form, good or evil, while imperial responsibilities were either left to deputies—praetorian prefects and chamberlains—or neglected altogether. This gross neglect of duty by Commodus led to changes, just as marked, but less beneficent than those produced by the judicious measures of good Emperors. The provincial armies began to nourish rivalries and express political opinions. Desertion became so common that a certain Maternus could stir up a war of deserters, which culminated in a serious threat to the person of the Emperor himself. The guard was demoralised by witnessing the degeneracy of a gladiator Emperor and by being subjected to a series of many prefects, appointed by Commodus out of fear and mistrust.

When Commodus at last met his doom, the way had been prepared for the second series of civil wars, which almost disrupted the Empire. Pertinax, the old general of Marcus, who succeeded to the empty throne, strove in vain to recover the good old standards of Marcus and restore order and dignity. The praetorians could not brook lawful authority. After several abortive attempts to set up a rival Emperor, they murdered Pertinax in his palace. Rebels without a leader, they were reduced to putting up the Empire for auction to the highest bidder. A distinguished senator, Didius Julianus, was ill advised enough to purchase the perilous honour at the price of 30,000 sestertii per man. But the guard was not in a position to deliver the goods for which it had taken the price. Now, as after the death of Nero, the armies of the Provinces took a hand in the game. It was the Pannonian army with its nominee, Septimius Severus, that finally triumphed over the Syrians with their Pescennius Niger and the Britons and Gauls with their Clodius Albinus. The praetorians were disgraced and dismissed the service. Septimius enrolled a new guard from the élite of his own troops ; but he also took the precaution of placing one of his new legions, the 2nd Parthica, on the Alban Mount.

Septimius was an African by birth ; he had gone through a distinguished senatorial career and had shown his ambition by marrying a Syrian princess, Julia Domna, who was reputed to have an imperial horoscope. He was a great general, a skilled intriguer, a man sure of himself and his purposes. But he was a disastrous Emperor for Rome and did more harm in his not very long reign than many of the worst monsters on the throne. In order to secure the unquestioning loyalty of his troops, he indulged and spoilt them. There certainly was a rise in pay, but we cannot define its exact amount. He allowed soldiers to live in quarters with their lawful wives, instead of forming irregular connexions which were only made legal after discharge. This seems to us very reasonable, but it was regarded as a relaxation of discipline. The life of the soldier

was made easier and more lucrative.   In the course of the civil wars
Septimius formed out of confiscated properties a new fund, the
res privata, which he used mainly to pamper the army.   He himself
followed out in full the advice that he gave to his sons on his deathbed, ' enrich the soldiers ; despise the rest of the world '.   For the
first time in the history of the Empire, the army was acknowledged
to be master rather than servant.   The evil crop sown by Septimius
took some time to mature.   Caracalla, by the murder of his
brother Geta, lost all sympathies in Rome and had to throw himself
on the mercy of his army.   Macrinus, the praetorian prefect who
succeeded Caracalla, did not last long ; he was overthrown by a
cunning intrigue, backed by the wealth of the royal house of
Emesa.   And so the dynasty of Septimius returned in the person
of the handsome, immoral young priest, Elagabalus.   This dis-
solute enthusiast was too much for Rome to tolerate for long, but
the dynasty was still saved by being transferred to a better cousin
of Elagabalus.   The gentle Severus Alexander reigned for thirteen
not inglorious years, but the army had now to be spoilt the whole
time.   Alexander was finally murdered in a military mutiny in
Gaul, because of the miserliness of his mother, Julia Mammaea,
we are told.   That sentence speaks volumes ; the troops, already
fattened out of the *res privata*, still grumbled because the entire contents
of the chest were not placed at their disposal.

The evil harvest was now ripe.   The new Emperor Maximin,
created by the mutineers, was a rough barbarian, a giant in strength,
a child in culture, a devoted soldier, but with a marked distaste for
all society above him.   The system of Septimius was working out
to its logical development—a spoilt rebellious army with an Emperor
to match them.   The policy of Maximin was to fight the barbarians
and plunder his own civilian population for the benefit of the army.
But the State was not yet reduced to such abject submission.   A
more or less accidental revolt in Africa led to the appointment of
two new Emperors, the Gordians, against Maximin.   The Senate
at once declared in their favour and, when they were speedily suppressed, took up the cause itself and appointed two Emperors of
its own, Balbinus and Pupienus.   Now came one of the surprises
of Roman history.   Maximin, rushing back from the frontiers to
take a quick revenge, was held up at Aquileia at the North-East
gate of Italy and after vexatious delays was murdered by his own
men.   It was a resounding victory for the Senate.   The world was
not yet ready for an Emperor and army that would openly defy the
old guardian of constitutionalism.   Perhaps this triumph of the
Senate gave Rome a short respite.   Under Gordian III and Philip

something like the old Empire still remained. Trajan Decius even tried to repeat the achievement of Trajan. But the way was now open for the military anarchy which was the logical result of the evil policy of Severus. If the praetorian guard was no longer as troublesome as it had been, that was only because the provincial armies often took the decision out of its hands. It became almost the rule that an Emperor should die by the hands of his own men. Statistics of the 3rd century show very few cases of natural death, one death on the field of battle, one in foreign captivity, many and many by the hands of men or officers, or by ' lightning '— which seems to have been a polite way of describing a murder that could be suspected but not proved. The premium on life insurance policies for an Emperor would have been exceedingly high.

Several features of this new age may be noted. The soldier gained in position and pay. He received the golden ring of the knight, as soon as he reached the rank of centurion. His life in camp was easier, softer than before. And, above all this, he began to throw his sword into the political scales and naturally expected some special reward if his candidate for Empire won. It may be assumed that the fighting quality of the army was not improved by these changes. The military career began to be distinguished sharply from the civil. The senators gradually withdrew from the higher military commands, which had been given them by Augustus, and were replaced by knights. The way in which this began to happen was probably by appointment of deputies to act for their senatorial superiors. By the reign of Gallienus senators were definitely excluded from the army command. It fitted well into the new age in which the Emperor, depending on the army, no longer necessarily cultivated friendly relations with the Senate. As the Empire began to descend into the valley of the shadow some reforms, long needed, were at last undertaken. The garrison of Rome was reinforced by the legion on the Alban Mount, and in North Italy at Mediolanum (Milan) or Ticinum (Pavia) the nucleus of a central reserve, consisting mainly of cavalry, was established. We have coins of the mint of Milan, celebrating the concord, loyalty and valour of the ' knights '. In the legions the Roman and Italian element was declining ; in the auxiliaries the element of pure barbarism was on the increase. Such new methods of fighting as became known were either barbarian or Eastern (Persian) in origin.

As soon as we begin to look for patterns in history, we are likely to recognise those that are familiar to us in our own time. This is legitimate enough—only we must be prepared to note what does not correspond as well as what does.   Today many students cannot look at a period of history without finding traces of a class war in it. So it has been in the 3rd century of the Roman Empire.   A great Russian scholar, Michael Rostovtseff, has invited us to see in the military anarchy that we have been discussing a veritable class war—the soldiers (the ' Reds '), as representatives of the pro-letariat, against the bourgeoisie, the lazy and comfortable civilians. Rostovtseff wrote earnestly from deep knowledge and sincere con-viction.   And yet his thesis breaks down at the first careful examina-tion.   It is quite impossible to show any solidarity of interests between the soldiers and the poor of the land and the cities.   The soldiers were out on their own quests against all civilians, rich and poor alike.   The fact is, there was little awareness of economic law in antiquity.   Obviously some men had the natural advantage, many more lacked it.   But people could pass from one class to another ; you were not predestined or fore-ordained to be either exploiter or exploited.   Even today the analysis of the great Marx is beginning to appear over-simple—as indeed it is.   The most obvious forms of exploitation are not the only ones.   We are seeing today how the mass of indifferently efficient and busy workers can combine to thwart the efforts of their more skilled brethren and stop them from working or earning as they could.   And there is another point.   The behaviour of that curious thing, money, from commodity to circulating medium, from that on to treasure, has never been, is still not fully understood.   The banker has a shrewd idea how to handle it for his own advantage, but who will admit that his advantage is necessarily always that of the com-munity at large ?   If sins have been and are committed in the economic sphere, they are far more often sins of ignorance than the Marxian theory allows.   In any case, the Roman army of the 3rd century was not a champion of Marxian doctrine.   It was a caste in the State, raised to a position in which it could exploit its fellows and mercilessly follow up its advantages.   Where we do find some-thing like modern Bolshevism, it is in quite a different direction— for example, in the distressed down-and-outs (the ' Bagaudae ') in Gaul towards the end of the century.   Their operations were definitely levelled against society as it stood, for the dispossessed against the propertied classes.   Like all ancient movements of the kind, they were condemned from the start to failure ; they attacked with insufficient forces along a front vastly too large.

The crisis of the Empire, as we have seen, came in the reign of Gallienus, when his father, Valerian, had been taken prisoner by the Persians, when the West revolted under Postumus, when almost every province threw up its pretender and the whole economic system collapsed under the strain. A succession of distinguished soldiers, following Gallienus, checked the rot and began to climb the steep path of recovery. Rome was still strong, had still good reserves and was not going to collapse under the first heavy blow. The military anarchy was not yet at an end, but there were signs of its clearing. The general staff, we might say, was beginning to make itself felt as against the unco-ordinated demands of single army groups. Out of the band of high staff officers, Pannonian by birth, came the great line of restorers of the world—Claudius who smote the Goths, Aurelian who recovered the East from Palmyra and the West from the Gallic Empire, Probus who restored the Rhine frontier and re-established peace, and his successor Carus who conducted a vigorous offensive against Persia. There could be no return to the old rules. The Senate no longer counted for much. It was consulted after the murder of Aurelian and asked to nominate his successor ; the army was for the moment sick of the officers who had murdered him. But this did not last long. Carus simply announced his accession to the Senate, without asking in the traditional way for its approval. The senators did not return to their high commands. On the other hand, the generals were no longer willing to be puppets, pulled this way or that by lawless privates. Aurelian, when his troops reminded him that he owed his throne to them, declared that he ruled by the divine grace of the Sun God. There is already a hint of Diocletian here.

If we look at the reforms of Diocletian as a whole, we get the impression of a man of towering genius, able to rethink and reshape almost every aspect of the State. A great man he certainly was, but there are two reasons why we tend to overestimate his personal contribution to Roman problems. Firstly, we attribute to Diocletian reforms spread over a long period which lasts well down into the reign of Constantine the Great. But, even more important, much of what Diocletian marked with the stamp of authority had already been in course of evolution during the 3rd century. Diocletian did not invent all his reforms ; he found some of them already more or less experimentally in use, recognised their value and established them as norms. The army must continue to be the basis of imperial authority, but it must be deprived of its worst powers of mischief. Diocletian reduced the size of the legions and increased their numbers. The troops could be more easily controlled in small divisions. The distinction between frontier and field army was made clear. On the frontiers stood militia, of little military value, but simply a watch on the spot. The main forces of the Empire, the *palatini* and *comitatenses*, were kept near the persons of the Emperors, ready to accompany them wherever they went.   The old praetorian guard disappeared for ever after the fall of Maxentius in 312.   To the legionary of the 3rd century the Emperor had been a *commilito*, a comrade to be cheered and supported as long as he was good, but to be removed if he ceased to satisfy expectations.   Diocletian changed all this.   He adopted much of the royal show of the Persian Great King and placed himself and his colleagues under the direct protection of the great god, Jupiter, and his hero son, Hercules.   These measures were effective. The murder of Emperors ceased to be a popular amusement of the army.   There was also a new method of recruiting.   Since all subjects of the Emperor were now equally free—or enslaved— anyone could join the legions—if he wanted.   Diocletian no longer relied on voluntary enlistment.   The military needs of the Empire, like all other needs, were carefully weighed and budgeted for. Each *iugum* (unit of assessment) had to supply so many soldiers.   It was more or less chance that decided who actually served.   If you were rich enough you could buy a substitute.   The law of hereditary succession was applied here as elsewhere.   The son of a soldier was expected to follow his father's profession.   Only by watching at each step that no one escaped could you make the failing manpower go round.

Constantine was a great general of a hard-headed type, a vicious and successful fighter, capable of outdoing his barbarian enemies in savagery.   He was loved by his troops, for he paid them well and did not force their loyalty too far.   But the Empire stood in greater danger than in earlier days.   There was almost continual trouble on Rhine and Danube and, in the East, Persia was such a menace as Parthia had rarely been.   There might be some risk in having a strong field army, but it was now essential if the Empire was to survive.   As a matter of fact, revolts beginning with the *palatini* and *comitatenses* were not common ; the Emperors seem to have succeeded in attaching their guards very closely to their persons. Under Constantius II the threat from Persia became a permanent one.   Civil wars in the West aggravated the danger.   When Magnentius revolted in Gaul and killed Constans, the brother of Constantius, two famous army groups, the Gallic and the Eastern, were brought into collision.   In the decisive battle of Mursa the losses were terrible, for the gallant troops of Magnentius continued to sell their lives dear long after their defeat in the field was certain. A few years later we find that Gaul had almost slipped out of imperial control.   Only by heroic efforts can Julian II win some relief from the invading Germans. This same Julian as Emperor a few years later made one heroic attempt to snatch the initiative from the Persians in the East. The effort was an individual one and it died away at his death.

Valentinian I was a great soldier, devoted to the task of defending his frontiers. What one man could do he did. But the tides of invasion were now flowing with a new force that no human effort could check. New peoples were surging against the defences of Rhine and Danube, and the first whispers were being heard of the coming of the Huns, those terrible little horsemen out of Central Asia. Valentinian did not live long enough to see the disaster. The Goths, hard pressed by the Huns, sought admission as federates within the Empire. Admitted inside and then swindled by imperial officials, they rose in revolt to burn and plunder. At the dreadful battle of Adrianople Valens with the flower of the army of the East was ridden down by the Gothic cavalry. Theodosius patched up the rent, but for a generation the Eastern army was more Gothic than Roman. For nearly a century more the tides continued to rise. The West was slowly engulfed—Britain, Gaul, Spain, Africa ; even Italy hardly escaped. The East escaped as if by a series of miracles and even succeeded at last in breaking the power of its great rival, Persia. The new Byzantine armies that gradually developed were distinguished by new qualities, by no means contemptible, but quite unlike the old Roman. Armies were small, very carefully provisioned and commanded, held back rather than driven into combat and taught to rely more on patience and cunning than on valour for victory. It was an economical and far from unsuccessful mode of warfare.

The question of naked force, however well it may be disguised, is vital to every state. Every government, even the best and most just, must have a final force to appeal to in case of challenge. In a well-ordered state, of course, force is kept in its right place, only used for protection, not for aggression, only called upon in the last resort. Under the Empire the imperial power rested ultimately on the support of the army. Tacitus knew what he was saying when he enunciated the principle that the quality of commander must be special to the Emperor. It was as the ' imperator ', to whom all ranks swore allegiance, that the Emperor could maintain himself at the head of the State. But, as loyalty is never impregnable, as troops can change their allegiance, what assurance had Rome against the anarchy of rival army corps ? The answer is ' none '. Augustus tried to reduce the danger to small proportions ; he could not eliminate it. It only made it worse that

the succession was never regulated according to any one principle.
An Emperor you must have ; the post cannot be left vacant.   But
is he to be a son by blood or a son by adoption of the preceding
Emperor ?   Is his acceptance to depend on the sanction of the
Senate ?   Or is the mere will of the soldiers, if effectually asserted,
enough ?   To all these questions part answers could be given,
based on practice ; there was no worked out, accepted theory.   The
Empire never had a written constitution.   Theodor Mommsen
worked out a theory by which an Emperor could be properly
appointed in either one of two ways.   He could be approved by
the Senate, the guardian of the constitution, to which in every
emergency ' the auspices returned '.   But he could equally properly
be appointed by the Roman people, exercising its ancient, never
surrendered authority, and, as that Roman people was no longer
represented in its ' comitia ', it must now have a new representation
—in the army.   If we ask next, what does ' army ' in this context
mean, we receive the astonishing answer that the army may be
represented by any portion acting for the whole—if only its action
finds approval.   The two privates who undertook to transfer the
Empire from Galba to Otho, and made good their undertaking,
were constitutionally impeccable.   No one will wish to challenge
the great Roman historian and jurist on his own ground.   But the
plain man will continue to regard Mommsen's arguments as no
more than an explanation and apology for military anarchy when
it raises its head.   A lawyer may be retained by a government to
give a legal cover to all its actions.   It does not follow that the
account of such a hired lawyer is the simplest and most accurate
account of what has happened.   No state can be assured of law and
order by a series of military upheavals.   If we began with any
doubts on the subject, the miserable tale of the 3rd century would
remove them.   The peace of the Empire depended on the Emperor's keeping its protector, the army, in order.   If the army
gained the upper hand, something like anarchy ensued.   For it
was not a case of government by a general staff ; that may be bad,
but it is not altogether intolerable.   The army spoke not with one
voice, but with many.   The only sound basis for the early Empire
was the approval of the Senate, sought and granted.   It was a
weakness of the Augustan system that the troops had to swear
allegiance, not to the Roman State, but to the Emperor in person.
No doubt Augustus knew what he was about ; he was not sure
enough of his position to do without this support.   But it would
have been far safer if the troops had owed an allegiance to the State,
which, in the temporary absence of an Emperor, would have meant

to the Senate. The insistence of the Emperor on having the oath taken directly to himself contributed to making the succession insecure.

The army of the Empire was asked to perform a number of varied tasks. It was to defend the frontiers ; it must maintain peace in the provinces ; in case of need, it must be capable of undertaking an offensive against enemies outside. It must uphold the government—the imperial system—against any rival, such as a restoration of the Republic, the reigning Emperor against any possible challenger. If we ask how the army performed these tasks at various periods, we shall have a very good measure of the health or malaise of the State.

The army of the early Empire was a fine fighting force, with its wonderful centurions as its backbone.[1] It suffered its disasters, but they were usually quickly repaired. If it was too fond of loot—and it was—what army is not ?—it kept the peace inside the Empire and protected the frontiers with much success. It was less successful in maintaining the prestige of government. Tiberius on his accession was confronted with serious mutinies ; concessions might be hoped for from the new Emperor, not quite settled in the saddle. The guard was conscious of its power in politics, but it had formed a habit of loyalty to the first imperial house and almost reluctantly departed from it when Nero committed suicide. The provincial armies were only half conscious of their power. It needed the elevation of Galba in Spain to give away that secret of Empire. The Romans still stood apart from the ally ; the legionary service was still a citizen one. The rough valour of backward peoples could be used—but only in their own formations. It might be found advantageous to spare the more precious Roman blood.

The army was probably at its best in the 2nd century under the great conqueror, Trajan, and the great organiser and disciplinarian, Hadrian. Never before or after did the prestige of the Emperor stand quite so high. For a long time peace reigned unchallenged—and not just any peace, but the peace that Rome wanted. When troubles came under Marcus Aurelius the armies did not let him down. Discipline and skill were high ; pretenders were few.

This happy state of things was corrupted by the dereliction of imperial duty by Commodus and the lawless dynastic ambition of Septimius. Septimius might have kept the able Clodius Albinus as his Caesar and heir presumptive ; that was what Rome as a

---

[1] There is some repetition here from Chapter I. But I have thought it better to pick out and repeat those features of history that specially concern the army than simply to refer back to the first chapter.

whole expected. He chose to fight a desperate civil war to get rid of this rival and to put the little Caracalla, and later, Geta, in his place. Caracalla murdered Geta and lived long enough to blot his record at every point. It was for this that Septimius had committed his grievous sin against Rome. He made life too easy for the soldiers and increased their thirst for money. The evil gradually grew to its height. Discipline went by the board. Money was poured out on the soldiers. Emperor after Emperor was murdered by his own men. Any man who could persuade a few soldiers to share in his gamble might throw the dice for Emperor. The fighting quality of his rabble of troops cannot have been formidable. Even in civil wars they showed little steadfastness ; they deserted their Emperors as readily as they made them. In foreign wars the army made a very poor show. Trajan Decius was left to die in the marshes of the Dobrudjska, Valerian fell into Persian captivity, because he could no longer trust his men. It was a time of deep military degradation.

The importance of allies and federates as against legionaries increases. So far as there was any development in the art of war, it was along the lines of barbarians or Persians that it took place. No new idea came out of Roman or Greek circles. Diocletian, here as everywhere else, produced some improvement. What came after him was not the excellence of the early Empire, but at least something better than the corruptions of the 3rd century. The army recovered some degree of efficiency—partly because discipline was restored, partly because the small value of the frontier troops was recognised and attention was paid to raising the standard of the picked army of the centre. It was seldom now that soldiers murdered their commander-in-chief. But there were strict limits to the efficiency of the new army. It was very much at the mercy of chance for its recruitment. The man who was pressed for a soldier and could not buy himself off must serve, but many found substitutes. What sort of way was this of finding effective recruits ? All one can say of it is what one says of the infamous press gang ; it worked after a fashion with an immense amount of friction and suffering. After Diocletian's system had taken root, things improved a little. Military service tended to become hereditary and that might mean that some liking, some aptitude for service was handed on from father to son.

The profession of arms was now balanced against the other imperial *militia*, the Civil Service. The two services stood out in contrast to the mass of subjects of the Emperor. At the head of the army stood the great marshals, the *magistri militum, magistri equitum*, each with his little band of personal retainers, the *buccellarii*, so called because they drew their little ' bits ' from their commanders. They were a little power by themselves. The Emperor, with all his pomp and show, had no such body of readily obedient soldiers at his command. He was therefore condemned to be the prisoner and puppet of his marshals. The occasional Emperor who still showed high spirit usually ended untimely by murder or suicide. It is a mistake to suppose that all the later Emperors were lacking in imperial courage or decision. The fact was that the cards were stacked against them. To make it worse, these masters of the soldiers who bullied them were usually barbarians. They represented the pressure of the barbarians on the civilian population of the Empire, as much to be dreaded in their own way as their wild brethren who, instead of infiltrating into the imperial army from the inside, attacked it from without. We have only to glance at the names of the great generals of the period to see that very many of them were Germans or, later, Goths ; they rose to the highest offices of the State, such as the consulship. If there was any real check on military caprice, it lay in the rivalry between the chief army groups—the Gallic, the Illyrian and the Eastern. The terrible civil war between Constantius II and Magnentius shaped itself largely as a trial of strength between Gaul and the East.

Down to small details the army was becoming barbarised. The Roman soldier was now summoned by those same dragon trumpets that had scared his comrades of old when they sounded out of the Cheruscan woods. All the new arms that were at all useful— the heavy knights in complete armour, the mounted archers, the javelin throwers—were all more or less barbarian. There was no corresponding advance on the Roman side. The art of war did not sufficiently interest the better brains ; they left it, much to their own loss, to the barbarians who loved it. We have one memorandum surviving from the 4th century, addressed to two Emperors (Valentinian I and Valens), in which an ingenious, but not very practical man puts forward a number of suggestions intended to make the defence against the barbarians easier. After reading his devices—some curious, some just absurd—we murmur to ourselves ' *non tali auxilio* '. But his work is at least a reminder that the faculty for inventions was not quite dead or asleep. Later, of course, the Byzantines *did* develop their much dreaded ' Greek Fire ', which played a not inconsiderable part in the defence of the capital on more than one critical occasion. Had the Roman world been able to achieve any such decided advance in warfare as that represented in modern times by gunpowder, the defence of the frontiers might have been made good for much longer. But even such a great technical advance could not have helped for long, if the interest in warfare on the Roman side had not revived. Any such invention would have become familiar first to the barbarians within the Empire ; by them it would inevitably have been betrayed, sooner or later, to the wild barbarians outside. In any case, such an invention could not have renewed the vitality of the Empire, even if it might have protracted for a short space longer its declining life.

When we allow for the inevitable imperfections of all human arrangements, we cannot say that the Empire was badly served by its army, though it was never large enough, never a matter of sufficient interest to the mass of the population. But, subject to these qualifications, it did its work economically and well. Professor Grant has recently argued that the Empire could have met the expense of all necessary foreign wars—and perhaps a few unnecessary ones too—if only it could have eliminated the waste of civil war. This may well be true ; but, where the equilibrium was never quite sure, how could you hope to preserve it without an occasional upset ? Certainly, if the Empire could have been spared all civil war, she would have had so much more unwasted life and energy. But we may observe that there was always a kind of self-defensive check in operation. Theoretically, a serious civil war, dividing large sections of the Empire, might have lasted for years, like the disastrous wars of religion in Germany. But, as it actually happened, all the civil wars were decided in comparatively short spaces of time—some of them very summarily indeed. There must have been a general agreement—unexpressed, but understood by all—that, if you fought too long, the prize of victory would no longer be there to enjoy. Yet the losses on such a bloody field as Mursa were ominous for the future. Some losses tend to be repaired by a sort of principle of compensation ; the losses in civil war tend only to weaken and depress.

CHAPTER VII

PRIVATE AND SOCIAL LIFE

Volume after volume has been written and will continue to be written about this fascinating theme. Many such works are of the highest interest and value ; hardly one lacks its own particular merit. The material to draw on is plentiful and one after another of us is tempted to give his own interpretation of it. Almost every ancient writer, be he historian, poet or satirist, supplies his quota of evidence. Inscriptions—and to a minor degree coins—increase the total. But, while the material is rich enough, it is very unevenly distributed. On some aspects of social life, particularly on the life of the wealthier classes in the cities, we are fairly well informed. On others—on the life of the poor, especially of the poor in the country—we know very little beyond what we might on general principles guess. Of the provinces, of course, we know far less than of Rome. Our chief source of literary evidence are works like the satires of Persius and Juvenal, the Satyricon of Petronius, the epigrams of Martial, the Golden Ass of Apuleius. It is difficult to distil the essence of Roman social life into some twenty odd pages. Reference must be made to the full treatment in larger works, which add the illustration that is really needed. We shall concentrate here on the life of Rome and the cities, adding at the end the little that can be said about life in the country.

The round of private life was, of course, much the same as it has been in all civilised societies. The birth of a child, if ' taken up ' by the father—if not ' taken up ' it was exposed—was an occasion of rejoicing shared by the friends of the family. As the child grew up, education began to be a matter of concern. The boy was placed under the charge of a slave, his pedagogue, and sent to school, first to learn grammar and literature, after that rhetoric. The girl would be taught at home, and music and dancing might be her chief subjects. The assumption of the *toga virilis* by the boy at the age of sixteen—the sign that he had reached man's years—was another occasion of celebration among friends and relatives. Betrothals were very often made at a very early age. The minimum age of marriage for a girl was twelve, for the boy somewhere near sixteen. The marriage was an occasion of splendid display along traditional lines. The bride, wearing a special flame-coloured headband, would be escorted through the streets to the flare of blazing torches. Arrived at her new home, she would be lifted over the threshold by her husband and would signify her devotion to him by the traditional words, ' where you are Gaius, I am Gaia '. Then would come the marriage feast, the bedding of the bride, the singing of the lusty Fescennine verses. At the far end of life comes the funeral, again an occasion for friends to meet and show their respect. In the case of a man of eminence, a formal eulogy (the *laudatio*) would be delivered by some close friend of the dead. The body would be cremated and the bones would be gathered up by the women of the family. Burial, however, steadily encroached on cremation—partly no doubt under the influence of Christian ideas.

The houses of the rich were magnificent—regular palaces. Walls would be cased in marble, the ceilings elaborately decorated. There would be paintings on the walls, mosaics on the floors. The furniture too would be elaborate and costly. The poor, of course, lived very differently—in mean tenements or in the *insulae* (islands), blocks of flats, where a minimum of accommodation was supplied at no very low cost. The clothes of the Romans were simple and tasteful—an undergarment, shirt or shift, an over-garment and perhaps a cloak. The toga—a sort of blanket elaborately draped and folded in a variety of ways for different occasions—was the official dress wear. Luxury in clothes no doubt existed. There were the transparent ' Coan ' dresses so popular in the fast set under the Empire. But there was not the immense multiplication of changes of raiment that later ages have seen. The comparative simplicity of Roman costume speaks of something sound in the popular taste.

Social life had certain features that distinguish it from the life of today. People, of course, paid one another visits—how could they fail to ? But social intercourse tended to be canalised in a number of set occasions. There would be the early morning levée, when friends and clients would assemble. Then again there were the recitations when the composer of some poem or speech invited his friends to hear him declaim it. For the rich and influential in Rome such occasions were frequent and could become a serious burden. How often does the harassed man sigh for rest in his country retreat ! But the true centre of Roman life was the banquet (*cena*), beginning in the late afternoon or early evening and sometimes prolonged in a drinking bout into the late hours of the night. The guests reclined on couches, normally three in number, with three guests on each couch ; the banquet hall was called *triclinium* from the number three. The guests, of course, were normally invited for their distinction or talents. But there would be an occasional obscure guest, just called in to make up the number. *Umbrae* (shadows) was what they were called. The meal began with a course of hors d'œuvre ; then came the main dishes—fish, meat and game—finally the confectionery and fruit. Wine was seldom drunk neat, mostly with an admixture of water, the exact proportions being determined by the ' master of the drinking '—but the Romans still contrived to get drunk on it. Entertainment of some kind was normally provided, but it varied enormously with the wealth and taste of those who gave the party. It ranged from discreet readings from classical writers to buffoonery of the most outrageous description. Petronius's Trimalchio, the vulgar, ridiculous, and yet not unlovable freedman, who has made his fortune several times over and is now busy inventing means of dissipating it, produces an amazing sequence of absurdity after absurdity at his banquet. Conversation would naturally run its course throughout the meal. It would be mainly on private matters, of personal interest but no serious concern. Under the Empire women might be present and there would be feminine gossip to match the male. Political discussion was dangerous. You could never be sure that no spy was present among the guests. On the whole, we get the impression that the Romans lacked re- finement of taste. They loved success and the ostentatious display of it. Horace's account of the banquet of Nasidienus shocks us by its revelations ; Horace knows that what he is describing is vulgar, but hardly seems conscious how *very* vulgar it is. No doubt things were better at the table of Horace's own patron, Maecenas ; but then Maecenas came of an old race, which had learnt a good deal about luxurious living, while the good Roman was still sweating behind the plough-tail. Imperial banquets varied with the Emperor, from decent moderation to colossal and grotesque extravagance. Invitations to them were naturally coveted.

The *cena* was by far and away the most prominent feature of Roman social life. It was the one main meal of the day, in fact the only regular meal. For the other meals the Romans seem to have helped themselves from bar or side table. It was not that they were abstemious, but that they could not be bothered with formal meals. It was only natural that the main meal was made the centre of Roman entertainment and that the ambitious vied with one another in the richness and rarity of foods and the variety of enter- tainments that they could supply.

Roman society, we must remember, was divided fairly rigidly into a series of classes, almost fit to be called castes.   Our information mainly concerns the top class of all, the senators.   It was their levées, their recitations that drew the largest attendances.   Those who followed them were not only friends, but also humble attendants, clients.   It lay at the basis of Roman social conceptions that the high man and the low man were naturally linked by the relationship of patron and client.   The patron gave freely of his counsel and protection, the client responded by supporting his patron by every means at his disposal and by rendering him a number of minor services.   The client would also receive his dole of food (*sportula*), which at times was commuted to a pittance in cash.   Under the Empire, we tend to form a very mean conception of the client, especially as he appears in the Roman satirists.   We see him as a starveling hanger-on, despised even by the slaves and freedmen of his patron.   The fact was that the Emperor was now the universal patron, the Roman people, dependent on him for food and entertainment, his clients.   Before him the private patron paled into insignificance.   Yet something of the old relationship remained ; it was too deep-rooted in the Roman mind ever to be completely eradicated.   The satirists concentrate on the meaner or more ludicrous aspects.   But something of the old worthier relationship of mutual trust and service survives, and hints of this may be found here and there, if we read our authors attentively.   For example, when the praetorians broke in on Otho's banquet and threatened to murder the senators dining with him, many of them found refuge with their clients in the obscurer parts of Rome.

The club plays a very important part in modern social life. Men meet in their clubs for the most varied purposes—for society and entertainment, for sport, for hobbies and interests of all kinds. A vast amount of useful work is done by these private and voluntary organisations.   It is a suggestion of what might be accomplished under the right kind of ' anarchy '—with compulsory government reduced to a minimum and private enterprise left free to work out its plans without interference.   In Roman life the function of the club was severely restricted.   The State, taught by the experience of the Republic that clubs might easily degenerate into foci of political agitation, refused to admit any that were not licensed by the Senate.   Licences were only granted as a rule to the most innocuous—friendly or burial societies.   When Pliny as special commissioner of Trajan in Bithynia, wrote to his Emperor asking for permission to set up a fire brigade in Nicomedia, which had just suffered from a devastating fire, Trajan refused permission and suggested that Pliny should rely instead on fire-fighting appliances and voluntary assistance in case of emergency ! This strict limitation of clubs completely shut out a whole range of possible interest and usefulness.

We have spoken so far of social life as lived in private, but it was a main feature of the Roman world that that life was lived largely in public in the open. Men thronged to meet at the great public occasions of the Roman year—the Vows on the 3rd of January, the celebration of events of importance in the imperial family—births, marriages, funerals—the comings and goings of the Emperor, magnificently staged for the benefit of the Roman people. And then there were the recurrent ceremonies of religion and occasional special services of intercession, *supplicationes*, when the attributes of the gods were set out on sumptuous couches, the sacred *pulvinaria*. But it was the great public entertainments that supplied endless opportunities of meeting and gossiping with your friends. People visited the shows, not only to please their own eyes, but also to offer themselves to the eyes of others. As Ovid writes of the girls of his time

ut spectent veniunt, veniunt spectentur ut ipsae
(' they go to see the show and to be part of it themselves ').

Public shows and holidays of one kind or another took up a good part of the year. It occurred to some observers that the whole world was keeping holiday. The austere might ask, as they might in some countries today, when people found time to do any work.

Gladiatorial shows of the arena came from Etruria to Rome and soon became acclimatised there. Gladiators, drawn from various classes—slaves, prisoners of war, occasional volunteers—bound themselves by oath to endure every rigour of their bloody profession. They were carefully fed, elaborately trained, but sacrificed mercilessly in the arena to gratify the bloodthirsty mob. Socially they ranked as the lowest of the low, far beneath contempt. Tacitus hardly dared to admit of one man who rose from below to distinction that he was the son of a gladiator. But they had their compensations. They won wealth and fame by their victories and were sometimes courted by ladies of rank—who ought to have known better. The influence of these shows on the masses who witnessed them must have been demoralising in the extreme, encouraging a cowardly delight in the sufferings of others and fostering every base passion. An occasional voice was raised in protest, but, for the most part, the games were accepted as a normal and necessary side of life. Defence of them might even be offered on the ground that they inured a people like the Roman, which depended so much on war, to the endurance of suffering and death. Even the influence of the Christian Church was for long unable to bridle this wild lust of the people. It was not until 404 that the monk, Telemachus, gave his life in protest against the shows and that the Emperor Honorius then forbade their continuance.

Gladiators were divided into a number of classes—the Samnites, the *secutores* (chasers) set against the *retiarii* (men armed only with a net and trident), riders and chariot drivers. The military value of gladiators, as tried out on occasion in times of civil war, was found to be slight ; they were no match for the trained discipline of the legionary. Apart from the gladiatorial shows there were the *venationes* (hunts), shows of wild or tame beasts, in which men might be pitted against beasts or one beast against another (elephant against rhinoceros, or rhinoceros against bull), or a variety of rare creatures might be exhibited to an admiring public. But even the shows of tame beasts ended in a horrid butchery.

Gladiatorial shows spread out from Rome to Italy and the provinces, even to the East. There, some opposition was encountered ; the Greek taste revolted against the senseless brutality. In the West, Marcus Aurelius found it necessary to impose restrictions on the number of shows in the Western provinces. It speaks volumes that Treves in the 5th century, sorely harassed by barbarian invasions, should petition its Emperor for restoration, not of its walls, but of its arena.

Second only, if second, to the arena came the circus. It was not quite as obviously bloody as the arena, but there was still danger enough in it to life and limb. Here again there was a vast outlet for popular interest and excitement, which the government rather encouraged than discouraged as providing a vent for passions that might otherwise have taken a political direction. The factions of the circus—reds, whites, greens, blues, yellows— were keenly followed by all Rome. They had their own charioteers, cars and equipment and expended vast sums on their maintenance. Very seldom indeed did these factions take a political turn ; the only notorious example is very late—that of the Nica riots in Constantinople between the Greens and the Blues which very nearly cost Justinian his throne. But the Emperors openly avowed themselves as enthusiastic adherents of this or that faction. The Circus Maximus was built by Julius Caesar and Augustus, rebuilt by Nero and improved by Trajan, Caracalla and other later Emperors. Its most notable feature was the great obelisk set up in the centre by Augustus. The circus accommodated from

180,000 to 190,000 spectators and like the arena provided unique opportunities for social meetings. Betting of course was the inevitable concomitant of the racing and fortunes were freely won and lost. Successful charioteers were the darlings of the public, won vast wealth and reputation by their victories and were overweening in their pride and their caprice.

In comparison with the burning passions of arena and circus, other entertainments seemed to pale. Athletic performances in the stadium were encouraged by Nero at his festival of the Neronia and by Domitian at his Capitoline contests. But, on the whole, the Romans despised the athlete as a lubberly lump, over-trained and over-specialised. It was in the Greek East that the athlete came into his own. There he might win universal admiration or honour, and victory in the games might secure him the supreme distinction of being welcomed back into his native city through a breach in its walls ; games that led to this honour were described as ' entry games ' (εἰσελαστικοὶ ἀγῶνες).

Musical and literary contests again were favoured by Emperors like Nero and Domitian, but were never more than mildly popular in Rome. Music played its part in all public ritual and ceremonies, but it was of a far simpler character than modern music and had nothing that can begin to compare with our great modern orchestras. The chief instruments were the flute and the lyre. Some kind of organ had been introduced by the time of Nero and fascinated that dilettante Emperor.

The drama was popular enough but it had sunk to a very low ebb. Straight tragedy and comedy were hardly ever written for the stage and were quite out of favour. In their place came the mime and pantomime, shows in which words and music were entirely subordinated to gesture. Preference was also shown for brutal or lascivious subjects. The most successful actors won immense wealth and popularity and, on more than one occasion, intruded adulterously into the imperial family. But the social reputation of the actor was of the lowest, and the word ' actress ' was almost synonymous with that of a follower of the ' oldest profession in the world '. The pantomime seems to have been comparable to our modern cinema, immensely popular and attractive, drawing to itself money and talents galore, but still impoverished too often by a lack of real life and integrity at its heart. Popular actors may have enjoyed just the same sort of reputation as our film stars ; could we investigate more closely, we might find the ancient equivalent of the fan mail.

This Rome of the Empire was a marvellous city. Its population at the highest may have been of the order of a million inhabitants. After Augustus it was no longer a city of stone, but of marble, embellished with fora, arcades, triumphant arches, temples, palaces, libraries—the queen of the earth and arrayed to suit her rank. Rome was not only the political centre of the world, but also the literary and artistic. Even in religion, which in its newer revelations had its roots in the East, the pull of Rome was gradually felt. The Bishop of Rome became the Pope, the father of all bishops. At Rome you could see all that was fair and wonderful in the world, not only the regular sights and shows, but anything strange enough that appeared anywhere—rare birds and beasts, prodigious gluttons, a satyr, a pigmy, freaks in fact of every kind.

The public baths were a very prominent feature of daily life. The ancients were very cleanly ; or was it simply that they made a luxury out of cleanliness? Some baths were private with a charge for admission, but the larger and finer ones were as a rule public. Supplying public baths was one of the quickest ways for an Emperor to win favour. Emperor after Emperor—Nero, Titus, Caracalla, Diocletian—expended money and ingenuity on improving Rome's facilities for bathing. The great baths were most elaborately constructed, the swimming pool, hot, cold and tepid rooms, gymnasium and additional quarters for rest, conversation and refreshment. Women might be admitted as well as men, and the baths not unnaturally became favourite places of assignation. They also did something to fill the places of the social clubs, the lack of which we have been deploring. As dangerous allurements, which certainly wasted your time and might wreck your morality, the baths were feared and loathed by the Christian Fathers. Much washing came to have an unhallowed savour ; godliness, retreating from cleanliness, came to hobnob with unwashedness. Naturally, this is not to be applied too seriously to the ordinary simple Christian. It certainly has a meaning for the zealots, the men who lived in filth and squalor, in deserts or on pillars. Not only Rome the capital, but all the great cities of the Empire prided themselves on the super-excellence of their baths ; Antioch, with its suburb Daphne, enjoyed a unique reputation.

It is impossible to sketch the social life of all the cities of the Empire ; it will have followed the same general lines as that of Rome, but on more modest scales. Classes there will have been comparable to those of the capital, but on a more modest design— a few Roman senators at the top, rather more Roman knights, the local senators, the masses of the population under them. Of the individual flavour of some cities we can still judge—of Alexandria in many an event of history and in the records of fanatical fights of monks and populace in early Christian days ; of Antioch in the Acts of the Apostles or in the bitter tract of Julian II, the ' Misopogon ' (the hater of the beard, i.e. the philosophic Emperor) ; of Carthage in the Confessions of St. Augustine. The Roman tended to look down on all less favoured cities. Even the Italian townsman was to him a mere ' municipal ', a word used by Roman writers as something near a term of abuse. Sejanus, who seduced the daughter-in-law of the Emperor Tiberius, is stigmatised by Tacitus as a *municipalis adulter*—and the sting is felt to be in the first word even more than in the second. It was something like a public disaster when Tiberius betrothed a grandniece to a Roman knight from Tibur.

Everywhere the scales were weighted in favour of old family, wealth, official respectability. It is easy to declaim against the evils of such rigid classification, but human nature seems to require it, as if society were not comfortable until it has set up separate pens for different types of social animal. The Roman world as a whole liked its snobbery, its strict division into classes, its regular path up and down, with no short cuts allowed. Perhaps snobbery is not quite the right word for this extreme class-consciousness. Our modern snob is all taken up with social precedence ; he has no strong moral background. The Roman snob, or whatever else we may choose to call him, is certain that he is right, that the principles that he maintains are deep-rooted in the nature of things. It is just as proper and natural for the senator to hold his superior position and honours as it is for Rome to rule the nations under her imperial sway.

Here is one reason for the long duration of the Empire, perhaps also a reason for its flagging energies. Ability there must always be, but it was forced to express itself through conventional channels. The Empire could seldom produce a great Independent. Its great men must shine, if they were to shine at all, in one of the services, civil or military. St. Paul asserted the essential equality of all men in Christ ; in Christ neither Jew nor Gentile, neither bond nor free. The Roman assertion would be almost the exact opposite ; under Caesar either Roman or subject, either noble or base, either bond or free.

If fortune had offered the modern lover of the Ancient World just one single wish, what might he have asked for ? A discovery of the lost poems of Sappho ? Or of the lost books of Livy ? Or, perhaps, of those many early Christian writers of whom St. Luke speaks in his introduction to his Gospel ? One of these perhaps ; or he might have been led to ask for the revelation of the life of a Roman city, as it was actually lived in the 1st century of our era. Well, that is what fortune has actually done for us. The eruption of Vesuvius in A.D. 79, which buried Herculaneum under lava and Pompeii under ash, has kept those two cities essentially unchanged from the year of their burial. We can still see the houses in which men lived, the shops in which they bought and sold, or read the election manifestos or the announcement of gladiatorial shows. Even the dead themselves were sometimes there, trapped before they could find time to escape. What we find, no doubt, is often more or less what we might have expected to find. But it is something to see it so clearly, all uncertainties removed. We realise more and more how relative the conception of time is. How long it is since Herculaneum and Pompeii lived ? Nearly 1,900 years. Yet, when we see the cities unearthed, the time between us has shrunk down to a mere span—just time enough to be covered over, not time for them to change essentially. It is much the same with coins. A hoard of gold coins, buried in that same year of destruction, A.D. 79, turns up clean and unworn except for a touch of volcanic patina. They might have been struck yesterday. And those coins give just the meaning I am after. In the special case of the coins and their finder there has been no interval. Time has done nothing ; today and that distant past are as days adjacent to one another. So with the two cities ; for once, a miracle has been worked for our instruction and delight. Time has not been allowed to lay its last hand on the cities ; we leap the centuries and are back with them in their life as they lived it. It is with a strange emotion that one passes on the road the ' sea gate ' of Pompeii. In imagination one can almost hear the sea lapping on the shore.

It is an excellent illustration of the urban direction of ancient life that our knowledge of life on the social side is mainly confined to cities. Life in the country might be pleasant. Many a poet and philosopher sighed for its relief from city distractions. But life in the country had little shape ; one day there was much like another. Life there must have been weary and monotonous—the daily routine of exhausting toil, the occasional holiday or festival, the rare chance of meeting with your friends. Of wealthy Romans we *do* know rather more. They liked to plant their country villas at strategic posts on the coast, on the hills or in the plain, where they could retire for the occasional holiday, entertain friends, break a journey in comfort when they had to travel. Much money, ingenuity and taste were spent on the lay-out of such villas, and we have elaborate descriptions of them from Pliny the Younger and Statius. The amenities of the position—morning sun, views of hill or sea—would be exploited to the full. There would be banqueting halls, libraries, studies, halls for exercise and the rest. In some provinces, such as Africa, great estates, with villas as their centres, steadily grew. Considerable remains of such villas have been found. These establishments were often on a very large scale. They were little communities, self-supplying, self-contained, more or less independent of the outside world. Hunting was the main amusement that relieved the monotony of the long daylight hours. In the late Empire, the owners who lived on the great estate became something like feudal lords, absolute masters in their own house, owing little more than nominal obedience to the Imperial Government, ready to give a very unfriendly welcome to the intrusive tax collector and willing and able to shelter many a fugitive from the law.

This was one form of detachment from the general life of the State. But there is another at which we must just glance—the flight of the hermits into deserts, the retirement of monks into their communities of the common life. However different the motives for the two kinds of retirement might be, they agreed in one thing, in a revolt against the ordered, too ordered, life of the State.

The conflict between pagan and Christian was largely fought out in the field of private life. It will be fruitful to examine this conflict a little closer, because it will throw light on the ethical ideas that underlay the social life of the ancients. The pagan ethic was often challenged by philosophers who were courageous enough in what they said. They seldom thought it necessary to go on to do anything about it. They said to the people ' how ridiculous, how wrong you are ! and let it go at that. Not so the Christians ; they had their new ethic, they believed in it, they planned in due course to impose it upon the world.

On rare occasions the conflict came to the official cognisance of the governor ; there might then be persecutions and martyrdoms. The preliminary skirmishing took place in market and arena. The Christian challenged the very bases of pagan life. He acknowledged the duty of obedience to the Emperor and his deputies, but not as to absolute lords ; there is only one Lord, the Father in Heaven. He accepted the organisation of society as he found it. Christian slaves continued to be obedient to their masters ; masters did not at once set their slaves free. But relationships had changed. There is something much more fundamental than where a man was born, into what nation, religion, class. All are sons of the Heavenly Father ; before that unity all earthly distinctions fade into insignificance. This cut very deep into pagan thought. The Christians condemned by implication, if not by explicit denunciation, so much that to a pagan was a matter of course and right. The Christians might appear to be so many troublesome killjoys, denying everything that did not suit their personal taste. Look a little closer into it and the question changes. If the things to which the Christians objected were so innocent, so indifferent, shall we say, to the wise man, why should the Christian refusal to conform have aroused such profound bitterness ? It is much the same as with the Quakers in the age of the puritans and cavaliers. It seems very odd at first sight that good Quakers should make such an ado about the use of the second person singular or of hat homage. But read of the transports of rage into which a worthy father was thrown when his son refused him the honour and you will see that these indifferent things were valued far above their real worth, that the protest against them was fully justified by the intemperance of the conformists. Far more effective was the quiet response of Charles II. When William Penn on one occasion failed to remove his hat in the royal presence, Charles took off his own remarking ' that in this presence it is unusual for more than one person to remain covered '. It was a very neat rebuke, but we do not hear that Penn was discouraged by it.

Perhaps it may be worth our while to look a little more closely into the differences between the pagan and Christian views of the world. We must seek on each side for average normal views, omitting all special extravagances. The pagans saw the world as a One, divided into many parts. The gods are very like men except in the one important detail that they are not subject to death. They are at the mercy of human passions ; they love, marry and beget children. They do not inhabit a different dimension from ours, or, at least, the dimension they inhabit is by analogy extremely like ours. They have food, as we do, but different—ambrosia ; for drink they have nectar, for blood ichor. There is no strong contrast between natural and supernatural ; both are parts of the same scheme. In conceptions of time, too, there is unity. There is no progressive revelation of God to man ; or, if that is too much to say, such revelation is the exception, not the rule. There is a divine past—before Jupiter Saturn, before Saturn Uranus and Gaia ; but that is a sacred history that hardly concerns ordinary life. The gods are characterised as ' the heavenly ones who live forever '. There is no future theodicy, no judgment, no millennium on earth. *Aeternitas* means simply indefinitely long continuance like that of the sun and moon in the physical universe. Inside this system of time and place there may be room for many shapes of human life and fortune—for kings and republics, for peace and war, for wealth and poverty. But, wherever you chance to find yourself, you are in a frame that does not change. The laws of your existence can be read with some sureness. Many generations of men have worked on the facts and you have all their *exempla* as precedents to direct you. There is conventional morality which is convenient for social life, which may be considered to have the approval of the gods. Flagrant breaches of it may bring down the divine wrath. But there is no general demand for a very exalted morality. The gods are tolerant, very tolerant ; you may even offend certain of the powers if you try to be too good. Witness poor Hippolytus in Euripides who offended Aphrodite.

Contrast with all this the Christian view. God is divided from man by an immense gulf. He is holy, mighty, eternal, only by metaphor to be described in human terms. It is His remoteness, His unlikeness that has always been stressed. And yet He sends down His Son to earth ; God becomes incarnate and, as if that were not enough, endures the worst indignities, death by crucifixion. The story must have seemed shocking to Roman ears, invented, you would say, to surprise and offend. The world is now divided into two distinct spheres, the divine and the human. There is constant communication between them, but not by any mere natural process ; no, by special divine mediation, by Grace. Time is no longer one continuous, unending process. God has revealed Himself in time to the Jewish people at various points of their history. He has now revealed Himself in His Son. The revelation once made to the Jews is now extended to all mankind. The Incarnation is the central point in history. Behind, lie the Jewish revelations and the prophets ; ahead, lie the Second Coming and the Judgment. The Christian can no longer steer his course by the pagan compass. He dwells in an earthly city, but his true citizenship is not there. He obeys an earthly lord, but the authority of that lord is only derived from God. He can live according to the rules of the society in which he finds himself, but they are no longer valid in themselves ; they are part of a world that is passing away. When you come to the moral law, we find a new order of requirements—much that was current morality marked down, some unpopular virtues marked up. All the things that excite men's cupidities and ambitions are decried. What really matters is Faith, Hope and Charity. The best of the philosophers, of course, made similar protests against current loose standards ; but philosophers, as we have observed, were seldom as courageous in their practice as in their preaching.

It is not surprising, then, that the Christian found difficulty in adapting himself to the society in which he lived. Let us look at his difficulties over a number of questions. The most obvious is that of religion. How is the Christian to behave in face of a religion in which he cannot believe ? He must clearly be a non-conformist ; he cannot worship idols that to him are mere wood and stone ; he cannot offer sacrifices to gods who are either nothing— or demons ; he cannot accept the attribution of moral evil to powers divine. Courtesy and prudence combined may lead him to avoid occasions of offence, to make his protest as secret and silent as he may. But he must betray himself on occasion—when the wine is poured in libation, when sacrifice is made to the Genius of the Emperor, at occasions such as births or marriages, when some little religious rite has its place. That he should practise his own religion in private assemblies would not trouble his neighbours very much ; it was well known that there was much variety of religious experience and practice, many a form, we may say, of specialisation. It was only the government that might be worried by the suspicion of a secret society with political ends. Society did not demand any enthusiastic or exuberant acceptance of its religious ways ; a very discreet conformity would suffice. But it was dangerous to refuse that minimum. Some scholars are fond of pointing out that such religious observances are of mere formal character, not in the least emotional. It is like standing up to join in singing ' God save the Queen '. No one demanded that you should put your heart and soul into it. The analogy is not so bad, but let us work it out fairly. If a man today deliberately flouts public opinion by breaking the etiquette about such a matter as the National Anthem, he will soon find a surprising amount of emotion pent up behind the set form. Many a pagan will have first discovered his passion for the old worships when he thought he saw them flouted by the Christians.

This religious difficulty troubled the whole social life of the Christians ; for religion touched ordinary life at so many points. Let us look at one or two special difficulties. The victims offered in sacrifice were not all consumed by fire. The gods, it had been discovered, very conveniently liked the parts unfit for human consumption. The result, of course, was that meat from sacrifice regularly came on the market. A large part of the meat which

you ate had been ' offered to idols '. That troubled no pagan ;
but what was the Christian to do, if asked to eat such meat after
having been told what it was ? St. Paul shows the question as it
vexed his early converts. His advice was wise and moderate ;
don't make difficulties, but, if you can't escape the dilemma, be
true to conscience. Incidentally, we notice that the Christians
here came up against vested interests ; if the new religion made
idol meat a drug in the market, business was seriously in danger.
At the banquet the pagan would wreathe his head with myrtle or
flowers—an innocent, it may be even a charming practice, we may
think. The Christian refused to comply, for wreaths of bay might
be associated with the worship of Apollo. Or was the placing of
a wreath on the head an assumption of an honour not proper to
mortal man ? Certainly at the banquet you tried for a moment
to forget your pathetic mortality. At any rate, this was a point
of bitter conflict. We may imagine that the moral principle at
issue was often forgotten. The question became one between
Swift's Big- and Little-enders. Tertullian remarks caustically to
pagans who criticise the Christian refusal to wear the festal wreath
that he does not smell his flowers with the back of his head. But
we can see the clear difference of principle behind all this. The
pagan joyfully accepts life ; the Christian hangs back, not fully
trusting it, looking to faraway authority. Many a pagan must
have been infuriated by this refusal to accept what life offered,
and his fury would grow if he came to understand that the Christian regarded all these supposed values as so much stuff for burning.

Pagan ideas of domestic life were not so backward that there
need be any very serious clash with the Christians over them.
The family was recognised as the social unit. The round of life—
birth, marriage, funeral—was all regulated under the blessing of
religion. But the Christian would take a far more serious view of
love before marriage than would the pagan ; he would also
question the rightness of second or third marriages. More than
this, he would not countenance the exposure of unwanted children.
The pagans accused the Christians of shirking their natural duties
and not making their fair contribution to the population. This
was because of the Christian praise of virginity and insistence on
continence. But, if Christian parents reared all the children born
to them, they may easily have contributed more than the pagans
who could not be troubled to care for their own offspring.

It was in the social pleasures on the grand scale that the conflict
was most acute. The baths were one of the most beloved diver-
sions. They were used as clubs and places of assignation ; they

encouraged idleness and wantonness, and for both these reasons were denounced by the Christians. They were a typical sign of the world and we must never forget—what is only too easy to forget today—that to the early Christian the world was an enemy, not a friend. But think what a gulf opened up between Christian and pagan, when the former would not even show himself where the latter found his most congenial companionship. It was like cutting oneself off from the public house in the modern village.

The public shows were a standing ground of disagreement. The theatre was admittedly flashy and immoral. It accustomed you to look at shams and not very agreeable or elevating shams at that. It was loose in morals ; you would see and hear things that should bring a blush to any cheek. There must have been good pagans who shared the Christian objection. The circus was banned by all good Christians. It encouraged wild excitement and desperate gambling ; it taught men to seek their spiritual food in the adventures and dangers of others, not in their own wrestlings. It collected the crowds in their indiscriminate exuberance—and crowds as such can be very ugly things. Even worse were the gladiatorial shows and wild beast hunts. There was the same mad excitement, the same mob emotion, and, added to it all, the terrible thirst for blood. All these excitements were calculated to inflame the sexual passions that were never left long without sustenance in the Ancient World. Over these passions of the mob the conflict waxed hottest. The Christians protested and abstained ; the pagans growled at these attacks on their pleasures. When they succeeded in bringing the Christians to the lions, they could derive a double pleasure—in seeing their adversaries confounded and confounded in just that way, to make themselves one of the shows that they denounced. Tertullian's terrible pamphlet ' de Spectaculis ' helps us to feel the bitterness with which this fight was conducted. The bitterness is by no means all on the pagan side. Tertullian promises his brethren very satisfying spectacles in the future, far more exciting than those of circus or arena. The saints will look down from Heaven on the tortures of the damned and will derive a just and exquisite pleasure from the sight. He ends on a finer note when he suggests that the things that God has prepared for them that love him, ' things that ear hath not heard, eye hath not seen, nor hath it entered into the heart of man to conceive ', are far better than any show of beasts or contests of chariots. There is room for reflection in the fact that the Christian Church triumphant was very slow to make any impression on those shows that it had denounced. Gladiatorial fights had to go—but not for two generations after Constantine. The passion for the circus continued hardly abated. The theatre continued to droop on its low level. Theodora, consort of Justinian I, had been an actress ; that did not prevent Justinian from marrying her, but even the imperial purple could not quite cover her former disgrace.

It is a tragedy that one can so easily lose what has been fought for in the very hour of victory. Absorbing in masses converts, who continued in their inmost hearts to be pagan, the Church was conformed to its new material, when it should have transformed it.

I will conclude this chapter by borrowing a few thoughts from Lecky's great ' History of European Morals '—a subject not easily to be exhausted, but of perennial interest. Our comparison of pagan and Christian has already suggested thoughts about pagan morals ; we will now arrange them in more exact order.

One of the most conspicuous features of the Empire, and one of the ugliest, is cruelty, contempt for human life and suffering. It was fed from several springs. One was the institution of slavery, of a class of human beings deprived of elementary rights. The evils of slavery might be—in fact were—mitigated by kindliness between masters and slaves born in the house, by the possibility of manumission, by the insistence of the Stoic on essential human rights, finally, by legislation that removed the worst abuses. But that the honour or life of any man or woman should be at the mercy of others struck at the roots of right behaviour. Contempt for human life was seen at its worst in the amphitheatre, when it was expended to glut the lust for blood. It is hard to exaggerate the demoralising effect of such shows, continually and almost universally enjoyed. And the worst of it was that it did not stimulate courage, as some apologists might protest. The sight of other men bleeding and dying does not make a man brave himself. Even in the circus, where the excitement was comparatively innocent, the danger to life and limb was great, and that danger added an extra thrill to the partisanship of the factions. We live in a world of which death is a part ; it is possible to make too much of the inevitable exit from life. But to reduce the individual life in value is to debase the coinage, to lower the value of all that we possess. It is the worst result of prolonged war that it leads to a contempt for what we are instinctively taught to cherish. The cruelty encouraged by arena or circus made its way into private

N

life. Men, by exposing unwanted children, savaged against their own flesh and blood. To treat human life as sacred does not at once solve all moral problems ; but to treat it as low and profane solves even fewer.

The passions are closely related to one another. If you indulge one, you tend to encourage others with it. The connection between sexual licence and cruelty is well understood today. Laxity in sexual relations was fostered by the institution of slavery ; the master was free to indulge his passions without restraint. It was further encouraged by the cruel shows which men and women watched together. One form of excitement led on to another. Philosophy might impose some check, but not so religion, which has only too much to say about gods with very human passions. St. Paul's picture of the terrible decadence of the idol-worshipping world is bound to shock the lover of antiquity. He must find it extreme and one-sided. Vice did not reign unchallenged. There was room for many virtues of private life, for devotion of husband and wife, for firm family loyalties. But there was much to justify the Christian protest. Standards were too low ; immorality was taught by theatre and public shows, and marriages were too easily undertaken and broken. With the triumph of Christianity came a decided change for the better. The Emperors in many cases set an example of strict virtue. Legislation began to take account of the new strictness. When we read a Christian writer like St. Jerome, we may be repelled by what seems to us his abhorrence of human nature in some of its manifestations. But if we are willing to be honest, we also see something of those evils that drove him to such extremes as to prize virginity above all else and to admit of marriage only because it supplies the virgins whom he regards as the crown of life. No doubt the right balance is hard to find and the Christians did not at first find it. But they did much to redress a balance that had tilted far too far the other way.

The Romans certainly set too high a value on wealth. ' Wealth however obtained '—that was the first aim of many. Even a philosopher like Seneca had too much money for strict virtue. The good Roman had a great respect for what he called *fides*, right relations between men in points of responsibility. He must be true to a trust, he must not disclaim a just liability. The special temptations of modern times, the chances to gamble on the Stock Exchange, were perhaps not so immediate then. Financial relations were still uncomplicated. But trust and truth were in peril when men were too anxious to make money quickly. A regard for the truth is an important part of morality. It had various enemies under the Empire. It might be dangerous to speak the truth too freely, for fear of offending the powers that be. In the immediate entourage of the Emperor, there was the possibility of exploiting access to him or of selling reports of his intentions, as often as not false.

This matter of honesty leads us on to the intellectual virtues. We have learnt today to put a high value on the blessed trio, honesty, candour, care. We see in them the chief guarantees of that disinterested inquiry on which progress seems to depend. These virtues stood at a low ebb under the Empire. The scientific spirit was only feebly alive. Little fresh work was done on the advancement of knowledge. What was already known in different fields might be carefully recorded, but there was little careful scrutiny, very little that could be called research. The Empire could not reap what it did not sow. It held what it inherited from the past ; it did not go on to utilise it for further advance. It paid for its failure here in a paralysis of research, a sterility of invention.

The morality of society cannot only be judged negatively, by a chronicle of its weak points and omissions. It must also be judged in the light of what it *does* achieve, in the light of the total impression. It is much harder here to draw the picture accurately, to balance success against failure, to allow for what is attempted as well as for what is achieved. The great aim that the Empire set before itself and never lost out of sight was the maintenance of a peace and order within which men might live at ease. This aim it achieved. The problem of how a great society might live together and develop its common goods was largely solved. But the cost was great. Individual freedom was severely limited, and the free development of the separate parts of the Empire was hampered. But the task was a very difficult one and even partial success is remarkable.

The next point is : can the values which a society holds most sacred be kept under this unified system ? In the case of the Roman Empire we are left hesitating over the answer. Up to a certain point what was most important was secured. Beyond that point there was failure. Too much had to be paid for unity. Something of the driving power of free men was lost. The State that Diocletian rebuilt after the disasters of the 3rd century was too much concerned with survival at any cost. When the cost became too great for the subjects of the Empire to pay willingly, collapse soon followed. Here too we come to what is perhaps the most

ominous of the Empire's failures.   It honoured the past, it safeguarded the present.   Of the future it was incurious.   'There
was no rapture of the forward view.'

   The eyes of modern man have come to be focused on the future.
The immense advance of physical science, the vast increase of control of natural resources, the industrial prosperity that has followed
—all have combined to create the hope of unlimited advance in
the future—the ideal of progress as developed towards the end of
the 19th century.   It is an inspiring ideal.   You can find consolation for any temporary check, if you are convinced that man
does progress, that there is a steady movement upwards, that the
process of gradually unfolding advance can be trusted as a part
of the system in which we live.   Today, it is true, the ideal has
suffered a set-back.   We have had to realise that science may turn
in our hand against us, may become enemy instead of friend.
H. G. Wells, that great champion of the ideal, spent his last years
in despair of the power of the human intellect to solve its problems
in time.   It should have been safe to back it to succeed, for it is
its function to grasp and master difficulties.   But the problems
accumulated and became complicated too rapidly.   And there
seemed to be an adverse influence, which in older thought would
certainly be ascribed to the devil.   However that may be, the
hope of the future is far from dead.   We are still looking to the
future to justify and explain the past.

   The Roman world was far from any such ideas.   It held firmly
to the belief that the past had already revealed the best of what
could be accomplished.   Its favourite myth is that of the Golden
Age—happiness and virtue once realised on earth in the distant
past and perhaps to be restored.   It is the dream that haunts
the poets and artists of the Empire.   The examples of great men
were constantly being quoted, the events of past history frequently
recalled when they seemed to have some relevance for the present.
Professor Michael Grant, in a fascinating book, has invited us to
see on Roman coins a long series of direct anniversary issues,
struck when some famous occasion came round for celebrating
some great day of the Empire or some temple foundation.   Whether
or not he is right in many of his suggestions, his underlying idea
is sound.   The Romans chose to live under the spell of the past
For the future they had little care.   If they thought of it at all
it was as *aeternitas*, unbroken continuity like that of the natural
order.   They show little consciousness of the very idea of progress
Or progress, if it is envisaged at all, is progress backwards ; listen
to Horace :

> *damnosa quid non imminuit dies ?*
> *aetas parentum, peior avis, tulit*
> *nos nequiores, mox daturos*
> *progeniem vitiosiorem.*

An encouraging prospect !

The Christian Church had a new view to offer. The future holds its great events as well as the past. Since the coming of Christ we live in an intermediate state. The world judgment is to come, the Second Coming of the Saviour. But those great days are to be heralded by such sufferings as the race has never yet known. It is only natural to rejoice that those terrible days are far away, warded off under divine providence by the watchful care of the Roman Empire. Christianity, then, never ceased to be apocalyptic ; it looked not to unlimited progress, but to catastrophe, as far as the view of this world is concerned. But it is hard to find places where this new idea made any impression on the world. The last of the pagans continued to deplore the innovators, who destroy the ancient good for unknown goods of their own.

It is interesting to speculate how we stand in relation to this circle of ideas today. Those who are qualified to speak with authority on the long-term sciences, astronomy and geology, hold out the prospect of times that seem almost endless on the human scale. Do we assume then that mankind has an indefinitely long future on this planet ? It is in some ways a grim thought. After all, the historical period up to now is relatively very, very short, a few thousand years against the millions upon millions of astronomy. What could man make of history, art and literature, if they were to stretch over centuries upon centuries ? Does it not look as if a civilisation, like a human individual, might live too long, beyond its powers of memory and connected thinking ? Curiously enough, the apocalyptic idea—the thought that the world might end in catastrophe—has been revived from a new quarter. It appears to be a possibility—not as remote as we should like—that our new scientific powers might be turned to destruction, that the elements might even melt in fiery heat. Or, failing anything quite so dramatic, that too many atomic explosions might render large portions of the globe uninhabitable. History often follows set courses for long periods, then suddenly takes a turn. Have we reached one of those points of crisis today ?

It is possible that we have been getting our values wrong. Whether we are to be here long or not, we shall continue to believe that we are here for some purpose. We cannot prove it, but we assume it as a reasonable postulate. But suppose that what we are really here for is not the advance of wealth and prosperity, not even the noble search for widening truth, but the development of character, the unfolding of the possibilities of our species. If that is so, there might come a point when the development was complete as far as it ever could be here—when catastrophe was bound to come. I think that these are possibilities that will not cease to interest the curious. Sir Bernard Darwin, in his fascinating book on the ' next million years ', seems to assume that mankind will last that long. It is interesting to note that he makes the assumption, apparently without thinking it necessary to justify it. Within a certain train of reference the assumption justifies itself. But what if anything comes in from outside that frame ?

I do not think these speculations are as irrelevant to our own theme as they may at first seem to be. When we try to sum up what a civilisation amounts to in the total, we have to forget details and search for general conceptions, held without being stated or realised. We find certain such conceptions in the Roman Empire, which seem to be obsolete today. That means a certain bar to our understanding of it. Unless we can reach an imagination of those conceptions, we shall be unable to realise why the ancients felt and acted as they did. Then, in justice to them, we shall have to review our own general postulates and decide whether we really are so sure of them. If we can decide to regard some of these questions as still open, we may more readily enter into sympathy with the Roman Empire and its different hopes and ideals.

CHAPTER VIII

ECONOMIC LIFE

Interest in that somewhat dry subject, political economy, is very much alive today. Even those who cannot honestly feel interest are led to believe that they ought to simulate it. Since Marx and his disciples have preached to us, we have had to admit that a sound economic system, under which men can earn and receive enough for their requirements, is an absolute necessity for the good life. It is of little use preaching ethics and religion if that is missing. But it is not quite a modern discovery that you cannot be perfectly good and happy on an empty stomach. The poor have always known as much.

Political economy is a very difficult subject. Its laws are hard to determine and are disputed even among experts. Those laws have certainly been very imperfectly understood by states and statesmen. Grievous harm has often been done without deliberate malice, simply by taking the wrong measures to meet immediate difficulties. Taxation and coinage, for example, have often been handled with a view to the present only, the future being left to take care of itself. This was very true of the Romans. We shall find again and again Roman Emperors fighting vigorously against economic difficulties, without realising who their real enemies were.

Herein lies one reason why it is hard to write a history of the economic life under the Empire. The picture is in itself confused, even before we contribute anything to its confusion. But there is a second difficulty even more serious. A true account depends on a vast accumulation of details. Even with a full length account, such for example as that of Heichelheim, this does not make for easy reading. In a short sketch like ours, most of the detail must simply be taken for granted. All that is reasonably possible is to trace the main lines as simply and accurately as may be, referring for the detail to the authorities behind us.

It will be convenient to make a rough division between public and private economics, though the two fields overlap. How were the finances of the Empire controlled? The Senate, as far as it continued to govern, kept its own treasury, the *aerarium Saturni*. It was controlled by a succession of officers—quaestors, praetors,

finally prefects of the treasury.[1]   Like everything else senatorial it
was not exempt from the influence of the Emperor, exercised
through the Senate.   Tacitus observes contemptuously that it was
a farce transferring confiscated property from *aerarium* to *fiscus*, ' as if
it made the least difference '.   Into the *aerarium* went the receipts
from the senatorial provinces ;   from it were paid the expenses of
the administration as far as it still stood under senatorial control.
In practice the Emperor often sustained the treasury with grants.
All the other finances were under the Emperor.   To him came the
taxes from the imperial provinces, the yield of the indirect taxes
and various odd sources of income—vacant inheritances, treasure
trove, etc.   He had to pay for the army, the Civil Service, the costs
of the special charges which he undertook.   The imperial finances,
from Claudius onwards, were centred in one great chest, the *fiscus*.
Before him there may have been no central purse, only a number
of separate *fisci* such as can be traced even later.   The *fiscus* was
essentially a public chest, though under no control but the Emperor's.   It was fed from public sources and had to meet public
charges.   In fact, the Emperor could abuse it if he willed.   Who
was to call him to account while he lived ?   But it was not really
the Emperor's to handle as he pleased.   The private fortune of
the Emperor, the *patrimonium*, was quite separately controlled.
You might even speak of a *patrimonium privatum*, which represented
the private fortune of the Emperor apart from what belonged to
him as holder of the crown.

The chief officer of the *fiscus* was the *a rationibus*, originally an
imperial freedman, from Hadrian onwards a Roman knight.   Many
posts round the Emperor were at first committed to freedmen,
not because they were not of the first importance, but because they
were so personal.   The *patrimonium* had procurators of its own.   The
private wealth of the Emperor might be very great.   There were
huge landed properties, such as the Hellespont, once the property
of Agrippa and then left by him to the Imperial House.   There
might be vast legacies.   Many rich men left fortunes to the Emperor,
either out of ostentation, or of fear, or of genuine admiration and
wish to assist in his work.   Septimius Severus, victor in the civil wars,
created a new chest to receive the vast sums brought in by con-
fiscation after the fall of Albinus.   This was on all counts objection-
able.   The brutal punishment of the adherents of a rival was in
itself hateful.   The plunder, if it was to be levied at all, obviously
belonged to the Emperor's public chest, the *fiscus*.   The monies
were due to be used for the State.   Septimius made a new private

[1] More is said of these officers in the chapter on the Civil Service.

fund, which he used mainly to bribe and pamper the troops. The head of the *res privata* was a procurator of the first rank. There is much discussion among scholars about the distinction between *fiscus* and *patrimonium*. The distinction which we have drawn between the two will not fit all passages in our authors and is rejected by some scholars. It seems to me that the importance of the *res privata* for this discussion has been neglected. It is really a part of the *fiscus*, which the Emperor for his own ends uses as if it were *patrimonium*. The view of the lawyers, as applicable to the early Empire, may be blurred by this complication of the 3rd century. One special treasury must be mentioned—the *aerarium militare*, created by Augustus in A.D. 6 to meet the pay and pensions of soldiers, fed by the 5% on inheritances and the one (or half) per cent on sales. It was under its own prefects and seems to have functioned effectively. Its importance is obvious.

Let us now look at the budget of the Empire—at its income first, then at its outgoings. Direct taxation was not for Roman Italy. Under the Republic the direct tax, *tributum*, had been something like a war loan, rarely levied and, at least in theory, repayable. It had been abolished in 168 B.C. It was not revived under the Empire. Rome and Italy continued to enjoy a great financial privilege. For the provinces it was different. They paid direct taxes, either as *tributum*, quota levied on land or trade, or *stipendium*, a lump sum calculated for province or district. This tax might be regarded as a natural toll levied by the conqueror ; you could rationalise it by saying that provincial land passed into the possession of the Roman people and that that people allowed the provincials, as an act of grace, to retain it, but required the tribute as a rent. To assist the distribution of taxation, a census was begun by Augustus, which, step by step, covered the whole Empire and was repeated, at intervals, under his successors. The Republic had entrusted much of the collection of taxes to private companies of Roman knights, who bought the taxes for lump sums down and then tried to make as much as they could out of the collection. It was an essentially vicious system, unjust both to State and to tax-payer. The Empire, by abolishing it and collecting taxes directly, contributed seriously to the welfare of the provinces. The change from indirect to direct collection could not be immediate, but the movement was steadily in that direction. We can trace an intermediate stage when a company promoter, like one of the *publicani* of the Republic, undertakes the collection of the taxes but does so as an imperial employee himself.

Taxation in the early Empire was not exorbitant. In a few cases we hear that the Roman tax contrasted favourably with what had been paid before. Complaints of oppression were not particularly violent and not very frequent, though we hear of them, for example, in Gaul. Of course, the tax-collector was unpopular ; of course he exacted more than his legal due ; but the initial scale was not hopelessly out of proportion to ability to pay. But what really convinces us of the 'honourable poverty' of the Empire is the certain fact that the receipts were barely adequate to meet the needs, that the army was kept at a low establishment and in danger of being starved. The 3rd century, that age of misery and uncertainty, changed the picture. With the abnormal demands on the finances taxes must have swollen above the normal. Money lost its certain value and the State, in self-defence, began to demand kind instead of cash, *annona* instead of *pecunia*. Diocletian based his financial reforms on a carefully revised census of the Empire, such as Augustus had instituted. But Diocletian aimed at more exact knowledge than before. The Empire was plotted out into *capita*, human units of work, and *iuga*, units of property. With this beside him the Emperor could calculate with scientific precision just how much he could demand. The taxation period was one of fifteen years, the *indictio*, after which taxes were fixed anew ; but, if the first estimate proved too light, the State recouped itself by an extra demand, a *supraindictio*.

The indirect tax had a great appeal to the Roman as it has to the Frenchman today ; it seems less of a personal slight, more of a voluntary choice. The Roman was not exempt ; in fact, for the inheritance tax he alone was responsible. The chief indirect taxes were the 5% on inheritances, the 5% on the enfranchisement of slaves, the 5% on the sale of slaves, the one (or half) per cent on sales in the market. Apart from these there were custom duties, levied not only on the frontiers but also at fixed points within the Empire. The possible advantages of internal free trade had not been realised. The government saw in such duties an easy source of revenue and looked no further. These *portoria*, as they were called, bore different names in different parts of the Empire ; there was a 2½% in Gaul ; Africa had four main taxes, always known as the *quattuor publica Africae*. We have seen that in the early Empire the level of taxation was not very high. Of the later Empire it is no longer true. Conditions had become vastly more complicated and expensive. The new census of Diocletian should have given a much closer view of what the Empire could stand. But there is no doubt whatever that overtaxation was now normal. When sudden invasion presented a new demand on the budget, the excess had to be squeezed out by any and every vile method.

Some account can be given of regular taxation. No such account can ever be given of the irregular—the abuses that attached themselves to the system. There is evidence to show that, when Romans swindled, they did it with a lack of heart and lack of shame to take the breath. The disclosures of Cicero in his Verrine Orations show us to what lengths a governor might go in abusing his subjects and taking unwarranted gains from them. When Nero conceived the generous plan of abolishing all indirect taxes, he was indeed restrained by the wise warnings of his counsellors ; but, Tacitus tells us, some of the worst forms of fraudulent collection were permanently abolished. When the Iceni revolted under Boudicca in Britain, they were driven by the illegal extortions of the imperial procurator. Suetonius Paulinus, the governor, rather than restrain him, preferred to go off to the conquest of Anglesey. We would give a lot to be able to measure the harm that Rome suffered from these abuses. In the end, it was certainly excessive taxation that broke the heart of the provincials and opened the way to the barbarian invader. Even before the end, conditions had become bad enough. In Illyricum, as we chance to hear, the tax-payer had been well nigh crushed by the iniquitous extortions of the praetorian prefect, Probus. Valentinian I, for once, chanced to hear that all was not well and intended to avenge the wrongs of Probus's victims—only sudden death forestalled him.

We have now surveyed the main regular incomings of the State. What of its expenses ? The chief of these, of course, were the expenses of army and Civil Service, regular and inevitable. The military pay was not high—about nine golden sovereigns a year for the legionary under Augustus, raised to twelve by Domitian and higher by later Emperors ; out of that the soldier had to pay for food and kit. Salaries of governors were relatively high, those of the imperial procurators were on a more modest scale. But the charges in the total were not really heavy, as the numbers in question were not large. It was the multiplication of offices in the 4th century that aggravated the burden. The Ptolemies had made a science of exploiting their rich land and the Romans continued their practices in the same spirit, but possibly with less scientific efficiency. The city of Rome was a continual charge on the revenue. Provision of free corn for the 150,000 on the list (*aere incisi*) cost a good deal ; above and beyond that, the government was at much expense to maintain a plentiful supply of corn at moderate prices to the capital. The popularity of the Emperor was at stake, if he neglected this essential duty. The costs of the corn supply could be more or less calculated in advance. But what of the other demands of the Romans, for *circenses*, games in the circus, in the amphitheatre and the rest? The cost was always heavy and it had no ceiling ; it might rise towards infinity, if the Emperor had a special need to win good opinions. The occasional distributions of money to the civil population meant a heavy extra charge. The donatives to the army were even more serious ; the Emperors deliberately abstained from advertising them on the coins. It is just here that we reach the frontier between normal expense and *largitio*, free-giving by the Emperor. He could put his hand as he willed into the public purse ; for the time, no one could check him or call on him to draw the line between his private funds and those of the State. A careless Emperor, then, could squander the revenue of years and bring the State to the verge of bankruptcy. Committees were from time to time appointed to control expenditure or even to recover monies squandered in lavish generosity to individuals. In all such cases, the stable door was locked too late.

It is interesting to speculate what a difference it would have made, if the Roman Senate, like the British House of Commons, had had the power of the purse. In that case, the whole system of Augustus would have been something very different from what it actually was. The better Emperors showed some sense of responsibility about these grave matters of finance and often informed the Senate of the needs of the State. But unscrupulous Emperors could waste public money unchecked. Septimius made the bad even worse when he turned over what should have been fiscal goods to his new ' private fund '. A history of that fund—from the inside—which we have not got, would throw light on much that baffles us in the history of the 3rd century.

Augustus, when he died, left careful records covering the whole Empire. One document was devoted to receipts and expenses—a kind of imperial budget. It was read aloud in the Senate after his death. No such budget was presented regularly later, though the Emperor would occasionally inform the Senate of the state of the finances at some particular moment. It is beyond my ability to offer a budget of the Emperor here ; I can only hint at the way in which it was made up. On the credit side stood the taxes of the provinces, indirect taxes, income from sundry additional sources such as vacant inheritances or treasure trove. We know the rates of a number of the indirect taxes and have occasional information about the amount of direct taxation. On the debit side stand the pay and pensions of the army, the salaries of the Civil Service, the costs of administration. Of these much is known in detail, though the calculation of the total remains hard. A vague guess at the budget in the reign of Augustus might be of the order of £20,000,000. Now and then, we have information about the state of public finances at particular moments. Tiberius left a handsome balance which was squandered by Caligula. Vespasian after the civil war could tell the Senate just how much the State required to recover solvency. We have figures of the amount of bullion lost each year in luxury trade with the East. From all these data we can form an approximate idea of scale.

The Roman Republic had been familiar with the policy of *laissez faire*, taking over a minimum of actual management itself and leaving the rest to private enterprise. From such a policy the Empire steadily moved away. It replaced indirect by direct collection of taxes. When the cities ran into debt, curators were appointed to advise and supervise. By the time of Diocletian the State had its finger in every pie. We find state factories working on a large scale, primarily to satisfy public requirements, but also able to work for profit and compete with private enterprise. Many great corporations, such as those concerned with transport by sea or bread-supply in Rome, were to this extent nationalised, that the members were kept under strict control, and tied to their posts, while their rank was made hereditary.

By establishing the Augustan peace the Empire did an immense amount towards fostering trade. It also assisted it enormously by its development of communications, by road, river or canal. Though it worked solely with its own needs in mind, the trader was bound to share in the profit. The customs duties levied at particular points in the Empire were naturally unfavourable to trade. But here the government was mainly concerned with its own profit. Apart from this we hear little of interference with trade, except in so far as Diocletian's Empire brought some parts of it under its own control. Restrictions on particular callings might be imposed. Domitian, for example, forbade the development of vine-culture in the Western provinces. Senators were required to invest a proportion of their fortunes in Italian land. The income for the orphan foundations, the *alimenta*, was secured by mortgages on Italian land ; two purposes were served at once, one the charitable, the other the encouragement of Italian agriculture. The State itself was the great holder of capital and might act as banker, lending out of its immense resources to the public. When prices rose to abnormal heights, the government took steps to check them. We hear of a number of such actions in the 4th century—the most famous being Diocletian's edict *De maximis pretiis*, designed to check the ' enormity of prices ' in 301.   The real causes of the troubles being unknown, these attempts at remedy were naturally unsuccessful.

When we come to the coinage we are fortunate enough to have under our eyes a large proportion of the ancient evidence. For the great mass of coins in common use have survived to our day.   Up to a point we can read the story of the coins with certainty.   Beyond that there are problems which we can partly see, but only very imperfectly solve.   Augustus began with an excellent system of bimetallism in gold and silver.   The lower coinage, in brass and copper, was probably part token, but represented values above the metal.[1]   The Emperors chose to keep this part of the coinage under the nominal control of the Senate, thus imposing a check on their power to inflate.   Gold stood to silver at something like $12\frac{1}{2}$ to 1.   Nero reduced the weight of standard coins both of gold and silver.   It is improbable that this was anything more than a mild inflation.   It occurred at a moment when Nero was beginning to need money for his extravagances.   He also debased the silver to the extent of 10%—a dangerous move, ominous for the future.   This method of finding easy relief could be used again and again, and the bimetallism of Augustus ceased to be real ; the coinage came more and more to depend on gold.   Further debasement of the silver followed under Trajan, Septimius and other Emperors.   By the time of Gallienus the good silver had sunk to the level of bad billon,[2] containing no more than some 3–5% of silver.

Of what happened before the great crash, which came in 259 after the captivity of Valerian, little is known.   It is improbable that the deteriorating silver continued to keep its position in relation to the gold.   By the time of Trajan Decius it seems that the denarius had sunk to half its original value of one twenty-fifth of the gold piece.   Decius overstruck his double denarii on old denarii.   For the fifteen years after 259 the whole coinage had shifted its foundations.   There was no decent silver left.   The base-metal coinage decayed ; it was probably worth too much as metal to circulate as fractions of the debased silver.   The gold, it appears, was issued only for the army.   In the market it probably commanded a large premium over any nominal value.   Aurelian, the great restorer of the world, tried to reform the coinage too ; in

---

[1] The system was :   1 aureus = 25 denarii = 100 sestertii = 400 Asses = 800 semisses = 1,600 quadrantes.   The aureus was about equal in weight to a gold sovereign, the denarius about equal to a silver franc.

[2] Much debased silver.

274 he called in the old bad money and issued new. His double denarius, still of poor billon, was marked XXI, twenty small units equalling one higher one. Perhaps the most likely guess is that the new piece was still a double denarius (20 Asses ?), with the return to the old value (ten) of the denarius, but that it also equalled a sestertius. The sestertius, as the unit of reckoning, would then reappear in a new and enhanced relation to the denarius.[1] But the Western provinces, only just recovered from Tetricus, fought against the reformed coinage. They were flooded with the base billon of Gallienus, Claudius and the Gallic Emperors and refused to surrender it for the new. The vast hoards that we find of this base billon may be less due to barbarian inroads, as we used to suppose, than to the fight to reserve the old money for better times. When Carausius made himself Emperor of Britain, he struck at first on the model of the bad old money. Only when he had won peace with Rome did he, as a part-payment of his recognition, set the mark XXI on his billon piece. As soon as he broke with Rome, he dropped the mark again. It was only when Constantius Chlorus brought Britain again into ' the eternal light of Rome '[2] that the rebellion against the state money ceased.

Diocletian introduced a new reform in 295. Its details are not yet known, but we have so many data that we may hope one day to solve the problem. Diocletian issued gold at a fixed standard, first 70, then 60 to the pound, pure silver again at 96 to the pound, and billon coinage below that. If we look at the system of Diocletian in the light of tradition, it looks as if he were going back to the system of Nero, with a gold piece equalling 25 silver pieces and 100 folles. The sestertius of Diocletian would then be the large billon follis, still double denarius ; it occasionally bears the mark XXI. At that rate the aureus would contain 200 denarii, the pound of gold 12,000 denarii. But in the edict of maximum prices the price of gold is stated as 50,000 denarii a pound—although the price of gold in other forms than the gold piece is much less. The problem still awaits solution.

At the causes of the great inflation that led to the edict we can make a shrewd guess. The follis of Diocletian was a much larger coin than the XXI piece that preceded it and now survived as a sub-denomination, the half(?). An Egyptian papyrus preserves a letter from one man to his friend, telling him how the ' divine

[1] This is all very controversial : I give the account that seems to me most probable.

[2] A quotation from a famous gold medallion, found after the first World War at Arras in France.

1. *Obv.* Titus (IMP T[itus] CAES VESP[asianus] AUG PM TRP PP COS VIII). *Rev.* The Colosseum. Sestertius. 80. Rome. For the inscription cp. Pl. IV, No. 11. (p. 165).

2. *Obv.* Trajan (IMP CAES NERVAE TRAIANO AUG GER DAC PM TRP COS V PP). *Rev.* The Circus Maximus (SPQR OPTIMO PRINCIPI SC.). At foot : s[enatus] c[onsulto]. Sestertius. *c.* 108. Rome. (p. 166.)

3. *Obv.* Nero (IMP NERO CAESAR AUG P MAX). *Rev.* Wild beast show. Contorniate. *c.* 390. Rome. A hark-back to the memory of the notorious Nero.

4. Augustus. *Obv.* Civic Oak (OB CIVIS SERVATOS). *Rev.* SC and inscription (C. GALLIUS CF LUPERCUS III VIR A[ere] A[rgento] A[uro] F[lando] F[eriundo]). Sestertius. *c.* 11 B.C. Rome. (p. 190.)

5. *Obv.* Antoninus Pius (ANTONINUS AUG PIUS PP TRP COS III). *Rev.* Third largesse (LIBERALITAS AUG III). Aureus. *c.* 144. Rome. (p. 164.)

6. Augustus. *Obv.* Civic Oak (AUGUSTUS TRIBUNIC[ia] POTEST[ate]). *Rev.* SC and inscription (T. CRISPINUS SULPICIANUS III VIR AAAFF [cp. No. 4]). Dupondius [= 2 Asses]. *c.* 20 B.C. Rome. (p. 190.)

7. *Obv.* Augustus (CAESAR AUGUST[us] PONT[ifex] MAX[imus] TRIBUNIC[ia] POT[estate]). *Rev.* SC and inscription (P. LURIUS AGRIPPA III VIR AAAFF [cp. No. 4]). As. *c.* 10 B.C. Rome. (p. 190.)

8. Augustus. *Obv.* SC and inscription (III VIR AAAFF [cp. No. 4]). *Rev.* Clasped hands holding caduceus (TAURUS REGULUS PULCHER). Quadrans. *c.* 8 B.C. Rome. (p. 190.)
   Nos. 4, 6, 7, and 8 are the four denominations of base metal under Augustus.

9. *Obv.* Caracalla (ANTONINUS PIUS AUG GERM). *Rev.* Sol as charioteer (PM TRP XX COS IIII PP). Antoninianus. 217. Rome. Caracalla was named Antoninus by his father, who deliberately linked himself to the great Antonine dynasty. Elagabalus had a similar name, and is very commonly confused with his cousin Caracalla. (See Pl. VI, No. 14.) (p. 190.)

10. *Obv.* Aurelian (IMP AURELIANUS AUG). *Rev.* Sol (ORIENS AUG). At foot : XXI (see p. 191). Antoninianus. *c.* 273. Siscia. (p. 191.)

Plate V

Plate VI

1. *Obv.* Augustus (AUGUSTUS DIVI F[ilius]). *Rev.* Apollo of Actium (IMP X). At foot : ACT[iacus]. Aureus. *c.* 14 B.C. ? Lugdunum. (p. 210.)

2. *Obv.* Nero (NERO CAESAR). *Rev.* Nero as Apollo (AUGUSTUS GERMANICUS). Aureus. *c.* 65. Rome. (pp. 50, 214.)

3. *Obv.* Domitian (DOMITIANUS AUGUSTUS). *Rev.* Minerva (GERMANICUS COS XIIII). Aureus. 88. Rome. (p. 210.)

4. *Obv.* Trajan. *Rev.* Jupiter preserving Emperor (CONSERVATORI PATRIS PATRIAE). Aureus. 115. Rome. (pp. 210, 216.)

5. *Obv.* Vespasian (IMP CAES VESP[asianus] AUG PM COS IIII). *Rev.* Neptune who brings home (NEP[tunus] RED[ux]). Aureus. 72. Rome. (p. 210.)

6. *Obv.* Septimius Severus (L. SEPT[imius] SEV[erus] PERT[inax] AUG IMP IIII). *Rev.* Mars the Father (MARS PATER). Denarius. 194. Rome. For the name Pertinax see Pl. IV, No. 4. (p. 210.)

7. *Obv.* Hadrian. *Rev.* Rome the Eternal (ROMA AETERNA). Aureus. *c.* 135. Rome. (pp. 45, 180.)

8. *Obv.* Septimius Severus. *Rev.* Fortune (PM TRP III COS II PP). Denarius. 195. Rome. (pp. 54, 211.)

9. *Obv.* Hadrian (IMP CAESAR TRAIAN[us] HADRIANUS AUG). *Rev.* Pax (PM TRP COS II). Denarius. 118. Rome. (pp. 53, 211.) Hadrian began by incorporating the name Trajanus in his title. He dropped it later. (p. 210.)

10. *Obv.* Domitian (IMP CAES DOMIT[ianus] AUG GERM PM TRP VIII CENS[or] PER[petuus] PP SC.). *Rev.* Citizens offering produce at secular games (LUD[i] SAEC[ulares] A POP[ulo]). On base of dais : FRUG[es] AC[ceptae]. Sestertius. 88. Rome. (p. 20.)

11. *Obv.* Hadrian (inscription as No. 9). *Rev.* Felicitas (FELIC[itas] AUG[usti]). Denarius. 119. Rome. (pp. 52, 211.)

12. *Obv.* Hadrian (inscription as above). *Rev.* Providentia (PRO[videntia] AUG[usti]). Denarius. 119. Rome. (pp. 54, 211.)

13. *Obv.* Commodus (L[ucius] AEL[ius] AUREL[ius] COMM[odus] AUG P[ius] FEL[ix]). *Rev.* The Roman Hercules (HERCULI ROMANO AUG). Aureus. 191. Rome. (pp. 50, 210.)

14. *Obv.* Elagabalus (IMP ANTONINUS PIUS AUG). *Rev.* Emperor as priest of the Sun-god Elagabalus (SACERD[os] DEI SOLIS ELAGAB[ali]). Aureus. *c.* 219. Rome. (p. 214, and Pl. V, No. 9.)

fortune of the Emperors has decided to reduce by a half the value of the coin ' and instructs him to turn all his money into commodities. Scholars seem to be reluctant to relate this papyrus to this moment of coin history, and yet the agreement seems to be very close.   The coin evidence is just this—that Diocletian *did* reduce the coin in just the way described in the papyrus.   If we accept this view, we have in our hands one of those unseasonable actions by which Diocletian, if we may trust Lactantius, precipitated the financial disaster which he deplored.   The double denarius was not established in public confidence.   Diocletian, with the best intentions in the world, tried to put matters right by halving the value of the coin.   But he had not calculated on the chancy effects of such a legislation on the public.   His measure of deflation was misunderstood.   Instead of recovering confidence in the revalued coin, people began to fear that further devaluation would follow.   Hence the rush to turn money into goods and the inevitable soaring prices.

Subsequent history is clear in its main points, quite obscure in many of its details.   The gold and silver, being pure, can be estimated close to their actual values.   The lower coinage bears no marks of value.   It usually contains silver in small variable proportions ; in some issues it seems to contain none.   Yet to the student of imperial coins it will appear that it is never a true base-metal coinage ; the admixture of silver, even if it sometimes drops to almost nothing, was always supposed to enhance the value.   We have what may conveniently be called a ' nickel ' coinage, intermediate between silver and bronze.   Anyone who compares all this base-metal coinage of the 4th and 5th centuries with the large bronze of Augustus before and of Anastasius later will soon see what is meant.   If this is so, the weight of these coins will only give us a very general view of their value.   We shall not know how they were tariffed, until we can harmonise with one another the somewhat conflicting statements in our authorities or until new sources of information are unsealed.

The gold piece was issued regularly and in mass.   Constantine reduced the ' sixtieth ' of Diocletian to a seventy-second, and his coin, the famous ' solidus ', dominated the world market for centuries. Pure silver was still struck, sometimes in small volume, sometimes in great.   The gold-silver ratio stood at about fourteen and a half to one ; it tended to rise still further, to eighteen to one.   Gold and silver coins were probably tariffed in accordance with the market values of the metals.   With the base metal it was different. The solidus may have had a par value in small change.   But what actually happened when you had a solidus, was that you took i to market and sold it for what it would fetch ; it will usually have commanded a high premium. The solidus, in fact, was treated as a privileged piece of bullion, not as a coin denomination. The solidus served as an index of prices. As its price rose, so did the general level rise ; as it fell, the level fell. At intervals, the base-metal coinages were replaced by new. On each occasion, it seems, the old issues were demonetised. We can only guess at what the government hoped to gain by these manœuvres ; it may have meant to raise new credit easily, leaving the owners of the old demonetised coin to pay the price. Probably, each new standard piece of bad billon fell steadily in weight and fineness, till a new issue set the whole process moving again from the start. Thus the ' centenionalis ', which began life as a ' second bronze ',[1] seems to have finished as a ' fourth '.

The Emperors of the 4th century gave their subjects what they had lacked for a long time—a coinage in the precious metals that could be relied on. Some benefit from this improvement must have been experienced. But much of the benefit was lost when the government tampered with the base metal—which, after all, was what the common man mostly used. And the government was greedy in its handling of the gold. It required payment of many taxes in gold and would not even accept its own solidi—they might be debased ; the solidi tendered had to go into the melting pot, so that the exact quantity of the metal might be determined by assay. As if this were not enough, abuses were added ; as the tax-payer poured his solidi into one scale, some scoundrel would keep the counter-scale depressed. It was also possible for the government, through a guild working under its orders, to make a profitable business by selling solidi to the general public ; something could always be made on the exchange. The issue of solidi, of course, was in the hands of the government ; there is no reason to think that the mints undertook, as modern mints sometimes have done, to convert the gold of the private holder into coin gratis or at a small charge.

There is one feature of the 4th century which we can observe clearly, but not so clearly explain. In the early Empire—in fact down to the 3rd century—gold and silver had both been flowing in full current. Then, as we have seen, the silver fell into debasement ; a great deal of good metal was immobilised in tiny percentages in the base billon. The issue of gold became irregular and declined in mass. Some Emperors hardly struck gold at all—Maximin I

---

[1] ' 1st, 2nd, 3rd and 4th bronze ' are convenient descriptions, by size, of coins whose denominations we do not know.

for example. The experience of our own time warns us that the
absence of gold coinage does not imply an absence of the metal.
But why was it not coined ? Was it that the Emperor chose to keep
the precious reserves in his own hands, only jealously releasing a
little for his fellow soldiers ? From Diocletian onwards the stream
flowed again—gold steadily and in mass, silver also in mass but with
occasional intermissions. What does it mean ? Just a change in
policy ? Or some drastic change in the supply of the precious metals
available ? Every collector of coins is familiar enough with the
phenomenon. The prices of gold coins drop abruptly after Constantine. But again what does it all mean ? Gold and silver again
appear in mass. Where do they come from ? From reserve ?
Or from some new source ? There is no evidence of the discovery
of new mines at this moment or of enhanced production from old
mines long in use. No new treasures came into Roman hands.
Something may have been won from Persia—but not on a scale
sufficient to change the whole national economy. Such windfalls
could hardly be on a sufficient scale for that. Trajan, it is claimed,
gained the treasure of Decebalus the Dacian. But could that
treasure, however jealously hoarded, amount to any serious per-
centage of the total gold supply of the Empire ? Surely not. The
writer of the anonymous pamphlet of circa 370, who proposed
inventions and reforms in war and finance, declares that Constantine
made a ridiculously free use of gold and thereby brought on many
evils. The writer does not appear to understand very well what he
is saying. But his statement *does* agree with the evidence of the
coins—the circulation of gold in a new abundance. The 3rd
century had witnessed the hoarding of gold. A new policy now
released it again. The will of the Emperor by itself could doubtless
effect much ; it could bring into the light of day long reserved
treasures. But there is one possibility by which new resources could
now be tapped. From ancient times the temples of the gods had
accumulated masses of treasure in the precious metals. After the
religious reform of Constantine paganism must appear doomed
sooner or later. Even before anything drastic happened there might
be a movement to release the long-hoarded temple treasures. We
have no means of estimating amounts, but it would not be ridiculous
to suppose that the gold and silver hoarded in all the temples of
the Empire might represent a very considerable addition to the
stocks available. If a country is in a sound economic position
increase of the money in circulation may safely be made in reliance
on the wealth and industry of the nation. But gold and silver have
so long been worshipped as idols that such increase has been sup

posed to depend on increased supplies of them. The Empire, then, may have gained enormously by the mobilisation of long frozen assets. The question is of such importance as to demand much further enquiry.

In the troubles of the 3rd century, the decay of the coinage led to a partial return to dealing in kind. The State demanded many of its requirements direct from the producers. The pay of the soldier and civil servant was made mainly in kind. To use the Roman terms, *annona* grew at the expense of *moneta*. Later we find officials clamouring for payment in cash, *adaeratio*. In the cities, as a whole, the money régime must have been in vogue. But in the country, on the large estates, where many a great landowner maintained a little estate within the State and sheltered many a refugee from the law, a natural economy must have reigned. You produced for your own use and had comparatively little to do with the commercial means of exchange.

The wealth of a nation consists not in its coin alone or in its trade, but in its man-power. The early Empire still used slave labour without sparing or discrimination. As long as slaves could be bought, there could be no lack of hands for menial work. The Romans had learned to regard immense establishments of slaves as a necessity of civilised life. But slave labour was economically wasteful and the supply of slaves decreased. Foreign war no longer brought in the same regular stock, and slaves acquired from civil war were invidious and hard to sell. One might expect a sharp rise in the status of the free labourer with the increased demand on his service. This must to some extent have occurred, but not to anything like the extent that we should have imagined. There was some check operating on the natural trend of events. It may have had something to do with the free labourer himself. He may have been, in the mass, lazy and unenterprising and incapable of taking full advantage of the movement of events in his favour. He was certainly not organised in anything like the style of modern trade unions. But there was at least one more cause at work. The State, it seems, for its own ends interfered in the labour market, checked free movement from place to place and sought to tie men in a series of serf classes. With the State setting such an example, private enterprise, even beyond the State's control, will have tended to take the same track.

It will be of interest to investigate this point more closely. We are suggesting that the Roman Empire suffered from a deficiency of man-power and was therefore driven to try artificial means of maintaining, if not increasing it. This is not the difficulty of the modern state. Since Malthus, we have all been afraid of the increase of population over means of sustenance. The Malthusian doctrine may possibly have been accepted too readily as being necessarily and universally true. There is at least enough truth in it to worry the practical economist. Prophets of the future seem to be confident that the population will continue to increase by geometrical progression while the food supply is tied down to arithmetical. Hence the pessimism that still regards wars as our natural protection against over-population—simple variants of the other safeguards, pestilence and famine. In the Roman Empire things seem to have been very different. Statistics of population are very hard to collect, but we have clear indications on some points. We have already seen that the Roman army was very small for its tasks. Reluctance to undertake military service was a part cause ; but Augustus's restraint is easier to understand if the man-power at his disposal was not over-abundant. In the 4th century the anxiety about the deficiencies of labour was too evident to be mistaken. The State forbade all freedom, for fear that a gap might be left which could not be filled. Of plagues we hear enough under the Empire, of famines very little. The careful organisation of the corn supply will partly explain this, but it argues against excessive population. If this is really true, if, as has been conjectured, the population of the Empire dropped abruptly in the disorders of the 3rd century, to what are we to attribute it ? Deliberate childlessness, refusal to bring up children, would operate on a large scale only in the upper classes. It certainly helped to destroy the old aristocracy of the capital. But, in all classes, refusal to bring up unwanted children—the exposure of unwanted girls, in particular—relieved poor parents of the burden of education and acted as an almost automatic check on over-population. The rate of exposure would naturally rise in hard times. Christians, who were so often accused of shirking their duties to society in not bringing up enough children, for example, abstained from exposure and may therefore have made at least as good a contribution as their pagan critics. There was at times a lack of tension, of energy in the Empire, which may have made parents indifferent to their duty to the coming generation. It is hard to estimate how far this operated to keep numbers down. The great pestilences, those of the reigns of Marcus Aurelius and Trebonianus Gallus, for example, took heavy toll. Normally we should expect the loss to begin to be made good almost at once. If this did not happen in this case, we shall have to think of the miseries of the Empire, at home and abroad, which added to the loss of life and contributed to loss of heart. Otto Seeck has stated the case in a peculiarly pessimistic form ; he traces a process of definite ' Ausrottung der Besten ', a radical extirpation of merit. We are seeing in our own times the danger that arises, in doing justice to the ordinary man, of doing injustice to the exceptional. Seeck exaggerates certain tendencies that *did* exist ; in a society like that of the Empire a small highly cultured top level has to civilise a great underlying mass. The small élite is always liable to collapse before its work is done. Seeck attributes too much to deliberate malice what was the result of natural causes. The fact remains with us that the Empire suffered from declining energy, evidenced by a declining population. The barbarian world, with its brimming masses, could less and less easily be halted at the frontiers. The Empire was like a beleaguered garrison. No hand could be spared, every man must be directed to his special post and must not leave it. The life of the later Empire was, we might say, lived under a severe medical regimen. It made it possible to survive, but quite impossible to survive with any comfort. It is a sad picture, but one so unlike the bogies that our prophets conjure up for us that we can even find a little satisfaction in it.

So far we have been speaking mainly of the economic system of the State. We have still to attempt to survey private life. Between the most primitive and the most developed states of society many varieties of economies exist, from primitive barter to a highly developed system of metallic currency and credit. In the vastly varied Empire many different forms of life, with economies to correspond to them, existed side by side. In the backward parts of the Empire, among woods and mountains or along the fringes of the desert, life was still wild and unformed, pastoral rather than agricultural, trading very little far afield and therefore having very little use for money. The wealthier lands, lands that knew the culture of grain, olive, and vine, stood on a higher level ; their products were needed and they could sell them and buy their own requirements from abroad. But, right out in the country, there might be large establishments, which aimed at producing their own requirements and clung to the old ' house ' economy. As soon as we touch the cities, we approach an advanced money economy. Exchange of goods is a natural matter of everyday life and coin is naturally used to facilitate exchange. The minor, but often lucrative, forms of agriculture, especially the culture of choice vegetables and fruits, were mainly linked to the towns that took their produce. Finally, the great cities of the Empire sold and bought freely, sending out their own manufactures and receiving those luxuries that they could not themselves produce. This was the furthest that the Empire advanced—an advanced money economy with some slight development of the system of credit. Down to the beginning of the 4th century there was a growth of exchange. The Empire, as far as trade went, is found to fall into a number of economic blocks—the Western provinces, Italy and the islands, Africa as far as Cyrenaica, Greece and Asia, Syria, Egypt. Many cities of Gaul and Spain traded far abroad. The cities of Italy had begun even before them, while the cities of the East inherited much of the tradition of those men of genius at trade, the Phoenicians.

The principles of agriculture and the keeping of cattle and sheep had long been studied ; a good living could be made out of them and still was. The Carthaginians had devoted special attention to the growing of grain and the Romans had not been slow to learn out of their book. What was new under the Empire was the close control of the movements of grain on the grand scale for the needs of Rome and, in a minor degree, of other cities of the Empire. The *annona* belongs rather to the other side of our subject —the side of the State—but private enterprise also comes in. Shippers and carriers were enrolled in masses in these essential services. They were encouraged by good pay and some privileges and were held bound to their tasks. In the 4th century these guilds became compulsory and hereditary. There was a great development of the growing of choice fruits or the fattening of choice birds for the table. Private fortunes could be made by a close study of the turns of fashion and the greedy caprice of the Roman gourmand. It was chiefly country districts near great capitals that came under such development, and this was specially true of the country round Rome. It seems likely that the later Emperors had at their disposal a far better knowledge of the productive capacity of the Empire than had ever been known before, except in the special case of Egypt under the Ptolemies. The *praefecti praetorio* and their *vicarii* must have been something like controllers of food and production such as modern ages seldom see except in time of war. The late Empire never got far from a war basis.

Under the peace of the Empire trade was bound to prosper. There were now as a rule no political frontiers to cross. The economic frontiers *could* be crossed. The Empire made its profit out of the customs, but did not use them in a restrictive sense. Carriage by land for long distances was expensive, carriage by sea comparatively cheap and therefore to be preferred wherever possible. There was an open field for individual enterprise. Many a lucky adventurer, like Petronius's Trimalchio, made and lost fortunes in hazardous voyages—and made them again. Augustus, near the close of his life, was delighted by the hymn of praise that Alexandrine merchants off Puteoli raised to him ; ' through him they sailed the sea in safety, through him they could make their wealth, through him they were happy'. Private enterprise had this field almost to itself. State manufactures belong to a later period. But many small cities began to claim their share in the general prosperity by developing particular kinds of production. Many Italian cities were known for their special manufactures, and Gallic and Spanish cities soon came to join them.

Mass production for export was of course known, especially at the great Eastern capitals, Antioch and Alexandria. In the West the Samian pottery, mostly of Gallic makers, had a wide market. For the most part the rule seems to have been—many businesses of moderate compass rather than a few of great. Even so we might have expected a vast growth of enterprise and the formation of great trading interests. But we certainly do not find it. We do not find private corporations with such economic power that the State must pay heed to them. Even the great corporations that were drawn in towards the fringe of the Civil Service seem to have had little, if any, power of collective bargaining. Why was this ?

The State, as we know, was very jealous of private *collegia* of every kind ; the only general exception was made in favour of friendly burial societies, essentially harmless and restricted in their aims. This suspicion of the State will have operated against the formation of large companies. It will have been a matter of many moderate fortunes made by individuals. What happened to the lucky maker of money ? He might, like Trimalchio, devote the rest of his life to devising means of squandering his fortune. But he would also be likely to seek social advancement. In the provinces he might buy with his surplus the favour of his fellow citizens and their suffrages in return for his munificence. He might become a Roman knight, perhaps in time even a senator. If a senator, he must invest the third of his property in Italian land. In this way much of the hoarded wealth would flow back in familiar channels. There was no class of the new rich as such. The Emperor might naturally be jealous of over-great wealth. A number of instances of confiscations of great fortunes are known. Excuses could always be found. A certain Sextus Marius was executed under Tiberius, ostensibly for a horrible crime, incest with his daughter, actually, men said, because he owned too many mines in Spain. The 5%

tax on inheritances brought back some of the money into the exchequer. Often, the wealthy man would make the Emperor an heir in part, in order to save the remainder for his kin.

We come to the next point. The immense development of trade might naturally lead to a correspondingly great development of credit. Trade on the grand scale requires free movement of capital. It becomes most convenient, if not absolutely essential, to be able to transfer wealth without the actual transport of bullion or coined money—the development of banking in fact. At this point progress halted. Letters of credit could not remain unknown. Money owned in one quarter could be transferred to another, when the traveller took with him some token to establish his rights to draw on it. But there is no evidence of great banks, drawing in to themselves money from many sources and acting as managers of the whole credit of the Empire. We have seen in modern times how great businesses, nominally private, may control what are really the state resources. Perhaps the possibilities of management on this grand scale had not yet been realised. But it was probably the jealousy of the State that checked this growth near its source. The Emperor himself was the great financier. A large part of the wealth of the Empire flowed through his treasuries. A great deal more fell in through the confiscations which began on a grand scale under Septimius Severus. With the Emperor as chief banker in fact no private individual could dare to compete. The *fiscus* itself, as we have seen, could act as banker. There was a limit, then, to development, and the mysterious field of exploitation of capital was not fully explored.

Trade with the peoples outside the Empire on most of its frontiers was not unprofitable. The barbarians had raw materials and slaves to deliver ; they were glad to take in return various articles of use and even of luxury. With the East the case was otherwise What the Empire imported was mainly articles of luxury—precious stones, perfumes, aromatics. The costs of transport and the duties were enormous, the dangers serious. The cost was colossal in proportion to what actually came in, and it had to be met mainly through the export of bullion. Roman gold and silver drifted in masses to India, as is still evidenced by hoards of the precious metal found there. Roman observers were shocked, and with good reason at this dissipation of wealth that could not easily be replaced. I might have been wise for the Empire to impose restrictions on the export of bullion. But the State took its share in the prize and chose here to pursue a policy of *laissez-aller*, when actually firm control was demanded of it. The loss of bullion leads toward deflation, while many other tendencies worked in the opposite direction. It might have been hoped that the two sets of tendencies would have balanced one another out. A shortage of precious metals is a symptom of the inflation of the 3rd century.

Wealth, by modern standards, was very modest. The census of a senator was a million sestertii, about £10,000—a fortune of that amount, not an income. A hundred thousand sestertii entitled a man to count himself moderately well off. Individuals, of course, might own much more, but the average was not high. Throughout the provinces wealthy men could be found, sometimes multi-millionaires. As we have seen, they often let their money flow back into the coffers of their cities. The masses of the citizens were anything but rich. In Rome we hear much of the clients, free indeed, but dependent on very grudging doles from their patrons. The imperial liberalities, often on the scale of three pounds per person, were appreciated as a serious contribution to the cost of living and rearing a family. There must have been thousands in Rome and other cities who lived more or less from hand to mouth, earning a little by small trade or casual labour, but always hoping for a little more from imperial munificence. In the country, poverty will have been the rule—except that, where needs are small and easily satisfied, not much money is needed for happiness.

There is material in plenty for the study of wages and prices in the Empire, but there are difficulties in reading it. Egypt has given us its papyri, to enlighten us about social and economic conditions. But papyri are often imperfect ; the exact size of measures of capacity is subject to some uncertainty ; the coins cannot always be interpreted with assurance. Evidence of prices often comes from times of abnormal scarcity. We cannot yet use the edict of Diocletian on maximum prices to the full, because we have not yet determined the value of his basic denarius. We need not wait before drawing some conclusions, but they are not yet as precise as they might be. In general, we seem to see that average prices and wages, though lower than in modern times, were not so to any enormous extent. As the purchasing power of money was certainly much higher, it might look as if the ordinary man commanded more from life than his modern successor. The prices that we find recorded must be mainly exceptional ; the average will have been lower. In the course of the Empire the tendency was for prices to rise. We find one great inflation in the 3rd century and another, even more extreme, in the 4th. Whether the enormous inflation noted in that century in Egypt was confined to that country is hotly debated. As long as the country was reasonably rich in natural resources, the standard of living may have been relatively high, even though money was scarce. What was needed could be easily obtained. But money for special purposes may have been very hard to come by. Luxuries were for the few. The prices were enormous, often quite ridiculously high, and the competition for them was limited to the very few.

We have touched on a number of themes that excite our curiosity without fully satisfying it. The early Empire was obviously fairly prosperous and used its prosperity not unwisely. The 3rd century brought acute economic sufferings. The 4th century found relief from its most urgent necessities at a terrible cost. The existence of wealth is not enough ; it must be capable of being applied where it is needed. The late Empire seems to have been permanently embarrassed both through shortages of goods and through imperfect distribution. We can point to several causes—loss of bullion to the East, loss of silver in minute amounts in the debased bronze coinage, excessive demands by the State, exhaustion and despair among the tax-payers. All these contributed to the decline of the West.

The possibilities at the disposal of an all-powerful state are enormous, if it can estimate its resources in money, natural wealth and man-power. If the Roman State could have been administered by a syndicate of men of modern capacity in banking and industry, there might have been rationalisation on a magnificent scale. The State might have been able to meet all demands upon it and still have left its subjects to enjoy a very fair measure of prosperity. If it failed to realise all these possibilities, that will have been due to lack of knowledge as well as lack of interest. The Emperors were not blind to the decline of the prosperity of its cities and to the threat thus offered to the prosperity of the State. They did what they could by appointing their own special commissioners to supervise local finances. But the deterioration went on unchecked. By the 4th century the situation was desperate. The State had great difficulty in collecting its dues and martyred the local senates in collecting them. With the cities individuals suffered too. All men drew uneasy breath, unhappy and discontented where they stood, hampered whenever they tried to better their condition by change.

What have we to say of class warfare under the Empire ? Can anything like it be traced ? Divergence of interests there must always have been. We can trace the fight between the Senate and the knights, between the knights and the freedmen. We can see the country districts at first subordinated to the cities—but tending in the end to triumph—the Empire as a whole treated as less privileged than Rome and Italy. But can we find any trace of an oppressed underprivileged proletariat, fighting to maintain its interests against a happier bourgeoisie? It is tempting for us, full of Marxist ideas, to look for such a fight. But can we find it? Rostovtseff, in his bitter experience of the clashes in modern Russia, has found abundant evidence of such a fight in the 3rd century. To him the rise of the army appears as an upthrust of unprivileged sections of the community against the bourgeoise in the cities. The general verdict of scholars has gone against him. The insolence of the army is unquestioned. But was it the insolence of a profession or of a class? Of a profession, surely. The army does not discriminate much in its hostility to other interests than its own. It shows no particular indulgence for the poor civilian. All civilians are despised in contrast to those who wield the sword. Of all the pretenders of the 3rd century not one inscribed the slogan of social and economic reform on his banners. Some traces of such movements might be found, if our knowledge were not so scanty. But, if they were ever of serious importance, surely we should have heard more of them. Discomfort was general. Every class no doubt felt with peculiar acuteness where the shoe pinched. But the enemy, if an enemy must be found, was looked for in the tyrant state or in the restless barbarian invaders, or even in the Christians, whose newfangled ways were disturbing all the old norms of life. That any class ever felt that its chief enemy lay in some other class is not to be proved.

Class or caste was part of the set-up of the State and yet, economically, the State was not markedly class-conscious. But this does not necessarily mean that sharp economic clashes between classes might not sometimes arise. Some of the suffering of the later Empire might have been allayed if its causes had been better understood. As it was, there was much blind discontent, but little struggle against definite obstacles. When we search for economic roots of known evil, we are searching for that of which the sufferers were barely conscious themselves. For all that, the search is stimulating and may lead to results of value.

CHAPTER IX

RELIGION AND PHILOSOPHY

We have already had occasion to observe more than once that a civilisation cannot properly be judged except by its whole content ; it is not just a matter of political form or social organisation, but of a whole, including literature, art and religion as well. It is particularly important to remember this principle as we approach the question of how the Roman of the Empire thought in large terms of human life and destiny. For we have reached the domain on which, if on any, the Empire has a great and permanent importance.

It does not take long to discover that the Empire was not one of the great ages of creative literature or art. There is nothing in the social build-up to command any great admiration. Its technical achievement was not brilliant except along one or two special lines. Its science was on the decline rather than on the advance. It produced nothing of distinction in the economic field. Its political achievement—the building up of a society of peoples that could live together in peace—is perhaps too often underrated ; however high we may rate it, it failed far more than it succeeded. But, when we come to religion, it is clear at once that we can no longer talk of lack of vitality and decline. An age in which the great Jewish tradition attained its world form in the last and greatest of its prophets, in which the conditions that were to produce Islam were being prepared in the Arabian deserts, in which, a little beyond the bounds of the Empire, the noble faith of Buddha was spreading in India, in which the old Persian religion was to enjoy an official revival and produce its great heretic in the person of Mani—how can one deny to such an age the title of high religious significance ?

With philosophy the case is somewhat different. No one could claim for the Empire that it was a high tide of philosophy. Even a Plotinus will not bring back the great age of Greek philosophy, of the Pre-Socratics, of Plato and Aristotle, of Zeno and Epicurus. But the love of wisdom still persisted. If philosophy now lagged behind religion it was because the drift of the age was in that direction—towards the intuitive, instinctive reaction to life rather than the intellectual. Philosophy and religion are alike in that both address themselves to life as a whole—what is the nature of the world and of man, what is man's destiny, what his duties and his aims. But philosophy tries to find answers that will satisfy the understanding ; religion is concerned with the satisfaction of the emotions, the imagination, even the instincts, we may say. The two are of course seldom found quite apart. A religion tends to develop an appropriate philosophy, a philosophy may suggest moral teachings that amount to a religion. The two may be friendly to one another or they may be hostile. The people of the Empire, living more on their emotions than on their cold reason, tended to prefer religion.

The absence of serious political discussion, when the main questions have been settled once for all, left a void which needed something new to fill it. The something new might have been, as in our own day, the natural sciences. In the Empire they were in no way ready to take the lead. Religion was the natural substitute. It had a deep interest, an almost universal appeal and, normally, it was fairly safe politically. We shall note exceptions later. The importance of the new religious development has long been recognised. What has taken longer to recognise is the vitality that still persisted under the forms of the old pagan, polytheistic religion. We used to be told that the old Olympian religion was already moribund in the time of Augustus. We can see more clearly today. Much of the old myth was being discarded ; new meanings were found in the old stories and practices. No doubt, the wine that was poured in was likely to break the old bottles ; but it was into the old bottles that many insisted on pouring it. Perhaps for all these reasons the present chapter should be the central one of this book. Religion and philosophy have this to be said for them : that they set themselves worthy problems, the problems of nature and destiny in their widest sense, that they are universal in so far as they ask questions that are of concern to every man, that they are humane and democratic, in so far as they move outside the ban of ordinary custom and convention. Our own age, triumphant in its exact knowledge, its conquest of the material world, tends to dismiss both religion and philosophy with the observation that they attempt too much and miss their mark most of the time. But are not we in danger of completely missing the synoptic view ?

For convenience we will separate religion and philosophy and will take religion first. In no field is it easy to offer generalisations that will hold true of the whole Empire, at all times and in all places. Nowhere more so than in religion. There cannot be only one way to the supreme mystery ; so said Symmachus, and

1. *Obv.* Philip I (IMP PHILIPPUS AUG). *Rev.* Lion shown at secular games (SAECULARES AUGG). At foot : I [i.e. 1st officina]. Antoninianus. 248. Rome. (p. 230.)

2. *Obv.* Philip I (inscription as above). *Rev.* She-wolf shown at secular games (inscription as above). At foot : II [i.e. 2nd officina]. Antoninianus. 248. Rome. (p. 230.)

3. *Obv.* Salonina, wife of Gallienus (SALONINA AUG). *Rev.* The Empress in peace (AUGUSTA IN PACE). Antoninianus. *c.* 260. Milan. (pp. 53, 233.)

4. *Obv.* Gallienus (GALLIENAE AUGUSTAE). *Rev.* ' Peace on every hand ' (UBIQUE PAX). Aureus. *c.* 267. Rome. (pp. 50, 53, 233.) The feminine is very curious. It was once supposed that this coin was struck in derision by the enemies of Gallienus, referring to his supposed effeminacy. More probably it represents him as Kore, the goddess of the mysteries. But it remains a curiosity.

5. *Obv.* Diocletian (DIOCLETIANUS P[ius] F[elix] AUG). *Rev.* Jupiter the Preserver (IOVI CONSERVAT[ori] AUGG). At foot : P[rima, sc. officina] ROM[ae]. Aureus. *c.* 296. Rome. (pp. 50-1, 233.)

6. *Obv.* Diocletian (IMP C[aesar] C[aius] VAL[erius] DIOCLETIANUS PF AUG). *Rev.* Jupiter the Thunderer (IOVI FULGERATORI). At foot : P[rima] R[omae]. Aureus. *c.* 288. Rome. (pp. 50-1, 233.)

7. *Obv.* Diocletian. *Rev.* The Genius of the Roman People (GENIO POPULI ROMANI). In centre : B Γ (mint-marks, probably denoting periods of mint-working). At foot : TR[eviris]. Follis. *c.* 296. Treviri. (p. 283.)

8. *Obv.* Constantine I (CONSTANTINUS PF AUG). *Rev.* The Sun-god (SOLI INVICTO COMITI). At foot : P[rima] L[o]N[dinii]. Bronze coin. *c.* 310. London. (p. 214.)

9. *Obv.* Constantius II (D[ominus] N[oster] CONSTANTIUS P[ius] F[elix] AUG). *Rev.* The Vows—' thirty paid for, forty undertaken ' (VOTIS XXX MULTIS XXXX). At foot : LUG[duni]. Silver coin. *c.* 354. Lugdunum. (p. 223.) The vows were undertaken yearly, but with emphasis for particular terms, e.g. VOT V when four years of rule had been completed, X when nine had been, and so on. The common formula—VOT X MULT XX —can unfortunately bear two meanings : (1) vows undertaken for ten years, with enhancement (MULTIS) for twenty—such vows could begin a reign ; or (2) vows paid for ten years, undertaken with enhancement for twenty—such vows began at the expiry of nine years. The second meaning holds for Constantius II, the first for Valentinian I (Pl. I, No. 16).

10. *Obv.* Aurelian (SOL DOM[inus] IMP[erii] ROM[ani]). *Rev.* Worship of Sol, Lord of the Roman Empire, set up at Rome by Aurelian (AURELIANUS AUG CONS[ecravit]). Bronze coin. *c.* 274. Serdica. (p. 214.)

11. *Obv.* Vetranio (DN VETRANIO PF AUG). *Rev.* Emperor victorious with the Christian standard (HOC SIGNO VICTOR ERIS). At foot : SIS[ciae]. Centenionalis. 351. Siscia. (pp. 51, 234.) The motto on the reverse perhaps represents Constantine I as the pattern of Vetranio.

12. *Obv.* Magnentius (DN MAGNENTIUS PF AUG). *Rev.* Monogram of Christ, with alpha and omega (SALUS DD[ominorum] NN[ostrorum] AUG[usti] ET CAES[aris])—' the salvation of our Augustus and Caesar '. At foot : AMB[iani]. Centenionalis. 352. Ambianum. (pp. 36, 51.)

13. *Obv.* Julian II (DN FL[avius] CL[audius] IULIANUS PF AUG). *Rev.* Apis as sign of the ' Security of the State ' (SECURITAS REIPUB[licae]). At foot : CONS P[ercussus ?] A[i.e. at 1st officina]. Follis. 363. Constantinople. (pp. 36, 51.)

Plate VII

Plate VIII

1. *Obv.* Theodosius I (D[ominus] N[oster] THEODOSIUS PF AUG). *Rev.* 'The Salvation of the State', with monogram of Christ (SALUS REIPUBLICAE). At foot : CONS. Bronze coin. *c.* 393. Constantinople. (pp. 51, 235.)

2. *Obv.* Marcian (DN MARCIANUS PF AUG). *Rev.* Victory with cross, as Christian angel (VICTORIA AUGGG). At foot : CON OB[ryzum]. Solidus. *c.* 455. Constantinople. (pp. 53–4.) For obryzum see Pl. I, No. 16.

3. *Obv.* (below). Justinian II standing facing, holding cross (D[ominus] IUSTINIANUS SERVU[S] CHRISTI). *Rev.* (above). Bust of Christ facing, holding the Book of the Gospels (IHS CRISTOS REX REGNANTIUM). At foot : CONS. Early 8th century. Constantinople. (p. 51.)

4. *Obv.* Horace. *Rev.* The tragic poet, Accius. Contorniate. *c.* 390. Rome. (pp. 247, 266.)

5. *Obv.* Augustus. *Rev.* Cow. Aureus. *c.* 20 B.C. East. (p. 286.)

6. *Obv.* Nero (NERO CLAUD CAESAR AUG GER PM TRP IMP PP). *Rev.* Annona and Ceres presiding over corn-supply (ANNONA AUGUSTI CERES SC.). At foot : s[enatus] c[onsulto]. Sestertius. *c.* 65. Rome. (pp. 54, 287.)

7. *Obv.* L. Aelius Caesar. *Rev.* Concordia (TRIB[unicia] POT[estate] COS II). At foot : CONCORD[ia]. Aureus. 137. Rome. (pp. 21–2, 287.)

8. *Obv.* Postumus (full face, instead of in profile). *Rev.* 'The kindliness of the Emperor' (INDULGENTIA POSTUMI AUG [usti]). Aureus. *c.* 266. Gaul. (pp. 288, 291.)

9. *Obv.* Septimius Severus (SEVERUS PIUS AUG PM TRP VIIII). *Rev.* Julia Domna, Caracalla and Geta, 'the Bliss of the Age' (FELICITAS SAECULI). Aureus. 201. Rome. (pp. 23, 288.)

10. *Obv.* Constantine I, with face turned upwards. *Rev.* Emperor as conqueror (GLORIA CONSTANTINI AUG). At foot : SIS[ciae]. Double Solidus. *c.* 330. Siscia. (pp. 234, 288–9.)

many are the ways that we find the peoples of the Empire taking.
Yet there is one important feature common to most of the religions
of the Empire—they were polytheistic, systems of many gods.
Some trace of henotheism—with the belief in one god supreme
over the many—is usually found. But the supreme god is often
like a Great King ruling over many provinces, governed by his
satraps. The gods are conceived of as ruling the natural world.
They preside also over the destiny of states and cities. To a limited
extent they may be the guardians of morality. Themselves, they
may appear to us both immoral and capricious and may even
make unethical demands on their worshippers. But they commonly
have one attribute, without which we should seriously misconceive
them—their ' numinous ' power. They belong to another order
than the human. They are not subject to many human limitations,
they are not subject to death ; they are the ' dwellers in heaven
that live forever '. They are the great example to man of Other-
ness, of a nature distinct from his own. In spite of all the anthropo-
morphism in the old religion, this difference persists. It follows
that man cannot judge these beings by his own standards. It is a
part of the religious revolution, brought in by Christianity, that
the gods are called to the bar of morality and law, that it
is decided that a heaven that has forgotten these is no true
heaven.

In the centre stand the great gods of Greece and Rome. Originally the gods of Greece and Rome had been far apart—the gods
of Greece, figures of wonderful beauty and attraction, the chosen
themes of art and poetry, surrounded with strange and exciting
myth—the Roman remote powers, known in their workings, their
numina (gods), but only imperfectly realised as man-like and with
very little legend or myth. In course of time, chiefly through
the surrender of Rome to the superior attractions of Greek imagination, the two systems have been very perfectly concorded. The
equations have been nicely worked out. Zeus is Jupiter, Hera
Juno, Athene Minerva, Ares Mars, Hermes Mercury, Aphrodite
Venus and so on. . The translation extended to deities of slightly
lower rank, especially to the heroes raised to deity for their services
to the world. Thus we have Dionysus equated to Liber, Heracles
to Hercules, Asclepius to Aesculapius, Castor and Polydeuces, the
Heavenly Twins, to Castor and Pollux. The process of equation
goes far back into Roman history, far earlier than was once supposed.
The ancient ' religion of Numa ' belongs to an almost forgotten
past. At least as early as the Etruscan kings of Rome, Greek
deities were coming to Rome under Etruscan forms. Later influ-

ence was more direct ; Asclepius, brought to Rome as Aesculapius near 300 B.C., is a good example.

It is round the figures of the great Olympians, the central Twelve, that Greek-Roman polytheism revolves. Modern scholars often find them hard to interpret. They miss in them the personal appeal that should be a part of any vital religion. One explanation is that they are the gods of a conquering race, the official protectors of its supremacy. The worship of the heart, it is argued, was given by the masses of the socially unprivileged to older and quite distinct powers. In all this there is a large amount of truth. But we must not insist on this aspect of truth to the exclusion of others. Even the Olympians were not only powers of nature and the State. They were concerned with some sides of morality ; they were capable of inspiring private devotion. Their forms, once defined by myth, poetry and art, dominated the imagination of the world. The whole was seen under a number of aspects, each aspect represented by one or more of the chief gods. Jupiter stood for the majesty of the natural order, for the dignity of the great State. Apollo was the symbol of youth, beauty and healthy activity. Bacchus represented the joy of life, inspired by his great gift to man, the vine. Venus was the expression of the great passion of sexual love. Heaven was spanned by a rainbow of many colours ; the white light to which they all added up was not so clearly seen.

For the Greek and Roman there were 'many forms of things spiritual '. Apart from the great Olympians and their train there were gods of the country—Silvani, fauns, satyrs, nymphs of hill, wood and stream—Oreads, Dryads, Naiads and Nereids. The nymphs may be regarded as so many distinct forms of the one great Earth Mother. There were spirits presiding over individuals and institutions, genii and Fortunes. There were moral powers, immanent in human life and directing the activities suggested by their names—Peace, Felicity, Salvation and a host of others. The Virtues we often call them ; they still lasted on into Christian thought as one of the orders of angels. Some kindred powers are more properly defined as *res exoptandae*, objects of desire or blessings. *Spes*, Hope, is a good example. A peculiarly Roman conception was the *numen*, the god of the pure, single act, seen in his activity and in nothing more. It is probable that this was the key thought of early Roman belief. Divine power was observed in its single manifestations. Some of these *numina* remained isolated ; others could be grouped together, until from them was created the conception of a great divinity with many manifestations ; thus the

Juno of Virgil's ' Aeneid ' has many *numina*. There were gods of
the fields and the woods, presiding over every detail of the farmer's
work—the gods of sowing, harrowing, reaping—the gods of felling,
clearing, burning. And there were countless minor deities who
watched over every phase of human life ; who tended the child
from his cradle, taught him how to suck, how to crawl, how to
talk ; who presided over marriage, or presided over birth. In
one sense these godlings may be regarded as so many fractions of
the one genius (Juno for the woman), the spirit of the race in the
individual, who goes with you through all your life, whom you
honour with special care on your birthday, who in some sense
may be thought of as surviving death. This religious atomism
seems rather absurd ; it has been questioned whether it was really
a part of serious belief. The evidence is that it was. It lies very
near to the primitive Roman conception of the divine. St.
Augustine, writing very near the end of the ancient paganism,
still finds it worth his while to devote some time and trouble to
ridiculing just such beliefs. He would hardly have done so if they
had not been deeply rooted.

The gods of the barbarian world are known to us from chance
references in literature and from thousands of inscriptions of the
imperial age, chiefly dedications made by worshippers. Their
strange names may be read and marvelled at in the pages of
Dessau's great Sylloge of Roman Inscriptions. In many cases they
were associated with the country, with this or that grove, hill or
stream. We have recently had new light on one from Britain,
Nodens the god of woods and water, worshipped on the Severn.
Some of them were great gods presiding over larger provinces.
Such were the German and Gallic Triads. Their cults were
primitive and human sacrifice was not infrequently included. It
was for this abomination that the Romans broke their rule of
toleration and suppressed the Druids. Of those mysterious priests
it must be said that, apart from their cruelties, they had a discipline
and a philosophy that inspired great reverence and they have truly
deserved respect. What we have been saying applies not only to
the barbarians of the West, of Britain, Gaul, Germany and Spain,
but also to those of Africa and the Balkans, and to many ancient
deities of Asia Minor and Syria—old Hittite or Phoenician powers,
who held their place in worship, but were not clearly enough
defined to keep their own individuality distinct. What happened
almost everywhere was that to all these gods an *interpretatio Graeca*
or *Romana* was applied—that is to say, that the native god was
equated to one or other of the Greek and Roman gods. By the

side of the native name appears a new one, Greek or Roman.
Where it seemed uncertain what the right equation was, several
alternatives might be suggested. Thus a goddess might be interpreted either as Minerva or Diana or Luna, the goddess of the
moon. The chief god of the Germans was taken to be Mercury ;
Thor became Hercules. When Paul and Barnabas visited the
cities of Southern Galatia and the inhabitants of the cities took
them for gods, Paul was taken to be Mercury, as being the ready
speaker, the mighty Barnabas to be Jupiter ; what they certainly
had in mind were local deities, equated with Mercury and Jupiter.
When Christian martyrs in Asia Minor or Syria suffered for their
refusal to worship Venus or Apollo, what they were up against
really were ancient idols of the heathen, not the radiant figures
of Greek and Roman myth.

From this welter of diverse powers, grouped with more or less
appropriateness around the great Olympian figures, a certain few
great cults stood apart. We must look briefly at some of these.
Cybele, the Great Mother of Anatolia, the Mother of the gods,
came to Rome near the end of the second Punic war as bringer
of victory. Despite the most un-Roman features of her cult, especially her eunuch priests, she was accepted into the Roman state
system and even among the high nobility. Under the Empire
her sway was extended. The worship of Cybele and her young
male consort, Atthis, spread far and wide. The cult had its colour
and its drama—its great festivals, the day of blood, when Atthis had
sacrificed his virility, the entrance of the tree—of the reed, the
ceremonial washing of the image of the goddess. The great
sacrament of the *taurobolium*, the drenching of the worshipper in
the blood of a bull, was supposed to confer a rebirth on the initiate ;
to the Church Fathers it seemed to be a blasphemous parody of
the cleansing blood of the Saviour. This was perhaps the most
popular of all non-Roman cults.

Mithras, the Persian god of light, came to Rome first with the
Cilician pirates. His cult spread slowly, but with the 2nd and 3rd
centuries he enjoyed great reputation as the god of manly valour
and mystic sanctification. He was especially popular in the army.
In the last few years shrines of Mithras have been found on the
Roman wall and in London and have attracted an extraordinary
amount of public interest. His worship was colourful and dramatic. There were grades to be reached in turn by the initiate—
soldier, gryphon, lion, raven, sun-runner and father. Each grade
could only be reached after ordeals that might appear quite terrify-
ing. He had been born in no normal way, but out of a rock.

As companion of the sun-god he had first had a serious quarrel with him, but had been reconciled, had celebrated a sacramental meal with him and had ridden with him in his car. The central act of worship was the slaying of the great bull—a re-enacting of the scene when Mithras sacrificed the great bull to give fresh life to the world. The drenching in bull's blood reappears in this cult, though it may have been derived from the cult of Cybele. Here too, as with Cybele, the Fathers could not fail to see blasphemous imitations of Christian truths. The importance of Mithras in the ancient world has perhaps been a little exaggerated—largely a tribute to the life work of a great Belgian scholar, Cumont. It is not exactly probable that Mithras would have inherited the vacant place, had Christianity failed. But his influence, especially in the Roman army, was great and extensive. The grades of the initiation, the ordeals, the solemn sacrifice of the bull, the serious moral tone and manliness of the cult—all had an irresistible attraction. It was a weakness, however, that there was almost no place at all in it for women.

We have just said that Mithras was hardly qualified to replace a failing Christianity. This ceases to be true if we extend our view and include with Mithras the various forms of sun worship that came to Rome, mainly from Syria. The sun-god was worshipped under varying forms in various places, such as Emesa and Heliopolis, but he could be included in one view and he was not unfamiliar to the Greeks and Romans who already had their Apollo. In the 3rd century the worship of the 'unconquered sun-god' struck its roots deep in Roman soil. Elagabalus, priest of the god of the same name at Emesa, tried from 218 to 222 to make his god the centre of Roman worship. This premature attempt died with the worthless Emperor. But Sol remained in favour with the masses and, in 274, Aurelian, victorious over Palmyra by the aid, as he thought, of that same Emesene god, set up Sol beside the old cult of Vesta in Rome with flamens of his own. The coins are full of the unconquered sun ; one coin of Aurelian expressly names him ' lord of the Roman Empire '. Sol was the favourite divinity of Constantius, father of the great Constantine, and Constantine himself, even after he had proclaimed his personal devotion to the Christian God, still maintained the cult of Sol for a little longer. Was he temporising ? Or did he really imagine that the concept of the pure sun-god might be a step from paganism to Christianity ? We cannot be sure. At any rate, Sol disappears from the coins after about 317. Julian the Apostate inherited the family worship of Sol and tried to make him the centre of his restored paganism. We can read in Julian's own words the curious mystical system in which the old mythology was explained around his person. But Julian died and sun worship died with him. Yet even today our Christmas Day, the 25th of December, is taken over directly from the *natalis invicti Solis*.

Egypt was one of the great centres of ancient religion. The strange worship of animals excited mingled wonder and repulsion. But two Egyptian deities gained world rank. These were the tender Isis and her majestic consort, Serapis, the new Greek god introduced from Sinope by one of the early Ptolemies, but equated with the traditional Osiris, the god of the dead. Serapis himself was a great god—a combination of Jupiter, Dis Pater (the god of the Underworld) and Sol. But Isis overshadowed her partner. The centre of her worship was the sacred mystery—the dismembering of Osiris by his enemy Set, the search for the scattered limbs by the faithful Isis, the restoration. All these were celebrated in the solemn ritual of the goddess. The service of the temples, the solemn processions were all marked by dignity, simplicity and purity—even if the worship was occasionally shamefully abused for immoral purposes, as in the notorious case under Tiberius of the Roman knight who abused the opportunities of the worship to debauch a noble Roman matron. The cult came to Rome during the late Republic, but was not officially recognised and was occasionally suppressed. It gained new favour when Vespasian arrived victorious in Rome from a residence in Alexandria. Thereafter the cult was admitted within the city walls and spread over the provinces. More than any other goddess Isis became to many the one reality behind the many names, Panthea, worshipped by many a people under their local name, but known in Egypt in her true nature as Isis. She was the Great Mother goddess, more beloved even than the other Great Mother, Cybele. The 'Golden Ass' of Apuleius gives us a vivid impression of the emotion, the excitement and devotion that her cult could inspire. In many respects she is the prototype of the Virgin Mary. Like Her she is *stella maris*, the star of the sea. Once a year, early in March, the opening of the seas to ships after the winter storms was celebrated by the festival of Isis, the *ploiaphesia*, the release of ships— perhaps the origin of our modern carnival (*currus navalis*).

The great province of Syria had its own special goddess, Atargatis, known commonly as the *dea Syria*. Lucian has left us a little essay explaining her worship. In a rather less degree than Isis she was regarded as a Panthea, the one true form under the many names. To the Roman world she seems to have passed

mainly under the more general name of Fortuna. Other deities
were connected closely with their individual cities. Diana of the
Ephesians was familiar far beyond the province and finds her
way on to Roman coins. Apollo of Claros gained great fame as
an oracular god ; he was consulted by Diocletian when he debated
whether or not to persecute the Christians. Jupiter of Doliche
had an interesting and picturesque cult that travelled far into the
West. He is a survivor of the old Hittite deities, who ride standing
on the backs of their favourite animals. There were Jupiters of
Heliopolis and Seleucia and, as we have already seen, many forms
of the sun-god. Punic Africa too had its special divinities. The
grim old god, whom the Romans knew as Saturn, was none other
than the Moloch to whom the abomination of child sacrifice had
long been offered. He was never acceptable at Rome. But to
Rome came, near the year A.D. 200, with the Emperors of African
birth, the Hercules and Mercury of Leptis Magna, home of Septimius Severus, and Saeculum Frugiferum, the strangely named
god of Hadrumetum, home of Clodius Albinus. More permanently
important was the Dea Caelestis, the patron goddess of Carthage.
She was worshipped far outside Africa and, when Elagabalus sought
a consort for his sun-god, it was the Dea Caelestis that he chose.

It may be useful here to sum up the results of a rather wide
survey. The world thought mainly in terms of the many gods,
representing so many different functions and provinces. The
thought of one god, supreme over the rest, was there, but unity
was usually allowed to recede behind the plurality of divine powers.
The Roman Jupiter never became popular throughout the Empire.
In the 3rd century Sol came near to displacing him from his rank
as supreme. Then Diocletian placed himself under the guard of
Jupiter and his colleague, Maximian, under that of Hercules.
This system of God the Father and God the Son was probably
designed to act as a formula that might satisfy such a powerful
minority as the Christian Church. The gods represented the powers
of nature, the State, the various phases of individual life. As the
Empire and the office of Emperor bulked more and more largely
in men's thoughts, the gods were called on to become their companions and preservers, *comites et conservatores*. This meant, of
course, that the divine retreated behind the human ; the Emperor
had his earthly companions and the gods must lose something of
their splendour in being placed on a level with these.

Some attempt to reduce the bewildering multiplicity of gods to
some kind of system is seen in what we call ' syncretism ', the mass-
ing together of attributes of many powers. Here is betrayed a

lurking uneasiness, a sense that there must be an underlying unity that is veiled by the many forms. Personal religion had its place in the Olympian scheme. Scipio Africanus the Elder was known for his special devotion to Jupiter Capitolinus ; he would spend long hours in the temple in meditation. The Greek rhetorician, Aristides, in the 2nd century A.D., devoted a heartfelt adoration to his special patrons, Aesculapius, god of health, above all. A special vent for personal emotion was provided by the ' mystery ' religions. The chief recurring feature in them is the conception of a divine protector and friend who guides and guards men in life and leads them to a happy immortality after death. In general we know much, in detail very little. The secrets of the initiates were well kept. In the most famous of all mystery religions, that of Demeter and Kore at Eleusis, the initiates shared with the goddess the search and finding of the lost Persephone, and the hope of immortality was shadowed forth under the symbol of the grain that is sown and dies to be reborn.

We have already spoken of the religious atomism of early times in Rome, when the divine world was seen as a vast number of isolated activities. It shows just how far you can wander, once you abandon belief in the unity of God. Under the Empire we find something like the same belief, but in a new form, probably rather Greek than Roman in origin. There were thought to be multitudes of spirits, demons—not exactly devils, though they often behaved as such—intermediate between gods and men, dwelling in the upper air, interfering at every point in mortal affairs, the cause of such visitations as illness and mental disorder. The superstitious—and the age had many such—lived in perpetual dread of these mischievous and unkindly spirits. The horrid practice of magic, which lurked ever in the slums of the religious world, largely depended on belief in these wretched little creatures, who could be conjured either to win the affections of the loved one or to destroy the body and the spirit of the hated enemy. Thessaly was from time immemorial the home of witchcraft and horrible tales were told of the Thessalian witches who haunted graveyards and called up the dead. From the contemptible enslavement to such beliefs Christianity set men free. The theory of demons was developed by some thinkers to explain certain phenomena that demanded elucidation. A lot could be explained by the theory that there was a class of being intermediate between the divine and the human worlds. Mysterious activities, not explicable on the human plane, but hardly dignified enough to be assigned to the great gods, might properly be attributed to demons.

Pushing enquiry further, one might argue that these demons were always coveting the divine honours to which they had no strict right and were always trying to cajole or bully men into giving them what was not their due.   The Christian Fathers found in this theory of demons a convenient, even a convincing explanation of the true nature of the pagan gods.   True gods they certainly were not. Powers of some kind they obviously were.   It seemed to explain so much if you assigned them to the intermediate sphere.   Astrology, though it might have a semi-religious aspect, will better be treated in connection with philosophy.

Classical paganism was by preference tolerant.   Where there were so many forms of the divine, what objection to admitting a few more ?   What wonder if you found someone worshipping a god who did not correspond exactly to any figure in your Pantheon ? Perhaps it was a new revelation of what a god could be, or again it might be a familiar god under a new name.   In either case, as long as the ritual prescribed was within the normal range, you were inclined to tolerate, if not to accept the worship.   We shall see later how this general tolerance broke down under particular conditions, as with the Jews and Christians.   To readers who know of the horrors of the wars of religion, there is something attractive in this toleration.   Its value should not be underrated, but it should not be overrated either.   It was easygoing ; it had not much heart or confidence behind it.   When the tolerant *did* chance to get excited by some innovation that seemed to him silly or dangerous, his tolerance, always brittle, would suddenly crack.   There was no willingness to differ on things that mattered— only on those that did not.   But let us throw no stones ; we have not learnt that lesson yet.

What verdict are we to pass on the polytheism which formed the background of belief in the minds of the vast majority ?   Its value for poetry and art need not be questioned.   The gods of Greece and Rome have vastly enriched the artistic vocabulary of the world.   The only drawback is that art and literature are not the main concern of religion—only sideworks, ' parerga ', as the Greeks would say.   Polytheism *did* supply a way in which our world, so amazing in its variety, might be explained, without complete loss of the unity which must somewhere subsist.   It was a most convenient form of thought, used by very many who could not be said to have any fervent personal belief in it.   We often find ourselves reverting to the pagan idiom today.   But paganism had two fatal defects, mercilessly exposed in the invectives of the Fathers.   These were moral laxity and intellectual muddle.   The gods to some extent guarded morality. They punished murder and perjury, for example. But they were, according to all accounts, so immoral themselves that their bad example overcame their sound precepts. Read the delightful, but frivolous, work of Ovid, the ' Metamorphoses ', and you will see in what a strange amoral world these radiant beings were thought to move. Now this will not do. A persistent instinct in man demands that his morality should be firmly based on the divine order. Morality is prized, not for any transcendental beauty it may have, true though that beauty be, but because it is salutary for the individual and necessary for society. The world of the pagan gods was always more or less anarchic. The supremacy of Jupiter was not as unquestioned as it should have been, and the gods, fighting, hating, lusting among themselves, troubled the order of the divine state. There was, it is true, one established principle : what one god has done another shall not undo. But one can show one's displeasure in some striking way. Aphrodite vexes Artemis by contriving the death of her devotee, Hippolytus. Artemis retaliates by sending the boar to slay Aphrodite's darling, Adonis. Some attempts were indeed made to purify the old religion, to explain the gross and brutal tales as allegorical figures of moral truths or natural phenomena. But cruelty and lust hung about the whole system of worship. In many places of the East grossly licentious rites stood under the direct sanction of religion ; they were survivals of the crude nature worships of primitive peoples. In the West, if lust was less aggressive, cruelty was even more so. The ghastly shows of gladiators were under the patronage of divinities, Mars and Diana. It would have been a task of Hercules to clean out these Augean stables and no Hercules was available for the task. Maximin Daza and, after him, Julian with even more effect tried to purify the old paganism and graft on to it some of the attractive features of Christian practice. Needless to say, the old tree could not change its nature so readily to bear such unaccustomed fruit.

Equally serious was the other fundamental defect—intellectual muddle. It gave the thoughtful man a headache to try to find a system in the chaotic world with all these variegated deities. Some attempts to clarify the picture were made. As we have seen, an interpretation was applied to all forms of polytheism as they came under view ; all gods were made to conform to the Olympian pattern. Syncretism, again, suggested larger divine realities behind the multitudinous forms. Later paganism, in particular, was busily engaged in trying to systematise belief. The elaborate scheme of Julian, in which the sun-god is the centre,

while all the other gods are grouped in concentric circles round
him, is a good example. But the task was too great for any energy
that could be brought to bear on it. The whole tale of paganism
was based on myth, not fact ; and who shall introduce logical
sequence into myth ?

Paganism is not yet dead. In our own times we have seen some
strange resurgences of it. We may admit its beauty on the lines
of art and literature ; but what other beauty can men find in it ?
I suppose that a modern pagan could claim that it is natural and,
to use a cant phrase of our day, uninhibited. Man is seen, not
as an uneasy alliance of body, soul and spirit, but, as he is and should
be, one. Well, there is something in this plea. Paganism may
suggest a healthy reaction against strained and unnecessary asceticism. But the reasonable man has soon enough of freedom.

‘ Me this uncharted freedom tires, I feel the weight of chance desires ’.

How truly Wordsworth expresses the craving for a discipline,
an order in life ! What man wants is not just lack of inhibition,
but a service that should be perfect freedom. Also, the modern
pagan needs to be firmly reminded that the picture that he paints
is largely a fancy one, that the colour of paganism in practice was
very different from the rosy hues that he paints. The Ancient
World was heartlessly cruel ; it was absurdly lax in sexual morality ;
even when it was free from these grosser evils, it set far too high a
value on immediate, worldly success. It was not a bad world,
when things went well, for the socially privileged. It was an age
of iron for the underdog. Let us try to keep the balance—to
admit the much of good that lived on in private lives, to discount
the wilder general denunciations of the age, but also to reserve
some scepticism for the lovely fancies of a Keats or a Shelley.
There are times when many of us can echo Wordsworth’s wish :

‘ Great God, I’d rather be, A pagan suckled in a creed outworn.’

But let us not forget that very true final word, outworn. For that
is precisely what paganism is. We may need to revise our religious
thinking to almost any extent ; to the old paganism we shall
never go back.

The religion of the State was well provided for under the forms
of the old paganism. Each state had its special tutelary powers.
Rome and the Empire stood under the guardianship of Jupiter
Optimus Maximus of the Capitol. But there was developed a
new form of worship, special to the State, the worship of the
Emperors consecrated, raised to heaven after death for services

done whilst on earth. The worship of the man as god is repulsive to modern ideas. It was familiar in the Ancient World. The kings of Babylon and Assyria were, if not divine, set in a specially close relation to the gods. The kings of Egypt were worshipped as divine themselves. The age of the great individual in Greece that had set in after Alexander the Great greedily welcomed the idea. The kings moved like gods on earth, powerful to hurt or bless. What if they were not gods in the making ? For, if some of the tales were true, the great gods themselves had once been men on earth, had done great deeds and had finally received divine honours from a grateful posterity. The Greek romancer, Euhemerus, developed this idea in a fanciful story which exercised a profound influence on all later thought. Many modern scholars, I am sure, tend to underrate the power of this hypothesis. It is not religiously edifying, it is not philosophically true, but it *does* recognise facts. And the great fact was that a number of mighty individuals were wielding such powers over their fellow men as are ascribed to the gods. What is shocking is not the belief in itself, but the deplorable circumstances out of which it was born.

Romans were familiar with the work of Euhemerus, ever after Ennius translated him into Latin, soon after 200 B.C. Roman governors, proceeding to their provinces in the East under the late Republic, found themselves welcomed with almost divine honours by the provincials. All was ready, then, for Emperor worship when the time came. Romans had a rooted objection to making a god of a man while he lived ; they had no objection to it once he had ceased to move amongst them. In a vague way the Romans had always ascribed a sort of divinity to the dead, the *Di Manes*. In the provinces worship of the Emperor, often coupled with that of Rome, became common form. After an Emperor died, it was for the Senate to decide whether his career justified this supreme honour for him. If the verdict was favourable, the dead Emperor was consecrated, enrolled among the gods of the State. He was beyond time and space, in Eternity, in the upper world of the stars, if you chose so to picture it. His title was now *divus*, the deified. All the adjuncts of divinity, the temple, the altar, sacrifice, the sacred couch, the car in the procession to the circus, all were his. It was for merit that the Emperors were thus glorified. They were treading the same path that Hercules, Bacchus, Castor and Pollux had once trod. The root idea is expressed at its highest by Pliny the Elder :

deus est homini hominem iuvare
(' it is divine that a man should help his fellow-man ').

This worship is, of course, primarily a worship of power. The one who could help or hurt in a supreme degree was a god. This debased conception of what the divine may mean is liable to arise when once divine power has been divorced from morality.

The worship of the Emperor never became a religion of the heart to the masses, though some simple souls will certainly have believed that the *Divi* could answer prayer. The worship was most useful as a token of official loyalty. Even in his lifetime the Emperor received a kind of minor worship in the form of libations poured to his spirit, his *genius*. The pouring of wine-offering or incense in this worship became a regular test for the Christians and over it the faithful must fall down. When Trajan Decius, in 249, tried to restore the old Roman *virtus*, he based his State religion on the worship of the *Divi*. Their ranks were checked over and coins were struck in honour of all who passed the review. Diocletian took a different path. He claimed to stand in a special relation to Jupiter and named himself ' Iovius '. His colleague, Maximian, at the same time, became ' Herculius '. Some difference between man and god was allowed. But it is a difference that tends to diminish. Diocletian and Maximian are on earth what Jupiter and Hercules are in heaven. Constantine, inheriting many of his ideas from Diocletian, considered himself under the special protection of the sun-god, the object of a family cult. But, when he gave his adherence to the Christian Church, the old conceptions must give way. The Emperor actually loses little. He may no longer be put on the level of the gods, but he rules by special grace of God, *dei gratia*, and is thus far removed from the common ruck. The hand of God crowns him from above. When he dies, a flaming car comes to carry him on high, as it had come for Elijah. Julian II had no special interest in the man-god ; his efforts were all directed towards restoring the worship of the old gods, Sol before all others. With Theodosius the Great paganism was doomed. The Emperor, like all his subjects, was the servant of God. But we have to look further along into mediaeval and modern times to realise how deep-rooted such ideas are. There have always been people—a minority, perhaps, but an enthusiastic minority—who delight in placing their rulers on some platform far beyond the human, on raising high their *fastigium*, as a Roman would have put it.

A word must now be said about the forms of pagan worship. They were not very different in every time or place. The god must have his house to live in, his temple. He cannot be actually present in quite the same way as a king ; otherwise, how can he

be present in so many temples at once ? But in some mysterious
way his presence is associated with his house. He must have his
altar for sacrifice. Were the sacrifices unbloody, the conception
of a spiritual offering lies near to hand. But, were the sacrifices
bloody, the flesh of bull, goat, or ram, the primitive idea that the
god needs his food as a man does is dominant. Only the less
useful parts were burnt ; the rest went to the market. The image,
the idol, might be made of precious material to show deep respect ;
it might be the tribute of some great artist. In some cults something very ancient, ugly and barbarous was deliberately preferred.
The idol was a suggestion of the god, not himself. No god could
be present in his countless idols, scattered over the face of the
earth. Otherwise how could the worshipper escape the scoff that
he in his blindness ' bowed down to wood and stone ' ? How
could he account for the undignified fate that might overtake a
sacred image—to be gnawed by mice, to receive the droppings
of birds, to be stolen and melted down by temple robbers ?

The usual form of prayer was the vow, the prayer accompanied
by the promise to pay some tribute named when prayer was
answered. It was a transaction with a legal flavour—

Do ut des
(' I give in hope of return from you ').

There were two main moments in each vow—the *nuncupatio*, the
solemn undertaking in set words with sacrifice of incense or wine
over the altar, and the payment, the *solutio*, when the prayer had
been granted, sacrifice with the victim named. On some special
occasions, as for instance national disasters, services of intercession
were held, when the sacred couches (the *pulvinaria*) of the gods
were set out in public with the divine attributes arrayed upon
them. There was one great recurring pageant, the *pompa circen-
sis*, in which a number of cars conveyed the images of the gods in
procession. Such were the normal forms of worship. They would
be put into use on the most varied occasions, public and private—
at the arrivals and departures of the Emperors, at the meetings of
the Senate, at private weddings and betrothals. All this was to the
Roman a part of his ordinary life. The forms were time-honoured ;
on them the right relation of man to god, the *pax deum*, depended.
Who could tell what might be the consequences of neglect ? The
legends had plenty to say about the vengeance wreaked by angry
deities on men who had denied them their due rights. Artemis
had sent the Calydonian boar to ravage the fields of King Oeneus
who had omitted her from his special sacrifices of thanksgiving

for a good year.   In time of calamity—invasion, famine or plague —men's thoughts turned naturally to this possibility.   Had something been done to offend the powers ?   The Christians in particular had to bear the blame for any unexpected calamity.   It did not cost much to show one's devotion to religion in this negative form of punishing the dissenters.

We come now to the two peoples who stood apart from the general polytheism of the Empire, the Jews and the Christians. If the Greek owes his place in history to his genius for philosophy, literature and art, if the Roman owes his to his flair for legal, social and political organisation, the Jew owes his to religion.   The Hebrews of whom we read in the early books of the Old Testament may have been like enough in their religion to many another Semitic people.   Their god was essentially a national god ; his chief attribute was power.   But the Hebrews were in some special way a chosen people.   The exile in Egypt, the deliverance out of the house of bondage, the long wanderings in the wilderness already gave them the sense of a peculiar destiny.   When, after the Babylonian captivity, the remnant returned from exile, they founded, under Persian protection, a little Theocracy, a state centred on the Temple and ruled by the High Priests.   The experience of exile and return, interpreted by the prophets, led to an enrichment and purification of the conception of Jehovah. He was now realised as the one true God, the God of the whole earth ; holiness even more than might was recognised as His chief attribute.   The struggles under the Maccabees with the Seleucid kings, who tried to make the Jews conform to the Hellenic worship, general under their rule, led to a quickening of spiritual life.   The Temple was the centre of worship not only for the Jews of Palestine, but also for the *diaspora*, the great body of Jews scattered over the lands.   Their peculiar religious destiny was thus confirmed.   Not that their development had been so completely different from that of other peoples.   But there was something in the way that that experience had been composed—times of blessing alternating with times of trial—that gave them a position of their own.   The Jew was an uncompromising monotheist.   His God was the only true God ; the gods of the nations were mere nothings, the work of men's hands, wood and stone.

From such a people we might forecast serious trouble with the Roman government.   But at first there was compromise to an amazing degree.   During the civil wars able and wealthy Jews contrived to render such services to Julius Caesar and Augustus as won their favour and an unusually friendly charter.   They won their right to exercise their religion undisturbed, to be exempt from military service, to pay the annual tribute of a shekel to the Temple. Caligula nearly raised a revolt by instructing the governor of Syria to set up his image in the Temple ; the Jews, like the rest of his subjects, must recognise him for the god that he was. His murder came just in time to save the wise governor who had delayed obedience to the fatal instructions. For the final break-down of compromise under Nero there were many causes—bad government in Judaea, secret impatience on the Roman side with the difficult people, a party of irreconcilables among the Jews themselves. The end of this first great revolt was the destruction of the Temple and the end of the Jewish State. When Trajan strained Roman resources in the East by his extravagant programme of conquest, the Jews rose in rebellion in many Eastern provinces. The revolt was drowned in floods of blood. One more desperate rising under Hadrian had the inevitable issue. No degree of obstinacy and valour could hold out against the massed might of the Empire. The wandering Jew entered on his long pilgrimage ; Jerusalem was buried under the new pagan city of Aelia Capitolina. Henceforward the Jewish religion lived on in the school of Rabbis at Joppa and in the hearts of the individual Jews, scattered without a national home over the Empire. And yet, as against the pagan world, the Jew knew that he was in the right. He had his ancient tradition, he had his holy Law. His vision of a one true God, righteous and mighty, was a true one as against the many gods of indifferent moral nature. That he was set against further revela-tion, that he could not advance from the Old Testament to the New —that was his national tragedy.

Christianity undoubtedly grew up in the world as a kind of sect of the Jews. Paul himself was a devout Jew. He turned by a natural preference to his own people first : it was only when they refused his message that he realised his mission to the Gentiles. There were also the strictest practical arguments in favour of preaching to the Jews. Seen as a sect of the Jews, the Christians could share in their charter of toleration and the infant churches could grow up unmolested by the Roman government. The question that Gallio in Achaea had to decide was just this : is this new religion just a variant of the Jewish ? Gallio decided that it was and that was an end of the matter ; he ' cared for none of these things,' sectarian disputes that mattered to no one but the disputants. We have to remember too that not all Jews declined the new teaching. Many of the first Christians were Jews them-selves. Even among those who were not Christians, there were

Q

classes of Jews, not entirely unfriendly to the Church. Such were the Essenes, the sect of ascetics who lived across Jordan. Such in some degree were the Pharisees, with their strict regard for the Law and their hope of the Resurrection. St. Paul could set them at variance with the Sadducees by insisting that ' concerning the Resurrection am I called in question among you '. It was the Sadducees, the politically minded Jews, who worked in touch with the Roman government and cared little for religion in any of its other-worldly aspects, who were the most relentless enemies. The zealots, the advocates of out-and-out resistance to the Roman rule, had no use for a body which disclaimed the use of force to gain its ends.

The persecution of Nero changed the whole picture. The occasion was the aftermath of the Great Fire of Rome, when Nero, squirming under the charge of being the incendiary of his own capital, sought scapegoats and found them in the Christians. A close investigation proved unfavourable to the victims. This new religion, it was decided, was unwholesome ; whatever else they were, they were the avowed enemies of the human race. The question then arose : granted that this is a new religion, is it to continue to enjoy the toleration that it has hitherto enjoyed as a sect of the Jews ? The answer was given against the Church. Christians as such were forbidden to exist. As a corporation without licence, they must disband, if called upon to do so, or suffer the consequences. Persecution ' for the Name ' had begun. Tacitus has seriously misled us by associating the persecution too closely with the fire. The decision went far beyond the initial occasion ; that was the memory that lasted on inside the Church. The Apostles, St. Peter and St. Paul, sealed their witness with their blood. Though it is not definitely recorded, it is so probable as to be almost certain that the Jews had a hand in getting the Christians separated from themselves in the government view. They had a powerful advocate in the person of the Empress, Poppaea Sabina, who was herself devoted to Jewish observances and exercised a decisive and baneful influence over the Emperor Nero.

The revolt of the Jews certainly accentuated the distinction between Jews and Christians, for the Christians of Palestine as a body withdrew beyond Jordan. The Jew was now compelled to pay to Jupiter Capitolinus the shekel which he had previously paid to the Temple. The chest, the *fiscus Iudaicus*, was administered with cruel chicanery, and brutal enquiry was made into the question whether a man was or was not a Jew and therefore liable to be taxed. In these investigations the distinction between Jew and Christian must have come out again and again. But the Christian profited little from the realisation. He had a bad name with the Roman government and could do nothing to improve matters. The decision of Nero was not regarded as one of his evil fantasies. Suetonius records it among his laudable measures. Later Emperors followed his lead. It is quite unnecessary to postulate unrecorded decisions against the Christians by Domitian or Trajan, when we have recorded for us the decision which covers the question. Towards the end of the reign of Domitian, about 95, came a second persecution of the Church. It is poorly recorded, but some Roman nobles, including some close kin of the Emperor, fell. It seems to have raged with special fury in the province of Asia, and the main ground of attack seems to have been the refusal of the Christians to join in the worship of the Emperor. The impression made by this persecution is preserved for us in that strange document, the Revelation of St. John the Divine. It is full of the emotions prompted by the persecution of Domitian, shot through with memories of the persecution of Nero. We find in it so many qualities combined—a powerful if lurid imagination, a fervour often rising to sublimity, a bitter and lingering hatred of Rome.

It seems unlikely that this persecution lasted long. There is a story, which may well be true, that Domitian sent to Palestine for any survivors of the family of our Lord. When he found that they were poor, simple, unambitious people, he dismissed them unharmed. Early in the reign of Trajan there was one famous martyrdom, that of the gallant fanatic, St. Ignatius, Bishop of Antioch. Later in the reign, in 111, Trajan sent out his friend, Pliny the Younger, as his special commissioner to Bithynia, to restore order to the distressed finances of the province. Pliny found himself confronted with a vast number of charges against Christians. He began by following the normal practice, allowing them to repent if they wished, but ordering them to execution if they persisted in their disobedience. But, as the numbers of the accused ever grew and as anonymous denunciations came into play, he became worried and made enquiry of two deaconesses under torture, to try and determine the rights of the matter. He found no evidence of the crimes alleged against the Christians— nothing but evidence of a ' base and immoderate superstition '. Why Pliny applies such terms to what consisted solely of hymns to Christ and oaths to maintain a high moral standard is hard to say. Pliny, unaccustomed to all the detailed procedure of trials of Christians—he speaks of them as something quite well known—appealed to Trajan for a decision. Trajan sent a noble but confused answer. There can be no one general formula. You are not to hunt out the Christians, you are to treat with contempt any anonymous denunciations. You may pardon them if they renounce their error but, in the last resort, if they persist they must be punished. The principle of Nero is maintained : ' it is not lawful to be a Christian '. This policy of partial and uneasy toleration was confirmed by Hadrian in a letter to a governor of Asia. Trials of Christians must be conducted with strict justice. There must be no tenderness for private enemies who try to black-mail Christians with such charges.

The first age of Christianity may be said to terminate with the persecution under Nero. There were no Gospels as yet, no litera-ture except the Epistles of St. Paul. The Christians were in the main people of little wealth, education or social standing. Their main fight was with the Jews, to win freedom from the Law. The Roman government was felt rather as protector than as enemy. The Church was simple and unworldly ; we hear of one short-lived attempt at communism. The Second Coming of the Lord was believed to be imminent and, with that in view, all earthly things shrank into small proportions. The second age, the sub-Apostolic, moves in a changed atmosphere. The Church actually spreads and gains some converts of high social rank. But the breach with the Jews is now complete and manifest. The Jew, though he still has his religious freedom, is despised and harried. The Christian exists only on sufferance ; he has no legal right to do so. The Gospels are now added to the Epistles. They seek to hold in a fixed form the traditions of the Church and the principles that form the base of instruction in the Faith. The fall of Jeru-salem—an event of grim apocalyptic import—seemed to be the prelude to the end. But it was not so. The world went on and Christians began to wonder whether they had not misinterpreted the words of their Master, whether His Second Coming was, by any ordinary human reckoning, imminent. The Church, in fact, began to reckon that it might be called upon to live on indefinitely beside the hostile State. At any rate, the Church began to improve and strengthen its organisation. The chief of the overseers began to develop into the monarchical bishop.

We may pause for a moment to ask whether it is really legitimate to devote so much space to Christianity in a book on the Roman Empire in general. I hold that it is and would suggest two main reasons for my opinion. The first reason is that this is a very good way of learning what the later paganism was really like. The part of paganism that was still alive and progressive can most suitably be studied in connection with the fight between Empire and Church. The Empire ultimately became Christian, but not because an entirely alien creed succeeded in forcing itself upon it. It was partly because that new faith gave prominence to many tendencies that had been trying to find expression under pagan forms—the demand for unity and goodness in the divine nature, the revolt against stupidity and immorality in religion. A second reason is more a matter of accident, but nevertheless vital. The history of the Empire is very commonly studied in two distinct compartments, secular history on the one side, Church history on the other. You seldom find a scholar who is quite in the first class in both disciplines. That means, of course, that a study which is essentially one tends to get broken into two sections which do not fit into one another. This dividing gap need not have been there—it is the result of a curious system of division in our teaching—but, since it is there, everything done to remedy it deserves a welcome.

The age of what we may call the uneasy truce lasted a long time, from Trajan and Hadrian down to Trajan Decius in 249. Christians were persecuted at intervals, but persecution was not official, systematic or continuous. Under the gentle Antoninus Pius there were some famous martyrs, Polycarp, Bishop of Smyrna, and Justin the apologist, among them. Under Marcus Aurelius there was a horrible persecution at Lugdunum, due to an outbreak of mass hysteria and a weak and evil governor. But Marcus, who, had he known Christianity better, must have found much to admire in it, can find no word of praise for the blind stupid courage of the Christian. Legend, it is true, tells of the miracle of the Thundering Legion, recruited from Melitene and consisting of Christians, which by its prayers procured a storm that discouraged the barbarian enemy and refreshed the weary Romans. Something did indeed happen, for there is a clear representation of it on the column of Marcus, and it was put down to supernatural causes; but it was to the Egyptian god, Thoth—Mercury—that the miracle was officially attributed. The striking name 'thundering' can have nothing to do with it, for the legion had borne it long before. Septimius Severus issued a ban against conversions to the Church. But the women of his dynasty, of the royal priestly house of Emesa, had more than the usual Roman interest for a new religion. We hear that Julia Mammaea, mother of the gentle Severus Alexander, the last member of this house to rule in Rome, had conversations with the great Christian Father, Origen. It is even recorded that this Emperor kept an image of Christ in his private chapel along with images of Orpheus and Apollonius of Tyana. The giant barbarian, Maximin I, who succeeded Alexander on the imperial throne, hated civilians in general ; his persecution of the Church may have been a part of his general war on civilians to enrich and aggrandise his army. Philip the Arabian, who ruled from 244 to 249, had a Christian wife and was himself not unfriendly to the Church. He was criticised by pagan enthusiasts for not putting more devotion into his celebrations of the thousandth anniversary of the city. His successor, the gallant Trajan Decius, felt that he had a mission to restore Rome to her old worth. He declared war on all modern weaknesses and insisted that all subjects should sacrifice to the gods and secure certificates that they had so sacrificed. The blow was not aimed only at the Christians as such, but they were bound to feel it ; it amounted to a general persecution of the Church. Multitudes lapsed—either sacrificed or, at least, bought certificates to say that they had. For a few years the persecution was abated, only to break out again under Valerian. The attack was now better planned and was directed largely against the bishops—the heads of the Churches. But Valerian was shamefully taken prisoner by the Persians and his son and successor, Gallienus, gave the Church peace.

This long period from Trajan to Decius saw far-reaching changes in the Church. It increases vastly in numbers ; it makes its way into almost every province ; it invades the higher social orders and the professions. The bishops govern their Churches with a firm hand ; the Bishop of Rome—the Pope, to use the later word— begins to be called in as arbitrator in disputes between churches in the provinces. Living in the Roman world, the Church begins to attract to itself men endowed with the Roman qualities of firmness, courage and organising ability. Apart from its religious aspect, the Church is developing into a highly efficient friendly society. At the same time the Church tries to come to grips with the thought of the age. Clement of Alexandria and his greater successor, Origen, interpret Christianity in a way that might appeal to minds versed in Greek philosophy. In the attempt to think out the Faith dangerous heresies were encountered, that many-headed monster that we call Gnosticism. The greatest of the Gnostic teachers, men like Marcion and Valentinus, were clearly men of great originality and power. Gnosticism, if we consider it as a whole, contained the most diverse elements—high soaring speculation, sublime imagination, vague mystical rubbish, the extremest asceticism and the wildest licentiousness. But its characteristic evils because of which the Church rightly banned it were its feeble grip of reality and its overweening spiritual pride. From the fight against Gnosticism emerged finally the Creeds. On a somewhat different level stands Montanism, a schism rather than a heresy. Montanism was touched with the wild emotionalism of Phrygia, where it had its birth. It stressed the continued inspiration of the Holy Spirit, as manifest in prophets and prophetesses, demanded higher moral standards than those asked of ordinary Christians and was very ready to refuse obedience to the Church's official representatives.

The Church had now settled down into an uneasy life in an Empire that would not approve it. Yet two Emperors, Trajan and Hadrian, had shown some personal disinclination to persecute. It might be worth while to improve on this beginning by making the Emperors more aware of what Christianity really was. Hence the stream of Apologies for the Faith, addressed to various Emperors. They may not have had much immediate success ; but they effectively show the Church in a new light—not only fighting against society, but trying to relieve the bitterness of that fight by removing current misconceptions. With Tertullian, the great African barrister, a new tone comes in—one of bitterness, scorn and defiance. The Church is too strong to be treated with contumely and contempt. That it is a serious problem for the State the Emperors themselves by their inconsistent regulations sufficiently prove. We can read Tertullian with intense interest and much sympathy ; but it is hard to imagine that his rhetorical tirades did much to convert the unconverted. Martyrdom continued to occur here and there. If we are to believe Tertullian—and he seems to know what he is talking about—there was little policy in these attacks. The mob might be disquieted because of natural catastrophes and demand victims ; a weak governor might grasp at an easy way of gaining popularity. The trials of Christians followed one normal, rather curious course. The first thing was to bring a Christian to a frank admission of what he was. That was the first step. The second was to induce him to recant. It was a contest of wills between the governor and the Christian— the one to gain a bloodless victory, the other to seal his testimony with his blood. If we ask why the Empire troubled itself to persecute what must for long have seemed a quite insignificant minority, we can find several answers. The Church was intolerant itself and thereby discouraged toleration for itself from others. The Christians were unpopular, suspected of horrible crimes, certainly awkward members of society, averse to its pleasures, critical of its morality. By the time of Trajan Decius they had become so strong and so well organised that they might seem to be a State within a State. Only at this point does official persecution become systematic. Before, it had been vague and inconsistent, leaving things to go as they might according to the tempers of the mob and the inclinations of provincial governors.

While the Church was trying to explain itself to the pagan world, thoughtful pagans were beginning to try to understand this new body, as they could no longer dismiss it as unworthy of consideration. The chief of these pagan writers, Celsus, is known to us very adequately in the refutation of his argument by Origen. Celsus examines the Christian claims and finds them insufficient. The miracles of the Gospels are not evidential of religious truth ; they may be no better than the tricks of Egyptian magicians. Celsus can see worth in the Christians ; they have courage, strength of purpose and devotion to their cause. But let them show a little commonsense. If they overpraise virginity and discourage marriage, how is the human race to be carried on ? If they refuse the profession of arms, how are the frontiers to be defended against the barbarians ? Celsus ends with an impassioned appeal to the Christians not to deny their services to an Empire that needs them. There is some hope of reconciliation, when an attack is launched with this amount of reason and courtesy. We can point to a counterpart on the Christian side—the charming little dialogue of Minucius Felix, entitled the ' Octavius '. Much of the argument is the same that we find in Tertullian. But how different is the tone—gentle, persuasive without bitterness ! The one real weakness is that the most characteristic parts of the Faith are left almost completely in the shade. The stumbling block of the Cross is hardly mentioned.

This is characteristic of the new age. Christianity had started as a religion of poor, simple people in general, of the socially underprivileged, to use a favourite modern cliché. It had been essentially revolutionary in preaching so uncompromisingly the equality of men in the sight of God and the meaninglessness of caste and social orders. That sounded almost blasphemous in the ears of a society which set the highest value on social position, which even carried its sublime snobbishness into the eternal world and supposed that the privileged on earth would continue to be privileged for ever. Christianity could not gain its hold on the higher social orders without undergoing some influence from them. Many Christians would now wish to be loyal to their new faith and at the same time retain as much as possible of the goods of the present world. It is easy to see how the extremists of both sides, pagan and Christian, were working up to the decisive break. It is not so apparent, but it is quite as important to realise how the moderates of both sides were taking up positions that might one day lead to compromise. This truth is partly veiled by the fact that there was a decisive battle and that Christianity came off clear victor. Actually, the victory was far less decisive than it seemed. There was a large element of compromise.

The captivity of Valerian shocked the Roman world. The pagan saw in it the mysterious doom of an excellent Emperor ; the Christians hailed it as the punishment of a persecutor. Gallienus reversed his father's policy and gave the Church a peace that lasted more than a generation. The Church was not fully recognised, but persecution was suspended. The wife of Gallienus, Salonina, was a Christian. We have a common issue of coins of hers with the legend, very Christian in flavour, AVGVSTA IN PACE. It is true, no doubt, that to Gallienus this ' peace ' was not the Christian one. Gallienus claimed to be ruling as a Prince of Peace in an Empire that had gone mad with war. Aurelian, the great restorer of the Empire, seems to have planned to renew persecution, but died before he could act. When Diocletian set to work to reconstitute the Empire, he left the Church for a long time unmolested. I think that in his system of Jupiter and Hercules, god the father and god the son, he must have been suggesting a formula of reconciliation for non-conformists like the Christians. Towards the end of his reign, the pagan extremists, led by Galerius, the Caesar of Diocletian, won the day. Christians were purged from the army and Civil Service. Then came persecution, at first bloodless, then with bloodshed enough. The attack was now consistent and thorough. The churches were to be destroyed, the sacred writings burnt, the bishops apprehended. Many lapsed and the Church seemed to be going down in irretrievable defeat. But first appearances were deceptive. There were enough courageous resisters to encourage the weaker brethren. Pagan opinion was seriously divided. Very many hated the attack on good citizens, whom they were prepared to like and respect. Constantius in the West did the least that in loyalty to his colleagues he must. The political position became more and more complicated. The elaborate arangements of Diocletian broke down. Finally, Galerius, the chief persecutor, must himself acknowledge the failure of the extreme policy. With undisguised anger and reluctance he yet accorded to the Christians the right to worship

God in their own way. Let them pray for their Emperor ! Soon afterwards he died.

Constantine the Great, the son of the merciful Constantius, inherited a liberal bias from his father. He came under the influence of a remarkable personality, Hosius, the Bishop of Corduba. As he thought over the happenings of his day he gradually came to the conclusion that the true *virtus*, the power, lay with the Christian God, not with the pagan deities. When he marched against Maxentius, ruler of Rome and Italy, he made the campaign a test ; if Christ would grant him the victory, he would serve him. Constantine saw the sign in the sky, the monogram of Christ and the words *Hoc signo victor eris*, fought under that sign and conquered.

The great revolution by which the Empire became Christian certainly began under Constantine. He confirmed toleration—only now it was even more important for pagans than for Christians to have it confirmed. He gave the Church wealth and favour and allowed the bishops to attend their congresses at the State's expense. He began the suppression of pagan worship in some of its more obnoxious forms. Whether he acted out of inward conviction or as a scheming politician is debated to this day. Myself, I share the view that Constantine was genuinely converted, that he did not become a Christian only to obtain a facile forgiveness for his horrible crime of putting wife and eldest son to death, that he only deferred baptism to his deathbed, because he feared the terrible consequences of post-baptismal sin if he were baptised before. But he did not cease to be a statesman. The Empire had failed to crush the Church. The other policy remained to be tried, to make of the Church a buttress of the united Empire. To that end Constantine fought against disunion in the Church wherever he found it—among the schismatic Donatists of Africa or among the heretical Arians of the East. Perhaps he had a very imperfect understanding of the philosophical points involved. He could see with absolute clearness that a divided Church was but a feeble ally. Arianism, whatever it may have meant to its author, Arius, and his friends, was a cloak for a certain pagan form of Christianity such as, we have suggested, Diocletian may have had in mind. It is significant that the barbarians welcomed Christianity in its Arian form. We may be sure that to many it was as bastard a Christianity as the ' German Christianity ' which Hitler fondly hoped to foist on his country. Constantine, though he maintained unity under the Athanasian formula at the Council of Nicaea, wobbled afterwards towards a modified statement of Arian belief.

Perhaps, if he could really have understood it at all, he was always an Arian himself.

The following age was marked by a continuation of the religious truce ; paganism was free to exist, but now definitely as the weaker party. The Church itself was rent by the unedifying disputes between Arians and Athanasians, the former strong in the East, the latter in the West. Then came Julian with his desperate attempt to turn the tide of history and restore paganism in his own favourite revised version. He did not actually persecute the Christians, but he showed marked disfavour to individuals in his service and tried to close the schools to Christian children—a futile gesture, which even pagans of the day found offensive and ridiculous. There were two roots to his enthusiasm—(1) his devotion to the sun-god, whose worship was traditional in his family, (2) a passionate hatred of the Christianity to which he had been forced to conform, but which had, he thought, sanctioned the horrible murder of most of his kin in the blood bath at Constantinople after the death of Constantine. But the Galilean conquered. Julian was too extreme, too eccentric to carry the masses with him. He did not make any strong appeal to the one constituency in which love of paganism was still strong, the city of Rome and its nobility.

After Julian the religious truce was resumed, until finally Theodosius the Great gave his complete consent to Christianity in its Athanasian form and led the fight to extirpate paganism from its last refuges. Two episodes in the final battles have been recorded for us. In the Senate House stood a statue of Victory, to which sacrifice was made before the meetings of the Senate. This was removed by Gratian in 378. Symmachus, the prefect of the city, in 383 submitted a formal proposal to the Emperor, Valentinian II, to put the altar back in its old place. He made a vigorous appeal to religious tolerance and ended by begging that Rome might be allowed to keep what was sacred to her, even if to others it seemed vain. Bishop Ambrose of Milan countered with a firm, but far less eloquent rejoinder and the altar stayed away, except for a short restoration by Stilicho. The other episode belongs to the year 410, when Alaric, the Visigoth, sacked Rome. The Romans were driven to adopt any and every expedient to pay the enormous ransom demanded, and even melted down such statues as still stood in the temples. Among them the statue of Virtus went into the flames and with it went all that was still left of manly quality and courage. It is Zosimus, that bitter pagan historian, who tells the tale. This statue was evidently a talisman, perhaps that mysterious tutelary power of Rome about which so much speculation revolved, and the destruction of it must have seemed a deliberate act of state suicide.

Paganism thereafter was a beaten enemy. It still survived in the heart of many an individual. It still had its roots fast in old Rome, which clung to her religion as a part of her great past. The Roman aristocracy, in particular, was slow to transfer its allegiance to the new faith. The schools of philosophy in Athens and other university cities continued to be little centres where interest in the old beliefs still clung ; for, by some chance and by no logical necessity, philosophy found herself at the last defending just those beliefs of which she had so often expressed doubts. But perhaps the place where paganism lasted most persistently was the country districts, the *pagi*, where the simple country folk held fast to their sacrifices and holidays in honour of gods of field and fold ; these were the true *pagani*, from whom our word 'pagan' takes its origin. The cities might give themselves wholeheartedly to the new ways ; the country could show what true conservatism was like.

And so after all these fights Christianity had won. It had had opposed to it not only the weaker and baser elements in the old culture, but also some of the finest ; many a good old Roman honestly distrusted the new morality with its softness (as he saw it) and its disregard for aristocratic values. It had begun with its precious inheritance from the old Hebrew traditions. It had its own tremendous initial drive, never quite exhausted. To these it had added in course of time an organisation, borrowed from the best Roman models, and a philosophy, partly learnt from Plato or Aristotle. But the Churches inevitably lost as well as gained. When persecution ceased, one of the main incentives to noble living was removed. When power and wealth beckoned to the successful churchman, new temptations beckoned too. The democratic spirit of the early Church began to lose its purity when Christianity came to take a prominent place among the higher as well as among the lower orders, the *honestiores* as against the *humiliores*. Imperial favour must have brought to the Church hosts of converts of the most questionable value. There were not wanting rigorists in the Church—the Donatists in Africa, for example—who regarded the new Church after Constantine as no true Church any longer, but a betrayer of its sacred trust to a State that could not be trusted.

State and Church in alliance must clearly exchange influences. If we ask how far the Church influenced the State, we can point to legislation on some matters of morality ; we can affirm a decided influence on the morals of the Emperor. But far too much continued just as it had always been. There were still the races of the circus, still the bloody shows of the arena ; they lasted down to the martyrdom of St. Telemachus under Honorius. Punishments were still horribly brutal. There was still corruption in the entourage of the Emperor, still injustice and cruelty in the exactions of the taxes. Nor was the Church exempted from the debasing influence of wealth and power. The position of Bishop of Rome came to mean such a height of opulence that it was furiously contested between rival factions. A satirist might have argued that it was not the Church that had converted the State, but the State the Church.

It has been a familiar doctrine since Gibbon that the barbarians and Christianity between them ruined Rome. Superficially there is obviously something in his dictum. Barbarians and Christianity were at least accompanying circumstances of the Decline and Fall. But is there any deep truth in the statement ? In all seriousness, I think, we must answer No. East Rome as well as West Rome suffered from both maladies—and recovered from both. From Christianity the East suffered—if that is the right word—for centuries and did not die of it. We shall never cease to read Gibbon for his admirable written style and his deep inborn qualities of historian ; as the bitter, malignant critic of Christianity we shall learn to discount him.

So far we have spoken of one great contrast in religious belief, between polytheism, the system of the many gods, and monotheism, the system of the one true God. There is yet another way of envisaging the problem—the contrast between the good and evil in the world, dualism. The ancient Persian religion of Zoroaster had pictured the whole world as the stage on which was enacted the great drama of good and evil in conflict—in the divine sphere between the good Ormuzd and the evil Ahriman, in the intermediate sphere between spirits of good and evil, on the human plane in the struggle between virtue and vice. Under the restored Persian Empire of the Sassanids, an eccentric religious genius, Mani, produced his system, which was based on this old conception. He was banned as an enemy by Diocletian and was finally martyred by a Persian king. But his doctrines found wide acceptance and, in the time of St. Augustine, were widely held in Western Europe. St. Augustine at one stage of his development was himself a Manichee. Since then Manichaeism has raised its head more than once in the form of a heresy in the Church. It has always a certain plausibility, recognising instead of trying to gloss over the conflicts of life and thought ; but it creates too many problems that were not there before.   To recognise evil as on equal terms with good lands one in the most deadly intellectual and moral difficulties.

We come now to the systems of thought that tried to interpret the world to the enquiring mind.   You may find philosophy anywhere, where men are thinking out the meaning of their existence. It may be in a priest of the old religion, speculating as to the real meaning of the ceremonies with which he is concerned.   It may be in a scholar and man of affairs like Cicero, devoting his leisure to a study worthy of every thoughtful man.   It may be in a wit and journalist like Lucian.   But here we may concentrate our attention on the professional philosophies, the adherents of the schools.   All of the famous old schools continued to exist under the Empire, but not all throve ; there is little now to report of the Lyceum of Aristotle, for example.   We may best spend our time on those that showed some new life and energy.
Most important for the Roman Empire was the Porch, the Stoic philosophy, founded by the noble Zeno.   The Stoics taught that moral good was the only absolute value, the wise man the only true king.   All goods of the ordinary man were ' indifferents ', more or less to be desired, but not absolute goods.   The chief defect of Stoicism was its spiritual pride ; it attributed to unaided human nature more than belongs to it.   But at its best it was a noble creed and made a strong appeal to the best Romans.   Its natural philosophy was a kind of pantheism.   There was a fiery soul of the universe, out of which all came, into which everything must return at the end of the long year of the world.   Yet some Stoics found in their creed room for a god whom they could worship with fervour and with truth.   Some too found room for a limited immortality—conditional, for it was only for the wise, and limited, for nothing could escape the final end of the world in fire.   Independence was the hall-mark of the Stoic.   The opposition to the bad Emperors was largely carried on by devout Stoics.   But in religious matters this independence was not often very vigorously asserted against the popular beliefs.   The Stoic could point out their inadequacy, but he would usually make concessions to the vulgar.   The popular errors were expressions of truths that they could not fully comprehend ; they were all right—with the masses The Stoics here were braver in their theories than in their lives. No Stoics were martyred for denying worship to Apollo or Venus.

Christianity, in some noble interpretations of it, has much in common with the Stoic ethic, but the Stoics of antiquity were slow to see it. Marcus Aurelius, the philosopher on the throne, sees nothing in the persecuted beyond the pathetic, blind courage of self-devotion.

Far different were the followers of the gentle Epicurus. The Epicureans were not the grovelling addicts of pleasure that their enemies made them out to be. Pleasure to them meant not mere physical enjoyment, though to it they *did* allot a place, but happiness, depending mainly on peace of mind. Religion was the chief enemy. It terrified men with fears of the supernatural, of punishments after death. Now Epicurus, following the Atomist philosophers, taught that the universe consisted ultimately of atoms and void : that all that we see in our world is chance agglomerations of atoms : that they come into being in time and in time dissolve. There are no gods in the ordinary sense of the word—busybodies, forever interfering in human affairs. There is no life after death, for the soul, like everything else, is only a chance union of atoms that must undergo the universal fate. No room then for fears of hell ! Epicurus had gods of his own—beings of superhuman beauty and power, living in paradises between the worlds, protected in some mysterious way, not fully explained, from the general decay. From them come images of grace and loveliness to men and impress their minds with something of the divine felicity. The followers of Epicurus tried to live a life of innocent retirement, not dabbling in politics, not worrying about the future, but finding such happiness as life allows in leisure and the love of friends. Epicureanism had not the same appeal for the Romans as Stoicism, though it was preached by one poet of genius. Some scholars think that we must not exaggerate those fears of death and hell of which Lucretius writes so movingly. It seems more probable that such fears were a real trouble to many and that Epicurus brought relief to many such suffering souls. Under the Empire Epicureanism was certainly on the wane. But Walter Pater may have seen a truth in his phantasy, ' Marius the Epicurean ' ; many a disciple of Epicurus may have found a new spiritual home in the Christian Church.

The Sceptics were not very influential in what was essentially an age of faith. They are well represented by the brilliant wit of the 2nd century, Lucian of Samosata, a sparkling writer of essays and tales who inevitably reminds one of Voltaire. He is essentially negative. There are all those strange tales of gods and afterlife ; well, you see what it all ends in—dust and ashes.

Meanwhile, we can be amused spectators at the human comedy—
no divine comedy here, but rather a dance of death.

The famous Academy of Plato, which by the time of Augustus
had declined into a somewhat colourless and lukewarm eclecti-
cism, enjoyed a remarkable revival in the 3rd century. Plotinus,
the favourite philosopher of Gallienus, restated the Platonic philosophy with a sublimity and power native to himself. The human
soul reaches up to the Absolute that is beyond thought and
emotion. Union with the Absolute, which may only be allowed
to a man a few times in a lifetime, is the supreme good. The
thought of Plotinus is difficult ; the air he breathes is too thin for
ordinary minds ; but he stands out in an age of mediocrity with
an authentic, individual grandeur. His school lasted after him,
though not on his level. It degenerated in the direction of theurgy,
the conjuration of divine powers. These successors, whom we
usually call Neo-pythagoreans in contrast to Plotinus, the Neo-
platonist, came to be prominent among the enemies of the Christian
Church. They found themselves committed to the task of apologis-
ing for the absurdities and immoralities of the old religion, by explaining that they meant something quite different from what they
seemed to say or do. Julian in his war on the Church had the
Neo-pythagoreans of his age on his side. One of the last shots
fired in the battle between the Church and paganism was the
closing of the schools of philosophy at Athens by Justinian.

Astrology was neither a religion nor a philosophy, though it
took the place of both for some people. It was very widely believed
in by many who had no other firm beliefs. By a certain natural
sympathy that binds the whole universe together in its parts, small
and great, the stars exercise an influence on human destinies.
The adepts of astrology can read horoscopes and deduce destinies
from them. Such a belief made an irresistible appeal to the
political adventurer. Many a plot was prompted by the advice
of some astrologer, many an execution resulted. It was, judged
by its fruits, an evil profession—destined, as Tacitus sardonically remarked, ' always to be banned and always practised in Rome '.
But, apart from the tragedies of political life to which it gave rise,
it had an evil and depressing effect on human conduct. What
room for courage and energy where everything is determined by
a court beyond appeal, the course of the stars ? And, to make it
worse, the tyranny of the stars can be continued after death.
The soul departing must pass by the gates of the rulers of the
planets, who are malignant and may do the most fatal harm,
unless the soul has learned the words of power that may win its

safe passage through. It is probably of these terrible Lords of the Planets that St. Paul is speaking when he writes of ' the world rulers of this darkness, spiritual wickedness in high places '. Yet Astrology had a tremendously strong appeal to many minds. But why a man, armed against credulity in matters of religion, should suddenly let down all his barriers for blind faith to pour in at this point—that is one of the psychological mysteries that meet one again and again in history.

Of pagan morality we said something in our chapter on social life. We will supplement that account by looking at two things that closely concern the conduct of individuals and yet are intimately bound up with religion—salvation and immortality. The dominant thought of the Ancient World was hardly democratic. The emphasis was directed towards the community or, if to the individual at all, the exceptional individual who overtopped his fellows. In religion, too, this principle ruled. It is the State, and the rare men who direct its destinies, that are the main concern of the gods. Salvation—the securing of the good, physical and spiritual, of the ordinary man—was not a main object in the State religion. The ordinary man, however, is always there and will not be entirely forgotten. Even in the conventional religion he found some place. As we saw, there was one particular development— the mystery religions—which catered specially for him. It is probably fair to say that this note, though never quite inaudible, was seldom dominant. But in the world in which Christianity grew and conquered the note sounded ever louder. Salvation, which is essentially an individual matter, takes a central position. There is loss here as well as gain. On the credit side we may set it that the values of life are enhanced, if they are to be looked for in every man, not only in the elect few. On the debit side one must note that a concentration on the importance of the average man may lead to a neglect, even to a dislike of marked excellence. And society *does* need its men of exceptional excellence—for its own sake if not for theirs. In one sense men are equal ; they are all born, they all die in the same way. In another sense they are different, with all kinds of difference. To keep a true balance we must take both points of view into account.

There remains the question of immortality ; does the human personality survive death ? The pagan world had no decided answer to this important question. Immortality, if promised at all, was usually given conditionally, to the man who enjoyed special divine favour or to the initiate who sought it by the service of his

R

special god. The Jews had among them both the Pharisees who affirmed and the Sadducees who denied. The philosophies were equally divided. The Stoics gave a possible affirmative answer in special cases; the Epicureans gave an absolute denial. The Christians made immortality a key note of their song—' Christ has brought life and immortality to light'. If we consult the thousands of Roman inscriptions for information on the subject, we get answers of every kind. Some funeral inscriptions deny any life after death : ' I was, I am not, I don't care '. In other cases, the forms of symbolism on tombs suggest the hope of survival. Recurrent themes—such as the victory in battle, the voyage over the sea, the scenes of translation, the Rape of the Leucippides and the like—strongly suggest analogies that were to be applied to the destiny of the soul. There is a very general desire to provide a lasting memorial to the bones or ashes of the dead. A man has been part of the great world of life and, even dead, he is reluctant to relinquish it entirely. The practice of inhumation, as opposed to cremation, undoubtedly points to a growing belief in survival. There is a decided shift of interest ; the present life is no longer the sole concern. There is a life beyond, and the thought of it has its effect on present ambitions and conduct.

In the triumph of Christianity the religious struggles of the ancient world found their solution. For a long time there was a very general uniformity of belief, only mildly diversified by the continued insistence of the Jews and by heresies within the Church. Thought on religious matters had been clarified ; morality in some vital respects had been reformed. But the old problems were still there, not finally answered in the new solution. If the belief in the one true God does justice to the order of the Cosmos, there is still the diversity of life to be explained. The Church baptised—invested with new Christian meaning—as much of the old paganism as it could. There was so much in ' natural ' religion that could be regarded as a blind groping after truth. In the orders of angels many of the minor pagan deities could be enrolled ; Victory becomes an angel of the Lord, Peace is now the armed Peace of God. The gods were more obnoxious, as they might still be considered as rivals of the true God. They retreated into the realm of fairy story and fable. Or they might be thought of as demons, who still hide in hills and corners, regretting their lost powers and still contriving to entrap the unwary. To some extent the role of the gods might devolve on the Christian saints. St. Cosmos and St. Damian, martyrs of the time of Diocletian, whose bones St. Ambrose discovered at Milan, are remarkably like the Heavenly

Twins—so like that a converted pagan could gladly accept them in their new form. The Christian world lays its emphasis on new points. But many notes that had been dominant, though now recessive, are still occasionally heard.

CHAPTER X

LITERATURE

There is hardly any way by which one can hope to get nearer to the mind of people of other times than through the books they read. And so the reader will approach this chapter with peculiar anticipation. Books are written and read for more than one purpose. They are written for the delight and instruction of trained readers ; they are also written for the instruction of specialists in various branches of learning. They are written for serious improvement of character or for light diversion. Literature means books, but books do not necessarily mean literature. By the time of the Empire the production of books was well advanced. There was as yet nothing like printing for the cheap and easy multiplication of copies. But the right materials had been found—papyrus for the cheaper kinds, parchment or similar material for the costlier. Teams of slave copiers multiplied the originals fast enough. Atticus, the friend of Cicero, had developed an important book business in Rome. Later, under the Empire, we hear of other firms of enterprising book producers and sellers.

And who were the writers ? Almost anyone who chose, from the lowest to the highest. Tacitus tells us that the early Emperors as a rule were trained orators. One might add that very many Emperors were historians too. Many of them wrote their memoirs. Romans of rank often joined the list of authors. There was nothing to prevent a man of low birth from trying his hand at what was admittedly mainly a profession for the notable. And who were the readers ? Men of rank and nobility, of course, for they would be interested in the themes of the major writers. But, clearly, a general public was beginning to grow up ; anyone who had a little money and a little interest in things beyond immediate daily needs might join in. Patronage of course counted for much. A wealthy patron might provoke the composition of a work of art, might push its advance when published. An Emperor would lend the weight of his authority to some favoured author. We shall find examples enough, when we come to speak of the Golden Age of Augustus. The point should however be made—not everything depended on patronage.

Not all of ancient literature survives today, rather a small fragment. Does what survives give us a fair picture of what was

originally there? The answer to such a question is always both
'yes' and 'no'. In this case the 'no' is more emphatic than the
'yes'. What we have, of course, gives us some idea of the mass that
is lost. But chance has had a good deal to do with survival or non-
survival. Prejudice has had even more—the prejudice of monks,
for example, against certain types of pagan literature. A good many
works of instruction have survived for no especial merit of their own,
but because they chanced to please the taste of ignorant generations.
Edification has preserved masses of Christian literature which we
feel we could well have spared. The books that were most greedily
read by the Roman masses have left few traces. We regret this, not
because of any possible literary merit—which was no doubt mostly
to seek—but because of the light that they must throw on social life
and on the taste of the readers. We know that the Romans of the
Empire were very fond of loose love tales (Milesian *fabulae*), wild
stories of adventure, works of silly gossip and scandal about the
mighty. In the case of coins—material that we can check with
some accuracy, as the bulk of mass issues survives—we can recon-
struct the trunk of the body but, even there, there will have been
issues enough, never of large extent, which with the natural waste
of time tend to disappear. The really rare issues have only the
faintest chance of survival. This applies also to books, but not in
quite the same way. Books are perishable in themselves; a
hundred thousand will perish almost as certainly as one. The mere
fact that the book was once in many hands will not necessarily
preserve it. Some rare books, on the other hand, may be deliberately preserved just because they are rare. The chief difference
between books and coins is that, with books, we can be certain that
we are very imperfectly acquainted with some of the commoner
classes, while, with coins, it is the rare or quite exceptional that we
can rarely hope to meet. In both cases, we have to try to estimate
the value and extent of the original mass by the aid of comparatively
small relics.

For literary purposes we must think of the Empire as essentially
bilingual. Latin and Greek both served the uses of the educated
classes. A few other languages, such as Syriac, Coptic and
Armenian, have a literature; it is mainly of a religious or historical
character and need not take up our time here. Punic was still
spoken, but no literature in it is left. The other languages of the
Empire which survived to some extent for speaking have left no
literature at all; it does not appear that they were ever much used
for that purpose. As far as it goes, this is evidence for the triumph
of the Empire over particular tendencies in the realm of thought.

If you really wanted people to listen to what you had to say, you used one of the two imperial languages. The study of the survival of the other languages by the side of Latin and Greek—of Celtic, for example—is full of interest. One must speculate about the chances that have made English so different from French in a neighbouring province, that have differentiated Italian, Spanish and Portuguese, that have left in Rumanian a Latin language across the Danube. As far as literature went the popular languages disappeared underground.

There is one other line of cleavage that must be heeded—that between pagan and Christian literature. In theory it might be better if we all mastered both branches, pagan and Christian, and could study them all the way side by side. As things are, scholars are usually definitely committed to one side or the other, and, as it happens, the two branches of literature diverge widely from one another, only touching at quite a few points. In so far as we study ancient literature in divisions by subject, pagan and Christian tend of themselves to fall apart. Only in the 4th century, when Christianity had become an integral, recognised part of the imperial scheme, can we readily compare pagan and Christian in the same fields.

What method are we to follow in using so vast a material as this for our special purpose? We need not essay the hopeless task of being exhaustive. There are excellent text-books of Roman and Greek literature of the Empire that will supply all necessary detail. The same is true of the Christian side. We may well select, only trying not to omit any name of really great importance. We may also, I think, depart from a rigid chronological sequence and prefer to take different kinds of literature in turn. But, in order to create some clarity at the outset, it may be well to sketch in very general outline the main course of development. We will put Latin literature in the centre of our scheme, relating Greek and Christian literature, Latin and Greek, to it.

The first age of the Empire has always been known as the Golden Age of Augustus. It is well named ; it is Augustan in deed as in name ; it is golden in its excellence. It looks back to past glories which it hopes to revive ; it is succeeded by ages of lesser glory. The great writers of this age share some common characteristics. They are serious in purpose, sober, moderate. Acutely conscious of the dangers through which Rome has come, they look with respect and gratitude to the New Order which has opened the door to a happier future ; they hold out good hope, conditioned by the need for reverence and discipline. It is amusing, but futile and unjust, to brand them as flatterers. They are not blind to sins of the past—not all on the side that had been defeated. But they see in Augustus the man divinely appointed to restore Rome, and to him in this capacity they give their full meed of praise. They do not simply follow his lead and speak smooth words for his benefit. They interpret for him the wishes and aspirations of the thousands who cannot voice them themselves. These are the great, the typical Augustans, Livy, Horace, Virgil. There are others who do not give themselves in the same degree to serious interests. The vexatious past has gone. A new future of hope and interest offers itself. That offers themes enough for writing. Propertius is more intent on his love for Cynthia than on any imperial concerns. Tibullus, the gentle poet of love and country life, followed his own true inspiration undisturbed. Ovid, the genius who could never learn self-discipline, ventured to give full expression to the licentious life of the generation of the Emperor's daughter, Julia, and her children. His ' Amores ' and ' Art of Love ' must have vexed Augustus from the first ; it may have been an accident that brought down on the poet a late nemesis in A.D. 4. Other writers of the age seem only to belong superficially to it. The style of the Augustan age is ripe— perhaps overripe. Latin has been carried a long way towards perfect accomplishment along a number of lines. It is in complete touch with the great Greek originals ; the vigorous, crude old Latin literature is severely criticised and allowed to slip into oblivion.

If we ask ' what follows ? ' no answer is easy to find. The Silver Age, the logical sequel to the Golden, may be dated from the death of Augustus to the accession of Hadrian. It is harder to define than the Augustan and has less unity. No Emperor is able to enlist literary support as successfully as Augustus, with Maecenas and Messalla, had done. Base and insincere flattery intrudes. New experiments in style and subject are tried. Rhetorical influence is very strong. There is a revulsion from the ripe perfection of Ciceronian prose. Seneca develops and often perfects a kind of superior journalistic style, with short, pithy sentences and variety of neat verbal point. The Augustan age had been an age of acceptance, with very little criticism. All that is now changed. The satirists complain of things as they are, even if they keep to generalities or take their examples from the past. Tacitus ventures to criticise the imperial scheme in itself. There is still talent in plenty —in poetry with Lucan, Statius, Martial, Valerius Flaccus, encyclopaedic knowledge with the Elder Pliny, satire with Juvenal and letters with the Younger Pliny. The literature is uncertain of its purpose and seems not to know where to turn.

After Tacitus and Juvenal follows a long period of silence or decline. There is no poetry of special interest, no history of high value. Only here and there can we point to something of special interest—to the romance of Apuleius, for example. There was a return to antique models, fostered by that stilted rhetorician, Fronto. There was much rather idle curiosity about the past as shown in Aulus Gellius's ' Noctes Atticae '. But there was no strong current anywhere running. I do not think that this decline of vitality can be quite an illusion in our view or an accident. One cause may be suggested. The attitude of Tacitus to the Empire could not please any Emperor who read him seriously. At Hadrian Tacitus seems to have permitted himself some spiteful gibes which must have given great offence. I think we may assume that the historian after his death was definitely in disfavour. Any attempt to carry on his work would be doomed to disaster. The lesson was not lost on the world ; any kind of independence would be unpopular in high circles and was just not worth while. Any history which still appeared hardly rose above the level of gossip. There was very little poetry of any merit, though the art of writing hexameters or elegiacs was no doubt not completely lost. In the ' Pervigilium Veneris ' there is a new note, of wistfulness and promise. The great lawyers were hard at work, but there is not much that is purely literary in their achievement. Technical works, none of great importance, continued to appear from time to time. Of the very popular literature very little has come down to us. It is quite certain that the age was not as barren as it appears to us today. Perhaps, like our own, it was an age of the novel.

To Greek literature the coming of the Empire meant very much less than to Rome. It was simply a new epoch in the history that could already show many. There was no Golden Age for Greece ; there was no Silver Age following, no sharp decline after that. Plutarch of Chaeronea is the great feature of the late 1st and 2nd centuries—not one of the greatest writers of the world, but one of the most familiar and beloved. In the 2nd century we meet one of the few great wits of antiquity, Lucian of Samosata, the Voltaire of the Ancient World. We shall not admire him or his heart—there is little evidence of one ; but his wit is admirable ; it shoots wide and pierces deep. A good deal of the serious thought of the age was going into Greek rather than into Latin. Marcus Aurelius addressed his soul in Greek, ' to himself ' ; Plotinus, the late exponent of rethought Platonism, naturally used his master's language. It is only when we consider Greek literature that we can truly estimate how great is the gulf that opens up in Latin.

Christian literature again has its own story, its own development. The first age produced the Epistles and, after them, the Gospels, both unique of their kind. We are not sure whether written records were set down in Aramaic. With the passage from the apostolic age to the next there is a decline in freshness of interest. Clement of Rome and Ignatius of Antioch are definitely inferior to Paul. The great new development of the 2nd century was Christian Apologetic—explanations and excuses for the Faith, addressed to Emperors or high-born Romans. The style of these works is usually humble, their interest considerable. Tertullian is the most remarkable of them all ; but he is ceasing to be apologist and is passing over to furious invective. There was a vast literature concerning the Gnostic heresies, expounding or refuting them. With the late 2nd to 3rd century came the philosophical work of Clement of Alexandria and the still greater Origen, the letters and doctrinal works of Cyprian and many more. Christian literature still moves mainly along its own lines, hardly competing as yet with secular.

The 4th century shows some change from the 3rd. The Empire has not recovered complete prosperity, but it has again some measure of stability. Dominant in literature is the new rhetoric, to us insincere and artificial, but with some dignity and consistency of its own. History is written once more. The Epitomes have some merit, but are limited by their very plan. The strange ' Historia Augusta ' seems to revive in a very indirect way the habit of historical criticism. Far more interesting is the bluff soldier, Ammianus Marcellinus. He is an astonishing apparition, an original mind in history after centuries of dry rot. There is also a court poet, Claudian, who has not forgotten the magic art of Virgil and can still write pagan poetry from the heart. The pagan reaction in Rome has given us the strange antiquarian work of Macrobius. After 400 the main track fades away, though a great name here and there still illuminates the darkness. We end with Isidore of Seville, Gildas of Brittany and the rest. The rhetorical style, which prevailed in the imperial chancellery, is preserved for us in the great Codices. The Greek orators match the Latin panegyrists ; we have considerable remains of two, Themistius and Libanius. At the very end of the age comes the strange luxuriant poem, the ' Dionysiaca ' of Nonnus. Julian II was man of letters as well as Emperor and general. His work shows all the faults of rhetoric, but some flashes of wit and insight. Its chief fault is that it wearies the reader. It is only now that Christian literature begins to flow in the same channels as pagan. Prudentius, the first true poet of the Faith, uses classical metres to defend the Church or glorify its martyrs. Ausonius is hardly more than a nominal Christian. His most charming poem, the ' Mosella ', is natural, neither pagan nor Christian. Christian historians now appear—not always very reliable, nearly always very dull. Controversy takes up an enormous space ; apologetic passes on into attack as we advance from our Arnobius to Firmicus Maternus. Many of the Fathers wielded their pen in letter-writing to very good effect. The great and versatile scholar, Jerome, produced one of the master-pieces of ancient literature, the translation of the Bible into Latin, which we know as the Vulgate. With Latin literature we are very near the hour of death ; the echoes of the great times are slowly dying away ; the new Latin is still to be born. Greek literature is simply turning over a new page in its age-long life. Christian literature is for the first time finding leisure to turn each way her fancy or inspiration leads her. In any case, we are now past the deadness of the 3rd century. The world is alive again, even if it does not yet know quite what way it will go. We will now balance the picture by considering literature in its classes—first, prose : history, law, rhetoric, essays, letters, works of instruction, novels, philosophy and religion ; and lastly, poetry, with satire as a special section.

For history we shall in the main follow the order of time and adopt the order—Latin, Greek, Christian. Livy is one of the great historians of the world in virtue of his glorious style and his noble conception of his task. He could not write an accurate story of the old Rome ; it had not been written soon enough and, when Livy came to his task, the record was hopelessly blurred. What Livy did was to paint a wonderful picture of old Roman character as Rome of Augustus's age conceived it. Later, where the record becomes plainer, Livy tells a straight story, still carrying with him his style and his interest in character. Livy has his place secured for him in the Augustan age. Velleius Paterculus writes curiously affected Latin and is an undisguised partisan of Tiberius. He preserves a good deal that would without him be lost and is often most unjustly disparaged. Valerius Maximus, who collected historical examples of virtues and vices, has no independence and only occasional interest. For the next age there was no dearth of historians ; we hear of many—Cremutius Cordus, Aufidius Bassus, Pliny the Elder, Cluvius Rufus and others. History was still vigorous and not yet muzzled, though Cordus suffered under Tiberius for his freedom. Pliny the Elder certainly could record the German wars from first-hand knowledge. Chance has denied us all of these.

Tacitus has made the early Empire what it is today in popular belief. A senator of Vespasian's new crop, he followed an official career with brilliant success, rose to the head of the Roman Bar and won fame in his lifetime. He wrote Histories and Annals, covering the whole period from Tiberius to Domitian, as well as several minor works. We have only part surviving and, accordingly, the light flickers on and off the imperial stage. Tacitus wrote with conscience and care ; he thought that he was writing without bias, without favour or malice. Wherever we can check him, he is almost invariably accurate in his facts. The doubt comes about his interpretations, which are continually being pushed on to us. We are not only told what happened, but what it meant, what the intentions of the actors were. Tacitus obviously risks going beyond the function of the historian here and becoming prophet or propagandist. How he can have believed that he wrote of Tiberius without spite is hard to imagine. Tacitus was a man of high principles and ideals, also of bitter and narrow prejudices. In the sum, he condemns the Empire not only for its sins but also for defects inherent in it. In this he is quite unreasonable ; he sees the necessity of the New Order for peace, but blames it for not perfectly satisfying the desires of his own class, the senatorial. Tacitus is a perfect Roman snob ; he admires or derides after the fashion of the Roman aristocracy. For a new minority like the Christians Tacitus has no glimmering of understanding ; he only repeats without either fully accepting or refusing what the mob says of them. But if we must speak with reserve of Tacitus as an historian, we can let ourselves go on his style. It is a marvellous instrument for compelling interest, conveying colour, rousing prejudice, pity or indignation. It is terse, varied, vigorous, poetical in colour, unusual and individual. Its famous epigrams have again and again penetrated deep into the heart and lodged there the thoughts and emotions that Tacitus wished to convey.

After Tacitus, Suetonius. As imperial secretary, Suetonius had unique opportunities for writing the lives of the Emperors. His work is full of interest, full of scandal, devoid of serious purpose and weak in plan. I believe that Hadrian forbade any attempt to continue the work of Tacitus and that Suetonius wrote what he thought to be safe. One might have thought that his scandalous gossip would give no less offence than Tacitus's moral indignation. This is a case where the old world differs from ours. Rome loved scandal, but did not take it too seriously. The Emperor need not regard the record as serious criticism. After this there is an almost complete gap. Lives of the Emperors were written by Marius

Maximus ; he was apparently an even more flippant Suetonius. Was there one great lost historian behind the muddled record of the Augustan history ? The case has been strongly argued, but is hardly proved. History then for a time passed into the hands of the Greeks.

The strange Augustan history has not yet yielded up all its secrets. But we know that it was written not before the fifties of the 4th century—some say even later—that it makes a mystery about its various authors, assigned to various earlier dates, that it comments most mysteriously on such questions as that of adoption or hereditary succession, of Christianity and paganism and so on. It style is curiously forcible-feeble. It seems to be brimming over with tendentiousness, but it is hard to find any consistent purpose in its bias. It is hard to take it quite seriously—and yet there is some trace of critical faculty, even if we do not quite know what the critic is aiming at. Clearer before us stands Ammianus Marcellinus, a soldier by profession ; admitted to senatorial circles in Rome, but not uncritical of them ; interested in the Emperors, but not a court favourite ; a pagan, but not a bitter one ; a man with a sense of public spirit and a natural love of what is noble. His style—painfully obscure but not obscurely painful—must not frighten us away from the sheer excellence of the man. He reveals a spirit that since Tacitus had seemed to be dead, the spirit of un-biassed historical enquiry. Epitomes, never lacking, flourished in the 4th century. Eutropius, a high imperial official, wrote one of the best. Aurelius Victor introduced into his short work some vivid touches and striking characterisations. Sulpicius Severus has left fragments which arouse a taste for more, while Orosius wrote a worthy, but rather dull ' Historia Contra Paganos ', to prove that the disasters of the time were not due to the Christians. One late writer, Nicomachus Flavianus, was certainly a supporter of the senatorial reaction.

There was much industry among the Greeks of the age of Augustus in compendia of history. Nicolaus of Damascus collected the history of the world. Diodorus has left in part that very dull compendium which is yet of such value to us. Dionysius of Halicarnassus devoted a long work to the ancient history of Rome, but he has no high merit of style or research. Strabo wrote a noble work on the geography of the Empire. Then comes a gap partly filled by the historical work of Plutarch, the wonderful Parallel Lives of famous Greeks and Romans. Plutarch gathered his materials from varied sources, most of them not available to us today ; he enlivened the whole with his intense humanity and wise moderate outlook. This has been one of the most read books of the world. Josephus, the able renegade Jew, used Greek to narrate the history of his people and, incidentally, justify his own career and praise his Flavian patrons. In the 2nd century Arrian wrote a valuable history of Alexander the Great ; we may note by the way that there is a Latin history of Curtius Rufus, of disputed date. Appian wrote chapters of the history of Rome, grouped under various subject headings ; the work rises and falls in interest, but is of great value to us. Herodian in an easy rhetorical prose narrated the history of his own times from 181 to 238. He is not contemptible and his local colouring is often good ; but when there is doubt about meaning and sequence of facts he is frequently wrong.

Of a much higher rank is Dio Cassius, to whom we owe a great deal of what we know of the Empire. He was a trained diplomatist and soldier of the Severan age and, even if he may import ideas of the 3rd century into the 1st, he had some political intelligence and a very considerable knowledge of the Roman State. I think he is hardly valued highly enough by most modern historians. We have only traces of one who must have been a considerable historian, Dexippus, the Athenian patriot who helped to defend his city against the Goths. After this, history tends to pass into Christian hands. Eusebius, the historian of Constantine, is not impressive either as stylist or as chronicler ; but he is often judged with a quite remorseless severity. Lactantius in the ' De Mortibus Persecutorum ' makes a short excursion into political invective, forceful and rather shocking. Sozomen, Socrates and the rest are dull ; perhaps it was not their fault that they had so many unedifying quarrels and interminable councils to chronicle. At the very end comes the bitter pagan, Zosimus, recording the Decline and Fall with a sincere hatred of the new that reminds us a little of our own Gibbon.

History is the branch of literature that touches government most nearly. The historian was usually under some kind of thraldom. Some few ventured too far in freedom and fell. Others, in happier times, took their chances without disaster. Such were Cluvius Rufus under the Flavians and Tacitus under Nero and Trajan— though Tacitus may have gone too far and affronted Hadrian. After that, servility or sheer flippancy was the rule. Ammianus is a wonder, almost a freak, in his age, a miracle of independence of judgment and spirit ; but even he probably had to compromise a little in order not to displease Theodosius the Great. It is idle to blame the Emperors too much. Some degree of censorship may be held necessary. Perhaps more might have been done to promote the better kind of official history ; as it is, we have to read it in short extracts on the coins.

Of the vast mass of Roman legal writing, comparatively little survives and that mostly in the great imperial compendia. The Roman mind was perhaps at its best in law and we must not neglect the legal writings, even if their interest is seldom literary. Gaius wrote an admirable handbook ; Papinian, Ulpian, Paulus and the rest of the Severan lawyers developed both the private law and the theory of State. We must read the Codices to understand the wealth of thought bestowed on the ordering of relationships and the spirit underlying the imperial government.

Rhetoric was a main Roman interest ; it had reached its zenith under the late Republic and had found its Demosthenes in Cicero. The order of the Empire no longer allowed the same field to rival orators, and rhetoric fled to the schools. There, its influence on literary style far exceeded its technical importance. Tacitus was a noted speaker, marked by his deadly earnestness ; but we have nothing of him except his ' Dialogus de Oratoribus ', an interesting essay in dialogue form, discussing why oratory has declined. Of his friend, the Younger Pliny, we still possess the Panegyric on Trajan, a work of tiresome eulogy and eloquence, but of great political interest. Quintilian, a great master of instruction, has left a noble work on the making of an orator. It is one of the great text-books, which retains its interest even when the special conditions for which it was written are gone. Of the artificial archaising style of the Antonine age Fronto is our only example, and we have little enough of him except some letters. The 3rd century, so far as existing work is concerned, is almost a blank. In the 4th century, we have a whole crop of panegyrists, who command a considerable range of flattery, whole flower gardens of speech, some liveliness of fancy—but seldom any deep sincerity or immediacy of expression. It is the darling style of the period and it found its way into the official language. There too floridity and rotundity flourish. Late in the century we have specimens of the rhetoric of Ausonius and Symmachus—fluent, facile but how sincere ? Only once, in the ' Relatio ' on the altar of Victory, does Symmachus really touch our hearts as his own was touched. ' You cannot approach the supreme mystery by one way only '. St. Ambrose could find nothing to equal that, even though he won the day.

The rhetorical style, divorced from the courts, flourished even more among the Greeks than among the Romans. Of authors of whom we can form an impression Dio Chrysostom, of the time of Trajan, is one of the most interesting. He travelled widely, discoursed with great acceptance to cities far and wide, taught lessons of moderation and concord and extolled wise monarchy. In the next generation, Aristides wrote an encomium on Rome, moving in its force and sincerity, and expressed his gratitude to the divine powers who had helped him in his physical infirmities and troubles. Of Philostratus, the great sophist of the Severan age, we have only a side work, the life of Apollonius of Tyana. The great rhetoricians of the 4th century enjoyed vast reputations and the approbation of the great. If we may judge them by Themistius and Libanius, they had immense facility, considerable powers of invention and formal eloquence; what they lacked was directness and simplicity ; they are desperately difficult even to understand. The Emperor Julian competed for the prize in this field too. He too is insufferably long and artificial, lacking in any convincing sincerity. When he attacks Christianity, his passion lends him a sort of eloquence. His fantasy on the Caesars has some amusing and even enlightening comments. His hymns to his favourite deities do not appeal to modern taste. His hymn to the Mother of the gods was written, he tells us, in a single night ; one might unkindly remark that one can readily believe it. There is a good deal of rhetoric in the Church Fathers, but *there* it is usually harnessed to serious debate and our discussion of them has therefore been reserved to our section on religion and philosophy.

We come to two minor branches of literature, the essay and the letter. Seneca developed the essay into a considerable literary form. He is mainly concerned with moral questions, which he treats with much sound humanity, mixed with some gross flattery of the great. His style is pleasant, a good deal more pointed than appears on a first careless reading. Aulus Gellius discourses easily, in his ' Noctes Atticae ', on themes of mild antiquarian interest. Lucian is a brilliant master of the essayist's art. He is interested in everything ; he has a vast capacity for detecting the more comical sides of the human play ; he can ridicule with a light touch ; he seldom touches the heart, but all who care for wit will love him and keep him on their shelves.

The letter, as a literary form, has a very wide range—from the simple, natural and sincere to the formal, artificial and affected. Seneca writes to his friend, Lucilius, on a variety of themes, of philosophy and natural history ; he is serious and sententious. Pliny the Younger writes in an admirably pointed style and displays his interests and character to good effect. Despite his deliberate art he reveals a good deal of himself. His letters to Trajan have serious historical interest and throw light on the characters of both parties to the correspondence. There is warm humanity in the letters of Fronto to Marcus Aurelius in spite of all the affectation of the writing. Alciphron gives us specimens of the purely artificial letter—the letter used to delineate types of character, the courtesan, the parasite, the fisherman. In Ausonius and Symmachus we have examples enough of the formal letter of the 4th century, stiff, artificial, stilted. Bishops Synesius and Sidonius Apollinaris write with some sincerity and charm, and convey vivid impressions of their age. The letter was a favourite form with Christian writers from St. Paul to St. Augustine ; it will be dealt with mainly later. The letters of the great Fathers of the 4th century tell us much of their character and circumstances. St. Jerome is very self-revealing.

Works of instruction of various kinds appeared from time to time. Some of them were technical treatises of considerable value—Frontinus on the aqueducts of Rome and on military strategy, Columella on agriculture, Pomponius Mela on geography, Ptolemaeus on astronomy. Pliny the Elder threw together into his natural history a vast medley of undigested information ; it was immensely influential in the Middle Ages. Celsus and Galen wrote admirably on medicine, Probus and Donatus on grammar. Chronology as a special subject was handled by Africanus, Eusebius and St. Jerome. Other works were of a more popular character—Artemidorus on dreams, interesting and delightful—Aelian on animals, full of curious information. We have the extraordinary miscellanea of Athenaeus who in his ' Deipnosophistae ' brings together much of interest and amusement on gastronomics, and Macrobius who preserved some very interesting literary criticism. Vitruvius's work on architecture preserves much detailed information for which we are grateful. But, even when instruction was offered, the intention to amuse was usually present. The Empire was not an age in which the purely scientific spirit flourished. Together with information of serious interest a good deal of hearsay is repeated.

We come to the novel, a form of art that was congenial to the age and may have played a far larger part than our scanty remains allow us to realise. Altheim has observed that the novel was the characteristic form of the Empire and he may well be right. Where the great forms of poetry have ceased to attract, and interests have been diverted from public life, scope may be found in the novel for the natural love of adventure, the curiosity about individual character and fortunes. If we are correct in our guess, we have only a fraction of what was once an enormous literature ; we must make the most then of what we have. Our first example, the ' Satyricon ', attributed to Petronius Arbiter, is alone of its kind. It is a picaresque novel about low life in South Italy in the reign of Nero. That seems to be the date, though some have placed it later. Whether it was written by Nero's 'arbiter of taste' is quite uncertain. The 'Satyricon' is amusing, varied, uncommonly low. It gives us some exciting tastes of Roman slang and the Roman vulgar tongue. The half-loving portrait of the incredible freedman, Trimalchio, has become world famous. Interwoven with the plot is some literary criticism of a fairly serious character. There can be no doubt that there were other works of this class, but the 'Satyricon' shows the talent, almost amounting to genius, that takes it out of the common run.

We may also mention a strange work that belongs to no particular genus, the 'Apocolocyntosis' ('pumpkinification') or the 'Ludus de morte Claudii'. This bitter satire on the dead Claudius is slickly written and has some wit ; but it is often in very poor taste, and the flattery of the young Nero is as offensive as the kicks levelled at his dead father. It is to be hoped that the attribution to Seneca is wrong. Seneca had been banished by Claudius, but had been recalled, had been made tutor of the young Nero and was a minister of the new Emperor when Claudius was consecrated. Anything more indecent than such a squib, written by a man more or less in the position of Prime Minister, could not be conceived. Then comes a gap in our tradition. The next Latin work of note is the 'Golden Ass' of Apuleius. It is a novel of wild adventure, encounters with robbers, witchcraft, loose love affairs, transformations and recovery of human form. Embedded in it is the most famous of all ancient tales, the story of Cupid and Psyche. The style is delightful but cloying. It is rich and intricate in construction, full of curious compound words. This odd work has a serious end. The enchanted ass is restored by special favour of the great goddess Isis, and becomes her votary. The vision in which Isis announces her nature and will to Lucius and promises him happiness now and in the hereafter is moving and beautiful. Of course, the effect that Apuleius makes on us is enhanced by his uniqueness ; there must have been many other works of this class.

Lucian is essayist rather than novelist, but we may take account of a few of his works here. The 'True History' is an amusing example of the wonder story of the Baron Münchausen type of the ancients. It is written with effective simplicity and soars from peak to peak of comic absurdity. As always, Lucian is fertile in invention. Other fanciful romances had a serious purpose behind their fooling, but Lucian rarely deviates into gravity. Other works like

s

the ' Timon ' and the ' Charon ' are like little novels, but are cast in dialogue form. The purpose is satire of human life rather than narrative for its own sake. The ' Menippus ' is another wonder story, of the philosopher who rode up to heaven on a strange new steed to get first-hand information from Zeus about some questions that were vexing him.

The love story, usually of a light and frivolous character, generally went by the name of ' Milesian ' ; Ionia always had a reputation for a refined immorality. Milesian stories were all too popular and widely diffused. A chance reference in Plutarch shows that they were current in Mesopotamia at the time of the tragedy of Crassus (53 B.C.). No true example of the genre survives. The story of Daphnis and Chloe is somewhat different—a fairly simple love story, set in a charming rural setting, with little more than the necessary minimum of adventure, showing the quiet development of the innocent affections of the two young lovers. The typical novel of adventure was more lurid in character. We know of it from some half a dozen suriving specimens by Achilles Tatius, Iamblichus and others. These novels, like modern thrillers, must move fast and furiously—that is their one main law. Nothing, however wild or improbable, is barred, provided only that it thrills. We have adventure by land and sea, perils from pirates, brigands and wild beasts, love potions and witchcraft, strange doings at the courts of Eastern kings. One rule is that the heroine shall be subjected to the most extreme risks, but neither her life nor her virtue shall be lost. The hero too is protected from the last terror, for he will be needed to be united in holy matrimony to the heroine on the last page. These were truly novels of release, taking the reader out of his known world into an unknown in which anything might happen. The plot of Shakespeare's ' Pericles Prince of Tyre ' owes much to such works. Marina in the brothel is a theme straight out of the Greek adventure story. Books of this kind are in their nature ephemeral ; it is no surprising that the monkish copiers were not concerned to preserve them in mass. There is a gap in our record here. A famous example that lies outside our period is the ' Baarlaam and Iosaph ' attributed to St. John of Damascus, a Christian version of the Buddha legend.

Our next section—philosophy and religion—embraces a mass of varied material. The only philosophy that took deep root in Rome was the Stoic. The moral code of the school appealed to the inherent earnestness and worth of a good Roman, and Stoic doctrine inspired many of the finest spirits of the early Empire. Seneca was a devoted Stoic and tried to practise his creed—as far as wealth and official position would allow it. A good part of his writings—letters and essays as well as purely philosophical works—is concerned with expounding various stages of Stoic practice. In the lost ' De superstitione', Seneca attacked popular beliefs with far more courage than he normally showed in his life. Something akin to Christianity in his noblest utterances led to the false belief that he had corresponded with the Apostle Paul. Of the famous Stoic teacher, Musonius, we have nothing left ; but his pupil, the satirist Persius, preaches Stoicism through his satires. Epictetus, the noble-hearted slave who, when emancipated, became a teacher in Epirus and won the hearts of many Romans of rank, is known intimately to us from the memoirs of Arrian, a Roman governor. Here we meet Stoicism at its loveliest—its harshness toned down, its moral integrity and courage shining bright, its pantheism appearing as a noble theism.

Of the Greeks, Philo of Alexandria was the most remarkable. As mediator between Jewish ideas and Greek philosophy he holds a position of real importance. The doctrine of the Word, which is the expression and wisdom of God, is developed in him. He is verbose and lacks charm, but his thought is not negligible. There is a good deal of religion and philosophy in the moral essays of Plutarch. He was a fine human being, devoted to the ancient religion, especially to the Apollo of Delphi, but more or less enlightened, willing to interpret old cults and myths in allegorical terms. We are not deeply impressed by the clearness or compulsion of his thoughts, but we feel that we are being brought into touch with what educated men of the age speculated on. Marcus Aurelius, when he wished to record his own spiritual history, chose Greek. The style is not easy or winning, but the matter holds us fast. Here is Stoicism again, still worthy of all respect, but sadder and gloomier. Occasionally, there is a cry of joy from the world citizen as he realises his portion in the cosmopolis. More often there is the resigned despair of the individual for whom the cosmos has no particular place—not even if he be the Emperor on his throne. Sextus Empiricus (*c.* 180) wrote Pyrrhonic Treatises that seem to us jejune and pedantic. More important is the work of Diogenes Laertius (*c.* 220) whose ' Lives and Opinions of the Philosophers ' constitute the basis of our knowledge. Somewhere towards the close of the 2nd century, an educated Roman, by name Celsus, set himself to examine and confute the preaching and practice of the Christians. We know a good deal about him from Origen who wrote in answer to him. Celsus thinks that he can establish the folly of the new Christian idea, but he realises their increase in numbers and position and realises too something of the power that had developed behind the movement ; he ends with an appeal to these perverse but potentially valuable citizens to remember their duty to the Empire of which they are part.

The Greek schools of philosophy continued to be active, with their centre at Athens. For some time the older schools, the Peripatetics and the Academy, produced nothing of note. But suddenly, in the reign of Gallienus, shot out that bright star Plotinus, the last of the great Platonists of antiquity, the first of the Neo-platonists. He is true to the idealism of his master, but develops his doctrine in his own individual way. What we can best grasp in his teaching is the thought of the union of the soul with the Supreme that lies beyond consciousness. Plotinus himself claimed to have enjoyed this Blessed Vision three times only in his life. Plotinus enjoyed considerable influence and the favour of the Emperor Gallienus. His thought is too austere and chill for the ordinary man, but even *he* cannot mistake the nobility of the personality. The followers of Plotinus, though men of ability, could not live on his heights. They decline from philosophy into theurgy, the conjuring of divine powers to work magic. We descend from the pure light of day into a murky and dubious dusk ; Neo-platonism degenerates into Neo-pythagoreanism. This was a philosophy that allured the Apostate ; it was in its wake that he spun his fancies about King Helios and his satellite powers. This was almost the last utterance of pagan philosophy ; for, though the schools of Athens were only closed by Justinian, they had long ceased to disturb human thought by anything new they had to say.

And so in due course we come to the Christian writings. As we are usually assessing them as documents of religion, it will be well for a change to let their literary character come into the foreground. The Epistles of St. Paul are the earliest Christian documents. They are true letters, written for special occasions to particular recipients. But they go beyond the limits of the private letter into doctrinal and moral teaching. A great German scholar once said that there were two main reasons for learning Greek—one to be able to read Plato in the original, the other to be so able to read St. Paul. The Epistles are great literature, peculiar and individual in form, but brimming over with interest and burning with passion. The other Epistles are not on quite the same level, but have something of the same appeal. The Gospels, following the Epistles, begin to set down the record and, in part, explain the new Faith to the world. They belong to the time after the Fall of Jerusalem when the apocalyptic ideas of the first age were fading ; or was the Apocalypse realised in the tragedy of the Holy City ? The Gospels are something quite new in literature—lives of an individual who had impressed himself on the imagination of his followers—records of facts and also works of edification. Matthew and Mark produce their literary effect without literary tricks. Luke seems to write for men of the world as well as Christians. John is not exactly simple, but his subtlety is one of thought rather than of expression. The sub-apostolic age is marked by a drop in temperature and interest. Clement of Rome is worthy enough, but dull after Paul. St. Ignatius impresses us with his courageous, fanatical enthusiasm ; but his letters are rather personal manifestos than documents of the Church.

The next age may be called that of the Apologists. Trajan had called off the active persecution of the Church and Hadrian had confirmed his moderation. It seemed worth while then to let the truth about Christianity be better known ; toleration might then be better secured. The Apologists—Justin Martyr, Aristides and the rest—had no great literary skill, but they discharged their task with conscientious accuracy and a sincerity that commands respect. The most attractive of them all is Minucius Felix in his little tract, the ' Octavius '. Much of his argument for the Faith and against the pagans is shared with Tertullian. But what a difference in tone ! Tertullian angry, even truculent ; Minucius gentle and persuasive. The weakness of the ' Octavius ' is that a lot of real Christianity is never expressed. We are faced with a gentle, rational reinterpreta-tion of belief—nothing hard to believe, hardly a word about the work and personality of the Founder. Tertullian, the bitter African barrister, cannot be accused of the same weakness. In form, he is still often Apologist ; in fact, he is on the attack, denouncing, ridiculing, goading on the pagans. Even as a Christian, he was immoderate and ended by joining the Montanist schism. His Latin is curious and distorted, often very hard to understand. But he hits so hard that you feel the blow, even if you cannot see where it lands. He is known for his wonderful epigrams, such as ' the witness of the soul which is by nature Christian '. His bitterness is shocking to us ; he gloats in his ' De spectaculis ' over the show that the pagans are going to make, when they are watched by the triumphant Christians from Heaven in Hell. But it is hard to believe that he made many converts.

During this time the Church had to fight for its intellectual and moral life with the Gnostics. The Gnostics were many and varied in belief. They agreed only in this—that they, in an access of intellectual pride, aspired to esoteric knowledge denied to the ordinary, and that, in satisfying this pride, they were prone to neglect the moral life as indifferent. No large remains of any

Gnostic writings survive, but we know quite a lot about the chief Gnostics, such as Marcion and Valentinus, from the confutations written by good Church Fathers.   Marcion saw clearly that God in the Old Testament is by no means the same revelation as God in the New.   He drew the extreme conclusion—they are not the same person.   Valentinus was more concerned with prying into the divine mysteries, discovering the ' Pleroma ' (or ' Pleromata '), the plentitude of divine powers surrounding the Supreme Being and expressing to man the sum of his nature.   There may have been a kind of lurid splendour about these wild imaginings.

Moved by the fight against these adversaries, the Church began to face the problem of thinking out its scheme and coming to some terms with Greek philosophy.   Clement of Alexandria begins the process for us.   His main work, the ' Stromateis ' ('bundles'), is formless and not easy, but the spirit of the man is delightful and he goes a long way on his chosen path, showing how Christianity fits into the world of thought prepared by the Greeks.   He was followed by a greater pupil, Origen, the greatest thinker after Paul in the early Church.   Origen was a thinker rather than an actor, though he crowned his long life of scholarship by martyrdom at the last.   He defended the Faith against the moderate and skilfully planned attack of Celsus.   He cleared the way for the formulation of Church doctrine, in doing which he fell into what were afterwards found to have been several heresies.   He had considerable adventure in his thought and a singular tenderness of feeling.   He seems, for example, to have looked for a final restoration of all things, in which even the Devil would be forgiven and restored. Cyprian was a man of a very different type, a bishop of a great city, Carthage, a man of affairs, skilled in business and administration. In him we see Christianity coming to terms with Roman experience and skill, as it had come to terms with Greek philosophy in Clement and Origen.   Arnobius, the African barrister of the school of Tertullian, who wrote ' contra paganos ' at the beginning of the persecution of Diocletian, is bitter, coarse and violent.   He has hardly a word to say about God the Holy Spirit ; it is doubtful if he could have defined the person of Christ in a way that would have satisfied St. Athanasius.   His chief interest for us is that he preserves a wealth of detail about pagan cults.

Arnobius is the last of the old age, the age of persecution. Eusebius and Lactantius are the first of the new age of imperial favour.   Eusebius receives very severe treatment from many modern critics.   They point out the obvious defects in his historical method, with distortions produced by his flattery of Constantine.

They proceed to belittle his whole achievement as revealing bias rather than any form of proof. The fairer judgment is that Eusebius, though no great man or historian, has yet given us a mass of useful information. Lactantius is a more interesting figure, versatile indeed if he wrote all that is attributed to him, not only his 'Institutions', but also, the 'Deaths of the Persecutors' and the pleasant poem on the Phoenix. The 'Institutions' is a serious and worthy statement of Christian philosophy, written in a style that may be called Ciceronian. The 'Deaths' is a fierce and bitter pamphlet, effective in its direct and sustained attack ; no one could imagine that it is entirely judicial or fair.

In this age the Christian takes over the pen from the pagan. The Church begins to out-write as well as out-pray its adversaries. The vast literature of the Church Fathers begins to unroll its endless length. Some of them, like St. Athanasius, are notable more for their personality and the parts that they played in controversy than for any literary merit. Some, like the two Basils, are notable for both reasons. Their letters, their doctrinal essays, reveal strong personalities, men who in an earlier age would have risen high in imperial service, but who now found an outlet for their abilities in the expanding horizon of the Church. Of two we must speak individually and in more detail.

St. Jerome was a scholar, not bishop or administrator, a lover of classical literature, tempted to be a follower of Cicero and not of Christ. He had influential friends in Rome ; he knew the pagan world, but could not trust it. His letters are rather grim, but very revealing. He it was who turned the whole Bible into Latin and set up a standard work that has its place in the great literature of the world. It was a mighty privilege to find the words in which the Christian message should be carried to the Latin-speaking world. St. Jerome discharged his task with a surprising success. He could not always arrive at the right interpretation or the best manuscript reading ; but his language has resonance and dignity. Faithful to his duty not to spoil or distort the original, he received the reward of his straight dealing. St. Ambrose is the typical great Christian functionary of the new Empire. Forced against his will into the see of Milan he soon found his destined career there. He established a complete ascendancy over the Emperor Theodosius and demanded penance from him for the massacre of Thessalonica. He encouraged him to advance to the destruction of paganism. He defeated Symmachus over the altar of Victory in the Senate House. As we shall see later, he was one of the first authors of Christian hymns. His is not the type to appeal to every man ; he was a manager, perhaps even an intriguer, as well as a man of God. But certainly the Church owed much to him and his peers.

St. Augustine was a convert of Ambrose. He outlived him and died when the Vandals were already conquering Roman Africa. Augustine, in fact, saw the end of that kingdom of the world, on whose destinies he had mused in his ' City of God '. Augustine was a scholar like Jerome ; he became in due course an administrator like Ambrose. He had a hot and wild temperament which makes him more interesting to a modern than either of the other two. His best known book, his ' Confessions ', is one of the few intimately personal books that have won their way into thousands upon thousands of hearts. Augustine, after a stormy youth, troubled with the passions encouraged by Carthage and by endless intellectual doubts, at last found haven for mind and soul in Christianity. We note with interest that for a long time he was involved in the dualism of the Manichaeans—a dualism that must have appealed to the schism in Augustine's own nature. After that come letters and treatises in their masses, mostly of minor interest to the general reader. The great work which, even more than the ' Confessions ', ensures his literary immortality is the ' De civitate Dei ', promoted by the shattering news of the capture of Rome by Alaric the Visigoth in 410.

When the Coliseum shall fall so shall fall Rome ; when Rome shall fall so shall fall the world.

So ran the old refrain—and now Rome had fallen ; what of the world ? Augustine braces himself to the task of thinking out the problem anew ; what happens to Christians if Rome really has fallen and fallen for good ; what of the world ? He fights his way to a new solution. There have always been two states in view, the State of the World and the State of God. They live by different laws, they go to different destinies. Rome, as the most remarkable example of the State of the World, was used by Providence in its plan of world government. But Rome was never more than the State of the World, and, as such, it was always doomed to perish however long its term. Christian people must lift up their hearts and face what the future may bring, sure that the special promises to them are in no way impaired. It was a grand effort to meet a pressing need and a real attempt to find an explanation for what baffles reason. The style is fairly plain and clear, rather wearisome in the immense length of the work. The argument, based on set ideas about the relation of the pagan world to the Jewish, is often unconvincing. But the whole is far greater than its parts. Occasional digressions, as, for example, the enquiry into the possible state of our parents in Paradise, are of exceptional interest.

St. Augustine is a suitable person with whom to stop. He marks the end of an epoch, or rather the watershed between two epochs. He looks back to Cicero and Varro ; he looks forward to the Schoolmen and Dante. Just one more philosophical work must not be quite omitted, the famous ' Consolatio ' of Boethius, minister of Theodoric and by him condemned to death. Boethius was, no doubt, a Christian, but his ' Consolation ' is essentially philosophical not religious. Written in alternating prose and verse it has won acceptance as a noble self-expression under circumstances of suffering and terror.

So at the last we come to poetry and, with it, many a reader may think, to literature in its most proper sense. Prose works may be wholly or partly due to practical needs, hardly literary at all ; poetry is, or ought to be, free, except as the muse drives. The poets of the Golden Age of Augustus have won their place in world literature. Virgil is not a Homer, but he is always named close after him. His was a gentle spirit, an *anima naturaliter Christiana*. He was sensitive to the pathos and uncertainty of human lot. Though he could under pressure produce a worthy national epic, he could not suppress everything that did not harmonise with that main theme, so both Dido and Turnus can command our love and respect. His Eclogues are too artificial, too full of little unsolved secrets, to appeal to most modern readers. For those that can feel it they have a strange artificial charm. The 'Georgics', whether or not of much value as a practical book on agriculture, reveal an intense love of nature, a close and loving study of what occurs in air or field. Virgil does not blind himself to the ugly things in the world, but he does not pretend to like them. He would rather be the bold-eyed philosopher who can face the truth of nature, or, if that is denied him, he can rejoice in the natural blessedness of the farmer. As for public affairs, ' res Romanae perituraque regna '—well, the ' peritura ' says all that may be said about them ; they will not last. What is most remarkable about Virgil is the sense that he has a secret that he has learned, a secret of supreme importance, signs of which meet him again and again. No wonder that he was claimed as a Christian before the time ; no wonder that Dante takes him for his guide in Hell. ' Sunt lacrimae rerum et mentem mortalia tangunt ', ' tendebantque manus ripae ulterioris amore ', ' pontum aspectabant flentes ', ' quisque suos patimur manes '—here and in many other passages Virgil from a special context passes over to the universal and whispers of the hidden truth. Those who love their

Virgil must love him well. To those who do not love him, it must be admitted, he seems insignificant, a mere copier, an artist at demand. The fact that some see is more important than the fact that others do not.

Horace comes close to Virgil in after reputation as in friendship during life. He is probably best known as the genial, tolerant philosopher, the poet of wine and love—neither to excess—of friendship, of country life, of dignified ease. His first poems, his Epodes, are coarse, bitter, crude, with only faint promise of the Horace who was to be. The Satires and Epistles give his philosophy of life and many a shrewd comment on social ways and morals. But it is by his odes that he must finally be judged. Horace follows the Greek lyric poets ; as they had turned their hands to the most varied themes, so Horace in Latin. But the essential point, very often missed by modern readers, is that Horace is a serious poet, a *vates*, a prophet with a message. He is not merely the writer of sparkling society verse into which some translators would turn him. He preaches manliness and patriotism, reverence for the gods and the old Roman pieties, simplicity in personal life. It is part of Horace's gift not to soar too high, not to lose touch with the plain man. But he can achieve what he himself describes as *proprie communia dicere*, saying with some special distinction something that might occur to anybody ; that is one of the things the dictum of Horace can mean. Horace is one of the most quotable of all poets and everyone wants to translate him—two considerable testimonies.

Virgil and Horace stand at the centre of the Augustan age. Others stand more or less apart. Tibullus, the tender poet of love and country life, has a pure, if not very deep, poetical vein. He is a poet certainly, a personality ?—perhaps not. That is what those who think lightly of his poetry miss in him. What Tibullus lacks Propertius has in excess. A member of the circle of Messalla, a noble patron who stood rather less close to Augustus than did Maecenas, he *does* touch at times on national and patriotic themes. But his main interest was in his love, the dazzling Cynthia—and in himself. Horace knew him and seems to have thought him vain and affected, and we might well have agreed with Horace. But, if we can get over his concentration on self, there are colour and form in his poetry that yield a strange delight.

Sunt apud infernos tot milia formosarum
(' there are so many thousand beauties in hell ')

—the thought is simple and has occurred to others before ; the expression suddenly lifts it into significance. Propertius died young ; one wonders if he would have had more to show if he had outgrown his hot youth. Of other poets of the age, regarded with admiration in their time, we have only the names—Varius, the writer of epic, Cinna, author in the Alexandrine style of the ' Scylla ', Cornelius Gallus, friend of Virgil, friend, to his bane, of Augustus, a notable figure in the field of love poetry. We would give much to have a specimen of his work..

Ovid comes a little later than the rest. He naturally takes on the tone of the second generation, born not to the civil wars but to the Augustan peace, not much interested in war or patriotism, but intent on all that life has to offer the young in Rome. His first offerings in poetry were made to the goddess of love. His ' Amores ' and ' Ars amatoria ' must have delighted the gilded youth of Rome just as surely as they must have offended the moralist Augustus. This duty performed, Ovid turned his mind to worthier themes— the ' Fasti ', the calendar of Rome versified with a wealth of mythical allusion, and the ' Metamorphoses ', a picture gallery of ancient myth. In A.D. 4 a thunderbolt from the Emperor suddenly struck him ; he was banished to the remote Tomi on the Black Sea. The secret of his disgrace was kept hidden ; it may have been connected with the banishment of the younger Julia for immorality ; at any rate Ovid's licentious poems formed part of the charge. For the rest of his life Ovid spent his poetical skill in pleading for return and letting his friends in Rome know in detail all the miseries of his exile. Ovid had a great natural ability, which he indulged but never learnt to control. His facility in verse was so great as to be a drawback ; in this he is something like our own Swinburne. There is in him much wit, much social sparkle, much observation, accurate though often superficial, not much heart. His observation of nature is sharp ; he notices colours and shapes, as if he were copying from a picture ; but he does not strike one as a true lover of nature. Perhaps it is in occasional passages in the late poems of exile that a deeper Ovid now and then shows. One poem of Spring reveals a touching homesickness for Italy. In another poem he steels his heart with the thought that his genius does not leave him ; he is still lord there ; *Caesar in hoc potuit iuris habere nihil.* He touches our hearts when he imagines his ghost still in exile among uncouth Scythian strangers. His tragedy, the ' Medea ', had a great reputation in antiquity ; we would dearly like to have it.

After Augustus came an intermission, broken only by the fables of the freedman, Phaedrus, a competent exercise in a side branch of poetry. There was a poetic revival under Nero, a poet himself, who collected a circle of poets around him and jealously criticised their

works.   The star among them was the young Spaniard Lucan, who
incurred the envy of the Emperor and passed from friendship to
opposition and complicity in the conspiracy of Piso.   The ' Phar-
salia ' begins with a grotesque eulogy of Nero, but develops into a
panegyric on the Republican cause that fell before Julius Caesar,
and its chief hero, Cato.   Lucan writes ringing, spirited hexameters, full of antithesis and epigrams, too rhetorical to be quite
sincere.   The straining at effect often leads up to and over the
brink of absurdity.   We think of scenes in the sea battle off Massilia
or of the centurion of Caesar, with so many endless spears in his
shield that it made an impenetrable barrier against more.   But
Lucan has his moments of triumph.   He has hit off some unforget-
table phrases—' victrix causa deis placuit, sed victa Catoni ' ;
' victurosque dei celant, ut vivere durent, felix esse mori ' ; ' nil
actum credens dum quid superesset agendum '.   There is a strange
force when the horrible old witch, after calling up an unhappy corpse,
promises him that, if he will tell her what she would know, she will
lull him to such a sleep as no charm shall again break : ' a me morte
data ', ' when I have given you death '.   His noblest passage is the
confession of Stoic faith, put into the mouth of Cato when he refuses
to consult the oracle of Ammon in the Lybian desert : ' haeremus
cuncti superis temploque tacenti, Nil facimus nisi sponte deum : '
' Jupiter est quodcumque vides, quodcumque moveris '.   The
eclogues of Calpurnius Siculus are correct and at times charming.
Persius, the satirist, writes in a stilted style of his stilted thoughts.
He is difficult and morose, not a person of charm.   But there is
nobility behind him, and we owe him the occasional glorious phrase,
such as the curse on tyrants, ' *virtutem videant intabescantque relicta* '.

The reign of Domitian, himself a devotee of Minerva, produced its
new crop of poets.   Apart from the greater poets who survived
there were many juvenile prodigies who made their mark at
Domitian's new Capitoline contests.   Statius wrote two epics, the
' Thebaid ' and the unfinished ' Achilleid ', and a number of
occasional poems.   He handles his metre with confidence and can
describe with zest and accuracy.   His chief faults are excess of
rhetoric, longwindedness and base flattery.   His little poem on sleep
is exquisite and deserves a place in any anthology of poems on the
subject.   His rhetoric *does* occasionally triumph ; look at Capaneus
on the wall of Thebes, struck by the thunderbolt of Jupiter and yet
defying heaven, as he and his armour fade to ash after the fire.   Had
he stood one moment longer

potuit fulmen meruisse secundum
(' he almost compelled the thunderer to strike twice ')

Martial, like Lucan a Spaniard, brings something new to Latin literature, a sharp bitter wit that expresses itself in barbed epigrams ; we owe to Martial the epigram in its modern meaning. Martial is immensely facile, varied, ingenious. He can be exceedingly coarse and malicious. His flattery of Domitian is absurdly gross. And yet, despite so much that is unlovely, most readers of Martial will confess to loving, if not respecting him. He shows signs of tenderness and loyal friendship. He is very human—all too human ; but there is a candour about him that redeems much. For the social life of Rome he is a main source. Silius Italicus, a senator of some note, devoted his leisure to an epic poem on the Second Punic war. The epic with all its formal machinery never comes to life. The style is correct, but essentially dull. Valerius Flaccus, author of a poem on the Argonauts, is a minor poet of considerable charm and quality. His theme is an old one, but it is enlivened by some delightful touches of fancy. Anyone who takes the trouble to make his way through the difficult diction will often be rewarded.

The drama as an art belongs to the past ; the old plays were sometimes revived, but not very much new was written. Augustus wrote an ' Ajax ' ; but the hero of tragedy, like the hero of life, despaired of fortune and ' fell on his sponge '. Of Ovid's ' Medea ', we have already spoken. It was the mime and pantomime that now commanded public enthusiasm, and in them all depended on the virtuosity of the gesticulating actors ; the text degenerated into a mere libretto. It was as if the movies and talkies should close the theatre altogether. A handful of tragedies of the time of Nero or thereabouts survive, to give us some idea of the last days of ancient drama. One is on a Roman subject, the unhappy Octavia, wife of Nero ; the rest follow themes of the Attic tragedians. They are attributed to Seneca; the ' Octavia ' at least cannot be by him. These tragedies are of an importance in literary history far beyond their actual merit ; for they brought the ancient drama to the Elizabethan world. There is much ranting, much tearing of emotions, much blood and thunder. The gross lack of good taste in such a play as that about the mangled Hippolytus is almost unbelievable. But there is vigour in the action, sometimes sincerity in the dialogue, sometimes true beauty in the choruses, as, for instance, when the prospect of a new world is opened up or when the quiet garden of Proserpine is conjured up before the imagination.

After the reign of Domitian there is one solitary great figure, the satirist, Juvenal—then a long silence. Juvenal is an enigmatical figure. He served as an officer in the Roman army ; he lived to a great age ; for some unknown reason he was exiled. He tells us very little of himself. He writes satire as Swift wrote it, stung by savage indignation. But caution forbids him to attack the living ; he finds all his examples among those ' whose dust is safely covered by the Appian Way '. Juvenal is a master of effective phrase and many of his epigrams have passed into general usage : ' Indignation makes one write verse ', ' It is we, O fortune, who make you a goddess and place you in heaven ', ' a boy of freeborn face and freeborn honour ', ' go, madman, and speed over the savage Alps that you may delight the boys and become a theme for declamation ', ' Thule is now talking of hiring a rhetorician '. Many readers of Juvenal will admire his penetrating insight, without being entirely convinced of his sincerity.

How are we to explain the long silence that now descended on the Italian muse ? It cannot be that the art of using the various familiar metres was lost. Pliny the Younger composed freely and even quotes a few verses for us—which do not make us ask for more. Many a noble must have written similarly, to please himself. The Emperor Gordian I composed a formal epic on the exploits of Antoninus Pius. What was lacking was an original impulse. These were only exercises on known models, no more destined for immortality than university ' prolusions ' in the classical metres today. One strange little poem, the ' Pervigilium Veneris ', suddenly breaks the silence. The date is about 300, fixed by an allusion in the poem ; otherwise we might wander far in our guesses.

> *Cras amet qui numquam amavit, quique amavit cras amet*
> (' let love's novice love tomorrow, love's initiate love again '),

that is the compelling refrain in trochaic tetrameters. The poem is sensuous, lovely, enchanting ; its rhythms remind us of the rhyming metres that lie ahead. And there is in it a note of haunting wistfulness, very rare in the Ancient World. ' Illa cantat, nos tacemus quando ver venit meum, Quando fiam uti chelidon, ut tacere desinam ? ' Late in the 4th century Ausonius, the professor turned statesman, produced poems as part of his enormous output. A man of his capacity and experience would now and then have something to say even in verse ; but the only poem that really lives is the ' Mosella ', a delightful description of a beloved and closely observed stream. Claudian, the panegyrist of Stilicho, recaptures something of the epic of Virgil. He is spirited, fluent, occasionally eloquent. His ' Rape of Proserpine ' still awakens echoes of a pagan world.

already half lost. Of later poets we would only mention the Rutilius who found noble words in which to express his love and admiration of Rome :

'Hail, Queen, loveliest of things in all your realm, O Rome, translated to the heavenly poles . . . it profited the evil to own defeat as you were ruler ; you have made a city of what was once a world.'

If new poetry was now sparsely produced, the old authors were still taught and studied. Some part of ancient criticism is preserved for us in the works of Macrobius and Servius. Though we find much in them that does not at once appeal to our judgment, we should read and ponder them attentively. They stood much nearer to their authors than we do and, when they seem to us off the mark, we need to make sure that it is not we who have not taken our bearings correctly.

What has been said of Latin poetry is even truer of Greek. Very few came forward to compete with the great established masterpieces of old times. Quintus of Smyrna wrote a continuation of Homer after the death of Achilles. The poem can be enjoyed, if you do not continually remind yourself that this is not the master. Babrius wrote rather flat fables in correct verse. Oppian discoursed of hunting and fishing. At the very end of our period—or rather just beyond it—Nonnus of Panopolis in Egypt narrated the adventures of Bacchus in a mighty epic, interesting at times in detail if intolerably weary in its bulk.

Poetry for the Christians was for a long time part of the forbidden classical world. When Commodianus wrote his uncouth hexameters in the 2nd century, his aim was to instruct, not to please. Prudentius was the first great Christian poet. He writes with a mastery of the old technique, but in the new spirit ; he looks forward as well as back. His defence of the Faith against paganism is clearly stated and firmly argued. His ' Psychomachia ' played a great part in later psychology. His praises of the martyrs introduced the new literary genre. They are horrific, pathetic, seldom dull. Sometimes we hardly know whether to laugh or cry, as for example over the very defiant little boy, whose offence was to be expiated by a spanking, if only he had not spat at the Emperor's image. The hymn also appears among the works of Prudentius. St. Ambrose took a great interest in congregational singing and to him belong several of our earliest hymns, very simple, yet effective in their very lack of ornament. The hymn looks forward rather than back. The movement is away from the formal, metrical verse of antiquity towards accented rhyming verse. It was in this new

Latin derived largely from popular sources that the great triumphs of hymnology were to be achieved.

It is a notable gain of our modern studies that we now try to grasp a civilisation as a whole, only partially to be understood from its political, military and economic history, needing to be known also in its art, religion and literature. There will be great differences between the various parts of the civilisation, but more often we shall expect to find agreements. In the Roman Empire agreement is the rule. In literature, as in political life, we find attachment to tradition, slowness to make innovations, lack of originality and energy. The slackening vitality, already evident in the 2nd century and accentuated in the 3rd, is seen in the decline of almost all the major forms of literature. The turning away from private interests is shown in the decline of history and oratory. We should probably see it even more clearly, were it not that the popular works that took their place were of such an ephemeral character that they seldom escaped oblivion. To understand the direction that the world was taking, we should be prepared to pay more attention to the Christian writings than we are at first inclined to do. Their prolixity, their concern with controversies that have ceased to be matters of burning interest, their occasional intolerance repel us. But they give us a true picture of the attempt to turn away from the frank enjoyment of the present that distinguished paganism and to grasp the world of revelation. In its hymns of prayer and praise the Church opens new fountains of fresh and sweet inspiration.

CHAPTER XI

ART

Art, like literature, is one of the adjuncts which complete the picture of what civilisation really is. Art, when used in the broadest sense, denotes the whole visual side of a civilisation—what is expressed in form not in words. Here and there, the two, the visual and the verbal, meet, as on coins. Visual art is not confined to articles made for their special beauty by artists for connoisseurs. It extends to articles of everyday use, where the practical need is dominant. Here, there might seem to be no special question of artistic sense—but rather of the average taste of a population. This may be so, but it makes the study of art more, not less, valuable, if it is going to lead us straight to some of the secrets of people's minds. We may not be prepared to accept any blame if we allow ourselves to be served with articles of poor workmanship and taste. But we ought to be. Artists may play tricks, tradesmen may try to foist the nasty and cheap on us ; but it is our responsibility if they continue to do so. You cannot fool all the people all the time—unless they are very ready to be fooled.

Our sufferings in this present time from certain artists who present us with nightmares and call them visions of significance, if not beauty, make one raise the question : had antiquity anything like that ? Did art ever cease to be representational and offer instead abstract ideas or incongruous patterns ? The answer for the Roman Empire is No. Whether it was ordinary human life or history or myth, still life or landscape, you could normally know at a glance what was being represented. There are some exceptions. Celtic art that lingered on was fond of drawing improbable horses with human heads or three-headed gods or beasts with limbs that knew little of anatomy. The animal art of the Russian and Asiatic steppes created its subjects with great freedom. Normal Greco-Roman art aimed at nature. How dull ! That will probably be the comment of the modern critic. But let us be sensible about it. Visual forms are symbols, as are words ; they are a convention generally understood through which ideas can be conveyed to all who see. As long as the forms, the symbols, are reasonably true to tradition, communication is uninterrupted. But what if an artist begins to leave the tradition and offer you something that, like the work of James Joyce, needs the study of a lifetime to understand it ?   I myself should say that such an artist is breaking all the rules and invites neglect.

Ruskin is not much read today, but we should do well to find some of his ideas again for ourselves.   In some of those passages, prophetic and a bit pretentious, which entranced his admirers and now infuriate his critics, he claims that art that copies natural forms, the tracery of twigs and boughs, for example, is essentially superior to art that relies on trick inventions of man—the pattern or the arabesque.   It is the superiority of what God does over what man can do.   We might do worse than ponder over the possible truth of this dictum.

Art has its own language, comparable to the language of words. Classical art had very clearly defined conventions.   All the chief deities and ' virtues ' have attributes and adjuncts that distinguish them from others (the attribute, by the by, is something held in the hand, the adjunct something less closely connected with the main figure).   You know that it is Jupiter when you see the thunderbolt, Neptune when you see the trident.   Peace has her branch, Victory her palm and wreath.   Clothing too has its conventions.   Absence of drapery takes one away from ordinary human life into the heroic or divine sphere.   The aegis on breast marks Minerva, the lion-skin on head Hercules.   Gestures and attitudes too are eloquent.   Leaning on a column and crossing arms or legs suggests Security. Drawing the veil over the head was a gesture of Pudicitia, chastity. The hand raised is a mark of address or response to such, the hand gently extended is a token of Mercy.   The hands raised, with palms upwards, distinguished Piety.   This language can be known if sufficient time is given to it.   The knowledge of it is at present confined to a few who study coins and kindred branches of art ; a book of introduction is badly needed for the general public.   Here in this world of history and myth, the artist had ready to his hand a fine instrument.   It was something like the equipment of a mediaeval monk with his legends of saints and stories of Holy Writ but more extensive.   If modern psychologists are correct, symbolism goes down to the roots of human nature in the unconscious. However much any special symbolism may be conventional in its own time, we are likely to find universal symbols occurring, which have some connection not fully explained with the basis of our existence.   Allegory is found as well as symbolism.   But allegory is more sophisticated than myth and may be simply telling its tale in the language improvised for the occasion.

What is the art of the Empire ?   Is it the art of a nation or of a period ?   Certainly the latter.   The inspiration of imperial art

was always Greek. The Greek genius flowered early and produced
works of glorious beauty which were accepted as norms for the
future. You might emulate them, you could hardly hope to
improve on them. That does not mean to say that all the good
imperial artists were of Greek nationality, though many of them
certainly were. An inspiration that stems from one people can
spread to congenial souls in others. The Roman added something
of his own, perhaps more as patron of art than as artist himself ;
he suggested new directions and interests—the interest in the
individual and the topical. Rome drew into herself the best talents
from every side and became the artistic capital of the world, however little she deserved to be.

By the time of Augustus this art was already ripe. The great
types of deities had been created by men of genius ; lesser men
repeated their achievements. We must not suppose that all
inspiration was dead. Men of great ability still arose, still produced
work that could amuse and delight. But there were too many
great models in existence. They made it harder to create new
ones—and less necessary. The Romans helped themselves freely
to the ancient masterpieces, as they got them into their hands.
Many a famous statue came to Rome, to embellish the temples or
libraries. But there was a demand far exceeding the supply and,
as a natural result, there was a great trade in the copying of the great
originals. It is no accident that so much of Greek art is known to
us only in Roman copies. That was the way of it ; for one or, at
best, few originals there might be copies galore. Some scholars
of great repute have seemed to think that there is something by
which you can distinguish the copy from the original—some touch
of the master's hand that cannot be imitated. But how near can
we ever come to that last hand of the master ? In the shattered
and weatherworn marbles of the Parthenon ? There is a moving
feeling of duration and suffering about their present greyness and
imperfection ; but how much has that to do with the dazzling, the
garish sheen of the originals ? We fall too easily into this pathetic
fallacy. We admire ancient art for accidental effects as well as
for intrinsic excellences. How then do we stand with copies ? A
bad copy is detected at a glance. Even a very good copy can be
spotted if the artist chances to give himself away by the use of some
technique unknown in the age of the original. But, if a highly
competent artist of the Empire, set to copy a 5th century original,
did his work well and introduced nothing of himself into his work,
his work for us after this interval of time is as the original and may
serve us almost as well. The erratic Dutch genius who tricked the

critics with his imitations of Vermeer is a warning to be heeded.   I
think that we need to do some drastic rethinking of the whole
problem.   The great thing about an artistic creation is the fixing
of a type ; the clothing of it in one special piece of marble or bronze
is of secondary importance.   There is, of course, a peculiar thrill on
the rare occasions when we can be sure that we are in the presence
of a great original.   But, where we have copies of the first class, we
have already a great deal.

We shall have more to say about schools of art and the importance
of Rome when we turn to the arts in detail.   We will first say
something about local forms of art, existing outside the main
current.   The art of the provinces is, for the most part, rather dull,
imitating at a distance the imperial form ; it is interesting for its
subject-matter more than for its technical skill.   In Gaul and
Britain there was a native Celtic art, the ' La Tène ', with its own
vigour and beauty.   It is recessive during the Empire, but not dead ;
for it could revive as the Empire fell.   The animal style of South
Russia is full of life and power and could exercise an influence on
imperial art.   Phoenician art was not impressive ; the Phoenician
genius lent itself better to trade and business.   Egyptian art retained
something of its ancient shape, but its vitality was declining.   From
the East came influences that were to be of importance in the
sequel.   The excavations at Dura-Europos have given us un-
suspected glimpses of an art intermediate between the Empire and
Persia.   Iranian art was to have a great influence on the art of the
period after Diocletian.   But what we shall be for the most part
studying is a late, but not unimportant, phase of the art that
developed in Greece from the 7th century onwards.   The art of
India and China was too remote to have much effect on Rome.
Where the influence is undeniable, as on the Gandhara statues, it
is the East that seems to be borrowing from the West.

We will begin with the noblest form of public art—architecture.
The Greeks had established the dominant forms and the Romans
followed them.   The temple to the Roman was what the Greeks had
made it, with just a touch of Etruscan influence from the kingly
period.   The Romans used new materials and introduced some new
forms ; for example, they preferred the ornate Corinthian column
to the pure simplicity of Ionic or Doric.   The chief innovations
were the dome and the arch, both with an earlier origin, but both
increasing their scope, until in Christian times they become dominant.   Architecture is always a practical art ; it serves immediate
purposes.   That is perhaps why the Romans, with their immensely
strong sense of the practical, excelled at it.   Where there was

necessary work to be done—an aqueduct to be brought across
the valley, a new Forum to be carved out in Rome, a Colosseum to
be built for the pleasure of tens of thousands—there the Roman
architect excelled. He produced the work that was required and
often reached that kind of beauty that consists in the nice adjustment
of a building to its end. Ruskin has laid down the main principles
of architecture in his ' Seven Lamps '. For the Roman several of
these lamps, if not all of them, were kept alight. He certainly
worked by the lamp of service. In one negative point the Roman
architect excelled ; on his works of utility he did not squander
meaningless and non-functional ornament. He knew what the
work was wanted for and kept that end steadily in view.

The Empire was in some ways a golden age for sculpture. There
was an immense demand for busts and statues, beginning with the
Emperor and the nobility of Rome and going down to the retired
freedman or centurion who desired to be remembered in the little
community that sheltered his age. The interest in the individual
will met us again. Gods and virtues—yes, they are not forgotten,
but it is the real man who commands more general interest. It is
to portraiture that most of the talent goes and it is there that we must
judge the age, if we mean to take it at its best. The mummy
portraits of Egypt repel some and delight others. They are crude
and vivid ; the people they represent are not notables, but just
ordinary men and women like ourselves. Official imperial art
called for story-telling on a large scale. The Emperor, returning
home from victory, would wish to have his exploits commemorated
for his public. It would be the permanent record in stone of the
story that was told in improvised form in the triumphs in the
streets of Rome. The development of the continuous style is one
of the main features of the Empire. The reliefs of the column of
Trajan tell the whole story of his Dacian wars. There is great
variety of scene—embarkation, building of fortresses, battle with the
enemy, addresses by the Emperor, the sufferings of Roman captives,
the final triumph over the enemy leader. The constant reappear-
ance of the central figure of the Emperor gives unity to a varied
narrative. The obvious merits of this form of composition are its
liveliness and variety ; its defects, equally obvious, are confusion
and overcrowding. On the great imperial monuments these defects
are kept in check. But on the many private sarcophagi the figures
are so crowded and thrown together that it is hard to collect a
general impression from the welter.

Rome certainly drew many notable sculptors into herself. But
there were local schools of which we know something and may in

time learn much more. One school, that of Aphrodisias in Caria, enjoyed a great reputation in the 2nd century. Close study of styles as we find them in the surviving works, combined with careful use of finds where they occur, will always be extending our knowledge of these local schools. Palmyra, the great desert city, has an impressive series of portrait busts, in a style of their own, in the characteristic frontal position, of which we shall have to speak later. The imperial art passed through many phases which can be noted in every branch in greater or less degree. We will discuss them under the coins ; there they are particularly clear and the dating and placing are much more exact than anywhere else.

Painting was a popular art, much in demand for the walls of private houses. The imperial triumphs relied much on painting for their effects. Paintings are in their nature perishable and, if it were not for the wealth of buried Pompeii, our knowledge of this widespread art would be poor. Of the work that survives little can claim any high artistic merit. Antiquity produced—or, at least, has left us—nothing to foreshadow the glories of the great Italian, Spanish and Flemish schools. The interest for us is mainly in the subject. There are many mythological scenes, often of doubtful interpretation. There are scenes from ' Iliad ' or ' Odyssey '. One villa in Rome has apparently preserved for us some of the symbolic representations of a sect of Neo-Pythagoreans. Still life was popular—pictures of animals, flowers and plants. So too was landscape, the typical Italian villa or the exotic Nile, with its ibises, crocodiles and hippopotami.

Much of the representation both in sculpture and in painting is direct and simple. There remain some themes that are much discussed today. Are they no more than what they appear ? Or do they carry deep symbolical meaning ? This is a favourite field for battle between the ' minimisers ', whose aim it is not to overstrain the evidence, and the ' maximisers ', who above all would not let any evidence pass unexploited. On sarcophagi, in particular, there are often recurring scenes : a passage overseas, with wind gods and Nereids ; the symbols of the upper sky, the Dioscuri, morning and evening star ; scenes of victory in battle ; the rape of the Leucippides or the leap of Sappho from the rock. Some say that these scenes are ornamental and no more. I think that our great Cumont is far nearer the truth when he sees in them allegories of the fortunes of the soul after death—its voyage to the Islands of the Blest, its rise to the immortality of the stars, its triumph after the long battle of life, its rapture, like that of the heroes and heroines of old, to a higher sphere.

Pottery is one of the oldest arts and one of the most universal. To it the archaeologist, digging up the past, owes more than to any one other source of evidence. But the pottery that is his delight has little artistic importance. Much of it is rough ; it has shape and elementary pattern—no more. Even the superior wares—first the Arretine of the Etruscan city, then the ' Samian ', mainly of Gallic potters—have significant styles, by which they can be identified and dated, but little artistic merit for all their varied figures. The Castor ware of Britain has a certain fresh beauty in its hunting scenes. Pottery of the Empire is one of the useful arts ; it made little call on the better artists. The same is true of various other articles of practical use—bronzes, lamps and the rest. They were produced in mass, they needed constant replacement ; the public did not demand any high standard of beauty. But, precisely because these things show us very ordinary tastes, they are valuable to us, if we wish to determine not the high spots but the average.

Mosaic, the forming of masses of little tesserae of stone into patterns and pictures, was a great favourite of the Romans of the Empire. Every villa would have its mosaic pavement, with some elaborate pattern or scene from myth. In mosaic there is a constant struggle between the shaping artist and his material, which is not plastic and resists his shaping ; the material often wins. The mosaics with which we are familiar are usually interesting, very seldom really effective or beautiful. It was not till the later Empire that artists discovered where mosaic could most effectively be used. In themes of imperial dignity or of religious reverence the hard still material seemed to catch just that half-natural, hieratic pose that perfectly fitted the occasion. Anyone who wants to realise what mosaic can achieve should visit Ravenna and, with the help of its mosaics, dream for himself of the formal magnificence of its court.

There are two other things—two if not more—in which art can express itself, music and clothes. Even experts do not know very much about ancient music. It had melody rather than harmony and its instruments were not very varied or exquisite in accomplishment. It had nothing remotely to be compared to the great modern orchestra. But it had its own importance. Music played a part at all sacrifices and state occasions. In the theatre, particularly in the ' modern ' theatre of the pantomime, music was a necessary accompaniment of the gesturing. We may think of the music of the Empire as immensely popular, but not artistically very important. But they had the organ, as early as the Emperor Nero.

It will seem strange to include clothes among objects of art. But many people study art in clothes more carefully than in anything else, and it can be argued that the many are not altogether worng. I have discussed this subject in the chapter on social life, and only observe here that ancient Greek and Roman clothing has normally a simplicity and a dignity that would lead one to be most hopeful of the artistic possibilities of people who could show such good taste in something that touched them so nearly.

Examples of luxury articles in gold and silver—bowls, goblets, plates, necklaces, rings, etc.—have survived in sufficient quantity to give us some idea of what could be achieved by the ancient gold- and silver-smith. Where there is figure work it can at the best rank with good sculpture, but often such work is absent and all that we can praise is the quality of the workmanship. The competence maintained was high. But there are curious exceptions. On the great silver plate of Mildenhall the scene of Bacchic revelry was largely conceived and richly sketched ; but, when we look into the detail, we find an amazing lack of conscientiousness in carrying out the design. Many figures are only hinted at, not fully rendered. It has even been thought for this reason that the plate cannot be ancient ; but that is out of the question.

The gem was very much in use in antiquity ; set in a ring it was used as a seal. This use, known from the early great Empires of the East, was still in full force in imperial times. The gem was the work of the graver, the 'scalptor', as distinct from the sculptor of stone or bronze. It is a twin of the art of the coin graver. Gems and coins are very often separated in modern museums, but quite wrongly, for they belong naturally together and the study of the one throws much light on the study of the other. The themes of gems are similar to those of coins, but less varied and more directed to private life—as the difference in their use explains. We will take for our guide the material that offers more scope with more certainty—that of the coins.

It will be well to begin by stating what the coinage of the Empire amounts to. In the first place there are the main series, struck for general use—gold and silver issued by the Emperor, brass and copper issued for him by decrees of the Senate. The Emperor tended to handle the two departments of central coinage differently, but in both his will was decisive. Apart from these central issues there were issues in silver and bronze for certain provinces—official but restricted in use. Further away again there are the city issues, nearly all of them of base metal only, but issued in vast masses, especially for the East of the Empire. In the West such city issues did not outlive the first hundred years of the Empire. In the East they continued down to the reigns of Claudius II and Aurelian and only disappeared when new imperial mints in the provinces were becoming general and making the old local issues unnecessary. Coins were articles of use, intended to circulate in wider or narrower spheres. Other objects of something like coin form are known. What we call medallions can occur in all metals ; where they are struck in coin denominations they may be coins as well as medallions, but we distinguish them from the common coin by their greater elaboration of workmanship and wider choice of subject. Medallions were probably gift pieces, given at New Years and other anniversaries to favoured recipients—high civil and military authorities, in later times also to foreign princes. There are some general truths about the development of art that could be traced in varying ways for each art separately, but that may for convenience be dealt with here. It may at once be conceded that one who knows and loves his coins better than any other class of evidence may reasonably seek his examples there, and that is one reason why I select coins for a general survey. But there are other reasons of weight, which are not yet understood as they ought to be and may therefore be set out here.

Coins are official records, dependent on decisions of authority, not on individual whim. Even the coin of a small city represents some decision on the part of local authority. Publicity was not the matter of course that it is today. There was no wireless, no swift travelling cheap press. If you wanted news to get round the Empire, the coin, passing on its inevitable course from hand to hand, was a useful messenger. And with publicity went propaganda. When you told people what was happening, you were inclined also to tell them what they ought to think about it. Hence, a series of little messages on the coins to the subjects of the Empire, telling them of the latest news and trying to condition them to it as the Emperor would wish. Historians who have neglected their coins in the past have undoubtedly believed quite honestly that what was said on the coins is no great matter—not like an imperial edict or letter. The evidence is accumulating that this view is quite wrong. Some Emperors may have neglected their coinage and left the decisions to their high officials or even to subalterns. All we can say is that this was not usually so and never meant to be so. Emperors were very sensitive about the right of coinage. Almost the first act of the usurper was to set his features on a coin for his people to see. The treachery of Perennis, praetorian prefect of Commodus, and his sons was proved to the Emperor by a gold coin struck in the name of one of the sons ; we have not got it today, but there is no reason for disbelieving the tale in Herodian.   When Constantine began to favour the Christian Church, Christian symbols—cross and monogram of Christ—begin to creep on to the coins.   They are not yet ostentatious ; they are not everywhere present.   But the idea that some have had that moneyers with Christian sympathies ventured to air them on the coins without higher authority is quite absurd.   As little could our Deputy Master of the Mint put a sickle and hammer beside the portrait of our gracious Queen Elizabeth.

The most distinguishing advantage of the coin record over others is its continuity.   Discontinuity in our general picture of antiquity is so constantly with us that we cease to be fully aware of it.   Tacitus throws his searching light on to a few periods of the Early Empire. The light goes off ; Tacitus ends his narrative or his defective texts let us down.   We suddenly lose focus and distinction in our vision. In trying to complete our view we naturally incline to fill in the missing parts from those that we have.   There is perhaps no better method, but the underlying danger is obvious.   We shall be inclined to make history repeat itself when it did not always do so. Some periods of the Empire are almost comical in their lack of record.   Is it really true that the stirring reign of Trajan has left us only enough historical records to fill a few postcards ?   Is the record of the crisis of the 3rd century so hopelessly ruined that we are in doubt about the crucial dates, that for many events we have only a bare mention ?   Alas, it is all true, so true that we prefer to forget it.   Under these circumstances the little extra help given by the coins is invaluable.   The coins are quite impartial ; they have not their favourite ranges, to be fully illustrated, while others are neglected.   They run on out of set periods into times of darkness and out of darkness into light again, all the time throwing their little rays of illumination.   Look again at the 3rd century.   Few historians yet realise quite how much coins are adding to the historical record.   On the reign of Macrinus they confirm the account of Dio Cassius against rival stories and explain just how Macrinus tried to solve his problems and how he met his end.   They help us to clear up the difficult chronology of the year 238.   They show us the inner meaning of the persecution of Trajan Decius.   His religious crusade is seen to be based on the worship of the *Divi*, that is to say on the religion of the Empire itself.   The coins show us how the authority of Trebonianus Gallus broke down in 252, how the East was lost to Sapor and how Aemilian rebelled far earlier than our epitomists realised later.   The coins enable us to decide the date of the captivity of Valerian.   They illustrate the rise of

Palmyra, its Eastern rule under Roman hegemony, its final bid for Empire. The coins show beyond doubt that Aureolus in Milan was fighting for Postumus against Gallienus at the end of his reign.

On the coins we can follow the religious revolution step by step : first, the defiant programme of the Tetrarchy, Rome needing only her gods and her own genius ; then the political confusion after the abdication of Diocletian, leading first to hesitation and, finally, to capitulation on the vital point of persecution. Then comes the decision of Constantine to give the Christian God a trial : the victory of the Mulvian Bridge and the new favour towards the Church : the disappearance of the old pagan gods—all but Sol, special favourite of the house of Constantine, who persists for a few years more : the appearance of the occasional Christian symbol. Then comes the neutral period, lasting down to Theodosius : the reaction of Julian, cautiously expressed : at last, the triumph of Christian thought.

In this one material of the coins we have the ancient record almost complete in its central parts and, from it, can begin to correct the irregularities produced by the accident of survival in other cases. If we speak of our coin record as complete, we ought perhaps to say something to justify the claim. Of course, we have not in our hands nearly all the coins and medallions struck in antiquity. Issues that were never plentiful will, except for rare exceptions, disappear. The really rare issues, consisting perhaps of a few hundreds to thousands of pieces, have normally no chance of survival. In spite of the durability of their substance the coins are subject to the general mortality. Large pieces of precious metal always gravitate to the melting pot. Perhaps the survival rate will be something like one in ten thousand ; this is a very vague guess, but may give some idea of probabilities. Of common double denarii of the time of Gordian III we have specimens of single types surviving in their thousands—nay, tens of thousands. In the great Dorchester hoard several types were represented by five hundred specimens each. What we *do* claim is that, in the case of any issue that was in common use, the probabilities are greatly in favour of some specimens surviving today. We claim that the centre of the picture is nearly perfect, that it is only on the fringes that the pattern begins to break down, only on the very edges that it is quite lost. Interesting as rare special issues are, from the point of view of general history the common issues are even more important. In this case, what survives is just what we most need. Where the pattern is broken, but not quite lost, we have good hopes of completing it in theory. Septimius Severus struck coins for the legions that supported him. If we compare the coins with what we know of history, we conclude that the record is fairly complete. The legions that are excluded from the celebrations are excluded for special reasons, because they fought for Pescennius Niger or because they stood under the banners of Clodius Albinus. The denarii were comparatively common and survived. It is different with the aurei ; specimens are only known for two or three legions. Yet it is probable they were struck for all. If the denarii went, as little commemorative medals, to the common soldiers, the aurei would be gold medals for the higher officers. We should postulate them then for all the legions in the list ; but, as they were always comparatively rare, their survival rate is low.

That is just the point. The survival rate is low for many classes of evidence. What a minute proportion of imperial edicts and letters may be read by us today ! How few in proportion to the lost are the extant inscriptions of major importance ! What tiny scraps are left of the rich artistic treasury of the Empire ! Some impressive remains, like the Colosseum or the arch of Trajan, give us pause for a moment. But we have only to begin to count up what is known to be lost, and we shall not overestimate the extent of our holding. It was not a case of destruction in a year or a generation ; ever since imperial Rome fell the destruction of her ancient monuments has been in progress. The survival of coins enables us to make good some little part of our loss. Coins preserve the bare record of many a fallen temple, many a collapsed arch. They give in their shortened version scenes that served as subjects for sculpture and painting on the grand scale. The medallions, in particular, with their larger scale and more ambitious treatment, clearly offer tiny copies of great works of art. The question has often been raised : do the coins copy other forms of art ? Not slavishly, not invariably. But the coin engraver draws on the general fund of subjects of immediate interest and naturally follows general lines of treatment. If we could more often compare the coin with other works of art of a major character, we should undoubtedly find differences of treatment. They would be mainly such as are conditioned by the minute scale of the coin. In a few instances we can set coins and other works of art side by side. The likeness can be striking. Scenes from the 'Aeneid'—such as Aeneas and Ascanius on the site of new Troy with the great sow—come out identical in all main points on medallion and sculpture relief.

It is strange that so profitable a subject of research has hardly been seriously attempted. But it is all part of the general strangeness—that coins, which are central to any true study of ancient art that goes beyond dilettantism, are never placed in the centre ; that students are taught their ancient art with a minimum reference to coins ; that coins, as a subject by themselves, are not even placed in the second part of the Classical Tripos at Cambridge. Coins are tiny objects. If some prefer to study temples we can well understand their preference. The peculiar interest of tracing styles of pottery engages the attention of many excellent scholars. Sculpture in the round appeals to many more than does low-relief engraving. But those who would know must go where knowledge is to be found, and, for the student who will heed, the signpost 'to the coins' is always catching the eye. For lack of obedience to this clear leading much is backward that should be on the advance. We have already spoken of schools of art under the Empire and of the tendency of Rome to draw all great talent into herself. On these subjects, coins can give some useful leads. The supremacy of Rome can be most fully illustrated. In the central issues there is a self-confidence, a firmness of conception and purpose that speak a truly imperial language. Emperor after Emperor is rendered with full attention to variety, but always with a suggestion of the imperial dignity. In Rome, in fact, a well established classical tradition unfolds itself without let or hindrance. The interest of the world is focused on Rome, to Rome most of the first-class talent inevitably flows, whatever the nationality of the individual artist. In the later Empire Rome loses something of this supremacy, but she loses it to the great competing capitals and resident cities, not to the provinces at large. The coinage, other than the central, gives us some impression of the state of art in other parts of the Empire. At some great Eastern mints there is evidence of independence in local style ; something of this will be seen at Ephesus, Antioch and Alexandria. It would not occur to any students of coins to place those cities on any level near the Roman. When Albinus struck at Lugdunum, he *did* find an artist to engrave his types, but only one who could scratch out something like a face or a figure, awkward and ugly. The short-lived issues of Uranius Antoninus at Emesa in 252–3 show an exquisite pretty style that has some attractiveness, but cannot be compared in solid achievement with the Roman. As for the city issues in their multitudes, style is not completely absent. The coin specialist can attempt with some hope to place coins by their styles when he cannot read them. But, though there is some individuality, there is seldom definite merit. It is as little documents of city history that these coins are rightly beginning to attract the attention of students.

In the case of all major works of art, dates are often only approximate. For the public monuments the Emperor often supplies the date. We know just where to place the Colosseum or the arch of Trajan. We know where we are with imperial portraits. But for most of our material—for paintings, for statues of private individuals, for sarcophagi—we rely on very vague indications of date. Even for pottery, in which ample material and close study have combined to produce astonishing results, precision in the first place depends very much on association with coins. The sure evidence that they give can be extended to cover places where their help is lacking. The coins supply us with a continuous series of closely dated pieces. The general development of imperial art is written down for us in close detail. No Roman coin or medallion is signed, but we shall no doubt in course of time be able to refer to certain masters of engraving by their descriptions if not by their names. We could at once begin to talk of the master of the Cow reverse of Augustus or the master of the Aelius obverse of Hadrian. But what at first may seem a defect turns out to be an advantage. Granted that the imperial coins show us rather the sound journeyman work of schools of artists than the brilliance of exceptional men, we are the more sure that we are following the line of general development, not the more erratic forces of individual geniuses.

We can now look at imperial art as seen period by period in the coins. The Augustan age has a firm Greek tradition, over-ripe perhaps, but worthy of respect. The Apolline features of the ruler are rendered in a variety of ways, always dignified, sometimes beautiful. Exceptional work is to be seen on Eastern aurei of the middle period and on a remarkable cistophorus with the reverse of the sphinx. If the reverses are treated with much less care than the obverses, that is due to the new tendency, imposed by Rome, of concentrating on the great individual. Rome has not yet taken her place at the head ; her style is rather stiff and clumsy, but that was soon to be remedied. The gold and silver of Tiberius continued to be struck at Lugdunum, but the interest of his coins is rather to be found in the Aes coinage struck in Rome. There we find strong portraits of Tiberius, Drusus and the deified Augustus, and reverses of great interest and dignity. A fresh batch of fine family portraits marks the coinage of Caligula. His own gaunt features are not attractive, but one cannot forget them. Claudius seems to impart something of his own careful, worrying exactitude to his coins. With Nero we find the peak of achievement. The early coinage, in gold and silver, is simple and decent. The later coinage of the tyrant, the Sun-god, the Apollo on earth, bears imperial portraits of remarkable force. Sometimes it is the proud lord who is a law to himself and the world, the Nero who was expected to return in triumph after death, that we see. Sometimes it is the veritable Apollo, young, beautiful, healing. The reverses of the Aes have some lovely types—the most attractive group of Ceres and Annona, the pleasing pattern of the port of Ostia, Nero himself as Apollo with the lyre, and the vigorous types of *decursio*, the exercises of the guard. Art had climbed under Nero. We know something of the great architects who served him ; there must have been men of similar ability among his engravers.

From this peak there was no sudden decline. The grave dignity of Galba, the doll-like neatness of Otho, the almost incredible brutality of Vitellius—all are rendered with gusto. The Flavians did not abandon the art of Nero, but, so to say, regularised it. Vespasian aims at a return to the Augustan age, but the art of the time, like the Emperor himself, may be termed prosaic. The strong realism of the portraits of Vespasian and Titus is replaced under Domitian by a touch of poetry. The reverses of the coins of Domitian show a new life and interest. The design of pieces like the great sestertii of the German victories or of the Secular Games is as good as anything of Nero. The great reign of Trajan did not lack a worthy coin record. We know the vigorous features of the Emperor as if we met him daily in the street. The coins are used to illustrate to the full the revival of Roman *virtus*, and there are many fine reverses on the sestertii. But we are more conscious of the careful use of a serviceable instrument than of any special delight in the use of it.

Hadrian was too original to leave anything just as he found it. Trajanic art received a new impetus. New artists, brought in from the East, rendered the Augustan features of Hadrian, the sad sensuous beauty of the imperial favourite Antinous, the dandified Aelius. The celebrations of the provinces and their armies near the close of the reign produced a whole picture gallery of attractive figures and scenes. Hadrian could not communicate his special gifts to his descendants. Antoninus Pius and Marcus Aurelius well maintained the imperial dignity and worth ; they did their duty at home and in the field, they recorded all with care. But there does not seem to be much enjoyment in it. The portraits of the two Faustinas are often beautiful ; there are some fine reverse types in the issues celebrating the nine hundredth year of Rome and in the consecration issues of the two empresses. The portrait of Antoninus Pius is just dignified—that and no more ; but, still, the traditional portrait of Christ owes something to it. Marcus Aurelius looks like what he often was, a good but very worried man ; Lucius Verus looks like what he was, an elaborate fop.

With Commodus comes distinct decline in merit, but a widening of interest in religion and elsewhere. The art of the reign is seen at its best on the medallions celebrating the exploits of the Emperor's hero Hercules. Septimius Severus, a provincial himself, married to an Eastern princess who was open to new ideas, refreshes imperial art. Judging from the coins, the Emperor brought back with him from the East in 202 artists of great ability, who rendered the features of the imperial family with fresh charm and so preached to the public the perpetual felicity that Septimius's new dynasty promised. There are traces of some more ambitious designs. A rare aureus of Geta, perhaps struck at his marriage, shows the nuptials of Bacchus and Ariadne ; it is surely a small copy of some painting or relief. From these beginnings Severan art declined towards mediocrity. If that unpleasant lad, Elagabalus, was really beautiful, his artists have not been very successful in rendering his beauty. Severus Alexander is a decent, rather dull lad, and his reverses share the same dullness. For the giant barbarian, Maximin I, the artist could do no more than produce a remarkable portrait, doing full justice to an amazing chin. The coins move on with no enhancement of interest, but with the unfailing series of worthy portraits. Gallienus gave a new impulse to art. Hard circumstances condemned him to spend most of his life in the field, but his interests were more in peaceful pursuits, in philosophy, in poetry and, we may add, in art. Under his sole reign there was a revival of art that may fairly be called Augustan ; there was a deliberate return to the models of the great founder of the Empire.

After Gallienus art moves on towards the period of Diocletian ; it is only when we arrive there that we become conscious of changes that have been slowly preparing themselves before. That is what distinguishes Diocletian everywhere. With him the process of change, half disguised, suddenly stands revealed. What exactly happens to imperial art under him ? There is a certain hardening and solidifying. The bullet heads of the Emperors, round, close-cropped, speak eloquently of the *virtus Illyrici*, the brave, unpoetic devotion of the Pannonians to duty. Through this hard exterior a second change came slowly to force its way—I mean the approximation to the ways of Persian royalty. The change certainly began under Diocletian ; the Persian Empire suggested to him how to protect the Emperor from his fellow soldiers. Under Constantine the change certainly finds expression. There is more subtlety in the imperial portraits ; attention is definitely shifted from the strong individuality of the Emperor to the supreme dignity of his office. The diadem, richly ornamented with pearls or gems, takes the place of the bare or laureate head. If we compare the coinage of the reign of Carus with those of the sons of Constantine, we shall find a change that looks like a revolution. Something new is being attempted. The record used to be that of an Emperor, able and worthy, performing mighty deeds and thus commending his person to his subjects. Now there is the Emperor, more symbol than person, seated among a number of eternal activities that protect and preserve the State. We stand ' sub specie aeternitatis '.

Later change only accentuates the revolution of which we have spoken. Art becomes ever more artificial and hieratic ; the Empire is seen under a number of permanent aspects, no longer as something vigorous in action. Think of the few meagre recurring types that cover the age when the Goths destroyed the Eastern army at Adrianople. The full development was reserved for Byzantium. Byzantine art is so far removed from the classical that the classical student may completely miss its significance. Wroth's disparaging remarks on Byzantine art in his great catalogue may be read with a sad wonder. The something new that had come in with Constantine triumphed and Christianity found in it a fuller expression of its nature.

Why does the pace of artistic change vary so much from time to time ? Take art in Greece between 480 and 420 B.C. If you compare the ends of the period, you might think that the interval had been one of centuries. The late archaic art has vanished and given place to a ripe classical. The old tricks of set expression have been abandoned ; the artist has found a full mastery of his medium and uses it without restraint. The tremendous impact of the unexpected triumph over Persia must have had something to do with it. But is there not something else in this sudden explosion of unrevealed faculties—a part explanation of why Greece so surprisingly won ? So too in our Roman sphere. The revolution in art between A.D. 280 and 330, say, is something quite out of the ordinary. We might say that art ran a more or less regular course from Augustus down to 280 : we might say with equal truth that after 330 it ran for centuries with only slow and minor changes of direction. In our Greek period we found the Persian wars the chief feature ; here we find the Christian revolution. Again we may formulate our conclusion in similar terms. The reserve forces of Greece that won the Persian wars expressed themselves in an art that suddenly soared up to the heights. The new energies that expressed themselves in the rise of Christianity from persecution to

U

power also burst through in a new art. The world of the 4th century is based on new conceptions, and men of a new type are making their impress on the age. But here the suddenness is more apparent than real. The forces of revolution had for long been sapping under the surface before they broke down the old forms and set new ones in their place.

I will now try to summarise the main results that come out of our enquiry. The art of the Empire was a late phase of Greek art, still far from contemptible, but stale and needing fresh inspiration. Rome, the capital, draws in the greatest talents by the magnet of her wealth and power. Provincial style survives, but cannot compete with the great concentration of talent at the centre. Later, the residencies and capitals take the position that Rome had monopolised. Other forms of art on the frontiers have little direct influence on imperial art ; but they may return and the way is left clear for them.

On the technical side the Romans themselves may not have done much for art ; the artists may still have been mainly Greeks and orientals. But what Rome *did* supply was direction. The tendency which we can trace from Alexander the Great, to divert interest from the world of gods and heroes to that of great men, now reaches its fulfilment. The Emperor is assimilated to the gods ; with many, in fact, he takes their place. He is the embodiment of power and many worshippers were more concerned with the power than with the goodness of their gods. This interest in the individual, beginning high up with the Emperor, descends down society, grade by grade. Every man, if he can anywhere distinguish himself, wants to have it set down on the artistic record. Only at the very end of our period does the great individual retire behind the great symbol.

The Romans had a vast interest in the topical, the practical— what is happening just in this way, here and now. The world of gods and heroes is not closed, but it no longer supplies so many scenes. Even when the old themes are still used, they are often related to persons and occasions of the present. One result of this interest was the development of the continuous style of sculpture referred to on page 277. In connexion with this we might glance at the question of perspective. Representation was often in the flat, the eye being expected to supply all the interpretation necessary. The continuous style forces you to think in three dimensions and should therefore help the observer to distinguish nearer or further distance. The problems that were thus being raised were not to be settled till very long afterwards.

Apart from the central current in imperial art there were many minor tides that did no t merge themselves in it, but still kept their place outside. When art took that abruptly new direction that we have been discussing, was any one of these arts on the fringe concerned ? There is only one art—or shall we say artistic direction ?—that can come into question here. We mean of course the art of the East—the East partly contained in the Roman frontier provinces, but seen more clearly in the great empire that lay beyond—the Parthian, or, after the successful revolution of Sapor, the new Persian. I think that we should be right in saying that Eastern influence was dominant here, not in the sense that this art came in as a stranger from the East, but rather that the Eastern elements within the Empire became dominant and readily met and combined with the new influences from outside. In what is this new tendency seen ? In a turning from the individual to the formal, from the immediate to the universal. The Emperor of the Early Empire is normally shown looking either right or left ; the bust may be nearly to the front, but the head is definitely turned one way or the other. In all such poses you may imagine that you see your prince engaged in one of his main activities—as chief citizen, as commander-in-chief or what not. But, when he is set directly before you, when you are confronted with him, he ceases to be a figure of daily life and becomes a symbol. ' En Priamus ' : ' Ecce homo '. When Constantius II visited Rome the people noted with admiration how he could stand for hours in his chariot, receiving the popular acclamations but showing no sign of human frailty—never needing to wipe nose or mouth. That was the kind of glorious idol that the Emperor had come to be. We are so much accustomed in later art to frontal representation that we easily forget that it is not the only possibility. The great religious pictures of the Italian schools usually show the Virgin and Child and Saint in direct frontal position. The Annunciation is an exception ; it is usually shown from left to right.

Imperial art, we have said, was not symbolic in essence ; it represented directly the subjects that interested it. Symbolical meanings were not excluded, but they came second. The later art is clearly changed in this respect. It chooses what forces on the mind a particular kind of view. It makes one think of the formal, the typical, the universal, the eternal. As we have suggested, this new tendency already existed inside the Empire ; there was no need to import it from without. In art, the East triumphed over the West, not as in politics with an external and more or less accidental victory, but with one achieved by merit and vitality.

The art of the Empire depended largely on the patronage of the great ; it was not a popular art. Articles of luxury were distinguished as much by the costliness of their substance as by the skill expended on them. Articles of common use stood on a low artistic level. Of the major arts architecture, of the minor engraving and mosaic, gained the chief triumphs.

EPILOGUE

The treatment which we have chosen—by subject—has rather thrown into the background the development in time. The short summary that we now give aims at making good this deficiency and also at suggesting to the reader how the different threads of our successive chapters are to be woven into one fabric. This last piece of co-ordination really belongs, as a private task, to each interested reader ; we can only make a few suggestions for his help.

We can see very clearly how the Roman Empire came into being. It arose when Rome attained a certain position of predominance in the world of Hellenistic culture. We have suggested that it is a mistake to regard it as no more than a late phase of that culture. The attempt to realise the peaceful co-operation of nations is something creative and of new promise—not simply one swing more of the old wheel. We have also suggested that, as the Empire develops, there is something like ' creation by emergence '. What comes out must certainly have been contained within, but it could not be accurately forecast before it emerged. The Empire developed a form of its own, which is fateful for it. Some of the shapes that we seem to see in it may be accidental, mere fantasies of our minds ; but there will also be significant shapes if we can see them.

In the Early Empire much of the old world is still recognisable under the new forms, and this applies to Rome herself and Italy as well as to her provinces. The old republican constitution is still precariously alive ; the office of Emperor is curiously grafted on to it. The constituent parts of the Empire still keep much of their ancient character. It is a world of rigid castes—the dominant Roman above all with his own class distinctions, under him the inferior layers, all tending to follow the Roman differentiations by birth and landed wealth. There is a breath of new hope—recovery after something very near to despair—even something of a moral and religious revival, though this does not move in any close relation to the political world.

The Antonine Age is the profound calm that follows the first stabilisation of the Empire. Answers to the most vital problems have been found, both in internal and in foreign politics. The Empire stands firm on its own foundations and imposes its majestic peace on the world. In one sense it is a time of great happiness. The world enjoys a perennial festival. It feeds on the traditions

293

of a great past ; but it is uncreative and makes no provision for the future, for those new dangers that arise even before it is ended.

Military anarchy grows out of the wreck of the Antonine Age. The Emperor becomes the slave of his soldiers. Step by step—not by any one violent convulsion—the old constitution is shattered and the military anarchy comes in. Empire ceases to be the reward of outstanding merit—under the sign of *providentia deorum* ; it is the great glittering prize awarded by fortune at her caprice. Disunion in the Empire is accompanied by and aggravated by new pressures on the frontiers. Under these combined strains economic life too collapses, and the ship of state narrowly escapes shipwreck.

A short period of restoration repairs the worst damage and promises better hopes for the future. But, though the great line from Claudius II to Carus ensures that the Empire shall have a future, it does not yet determine what that future shall be. That task is left to the builders of the new Empire, to Diocletian and Constantine. The troubles that had nearly sunk the Empire suggested their own remedies. Experiments in reform had occurred at intervals along the path of disaster. Diocletian and Constantine after him accepted the lessons and changed whatever seemed to require changing. The fact that Diocletian finally chose to champion the old in religion, while Constantine declared for the new, has led to an undue discrimination between them, the parents of the New Age. It is ridiculous to denounce Constantine as a reckless innovator, whilst sparing Diocletian any such blame. It was only that, in the sphere of religion, Diocletian failed to realise, as he did realise elsewhere, quite how much was changed.

The new Empire was firmly grounded, strongly governed. But it paid dearly for its new stability. Liberty was no more. All men were, if not slaves, little better than serfs. Uniformity, servility, inertia were the characteristics of the time. The Christian Church, while losing something of its first purity, received a great access of energy through imperial favour. But, as it spent most of that energy on its own internal feuds, it had little left to expend on any possible reform of the State. What has now emerged is the form that Empire was bound to take in the struggle through its bitter domestic problems at home and its unrelenting barbarians abroad. The ancient unitary view of life is being lost, the temporal is being forced apart from the eternal.

It is only in the Byzantine Empire that the new world finds its full development. We have suggested here that it is absurd to regard Byzantium as a sort of accidental continuation of Rome. No, it is in Byzantium that we see what the Empire had long been trying to grow into. Byzantium has certain defects—lack of independence, excessive conservatism, lack of new enterprise. But she was a civilised state, when our own ancestors in Western Europe were little better than savages. It is in the West that the idea of Empire was frustrated, because the political form containing it broke down under excessive pressures. But it is out of this collapse of the West that our modern civilisation was finally developed, and we are naturally biassed to some extent in its favour. But, even in the West, the idea of Rome still worked after her fall. We may still need to go back to Rome if we would learn how the nations may dwell together in peace.

CHRONOLOGICAL TABLE OF ROMAN EMPERORS

B.C. 27–A.D. 476

B.C.

27 *Augustus*

A.D.

14 *Tiberius* (his stepson)
37 *Gaius* (*Caligula*) (great-nephew of Tiberius)
41 *Claudius* (nephew of Tiberius)
54 *Nero* (stepson of Claudius ; committed suicide, June 68)
68 *Galba* (assassinated, Jan. 69)
69 *Otho* (committed suicide, April 69)
69 *Vitellius* (murdered, Dec. 69)
69 *Vespasian*
79 *Titus* (son of Vespasian)
81 *Domitian* (son of Vespasian)
96 *Nerva*
98 *Trajan* (adopted by Nerva)
117 *Hadrian* (adopted by Trajan)
138 *Antoninus Pius* (adopted by Hadrian)
161 *Marcus Aurelius* (died, 180) with *Lucius Verus* (died, 169) (both adopted by Antoninus)
180 *Commodus* (son of Marcus Aurelius ; died, 31 Dec. 192)
193 *Pertinax* (murdered, March)
193 *Didius Julianus* (murdered, 1 June)
193 *Pescennius Niger* (proclaimed by legions in Syria ; killed, 194)
193 *Septimius Severus* (proclaimed by legions in Pannonia, April ; died at York, Feb. 211)
     [*Clodius Albinus* (proclaimed by legions in Britain, 195 ; defeated by Septimius and committed suicide, 197)]
211 *Caracalla* (assassinated, Apr. 217) jointly with *Geta* (murdered, Feb. 212) (both sons of Septimius Severus)
217 *Macrinus* (killed, *c.* July 218) [His son, Diadumenian, proclaimed by him as Augustus, but never ruled]
218 *Elagabalus* (assassinated, March 222)
222 *Alexander Severus* (killed, March 235)
235 *Maximin I* (murdered, May 238)
238 *Gordian I* and *Gordian II* (father and son) (proclaimed in Africa, March ; confirmed by Senate, April ; son killed in battle, father committed suicide, April)
238 *Pupienus Maximus* and *Balbinus* (elected by Senate ; both murdered, ? July)
238 *Gordian III* (nephew of Gordian II ; proclaimed by army, July ; murdered, 244)
244 *Philip* the Arabian (killed in battle at Verona, Sept. 249)
249 *Trajan Decius* (proclaimed by troops, June ; killed in battle against Goths, June 251)

U*   297

A.D.

251   *Trebonianus Gallus* (proclaimed by troops, June ; killed by troops, 253) with *Hostilian* (son of Decius ; died, 251) and *Volusian* (son of Gallus ; killed with his father, 253)

253   *Aemilian* (recognised by Senate and in Egypt and the East ; murdered by his troops, 253)

253   *Valerian* (proclaimed by Rhine legions ; captured by Persians, 258-9) with his son *Gallienus* (appointed co-emperor by Senate, *c.* Sept., 253 ; killed, August, 268)
      [Macrianus and Quietus proclaimed in the East, 260, but both killed, 261]
      [Gallic Emperors : Postumus (259-68), Laelianus (268), Marius (268), Victorinus (268-70), Tetricus I (270-4), Tetricus II (274)]

268   *Claudius II* (died of plague, Jan. 270)

270   *Quintillus* (brother of Claudius, chosen by Senate, committed suicide, April)

270   *Aurelian* (murdered, *c.* April, 275)

275   *Tacitus* (chosen by Senate, Sept. ; died *c.* April 276)

276   *Florian* (brother of Tacitus ; seized purple ; died, *c.* June)

276   *Probus* (chosen by army ; murdered, autumn 282)

282   *Carus* (died near Ctesiphon, July 283)

283   His sons, *Carinus* (died 284) and *Numerian* (died, 283)

284   *Diocletian* (Nov. 284 ; abdicated, 305 ; died, *c.* 316)

286   *Maximian* (jointly with Diocletian, till 305 ; returned to rule, 306 ; died, 310)

[293   Constantius and Galerius invested as Caesars under the joint Augusti]

305   *Constantius I* (W. ; died at York, July 306) and *Galerius* (E.) on abdication of Diocletian and Maximian. Caesars : Severus (W.) and Maximin Daza (E.)

306   *Constantine I* the Great (son of Constantius I ; proclaimed by troops at York, July)
      Severus II (promoted by Galerius to emperor (W.) ; killed, summer 307)
      Maxentius (son of Maximian ; proclaimed in Rome ; acknowledged by Constantine, 307)

308   *Licinius* (made co-emperor by Galerius)

309   Six Augusti rule together : *Galerius* (died, 311), *Constantine I, Maximian* (returned ; committed suicide, 310), *Licinius, Maxentius* (died, 312), *Maximin Daza* (died, 313)

324   Constantine defeats Licinius and rules alone (died, 337)

337   *Constantine II* (Gaul and the West ; killed, 340), *Constantius II* (East ; died, 361), *Constans* (Italy and Illyricum ; murdered, 350) (all sons of Constantine I)

350   *Magnentius* (usurper in the West ; defeated by *Constantius II*, 351 ; committed suicide, 353)

353-61   *Constantius II* Augustus with
351-4   *Constantius III* (Gallus) Caesar
355-61   *Julian II* Caesar

361   *Julian II* (grandson of Constantius I ; died, 363)

363   *Jovian* (died, 364)

364   *Valentinian I* (W. ; died, Nov. 375) and *Valens*, his brother (E. ; killed in battle, Aug. 378)
      [Procopius, usurper against Valens, 365 ; put to death, 366]

367   *Gratian* (made co-emperor by Valentinian I, his father ; murdered by usurper Maximus, Aug. 383)

375   *Valentinian II* (succeeded his father, Valentinian I ; died, May 392)

379   *Theodosius I* (made co-emperor by Gratian ; died, 395)

WEST	EAST
A.D.	A.D.

WEST	EAST
395 *Honorius* (son of Theodosius I ; died, 423) [*Constantius III* (co-emperor, 421 ; died, 421)] [*Galla Placidia* (daughter of Theodosius I ; Augusta, 421 ; died, 450)]	395 *Arcadius* (son of Theodosius I ; died, 408) 408 *Theodosius II* (son of Theodosius I ; died, 450)
424 *Valentinian III* (son of Constantius III ; murdered, 455)	[*Pulcheria*, his sister, regent ; Augusta, 414 ; m. Marcian 450 ; died, 453)]
455 *Petronius Maximus* (killed, 455)	450 *Marcian* (died, 457)
455 *Avitus* (abdicated and died, 456)	
457 *Majorian* (deposed and died, 461)	457 *Leo I* (died, 474)
461 *Libius Severus* (died, 465)	
465-7 (Interregnum)	
467 *Anthemius* (died, 472)	
472 *Olybrius* (died, 472)	
473 *Glycerius* (captured and made bishop of Salona, 474)	
474 *Julius Nepos* (exiled, 475 ; assassinated, 480)	474 *Leo II* (grandson of Leo I ; died, 474)
	474 *Zeno* (father of Leo II ; driven out by)
475 *Romulus* (Augustulus)	475 *Basiliscus* (defeated and killed, 476)
476 End of Western line with the deposition of Romulus	476 *Zeno* (returned ; died, 491) (and later Emperors)

BIBLIOGRAPHY

This bibliography makes no claim to any kind of completeness. It simply records a number of books which the author happens to have met in covering his subject. Very full bibliographies may be found in such works as the *Cambridge Ancient History*.

Historical Sketch
Altheim, A. *Niedergang der alten Welt.* 1952.
Cambridge Ancient History, Vols. X–XII.
Gibbon, Edward. *The History of the Decline and Fall of the Roman Empire*, edited by J. B. Bury (7 vols.).
Methuen's History of the Roman World, edited by M. Cary. Vol. VI by R. P. Longden. Vol. VII by H. M. D. Parker.
Mommsen, Theodor. *Römisches Staatsrecht*, 3rd edition. Leipzig, 1887.
Schiller, H. *Geschichte der römischen Kaiserzeit.* 3 vols. Gotha, 1887.
Seeck, Otto. *Geschichte des Untergangs der antiken Welt.* 1910–1913.

The Empire and its Parts
Bouchier, E. S. *Life and Letters in Roman Africa.* 1913.
Bouchier, E. S. *Spain under the Roman Empire.* 1914.
Mommsen, Theodor. *The Provinces of the Roman Empire* (English translation by W. P. Dickson). 2 vols. 1909.

Cities and Citizenship
Coulanges, Fustel de. *La Cité antique.* 1888.
Jones, A. H. M. *The Cities of the Eastern Roman Provinces.* 1937.
Jones, A. H. M. *The Greek City from Alexander to Justinian.* 1940.

The Outside World
Altheim, A. *Die ausserrömische Welt* (Vol. 1 of *Die Krise der alten Welt*).

The Civil Service
Hirschfeld, O. *Die Kaiserlichen Verwaltungsbeamten.* Berlin. 1905.
Mattingly, H. *The Imperial Civil Service of Rome.* Cambridge. 1910.

The Roman Army
Cheesman, G. L. *The Auxilia of the Roman Army.* 1914.
Parker, H. M. D. *The Roman Legions.* Oxford. 1928.

Private and Social Life
Carcopino, J. *Daily Life in Ancient Rome.* Translated by E. G. Lorimer. 1941.

Friedländer, L.   *Darstellungen aus der Sittengeschichte Roms.*   10th edition. 1923.

Economic Life

Heichelheim, F. M.   *Wirtschaftsgeschichte des Altertums.*   2 vols.   Leiden. 1938.

Religion

Altheim, A.   *Römische Religionsgeschichte.*   Leipzig.   1931–1933.
Gwatkin, H. M.   *Early Church History to A.D. 313.*   1912.
Harnack, A.   *Die Mission und Ausbreitung des Christentums.*   2 vols.   1924.
Lietzmann, H.   *Geschichte der alten Kirche.*   3 vols.   1932–1938.
Toutain, J.   *Les cultes païens dans l'empire romain.*   1907.
Wissowa, G.   *Roman Religion and Worship.*

Literature

Altheim, A.   *Literatur und Gesellschaft des ausgehenden Altertums.*   Vol. I, 1945.
Teuffel, W. S.   *Geschichte der römischen Literatur.*   Leipzig.   1913–1920.
Wendland, P., and Lietzman, H.   ' Christliche literatur ' (in Gercke and Norden's Classical Encyclopaedia).
Wright, F. A.   *A History of Later Greek Literature.*   1932.

Art

British Museum.   *Catalogue of the Coins of the Roman Empire.*   Vols. 1–5. (H. Mattingly.)
                  Catalogue of the Engraved Gems and Cameos.   (H. B. Walters.)   1926.
Furtwängler, A.   *Die antiken Gemmen.*   3 vols.   1900.
Oswald, F., and Pryce, T. D.   *An Introduction to the Study of Terra Sigillata.* 1920.
Perrot and Chipiez.   *Histoire de l'art.*   (Vol. 9, *La Peinture.*)
Strong, Mrs. E.   *Roman Sculpture from Augustus to Constantine.*   1907.
Wickhoff, F.   *Roman Art* (translated by Mrs. E. Strong).   1900.

INDEX